DEER & DEER HUNTING

DEER & DEER HUNTING

The Serious Hunter's Guide

Robert Wegner

*With a Foreword by Leonard Lee Rue III and
an Afterword by Fred Bear*

Stackpole Books

Copyright © 1984 by Stackpole Books

Published by
STACKPOLE BOOKS
5067 Ritter Road
Mechanicsburg, PA 17055

First paperback printing, May 1992

Printed in the U.S.A.

Library of Congress Cataloging in Publication Data

Wenger, Robert.
    Deer & deer hunting.

    Bibliography: p.
    1. Deer hunting. 2. Deer. I. Title. II. Title: Deer and deer hunting.
SK301.W35 1984   799.2'77357   84-2413
ISBN 0-8117-2585-5

You can hunt the world over for trophies—
Far back of beyond you may go;
But one day you'll come back
To follow the track
Of the white-tailed deer in the snow.

—*William Monypeny Newsom, 1926*

Dedication

I dedicate this book to my mother and father, who gave me the best education money can buy and who instilled in me a profound love of the white-tailed deer. I also dedicate it to my wife, Maren Lea, my in-house critic who puts up with my writing sessions and all the time I spend in the field.

Contents

Part III   **THE DEER-HUNTING MYSTIQUE**

Part IV   **THE DEER HUNTER**

Part V   **WHERE TO FIND MORE INFORMATION**

Acknowledgments

I would like to thank the publisher and editors of *Deer & Deer Hunting* for allowing me to reprint many of the articles that first appeared in that magazine. I would like to thank Al Hofacker, in particular, for revising my prose throughout the years and for constructing charts, graphs and illustrations upon request. I would also like to thank my publisher, Jack Brauer, for encouraging me to combine scientific information on deer with high-level prose on the art of deer hunting. And finally, I would like to thank professors Orrin J. Rongstad and Robert A. McCabe for allowing me to use the Department of Wildlife Ecology's library at the University of Wisconsin—Madison, Wisconsin.

Robert Wegner
Deer Foot Road
March 16, 1984

Foreword

by Leonard Lee Rue III

I am both proud and very pleased to have been asked to write the foreword to this book. I want to state right at the very beginning that I am prejudiced.

I have known Rob Wegner and his colleagues at *Deer & Deer Hunting* magazine, Jack Brauer and Al Hofacker, for a number of years. If I were to publish a magazine on deer, it would be along the lines of *Deer & Deer Hunting*. I could only hope that I would be able to do the job half as well as they have. Their magazine devotes itself to the natural history of the deer: what the deer does, when it does it, how it does it and why. I am first and foremost a naturalist, and have devoted my life to trying to find the answers to those questions about many kinds of wildlife, but about deer in particular. That's what Rob's book is about.

Included in the table of contents is a selection of some of the finest basic research that Dr. Wegner has written about in the magazine. He is an exceedingly fine researcher, being very meticulous and thorough; he does his homework, he pays his dues. A couple of my favorite articles were not included, but this is a book, not an encyclopedia. It will whet your appetite for more, and that's one thing good books do.

The book also includes a large number of biographical sketches of men I have long admired because their lives, like mine, have been shaped by their contact with, and their love of, deer. Some of these men, such as Aldo Leopold, have been an inspiration to me since I read their books many years ago. The first book I ever read on deer hunting was *The Still Hunter,* by T. S. Van Dyke—a classic book, as Chapter Four well illustrates. I consider it a privilege to personally know Fred Bear who, together with Dr. Saxton Pope and Howard Hill, has probably done more to publicize bow hunting than anyone else. I would like to know Francis Sell and would liked to have met George Mattis personally, because they are my kind of men. Rob Wegner's sketches enabled me to know them better. You too will come to know them better after reading his portraits.

The last section of the book entitled *The Deer Hunter* is required reading for everyone who hunts deer. We are all on the defensive and we had better be, even though we should not have to be.

For years I have written and preached about the responsibilities of the deer hunter and the obligations we owe to the creatures we hunt. I do not concern myself with the so-called morality of hunting, as to whether we should hunt or not. Regulated sport hunting is one of the most important game-management tools that we have. My concern is rather with the ethics of the individual hunter.

Dr. Wegner has assembled a tremendous amount of data on deer and deer hunting and the ethics of the sport. Read his account, and you will be a better hunter; live by the precepts stated therein, and you will be a better person.

—Leonard Lee Rue III, 1984.

PART I
GIANTS AMONG DEER HUNTERS

Chapter 1

The Man with the Borsalino Hat

Robin Hood wore a felt hat in the Sherwood Forest in the 12th century. William Tell wore one in the Swiss forests of the 14th century. Saxton Pope and Art Young wore felt hats on their adventurous bow hunts in Tanganyika during the first decade of this century. Though the style and color may have changed, it seems appropriate that Fred Bear should wear one in the deer forests of the 20th century—more specifically a Borsalino felt hat, made in Italy.

The man whom we inevitably associate with the felt-hat trademark is now 80 years old. While some 80-year-olds might have difficulty seeing deer—let alone shooting them with a bow—Fred Bear, as the *Kansas City Star* outdoor editor recently remarked, "keeps things in perfect focus when it comes to deer hunting." Just mention the very words "deer and deer hunting," and he is a youngster at heart again.

"I still get the same thrill out of deer hunting that I did when I started at the age of 10." He says, "I think the reason I have always loved the sport of deer hunting so much lies in its inherent challenge, for the whitetail is the smartest creature to walk this earth. It has eyes for anything that makes the slightest movement, it has a nose that can pick up just about any scent, and it has ears that act like radar, warning it of any sound that is out of place. To outwit a creature as well-tuned to its environment as the whitetail takes some doing. They know where every tree, stump and twig is. We're definitely the ones at a disadvantage."

Despite the disadvantage, Fred Bear continues to hunt whitetails with all the vigor and enthusiasm of a 10-year-old boy.

Indeed, he still finds time to leave Gainesville, Florida, the new home of Bear Archery, to head north to Michigan where he enjoys bow hunting deer along the banks of his beloved Au Sable River. This fall we will surely encounter this long, lanky individual tramping the jack pine plain of northern Michigan as he pursues white-tailed deer with his bow and arrow in hand—a passion that Bear, still looking lean as a strip of venison jerky, has indulged in for the past 50 years.

In his work over the past 50 years as a pioneer developer of bow hunting equipment, in his films such as ''The Oldest Game,'' in his words, especially his *Field Notes,* in his philosophy of the chase—in the very essence of his outdoor adventures—Fred Bear, the soft-spoken, weather-leathered outdoorsman from the Pennsylvania highlands, represents one of America's greatest deer hunters. This chapter recalls the illustrious career of this master deer hunter who nearly always wears a sprig of fresh-picked greenery in the band of his soft felt hat.

Born on March 5, 1902, in Carlisle, Pennsylvania, Fred Bear grew up on a farm in the Amish country of the Keystone State. From his father, a toolmaker by trade, the young Bear acquired a love of building things and working with tools. From his rural surroundings, he gained a profound love of the white-tailed deer and the hunting of them. Indeed, in the rural area of Pennsylvania's Cumberland Valley where he grew up almost every mature male was a deer hunter, even though the deer population was at an all-time low at the turn of the century.

''My father, an expert with both shotgun and rifle, began taking me hunting when I was 6 years old,'' Bear relates.

''My first weapon was a BB gun, and at the age of 8, I became the proud owner of a 22-caliber rifle, a Quackenbush gun that was the pride of my life.

''Dad was very stern and drilled into me a proper respect for firearms and the responsibility that goes with their possession. Although teaching me these things, it was not until years later that I realized how pronounced were his leanings toward observance of the rules of fair chase, appreciation of the outdoors and the preservation of wildlife habitat. All this before ecology was even a word in the dictionary. There were no wildlife biologists and the term 'game conservation' was just beginning to be known.

''He deplored the coming of the farm tractor, with its ability to till the soil close to a fence. A team of horses pulling a plow could not do this, and the cover left along fences was a haven for wildlife.

''In those days, farm people toiled from daylight to sunset and the most that could be expected was a meager living, with the hope that the farm could be turned over to the next generation.

''The garden provided vegetables, but protein came mostly from rabbits, quail, squirrels, grouse and venison. Beefsteak was rare and it was available only when there was an abundance of butter and eggs to provide the funds for its purchase.

''In those days I was an inveterate gun man. In later years I turned to the bow and arrow for most of my hunting, but never abandoned entirely the use of firearms. Those rural beginnings and outdoor training proved to be a lifelong influence.''

Like most farm boys, the young Bear found school quite interesting, but his yearning to be in the field in search of birds and beasts was so prevailing that classes eventually lost the battle and had to be resumed in night school after he left the Pennsylvania highlands and moved to Michigan. Instead of sitting in a one-room schoolhouse, the boy preferred the peace and solitude of sitting with his back against a tree in the deer forest—studying animals, not arithmetic! One school boy lesson that Fred learned with great relish and never forgot, he found in Alfred Pease's *Book of the Lion:* "The most and best is known to the man who quits his bed before sunrise . . . who spends his days on the mountains and in the forests . . . who bears the heat and cold and hunger and thirst . . . for the love of nature . . . to visit the utmost refuges of beast and bird." Such things Fred Bear experienced on the family farm in rural Pennsylvania.

If you examine the first joint of the third finger of Bear's right hand, you will notice that it is missing—a permanent reminder of Fred's rural upbringing. Clare Conley, Editor of *Outdoor Life* magazine, tells us the story: "His sister cut it off with a hand-operated hay chopper. Young Fred and his sister were cutting hay to prepare a mixture of horse feed. The first step required chopping the hay

Fred Bear at the age of 12 with George Farthing, his early hunting companion. Fred used his dad's 12-gauge L. C. Smith double and is holding a quail and a rabbit. The photo was taken in 1914 at the Bear farm near Elliotston, Pennsylvania. The Ford Model "T" belonged to Farthing. *Photo credit Fred Bear*

into short lengths in a trough-like cutter with a shear handle, like a paper cutter.

"Fred fed the hay and his sister chopped. Soon it developed into a game. Fred would put the hay in and pull it back before his sister could cut it. With a little experience she began to plan ahead, and Fred's hand didn't quite clear the chopper.

"Fred rushed to the house, where his two Mennonite aunts treated the remainder of the finger with lily leaves and rosewater and then cleaned the boy up before going to see the doctor. Even the tips of his socks, which were sticking out of the holes in his shoes, were summarily snipped off with the scissors.

"Bear in later years became a left-handed archer, which meant he could draw the bowstring with his left hand. This may be a result of his childhood accident, because he shoots both a rifle and shotgun right-handed."

It seems quite natural that a master deer hunter should spend his childhood in the Pennsylvania highlands, for in 1912 Pennsylvania established the "high-water mark" for the noble sport of deer hunting when it harvested 1000 white-tailed bucks. According to Henry W. Shoemaker's popular *Pennsylvania Deer and Their Horns* (1915), 50,000 deer hunters participated in the deer season of 1912. One of those enthusiastic nimrods was the young Fred Bear, whose appetite for deer hunting was further stimulated by the results of the 1912 Pennsylvania deer hunt, which Shoemaker records for us in his deer hunter's journal: "More deer per square mile were killed in Pennsylvania in 1912, than ever bit the dust in the famed north woods of the Adirondacks." The young Bear, however, with part of a sock protruding through a hole in his boots, did not shoot a deer that year. As Fred Bear

will tell you with a straight face, "I went hunting once and didn't get a thing."

The Pennsylvania highlands not only provide the sport of American deer hunting with nostalgic myths, legends and famous tales of crafty old deerslayers, but set the historic background for one such deerslayer who remains a legend in his own time.

As a youngster at the deer camp of the Carlisle Gun Club on South Mountain, Fred surely heard the tales of such infamous deerslayers as Seth Iredell Nelson (1809-1905), who reportedly killed more than 2000 Pennsylvania deer and at least 100 elk. One of Bear's early hunting companions, George Farthing, undoubtedly told the youngster the tale of how the famous John Q. Dyce (1830-1904) of Clinton County killed three deer with one shot, as well as the tales of "Black Jack" Schwartz who presided over deer drives that encompassed a radius of 30 miles—usually resulting in the deaths of 200 deer or more. Yet, beyond these legends one basic principle of deer hunting from this early Pennsylvania period remains with Fred Bear to this very day. That principle we find most eloquently stated in Shoemaker's *Pennsylvania Deer and Their Horns*:

"Deer stalking, such as is practiced in Scotland, Ireland, and on the Continent, is by far the fairest and most sportsman-like manner of hunting deer. Unfortunately, it has been practiced by few Pennsylvania hunters. Those who hunt that way constitute the 'honor roll' of our deer hunters. If all hunted that way fewer deer would be shot, as it takes fully a hundred percent more skill than any other way of hunting. The idea is to enter the haunts of the deer 'off the wind' and approach close without being seen by them, and

Fred Bear with his first deer. Fred's buck is marked with an "X." This is one of the very few pictures of Bear without the traditional felt hat. *Photo credit Fred Bear*

then bring down the finest stag with a well directed bullet."

In 1916, the 14-year-old boy, already sporting the classic green-felt brimmed hat, brought down one of his first white-tailed bucks with a well-directed bullet from his specially stocked Winchester '94 in 30 caliber, a gun Bear still has in his collection today. That year Fred and his father, Harry Bear, arrive at their deer camp on South Mountain in their snazzy Maxwell roadster, the car Jack Benny made famous. During the 1916 deer hunt, the young boy with the thin, dimpled face

and the unforgettably big ears slept in the loft of an old line shack that a construction crew built at the turn of the century. When Pennsylvania's buck season ended that year, 1722 bucks went to the eternal meat pole—the young Bear's buck included. By 1916, deer and deer hunting had become an integral part of Fred Bear's life.

After settling upon a career as a patternmaker, Fred moved to Detroit in 1923, to work in the infant automobile industry. In truth, he was lured there not so much by the economic picture, but by the near-virgin deer hunting areas of northern Michigan. The year he left the Keystone State, the Pennsylvania Game Commission initiated its first antlerless deer season, thus ending the period of the "sacred doe" in that state. But the myth of the "sacred doe" continued in the land of Hiawatha when Fred arrived there in the fall of 1923.

After purchasing a deer hunting license for $2.50, Bear became one of more than 31,000 deer hunters to participate in the 1923 Michigan deer hunt. The bag limit consisted of one buck that year, and when the season ended 15,190 bucks were killed—with the Bear filling his tag. He now hunted deer in a state that harvested almost three times the number of deer taken in Pennsylvania. Like Pennsylvania, however, Michigan was a state rich in deer hunting stories and legends. Fred Bear now hunted in the land where William B. Mershon and Chase Osborn distinguished themselves as both deer hunters and conservationists—in the land of Deer Camp Erwin, George Shiras's Whitefish Lake Deer Camp and the E. C. Nicols deer hunting camps.

In 1925, Bear read Dr. Saxton Pope's *Hunting with the Bow and Arrow* (1923), a delightful book revealing the true excitement of bow hunting and the romance of deer camp life. In a recent reprint of that famous classic, issued by the Fred Bear Sports Club, Bear acknowledged that Pope's book, more than any other, contributed immensely to his early interest in archery equipment and hunting deer with the bow and arrow. Indeed, the sporting proposition of shooting deer with a bow struck the romantic fancy of the Bear, as it does for most men who read that book. The very exultation of the chase as Pope described it riveted itself into

Bear's consciousness, never to be forgotten:

"Despite the vague regrets we always feel at slaying so beautiful an animal, there is an exultation about bringing into camp a haunch of venison, or hanging the deer on the limb of a sheltering tree, there to cool near the icy spring. By the glow of the campfire we broil savory loin steaks, and when done eating, we sit in the gloaming and watch the stars come out. Great Orion shines in all his glory, and the Hunter's Moon rises golden and full through the skies. Drowsy with happiness, we nestle down in our sleeping bags, resting on a bed of fragrant boughs, and dream of the eternal chase."

In Detroit in 1925, Fred Bear met Art Young, one of the fathers of modern bow hunting, after Young's return from a notable hunt in Alaska. After seeing Young's film entitled "Alaskan Adventures" in a Detroit theater, Bear found himself at the point of no return with regard to his desire to learn more about archery equipment and bow hunting whitetails. In his *Field Notes* (1976), he fondly recalls how his interest in archery and bow hunting began in 1925, after seeing Young's film. "Later I had the pleasure of knowing Art Young and in shooting with him during the two years he lived in Detroit where we spent many happy hours making bows and arrows in my workshop. A hobby that was to become my life's work."

Since archery gear was practically impossible to obtain during the height of the Depression, Bear now turned to his hobby of making bows and arrows in earnest. His basement workshop and his inventive genius soon forced him to hire friends and neighbors to help him manufacture bows, arrows and other allied archery equipment for hunting purposes. This de-

Fred Bear and his deer hunting companions in the early 1930s in the Porcupine Mountains of Michigan's Upper Peninsula. Fred's deer is the second buck from the left. Note the arrowed rabbit hanging on the meat pole, taken for camp stew. *Photo credit Fred Bear*

velopment took place at a time when Bear's first bow sight was a kitchen match held to the bow with the aid of a rubber band and when Fred could have placed all of the bow hunters in the state of Michigan in a Model-T Ford.

In 1927, Bear made his first bow from a lemonwood stave that he purchased from the Stemmler Company at a cost of $2. "Immediately fascinated with this accomplishment, I spent every leisure hour working on bows in my basement workshop. With archers in the area unable to find good equipment in stores and with

my pattern-making experience helping me to turn out passable bows for them, it follows that I soon found myself in the archery business." Actually, in 1933, the auto plant in which Bear worked burned down, and the young deer hunter from the hills of Pennsylvania was out of a job.

A turning point in Fred's thinking about deer hunting came in the winter of 1933, when he shot a monster buck—dressing out at 285 pounds—with his rifle in upper Michigan. That year Michigan hunters harvested 25,500 bucks, but not many in that weight category. "It was so easy that there was no challenge, no thrill,'' Bear recalls. ''I decided that from then on I would do it with the bow.'' Indeed, in 1935 he downed his first deer, a spike buck, with the bow and arrow in the Upper Peninsula near Blaney, and has been downing them with the bow ever since. Downing a deer with a bow during the regular gun season is no mean task. In 1937, however, he no longer had to bow hunt during the regular gun season, for Michigan, following Wisconsin, initiated its first bow hunting season for deer. That first year just two counties—Newaygo and Iosco—were open.

That year Michigan sportsmen could buy either a bow or a gun license, but not both. Fred opened the bow-and-arrow deer season that year with a group of bow hunters from Detroit. ''We had rented an old cabin back in the woods, a large one-room affair with a big pot-bellied stove in the center. Except for one member of our group who had not yet arrived, we were bedded down comfortably by 10 o'clock, dreaming of the big bucks we would hunt at daylight on the following morning.

''Larry, the tardy member, arrived in camp at 2:00 a.m. He had stopped at the local tavern and, being in a boisterous mood, had filled the stove with dry wood to roast us out of our sleeping bags. It was two hours later that we got both the stove and Larry cooled down so we could get back to sleep.

''Our alarm went off at 4:30 a.m. From Larry's sleeping bag came only silence. Being a vengeful group, we decided he should not be coddled. He was awakened, dressed and taken out into the woods where we sat him on a stump in a cedar swamp where it was not likely he would be disturbed by animals. But as these things sometimes go, shortly after sunrise he shot a monster 8-point white-tailed buck. . . .'' One wonders about the justice of this sport! Larry was lucky indeed, for in 1937 only four bow hunters out of 180 participants filled their tags, with William Van Vorst of Lowell, Michigan, shooting the first deer taken that year with the bow.

During the 1940s, Bear struggled to win acceptance for the sport of bow hunting from the American public. He confined his deer hunting adventures during this time primarily to the state of Michigan— with the Porcupine Mountains of the Upper Peninsula and Allegan County of the Lower Peninsula being two of his favorite areas. Frequent jaunts, however, were also made into Wisconsin, where he downed a nice 6-pointer in 1941 while using a 75-pound ''bush bow'' and already sporting the familiar Borsalino trademark. Several years later, in 1946, his 8-pointer weighing 185 pounds dressed out won a medal for heaviest buck taken in Allegan County. He shot this buck while using one of his all-time favorite bows— a rattlesnake skin-backed 75-pound model. By 1946, Bear was one of 4360 Michigan bow hunters who harvested 170 deer that year.

During this time, Bear not only had to manufacture a product, but had to create a market as well. ''I quickly learned that newspapers weren't interested in any stories about scores at the tournaments, but if you could run down there with a picture of a deer or a bear that somebody had shot with the bow you might make the front page.'' Fred Bear soon began to make the front page, and thus entered the promotional business. Like a bear in a bull market, he tramped the sportshow circuit doing shooting exhibitions, com-

A successful deer hunt in northern Wisconsin, 1941. *Photo credit Fred Bear*

peted in numerous archery tournaments around the country, produced and directed a library of films on the sport of bow hunting, and spoke enthusiastically at dinners and sports clubs throughout America.

By 1947, Bear's business had prospered to the point where he was able to construct an 8500-square-foot plant on the banks of the Au Sable River in Grayling, Michigan, where he worked 14 to 16 hours a day developing and eventually mass-producing fiberglass bows. While developing glass bows and living in a tent on the banks of the Manistee River, Bear began to court a bride. As *Sports Illus-*

trated reported in 1976, "Rather than postpone the marriage until they could afford more conventional living quarters, they honeymooned in the tent and made the tent their home for the first two years of their marriage except in the deep of winter. When Fred brought guests home, Henrietta Bear recalls, he would toot the car horn the last mile through the woods to warn me that someone was coming." They have been married for over 35 years. Henrietta Bear, however, seldom accompanies Fred into the wilderness and just isn't as fond of the outdoors as Fred. "She went to Africa with me," Fred recalls, "where we had a photo-sightseeing

Bear's most memorable wide-beamed whitetail, which he stalked, shot and trailed in a howling blizzard. *Photo credit Fred Bear*

safari for two weeks. Following this, I hunted in Mozambique while she toured Europe.''

As Bear's business grew, he did more and more hunting and went to more and more places—always with camera and notebook in hand. During the 50s he filmed his adventures in stalking bucks in Arizona's Kaibab Forest and his experiences in hunting royal elk in the Wyoming Rockies, as well as his adventures in hunting mule deer in North Dakota and whitetails in Pennsylvania. As the decade wore on, he ventured into Canada for moose and bear and into Alaska for Dall sheep. He then tried his bow on elk and bighorn sheep in Montana. Before the decade ended, he left his footprints in

British Columbia and Africa. His films of these hunting exploits were soon viewed with enjoyment by millions of people. As John Mitchell observed in his highly controversial book entitled *The Hunt* (1979), ''With prints of his films circulating to Scout troops and service clubs, with Arthur Godfrey's microphone following him to the ends of the earth, with features in *Time* and *Life* magazines and the producers of ABC-TV's 'The American Sportsman' clamoring for his on-camera presence, and with his own likable, lanky, craggy-faced, cracker-barrel backwoods charm, Bear at last had something going for himself and for the sport of bow hunting.''

While Fred Bear enjoys the camaraderie of bow hunting camps and actively participates in deer drives, he prefers to solo hunt. Like T. S. Van Dyke, Francis Sell and George Mattis, Bear finds still hunting and stalking to be most gratifying methods of bow hunting. These methods of hunting allow him to pit all of his skill against the instinct of the deer he seeks. In *Fred Bear's World of Archery* (1979), he clearly distinguishes between these two methods of hunting: "Still hunting is the process of walking quietly and slowly through game habitat, trying to see an animal before it sees you. Stalking is the culmination of the still hunt, wherein the hunter, having located an animal, attempts to close to within bow range. This is the real essence of hunting and requires more skill than driving or blind hunting. It is by far the most difficult and the most satisfying way to hunt, for it places the bowhunter on more even terms with his quarry."

In November of 1969, Bear decided to still hunt deer on St. Martin Island, a densely wooded area in Lake Huron that stands as a kind of moated fortress for whitetails. Ray Kennedy, a one-time associate editor for *Time* magazine, accompanied him. Kennedy's report of that deer hunt needs to be quoted in full, because it captures the essence of a Fred Bear deer hunt:

First Day. *As dawn streaked across the amber and gold foliage on a heroic fall day, Fred was already prowling the beach, studying the heart-shaped tracks. "They're here," he whispered. A rangy, rawboned man with the weathered look of a backwoods sage, he was wearing a battered gray fedora. As he explored the island, half a dozen deer bolted from dis-tant thickets, their upturned tails waving like white flags. Later, sipping black coffee out of a tin can, he smiled: "Looks like this is going to be too easy for the bow. Maybe I should have brought my spear."*

Second Day. *Bow cradled under his arm like a violin, Fred moved through the bush like the prey he was pursuing— three steps, pause, slowly look around. Stepping in slow motion, he somehow worked his size fourteen hunting boots through the tangle of twigs without a sound. Coming upon a clearing, he pointed to deep ruts in the black soil and whispered: "That's as big a buck track as I've ever seen." As he sat statue-still behind a huge uprooted maple, a woodpecker's tattoo shattered the intense quiet like small arms fire. Overhead, squadrons of Canada geese flew south like dark arrows in the sky. They were the only signs of life the entire day.*

Third Day. *A chilly, gusty rain whipped through the trees. "This is good," said Fred. "The deer's vision will be dimmed by raindrops on their eyelashes." Toward nightfall, as the downpour subsided into a fine mist, Fred spied a big buck munching on ground hemlock eighty yards away. Slowly, silently, Fred positioned his razorhead arrow and watched for five, ten, twenty excruciating minutes as the buck worked his way toward the clearing. But suddenly, he jerked his head, wriggled his nose, and was off into the bush. "Damn!" exclaimed Fred as he huddled over the camp stove. "With this island's tricky wind, it's hard to beat a deer's nose."*

Fourth Day. *Fred peeped out of the tent flap at 4:30 a.m. to find four inches of snow on the ground. Then he slipped on an extra suit of thermal underwear and set out in the dark. In the near-zero temperature, the inlet rimming the camp was layered with ice, and the sand was frozen hard as concrete. Bending like a bloodhound over the maze of snow tracks in the clearing, Fred whispered: "They're moving out of that shintangle (thicket) over there just after sundown." At dusk, as he watched a deer 100 yards off through his binoculars, a red squirrel barked behind him. Turning, Fred looked straight into the eyes of a buck standing twenty yards away. Startled, the deer quickly thumped off into thick cover.*

Fifth Day. *After an uneventful day's hunt, Fred went to the mainland for supplies. At the Ponderosa on Interstate 75, he bought some smoked fish, and the proprietress, Mrs. Melina Hills, invited him into her kitchen for some homemade dandelion wine. She showed him a 20-lb. coho salmon she had "pulled outa the crick this mornin'" as well as photographs of the half-grown pet bobcat she had "potty-trained." Then, handing Fred a sponge soaked in anise oil, she confided: "Don't breeze it around, but that's the best buck lure there is. Just hang it on a tree near your blind." "How long will it last?" Fred asked. "For three rains," she replied.*

Sixth Day. *Fred was awakened by the violent flapping of the tent. Outside, an icy, 45-m.p.h. wind was screaming off the lake. In the clearing the trees were bending in the wind like drawn bows as Fred hung Melina's sponge in a spruce and sprinkled the trunk with a liquid lure made from the sex glands of a doe. Nothing worked. "The only thing left to do," said Fred, blackening his face with soot, "is hunt by moonlight and shoot by shade." Shortly after dusk, his eye caught the reflection of antlers in the moonlight.*

Again it was a big buck, and again he was moving enticingly close—seventy yards, sixty-five, sixty. Then the wind shifted, the buck snorted and disappeared into the night.

Seventh Day. *The hunt was over. Deer spotted: seventeen. Arrows shot: zero.*

"Boy, those whitetails are really something," said Fred as he headed home. "They're just smarter than hell. Reminds me of the time I was hunting mountain goat in Alberta with Bud Gray, the chairman of Whirlpool. After about three hours of panting up those icy mountains, he rested on his bow and said: 'Tell me we're having fun, will ya?' "

The essence of Fred Bear's character emerges most sharply in his weather-worn, battered notebooks that he tirelessly updates in the tradition of the classic outdoor writer. From the "dog-eared, rain-soaked pages" of his journals, we find a warm, humorous and compassionate man who at the end of the trail greatly enjoys eating fried venison tenderloins smothered in onions, beans, hot biscuits and jam; always finishing the meal with tea.

After eating such a delightful deer camp meal, and with a tarp stretched above him and a lantern swinging overhead, he reflects and writes about his adventures in his notebooks. At times, snow blurs the ink on his notebook; ink freezes in his pen. As he thaws his pen out and stokes up the fire, he thinks to himself, "It's my wife's birthday and as always I am hundreds of miles away. . . ."

The very remoteness of the wilderness in which he finds himself kindles the imagination of this adventurous bow hunter who "likes to think that he is perhaps the first white man to have climbed a certain ridge or looked down into a deep,

Sitting in the deer forest, thinking about deer and deer hunting, and writing notes in his journal on the behavior of the white-tailed deer. *Photo credit Fred Bear*

glacier-carved canyon." As a confirmed climber, he always anticipates the view from the next ridge. As he writes in his notebook, "from the top of any mountain the challenge extends, far and wide, until the mountains meet the sky." As soon as he plans a deer hunt, anticipation gets the best of him: "My legs are suddenly too long for my desk and I usually find myself on my way several days ahead of schedule."

At the end of a successful deer hunt,

it's not uncommon for a great celebration to take place outside the Bear's den. Even in a midnight rainstorm, Bear will participate in a shooting match by gas lantern, with the winner being the first to extinguish the flame of a candle, a candle protected with a tarp overhead. When he arises the next morning to fix his favorite blueberry pancakes, the bushes around his camp bloom with arrows.

As a master storyteller, Bear can spin an incredible yarn for you with all the

Hunting whitetails in the hills of Pennsylvania. *Photo credit Fred Bear*

finesse of Mark Twain. Here's one of my favorites:

There's a local fellow here in Grayling who's a confirmed duck hunter. He learned it from his dad. I guess I was instrumental in getting him to hunt near the Boy Scout camp where we have a nice lake. He felt obliged to me, and consequently invited me to go duck hunting with him. He has a dog, a black Spaniel of some kind, about 13 years old. When we got out on the lake, we hunted from a blind built on the point. We put our decoys out and anchored our boat in the brush.

He carries a pocket full of rocks because the dog's eyes aren't very good. He has to keep throwing rocks ahead of the dog until he gets the dog about 10 feet from the duck. That's a big operation. Geez, you even have to hold the dog

with one hand and get ready to shoot with the other. Well . . . some bluebills eventually flew in and we knocked a couple down. One of them dropped several hundred yards out in the lake. Dick said, "I'll take the boat and go get it." So he started rowing. Suddenly, the dog jumped into the water and began swimming after his master. He got entangled in a string of decoys and started towing them. Finally he realized that that task was too much for him and turned back. For a while I thought I was going to have to rescue him. But as things turned out, he did make it back to shore, and promptly shook the decoys off.

Because the wind had blown part of our blind away, I began to make some minor repairs. Since Dick had hip boots on, he stepped out of the boat to untangle the decoys. Well . . . we had an offshore wind and before either one of us knew it the boat was 30 yards out. You know, of course, that in duck hunting any time you're out of your boat the ducks are flying all over the place. Dick stood there looking and wondering how foolish a person can be, as the ducks circled overhead. So I said to Dick, "Oh, to hell with the boat, the wind will blow it to the other side of the lake. Let's go into the blind and get some shooting." He didn't say a word. He just came back and sat in the blind. Nothing happened for about 20 minutes, nobody said a word. Finally he looked over at me and with a very silly smile said, "My gun is in the boat."

Regardless of the name brand of the bow hunting equipment you use, it is more than likely based on principles which Bear discovered and implemented many years ago. An inkling of his personality and character reflects itself in his refusal to seek royalties from competitive companies that use his patented designs.

When asked some time ago how he would like to be remembered, he retorted, "that I was honest with myself and with others. And that I did my best at what I thought was important in my life. I am happy that I was able to grow up and live as a free man and to have the opportunity to work at what I enjoyed doing the most . . . hunting and fishing. It has always given me a great deal of pleasure to introduce new people to the outdoors and I am happy to have been able to do so over the years, as well as having been able to simply expose so very many people to the outdoor life through our films and books and travels. Anything else that I am remembered for will have to be decided by others."

Others, like Dick Lattimer, a long-standing personal friend of Bear's, have

decided that "Fred Bear's world is one of wood smoke, pawed acorns, the sweet smell of decaying leaves, the twitch of a deer's tail and ragged birch bark blowing in the wind. He is a man of the forests and mountains; a man who is equally at home with a prince of India or a nervous new bow hunter on opening day. It is said about some men that they do not walk where the path leads. Rather they go where there is no path and leave a trail. Fred Bear is such a man."

When the Hunter's Moon rises above the deer shack this October like a huge, orange ball of fire, many of America's 2 million bow hunters will be in the deer forest with Bear equipment in hand and with romantic images of the old master in the back of their mind. Actually, Bear bows and razorheads are as common in the deer forests as Fisher Bodies are on the American freeways that lead to them.

Fred shot this buck under an apple tree in Rolling Rock, Pennsylvania, in the early 1960s. It is the buck shown in the popular Fred Bear film, "The Oldest Game." *Photo credit Fred Bear*

Hunting deer in western Ontario, 1944. *Photo credit Fred Bear*

As long as the Hunter's Moon returns in the October sky, our thoughts will turn to Fred Bear, the man whom *Life* magazine once referred to as a cross between Natty Bumppo and Robin Hood.

Even though he has shot a four-ton bull elephant with a single arrow as well as polar bears in the Arctic and Bengal tigers in India, he still believes that "the wariest, craftiest and the hardest game of all to hunt is the white-tailed deer of North America." I agree. Why does the man with the Borsalino hat hunt white-tails? He answers this question for us in a classic essay entitled *Thoughts on Hunting:*

"I hunt deer because I love the entire process; the preparations, the excitement, and sustained suspense of trying to match my woodslore against the finely honed instincts of these creatures. On most days spent in the woods, I come home with an honestly earned feeling that something good has taken place. It makes no difference whether I got anything; it has to do with how the day was spent.

"Life in the open is one of the finest rewards. I enjoy and become completely immersed in the high challenge and increased opportunity to become for a time a part of nature. Deer hunting is a classical exercise in freedom. It is a return to fundamentals that I instinctively feel are basic and right.

"I have always tempered my killing with respect for the game pursued. I see the animal not only as a target but as a living creature with more freedom than I will ever have. I take that life if I can, with regret as well as joy, and with the sure knowledge that nature's ways of fang and claw or exposure and starvation are a far crueler fate than I bestow."

Chapter 2

A Solo Deer Hunter

Deer hunting still remains one of man's oldest pursuits. Even though the modern deer hunter no longer relies on venison to sustain himself, there nevertheless remains in each of us a heartfelt desire for basic self-sufficiency. What outdoorsman does not satisfy his own ego when he places trout or venison on the kitchen table? Fortunately, technology and modern civilization have not entirely destroyed the spirit for providing game for the larder. This heartfelt desire for self-sufficiency and independence best manifests itself in those free-spirited individuals who prefer to hunt deer alone. Although solo deer hunters represent a minority in the deer forest today (only 11 percent of American deer hunters hunt alone), there are at least a few individuals who—like many trout fishermen—need no camaraderie to enjoy their days afield.

George Mattis was such an individual. He died in August of 1982.

Mattis started to hunt deer at the age of 15. With the aid of a double-barrel shotgun, he killed his first deer, a spike buck, in 1920. From that moment on, he was a deer hunter for the rest of his life. During his life George Mattis studied, observed, photographed, hunted and wrote about deer behavior. Actually, his entire lifestyle literally reflected the essence of the white-tailed deer: a life of independence, self-sufficiency and simplicity, all underscored with an eternal yearning for the solitude of the November deer forest.

Born in Streator, Illinois, in 1905, the young Mattis moved to northern Wisconsin with his family in 1918, the year a 10¢ paper deer tag was required for all deer hunters. He grew up on a small farm situated in the middle of a logged-over

The young Mattis with a "brush wolf," October, 1921. *Photo credit George Mattis*

wilderness in Sawyer County, heart of the Indianhead area. His earliest impressions of the deer herd must have been bleak, for at that time the deer population was at a very low level. Game officials and deer hunters alike termed the 1919 any-deer season "a disaster." Yet, as George recalls, "the white-tailed deer was the most common form of wildlife to be seen during the early twenties."

As a mere lad during the early 20s, George was always fascinated with whitetails. "As children we saw them on our way to and from grade school. To me they appeared like over-grown cottontail rabbits with their supple bodies and continuous nibbling on browse as they filtered through the brush. Most every able-bodied man or youth was a deer hunter

during the twenties. But my interest in the whitetail went a bit beyond merely hunting them during the deer season. I used to take walks along a railroad track during the evenings just to observe deer that fed on the short browse along the right-of-way and at the edges of marshes and ponds. I must admit my interest in them during the off seasons was just as intense as during the deer hunting season. I studied them at their winter deer yards as well as at cattle salt licks during the early spring. I soon observed that they were most easily spotted during the summer when their reddish coats showed up in contrast to the lush, green foliage."

In recalling his earliest deer hunting experiences, George tells us that he attended a deer stand with his oldest brother. "I learned to sit quietly, be patient, and endure the weather. I felt I played a part in any kill he made. Later I made short drives for him and when I was successful in driving a deer onto him, I felt some measure of elation. I soon became a responsible member of our deer hunting group.

"The first buck I got was somewhat of a fluke. An older brother put me on a stand with directions to remain quiet until he came through. It was a chilly morning and I soon became a bit cold. So I moved about in an attempt to keep warm. I saw a spike buck come along, and he likewise spotted me. Suddenly I remembered I was to remain quiet. The buck was determined to cross the dirt road where I was stationed, so he ran parallel to it in order to avoid me. I likewise ran parallel to the buck. He decided to cross the road, and did so just a matter of a few yards ahead of me. I shot, undoubtedly from my hips, and down he went on the frozen road where he knocked himself out. The bullet

A typical northern Wisconsin deer camp, as Mattis encountered them when he moved to the Badger State in 1918. *Photo credit State Historical Society of Wisconsin*

just grazed his shoulders and stunned him momentarily, but the hard fall put him down. When my brother came through, the buck was on his feet and ready to go. My brother finished him off. I learned two early lessons here: one, to remain still at a stand, and two, to be sure your game is down to stay.''

The deer population changed dramatically for the better after the early 1920s, as evidenced by the many white-tailed bucks Mattis took during his lifetime. While the deer population changed, however, George Mattis did not. Throughout his life, he lived a bachelor's existence in a small one-story brick home near Birchwood, Wisconsin. He frequently explained his bachelorhood by saying, ''I just married the great outdoors.''

Like the whitetail, he rose early each day. But unlike the whitetail, he only spent half the day amidst wildlife and plants. That's one half day more than most of us accomplish in this regard, however! To make us even more envious, he always looked about 20 years younger than his age. I've got a feeling that good tracking snow, the sight of leaping bucks and prime venison roast greatly contributed to his youthfulness. Although he fit into the American deer hunting scene like any red shirt huddled over a bowl of venison stew, there was one basic difference: George Mattis made a living out of deer hunting and trout fishing—a dream most of us never accomplish.

Not only was Mattis unique in being able to spend 12 months of the year in the outdoors as an angler, deer hunter, naturalist and wildlife photographer, but he studied the white-tailed deer throughout its wide range, and lived in intimate

Patience as a solo deer hunter resulted in an easy, clean kill by Mattis of this fine 8-pointer. *Photo credit George Mattis*

contact with the animal in the upper Great Lakes area. From his North Woods retreat he wrote his regular column on outdoor recreation for the magazine *Sports and Recreation*. At the time of his death in August of 1982, he was writing a new book entitled *Excursions in Nature*.

In the summer, when he was not observing deer, angling for trout or writing, George Mattis did such things as visit small, isolated bogs in the depth of spruce groves, hoping to photograph pink lady's slippers. In the mellow sun of mid-September Mattis would make his annual pilgrimage to his favorite haunts in search

of the woodland jewels of autumn: the red baneberry, the scarlet berries of the jack-in-the-pulpit, the bunchberry and the shrubbery of dry, wooded hilltops. In the lavish blaze of October foliage, we would find the reclusive Mattis meditating to himself: "Where the reclusive blooms of spring and early summer shyly peeped, Mother Nature now splashes the withering greensward with fruits of bold and original color."

In mid-November we always found Mattis in the solitary, gloomy, colorless deer forests of the North; for the past half century he never missed a deer hunting season except for the years he spent studying journalism at the University of Wisconsin and for his term of military service. When it came to the deer season, he was about as regular as the deer themselves! Indeed, when one thinks of deer, one thinks of Mr. George Mattis. You will find his classic book on the white-tailed deer, (*Whitetail: Fundamentals and Fine Points for the Hunter*, 1980), in almost a half million homes, resorts, cottages and deer shacks across this country.

This chapter pays homage to this distinguished man of the deer forest . . . this small-in-stature and soft-spoken man with the shy-looking grin . . . this humble man who lived a very simple existence devoid of worldly possessions.

After spending more than 50 years tramping the deer forest, George Mattis recorded many observations on whitetail behavior. "I once found a very young fawn lying in my path along a trout stream. It was apparently born but a few hours before, for it lay a helpless thing, showing no fear whatever. It did not move or even bat an eyelash as I knelt beside it. When I returned down the trail an hour later, it was still there, only it had turned around, facing the other way. It takes a few hours for the very young fawn to develop its simple senses and make responses to the outside world to which it is a complete stranger. Indeed, hardly a year goes by when I do not come upon at least one fawn along my trout fishing waters. Maybe I am now more conscious of the presence of these spotted youngsters along my creeks, for I see them more often than I did years ago. Possibly this is because I have learned to expect more from my trout fishing trips than the mere taking of

The successful results of solo hunting. *Photo credit George Mattis*

fish." Indeed, like Henry David Thoreau, Mattis believed that a man might fish all his life and never realize that it's really not the fish he seeks.

Whether he's trout fishing or deer hunting, the sportsman rarely gets to see the frolicking and playful behavior of deer. The outdoorsman attuned to his natural surroundings does know that deer play consists of various types of activity: running, leaping, head jerking, butting, kicking, neck craning, mounting, head shaking and neck twisting. Yet, deer play remains one of the least understood categories of behavior. It's more easily described than explained, and generally takes place among fawns. One day while following a trout stream, and with a clump of foliage in front of him, Mattis encountered a playful incident with great commotion:

"There, in the middle of a shallow pool,

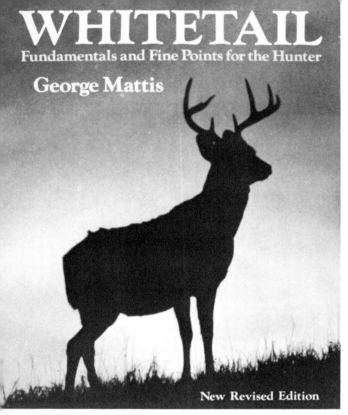

WHITETAIL
Fundamentals and Fine Points for the Hunter

George Mattis

New Revised Edition

You will find Mattis's classic book on the whitetail in almost half a million homes, resorts, cottages and deer shacks in this country. It blends a practical knowledge of hunting whitetails with an in-depth feeling for the mystery and mystique of the animal and the romance and challenge of the chase. *Photo credit Robert Wegner*

was a doe with her twin fawns frolicking in the water. Or, rather, it was the fawns at play while the mother looked on, occasionally coming to shore and straining her ears to catch any strange sounds above the low rumbling din of the nearby rapids. The fawns were uninhibited in their noisy romping, seeming to enjoy the feel of the cool spray on their bodies. Seldom have I seen deer so completely relaxed and off guard as during this warm and sunny August afternoon. After I watched them for about five minutes, my scent must have spread to the nostrils of the doe, for she became apprehensive and gradually led her youngsters downstream and then out of the water to a thicket. Indeed, it isn't often that deer are completely free to relax from possible danger.''

Throughout the years, whether in the field with rod or rifle, George Mattis remained a keen student of deer beds and bedding behavior. He summarized his conclusions on bedding behavior as follows: ''I used to believe that deer went through considerable purpose and ritual before they bedded down. This, I observed, is not at all the case. On several occasions, I have seen deer, including bucks, come down a runway toward me. I was all agog for a shot when the animals would pause a moment and then drop suddenly to the ground to bed down. Often this would be along the runway or else in a thicket just to the side of the trail. The modern whitetail might bed down in a farm field of alfalfa or corn, or very near farm buildings. The wilderness bucks, though, still prefer to bed down on a high vantage point from where they can be alerted to any threat to their safety.

''On two occasions I have seen deer that were completely at rest, or asleep, somewhat like you might find a cow dozing off with her head resting on the ground and eyes shut or half-shut. I approached a buck practically asleep under an evergreen tree in such a situation. I shot him at less than fifty feet away. I also observed a big doe in her bed that was so completely at rest with her eyes half-open and her head resting on the ground that it was only when I shouted that she awoke from her sleep and dashed off. It is rare, indeed, when one sees whitetails so completely off guard.''

I know several deer hunters (one particularly well) who score nearly every season. Why? Because they catch white-tails completely off guard. Because they go afield *alone* season after season. Needless to say, they are all very satisfied with their solitary roles. Restless legs and nervous anxiety are not attributes of these solo deer hunters. They are not members of the hurried crowd; they are not anxious newcomers or exuberant weekenders. They know that their best strategy revolves around intercepting deer rather than overtaking them. These solo deer hunters have several things going for them, attributes which they are not overly anxious to share with the vast army of red coats.

First of all, as Mattis observes, they are in *full possession of their senses*. In a classic article on the subject, he writes that "whoever is idle or resting, the hunter or deer, is the one that has full possession of his senses. It is the moving hunter or deer that is readily seen or heard by the other. If the hunter remembers this basic fact, he can expect to see more white-tails, especially bucks, for the good, clean shots that count."

Secondly, by being unattached to any group, solo hunters can be extremely *versatile* in their hunting practices. They can enter small timber patches overlooked by the gang hunters. They can change their hunting methods and grounds whenever conditions or the spirit warrant. They can appraise situations quickly and make the best of them—without a lot of needless opinionizing. Actually, Mattis's greatest contribution to the literature on deer and deer hunting revolves around his emphasis on the virtues of solo hunting:

"The science of still-hunting is being somewhat neglected today because of the trend of sociability in all our outdoor recreations. But the camaraderie of gang hunting is often maintained at the cost of the success of the individual; and the hunting pattern of the group becomes something of a standard ritual from which no single member must depart. Consequently, the routine hunt goes on day after day with little regard to weather conditions or any other situations that might suggest a needed change in hunting plans.

"In contrast is the flexibility of the solo hunter who plans his hunt from day to day and even from hour to hour to take advantage of weather change, deer movement or hunter concentration on his hunting grounds.

"If the solo hunter scores better, it is because he hunts better."

Mattis always believed that the solo hunter made quicker and cleaner kills of deer not running scared with high levels of adrenaline.

George Mattis never entered the forest *just* to get a buck. He went as a hunter, of course, but as a hunter-naturalist who kept his eyes and ears attuned to the activities of all woodland creatures. In his lonely vigil while trail watching, he took great delight in watching weasels, "the Lilliputian gangsters of the forest," prowl the snowshoe trail. With his back against an aspen tree, he witnessed ruffed grouse burst forth from dense foliage. His own behavior was frequently observed by beavers as they watched him in silence. Young porcupines clinging to small sagging saplings provided the lone Mattis with a pleasant break in the early morning hours. Red and gray squirrels, busy at work, ignored his presence. Indeed, animals, including bears, often learned to accept Mattis as just another denizen of the deer forest.

Not content to merely observe roaming bears while still hunting whitetails, he continued his childhood penchant for prying into dark hollow logs. One day he thrust his head into a black hole, "and almost collided with the swaying head of a drowsy bruin. He did not seem fully aware of any danger brought on by my intrusion, for he lay in his snug bed, his eyes less than wide open, and his head moving very slowly from side to side as though he were attempting to lull himself into sleep and thus dispel the hazy image before him. I knelt before the entrance to the den, and from less than two feet I uttered a few soft-spoken words in a low, monotone voice, but I got no reaction from the sleepy occupant. After a half hour I left my indifferent bruin to himself, feeling that if I loitered around much longer he might wake from his lethargy and decide to leave his winter quarters. I had nothing against this bruin or any other, and killing him would give me no satisfaction or pride."

Foxes frequently came down the deer trails George watched, as did brush wolves on very rare occasions. George fondly recalls the day he saw a mink wrestling with a large walleyed pike "in a mad fury of spray, fur, and fins." While on his stand, playful chickadees popped out of nowhere and consoled and amused the solitary Mattis as he patiently waited for the whitetail to appear. The solitary deer hunter, Mattis tells us, not only becomes a keen observer of wildlife, but takes a grandstand seat where he can observe the foibles of many deer hunters who pass by in an endless parade, still pounding the pavement and unfortunately remaining detached from everything that is wild.

Yes . . . Mattis enjoyed the utter silence of the autumn woods, the cherished hush of forested terrain. In the eerie silence of the deer forest, his senses became attuned to the muted activity of wildlife. Unlike the pseudo-outdoorsmen with all the accoutrements of the sport shop, Mattis traveled alone in silence with the bare essentials—in the simplistic style of John Muir. The lone still hunter, George Mattis explains, "gets as much satisfaction from the hunt itself as he does from bagging his quarry. He is actually more than just a huntsman out to get a deer; he is a man with more than an ordinary love for the solitude of autumn woods. So content is he with his lot that he is unwilling to share it with others."

The deer hunt for George Mattis meant much more than merely bagging a deer; it represented a meaningful excursion into nature. Getting a deer was merely an added bonus. "It's a great sport whether or not you get a deer . . . Enjoying the outdoors, having a safe experience and cooperating in a friendly manner with landowners is the important thing." Above all, he urges us to cultivate an esthetic appreciation of our remaining wilderness, and to study nature from an ecological point of view. He rightly insists that "we have spent the youthful energy of our pioneer past in striving to subdue the raw outdoors; and in our anxiety to do so, we overlooked the fact that we could do much better by learning to live with our natural heritage instead of subjugating it to shortsighted, selfish ends. Where ecology was once understood by only a few, today it is the concern of all of us."

George Mattis represents the classic woodsman, naturalist, trout fisherman and deer hunter, who strives for the ecological improvement of deer habitat and for the preservation of pure water for our trout streams. He visited the deer forest and the trout stream at every possible moment; he did so since he was old enough to hold a fishing rod and carry a deer rifle. Following his boyhood practices, he deliberately kept his trout fishing and deer hunting gear to a bare minimum and attributed his continued great passion for deer hunting and trout angling to the fact that his attachments lay with the stream and the forest, and not with the technological accoutrements that merely become a distraction and burden. Mattis did not pamper himself with a vast array of gadgets and extra attire for ease and comfort. He viewed deer hunting as a privilege of the hardy outdoor clan. "Only the lukewarm hunter needs to surround himself with many things in order to keep himself amused and occupied while in the field."

George Mattis clung to the traditions of the outdoor clan with a certain reverence, and like T. S. Van Dyke, Fred Bear and Francis E. Sell, he passed them along for future generations of deer hunters to nurse and perpetuate. Following the old traditions, for example, he read Jack O'Connor's books on big game hunting with great delight—greatly appreciating their practical lessons. Leaning toward the naturalist's love of deer, he preferred the deer books of Leonard Lee Rue III. It's not surprising that in deer rifle preference, George Mattis chose the 30/30 Winchester lever action. He hastened to add, however, that "my attachment to the 30/30 is not without some sentiment. The gun is the right weight for me, especially for still-hunting, but I am aware of and willing to accept, its limitations." Over all, Mattis believed that the nurturing of tradition is nowhere more pronounced than in the world of deer and deer hunting.

"Despite the ever-increasing number of men taking part in the hunt today, there is ample room for the individualist, the loner who derives his satisfaction from pursuing his quarry through knowledge he has gained from experience and observation. His is a total involvement in the chase. Where today's group participants hunt much the same every day, the inveterate solo hunter changes his tactics to conform with any change in weather conditions that might affect the behavior of his quarry."

—George Mattis
Photo credit George Mattis

George Mattis knew well the bend of many trout streams and the fork of many deer trails. He knew the deer forests of our eastern and western states. He sampled the trout streams and deer forests of England, Scotland and Germany as well. After 50 years of deer hunting and trout fishing, George Mattis brilliantly emphasized one basic fact of life: "There are more tensions released, anguishes soothed, and racking decisions realized on our fishing waters and in our deer forests than in the offices of psychiatrists or family consultants, or in the offices of all the other trouble shooters for our ailing humanity."

On August 13, 1982, George Mattis died at the age of 77. This blue-eyed, short and stocky deerslayer with the ruddy cheeks and white hair looked as if he were in his mid-50s. He died while playing cribbage with his brother in his hometown. In a eulogy, his friend Joel Vance wrote, "He died the way he had lived—quietly and without fuss. . . . Only in the woods and in the legacy of his heartfelt writing was he a giant." Indeed, he was a giant among deer hunters. Like the sudden crack of a 30/30 in the deer forest on a quiet, crisp November day, his words echo loudly and clearly among American deer hunters.

Chapter 3

An Oregon Backwoodsman

Few deer hunters live the life of Riley. Even those few who do would no doubt be envious of Francis E. Sell's picturesque situation in the wilderness of southwestern Oregon. Indeed, who wouldn't envy a life spent in top-shelf deer country? Who wouldn't admire living in a solitary, huge, old log cabin set in an apple orchard where numerous Columbian black-tailed deer help the deer hunting occupant harvest his fruit crop each autumn?

Yet, the harvest works both ways; for each autumn, when the hills around rural Coquille, Oregon, turn gold and crimson, it's an annual ritual for Sell ("Spud" as he is known to his friends) to take a trophy black-tailed buck. "Not just any buck," as Nick Sisley points out in his *Deer Hunting Across North America* (1975), "but a buck sporting a regal set

of antlers, one grown wise in the way of hunters and a worthy opponent of the most skilled woodsman." Yes, Sell fills his tag every year while still hunting or trail watching in the forested terrain around his frontier-style cabin—where wise old blacktails have everything in their favor. Sell wouldn't have it any other way.

Just to set the record straight—Sell killed his first deer when he was 9 years old with an old Model 73, 44/40 Winchester. During the 70 years since that exciting event, he has added immensely to his skills as a deer hunter, and has taken many fine trophies. His last nine shots produced nine trophy blacktails!

Sell was born in the Riverton wilderness area of southwestern Oregon in 1902. Ever since he was 17, he has been living with deer and studying them in the wilds of his native land. He could pass for a

Francis (Spud) Sell: trapper, backwoodsman, deer stalker and firearms consultant. *Photo credit Francis E. Sell*

man 30 or 40 years younger. He hikes the hills constantly, and pursues his quarry with camera in hand at every opportunity during the off season. As he proudly admits, ''my wife and I quit the rat race in 1926, bought 95 acres of wilderness, and have never regretted our decision. My wife, Ethel, is still with me after 56 years of married bliss. She was born and reared in Boston, but loves the western woods!''

Sell comes from a long line of frontier descendants. One of his forbears on his mother's side was Lewis Wetzil, the renowned Indian fighter, who was greatly feared and considered a better woodsman than Daniel Boone. Incidently, Sell's Indian name is Black Weasel, ''acquired from the Indians and whites because they said that I was the only boy who could eat as much as my Indian namesake.'' A Coquille Indian, named Tom Two Ridges, taught Sell woodcraft, deer hunting and trapping. With regard to deer hunting, ''he taught me that I must become one of the deer herd, moving and making noise where the deer expect movement and noise, that I must always be on a trail that the deer expect to be used at that time of the day, and that I must remain still when the deer are expected to be still.'' Spud can hardly remember when he got his first gun or fishing rod; they both have always been part of his existence.

Responding to a question that I asked him about what inspired or influenced him most of all in his love of deer hunting, Sell remarked, ''I think this is inborn. My family has been living with deer on the frontier since 1750—always moving a bit ahead of the so-called civilization. I have always been interested in the stories handed down in the family about my hunting ancestors. One great uncle of mine, for example, was hid in a hollow log by a squaw, so he could escape from being burnt at the stake after his capture by Indians. After the squaw removed the spider web from the entrance to the log, he eased in, making as little disturbance as possible. She then replaced the spider web and made some raccoon tracks going in and out of the log to account for the small disturbance. The Indians who were looking for him soon came and sat on the log—saying he couldn't be in there because the spider web hadn't been disturbed. They read *sign* as a matter of course. The wilderness was an open book to them, and it took an expert equally skillful in making sign to fool them." Indeed, Sell remains a fine product of the Indian tradition.

In addition to his Indian upbringing, Sell received his formal education in Oregon and Hawaii. It was, however, a backwoods education, to be sure. As Sell recalls, "I remember my first year of school. This required a walk of one mile through the forest to the one-room schoolhouse. No excuses for being late, and I always was. School started in April— a time when birds were nesting, rabbits birthing their young, and there were plenty of wildlife tracks on the trail. So . . . by the time I had gathered a few berries to feed the young robins, and looked in on a nest of rabbits, I was always late. I got my backside tanned every morning for being late for the full term of the school year. Later in life, I realized that I learned much more between home and school than I ever learned in school. For the most part, I ran a professional trap line and took my schoolbooks with me. I took my examinations *after* the trapping season. University schooling was all done by extension." He graduated from Honolulu College in 1925.

Sell's log cabin, where "Spud" has lived and studied deer for the past 55 years. *Photo credit Francis E. Sell*

Hard at work at the fleshing board with a carpenter's drawknife used for fleshing and removing hair and "grain" from the deer hide. *Photo credit Francis E. Sell*

Does his life of Riley in the western woods with mule deer and blacktail alike have any problems? Yes . . . indeed! "There are times when I have my troubles—situations which would try the soul of any outdoorsman. Last autumn, for example, I planned to hunt pheasants, when a friend called to tell me that the chinooks were almost jumping into the fishermen's boats on the lower Coquille, and suggested we go trolling the next day. Another friend stopped on his way back from the Sixes to report that there was an early run of steelhead in, and to ask me to return there with him. And on top of this a third friend, staying at the ranch, came in with a breathless story of seeing the tracks of three uncommonly large deer. If I would go with him the next day we could get one. SUCH ARE MY PROBLEMS!"

Indeed, Sell makes the life of the deer stalker sound like a happy existence. "We have good deer hunting. During the fall I have counted as many as 20 deer feeding on our apples, but I never kill, or allow anyone else to kill, a deer in the orchard. The deer know it too! As for fishing, my place is located within easy reach of the Umpqua, Coquille, Sixes, Elk and Rogue rivers. I manage to spend two or three days a week fishing or hunting, depending on the season, and Ethel, my trail partner, likes to cook, especially fish and wild game."

During the past 30 years, Sell has also been a full-time outdoor writer specializing in deer and deer hunting. He has published innumerable articles (well over 1000 of them), and 10 books on topics ranging from *Practical Fresh Water Fishing* (1960) to *Hunting with Camera and Binoculars* (1961). Several of his books appear in Japanese and Spanish editions. Asked about the circulation figures of his books, Sell remarked, "I do not have exact figures on how many books of mine have been printed—I'm too busy with deer hunting projects to keep count of them—but it has been a very large number!" Indeed, his deer hunting books were all selections of the Outdoor Life Book Club and of various sportsmen's book clubs throughout the country. Many of them are now collector's items with expensive price tags on them. Asked what his favorite book on deer hunting was, Sell replied, "The wilderness itself. The authors of the book, the deer themselves!" One thing is certain: when it comes to writing a book which makes the easy chair a ship to sail off into new lands of deer hunting delight, Francis E. Sell, a nationally famous author on sporting subjects, is a master craftman. People from all over the world not only read his books, but come to visit and study wildlife under his supervision.

Perhaps his greatest contribution and legacy to American hunting revolves around his reputation as an international authority on firearms, especially shotguns. He is well remembered as the designer of the Italian Gasperni 20-gauge Magnum double-barrel shotgun. In addition, Sell developed the first long-range loads for the 12- and 20-gauge. These special handloads enabled a gunner to do pass shooting with a shotgun of reasonable weight. His 20-gauge delivered good uniform 80-yard goose killing patterns, a range formerly reserved for the ponderous 10-gauge magnum weighing 11 to 12 pounds. All of the commercial long-range present-day loadings are certainly indebted to Sell's long-range handload. They use about the same type cushioning, and also buffer the shot charge with powdered plastic. In his design work on guns, Sell also introduced the long forcing cones, long choke cones and properly tapered ribs. He has also done considerable work in the custom stocking of shotguns—reducing the pointing element of gun handling so that the gun feels like an extension of the gunner himself. In coaching gunners to shoot, he frequently makes

Sell cleaning his 257-caliber wildcat rifle, which he developed for deer shooting in heavy cover. It pushes a 117-grain bullet at a velocity of 2575 feet per second. *Photo credit Francis E. Sell*

custom stocks for his outstanding students. At present, Sell is experimenting with new iron sights for brush shooting.

As a writer on the subject of guns, he has served as an editorial consultant for *Gunsport Magazine,* Associate Editor of *Guns and Game* and as a member of the editorial staff of *Gunfact Magazine.* Not surprisingly, ballisticians from many parts of the world seek out his advice on gun design.

Sell with one of his favorite rifles and a buckskin rifle case that he made from a trophy buck. *Photo credit Francis E. Sell*

His legacy goes far beyond his role as a firearms consultant, however. His life and work provide us with the highest caliber of professional hunting and fishing integrity. His legacy furnishes us with a brilliant definition of the universal meaning of deer hunting that he summarizes for us in his classic text, *The American Deer Hunter* (1950), a book which many still view as the greatest volume ever written on the subject:

"Under the drive of modern living, I am certain that deer hunting offers esthetic rewards that balance and often exceed the practical aspects of the activity. The hunter, his family and friends may quite easily share the satisfaction of dining on prime venison, but the hunter shares with no one the intimate contacts and sensations that are his in the field. Nature invites him to exchange days for memories; she bids him to fill the pockets of a magical hunting coat. These pockets never fill to overflowing. Into them tumble the flaming banners of autumn, the dew-diamonds of sunrises, the hundred little sounds of the solitude, and the silent beauty of the cover under a blanket of tracking snow. And never to be forgotten are the fine companionships; the comfort of the night campfire . . . the tang of burning resin . . ." Francis E. Sell, an American deer hunter *par excellence,* leads and points the way to these esthetic experiences of deer hunting.

Yet, Sell's legacy goes far beyond a mere definition of the esthetic experiences of deer hunting; for he has given us a tremendous amount of detailed information about deer trails in his writings and with a style as convincing as his superb shooting ability with the rifle. His theory of deer trails as found in his *Art of Successful Deer Hunting* (1971), revolves around 10 basic propositions: (1) Wind changes and prevailing air currents shape deer trails; (2) Change the wind and the trail activity changes; (3) Thermal wind is an air current set in motion by temperature changes; (4) As the temperature changes, the direction of the thermal drag changes. Under stable weather conditions the thermals go down slopes, creeks, and valleys from late evening until early morning; (5) From late morning until the evening reversal, thermal air currents move up slopes, valleys and draws, from the lower to the higher ground; (6) The inflow of game in late morning always travels from the direction of the more open feeding areas; (7) In the late evening it's just the opposite, with the deer traffic being toward the more open country; (8) Deer trails are always a primary consideration whether you still hunt, drive a section of territory or just trail watch; (9) When still hunting deer trails, duplicate in your movements both the sound and pace of deer; (10) Trail watching is a very exacting art.

As the long shadows of autumn evenings set on the moist, misty slopes behind his log cabin, you will find this trapper, backwoodsman, deer stalker and firearms consultant returning to his desk and fireplace to recapture in print his daily adventures in the art of trail watching. As he writes late into the evening, he knows that tomorrow he will again take the trail back over the hills with deer hunting in mind, especially the trail cut deep with deer tracks at its many turnings. Sometimes he is on the trail with his rifle; sometimes his only excuse for being there is his camera. He rightly acknowledges that "the inspiration for being abroad in deer territory in foul weather and fair, in spring, summer, autumn and winter, revolves around a lifetime desire

In the Oregon deer forest with his Winchester 358-caliber rifle. *Photo credit Francis E. Sell*

to learn everything possible about deer, the most canny of all big game." It is our great fortune that he shares with us his knowledge of deer. No finer deer stalker has ever emerged from the annals of American deer hunting.

Chapter 4

The Still Hunter

In the fall of 1882, Fords, Howard and Hulbert of New York published a unique book that was destined to become one of the greatest classics in the history and philosophy of American deer hunting. The book went through 10 editions between 1882 and 1944, and remained an all-time favorite of President Theodore Roosevelt, founder of the Boone and Crockett Club and lifelong member of The National Rifle Association. The book was entitled *The Still Hunter: A Practical Treatise on Deer Stalking,* and its author was Theodore Strong Van Dyke (1842–1923), a hunting companion and literary associate of President Roosevelt's. This chapter examines this famous treatise on deer stalking and the activities of this early American deer hunter, historian and naturalist.

Van Dyke was born in New Brunswick, New Jersey, in 1842. His father, John Van Dyke, was a lawyer and jurist, a member of the United States House of Representatives and a long-standing friend of Abraham Lincoln's. Like his father, young Theodore was born, raised and educated in the woods, and emerged as a student of the white-tailed deer. "From the earliest days the woods were to me the greatest of attractions. My home was in the corner of a twenty acre piece of forest on the edge of town, which connected with woods upon woods reaching miles away into the country. It was for the groves that I started when school was out and there most of my vacations and Saturdays were spent. Frequent trips to New York were mainly to explore the game departments of the museums and the novelties of the gun stores, and I always returned with a pitying contempt for the city boys who knew nothing of the woods.''

After graduating from Princeton University in 1863, the young Van Dyke moved to the woods of Wabasha, Minnesota, in 1867, where he practiced law for the next eight years. After establishing residency there he later became a member of the Minnesota State Assembly. During this time Van Dyke became so enamored with still hunting whitetails, both in Minnesota and northern Wisconsin, that his deer hunt generally lasted for several months, and was repeated every fall until he moved to California. Following the code of the ethical sportsman, he always considered deer hunting more of a charm than mere shooting; wild game that knew how to get away always remained his first choice of pursuit. By the time he was 25 he had 13 years of deer hunting experience behind him. As he put it in an autobiographical essay, ''I was distinguished for keeness of sight and skill with pistol, rifle, and gun at an early age, even among far older companions. Since childhood I had seen deer run before hounds and helped shoot many of them with buckshot. I was a natural still hunter that needed only opportunity.''

At the age of 25 he roamed the finest shooting grounds of Minnesota at every possible opportunity. Yet he always longed for bigger and wilder forests, not pine woods, but the old hardwood timber that Daniel Boone so admired. After years of longing, the opportunity arose in 1867 when an obstinate case of ague gave him an excuse for spending seven months in the great virgin forest of northwestern Wisconsin. He recalls the event in an essay entitled *The Forest Primeval*. ''A dim wagon road wound forty miles into the north, on which were five new settlers, each going eight or ten miles beyond the last, looking for something better. Like them I wanted the last and best and started for the end of the line with nothing but a rifle and blanket. As I left the lovely oak openings and the heavy timber closed in around me, I felt like the prince in a fairy tale, just come to his own.''

He so enjoyed the northern forests that when ill health struck again in 1875, he sought solitude and tranquility, but this time in the mountains and wilderness of southern California. There, he lived 60 miles from anything that could even be called a village, in one of the wildest parts of the country. During this time he lived among game, camping daily, and loafing

T. S. Van Dyke (1842–1923), deer hunter, historian, naturalist and author of that famous book entitled *The Still Hunter: A Practical Treatise on Deer Stalking* (1882). *Photo credit San Diego Historical Society-Title Insurance & Trust Collection*

The end of one hunter's successful still hunt near Donald, Wisconsin, 1904. *Photo credit State Historical Society of Wisconsin*

or walking in its haunts. Morning, noon and night he was rarely out of sight or sound of deer, for amidst the trees where he wrote, read and dozed, they trotted about within a few yards of him. "Often when no venison was needed, I spent the day in the tumbling hills on the trail of the deer just to study the habits and tricks of this most mysterious of big game animals. No book is more interesting than the record of his daily life when you have cultivated the eye to the point where you can read it on dry ground and follow it through dead grass and fallen leaves. And when at last you find where the deer has lain down for his siesta, there is almost as much pleasure in seeing the dust fly from his plunging hoofs as there is in

stopping them with the best of modern rifles."

There, in the mountains and wilderness of southern California, his greatest love not only centered around deer hunting, but hunting the blue plumed quail of the Pacific Coast as well. The valley quail of California, he wrote in 1888, "abounded in numbers quite inconceivable to Eastern sportsmen. One hundred and fifty to two hundred a day was an ordinary bag for a good shot, and in many of the canyons within a mile from the post-office one could quickly load himself down with all he cared to carry back on foot." As a hunter, Van Dyke loved game animals and birds that knew how to escape. He quickly tired of shooting that was too easy.

In fact, when hunting quail with his shotgun became too easy, he took to shooting them with his bow and arrow and his 22-caliber rifle, but freely admitted in a superb essay on the ethics of hunting that he never really mastered the inherent difficulties of this "fine sport."

Van Dyke was, incidentally, one of the early American bow hunters. Even the famed Thompson brothers, Will and Maurice, the patron saints of American archery, were admirers and careful readers of Van Dyke's philosophy of hunting. Like the Thompsons, during his early days he too roamed the woods and sent many an arrow after every squirrel and rabbit that crossed his path. From early childhood on, he loved bow hunting as dearly as he loved his dog and gun. With regard to bow hunting in the mountains and wilderness of California, he has this to say: "Where the bow can be used with any reasonable chance of hitting, as on hares, etc., and without danger of losing too many arrows, it will afford much more pleasure than the gun to that class of sportsmen whose pleasure lies not in a big bag, not in the tickling of the almighty palate, and not in mere murder, but in the skill required, the scenery and associations of the chase, etc. That class, too, is fast on the increase. I joined it years ago, and have no disposition to leave it. On the contrary, the changed taste grows upon me. Year after year I care less for game and counts, and more for the way and manner of securing a little. And herein lies I believe the truest pleasure of hunting."

Indeed, the outdoor sports of San Diego County greatly touched his fancy. Although his major preoccupation was still hunting for deer, he also enjoyed hunting rabbits. "The small hare, commonly called 'the cottontail,' abounds in incredible numbers. A bushel or two of them could be shot from a wagon in a few miles' drive along any of the roads. They run with a swift zigzag motion that makes very pretty shooting, especially on bright moonlight nights, the flickering white tail making a fine mark for snap-shooting." Like other sportsmen before him, he soon became so enchanted with the hunting opportunities of southern California that by the summer of 1876, he decided to make San Diego his future home. Thus, with bedroll, bow and gun in hand, he took to the backcountry of San Diego County. For the next 10 years he lived outdoors for most of the time.

Throughout his life Van Dyke not only enjoyed the truest pleasures of hunting, but remained a prolific outdoor writer. As he tramped the primeval forests of southern California, he used his eyes and ears, his pencil and notebook, and gave to the sporting world the vivid results of his wildlife observations. His writings in this regard combine a rich blend of natural history, adventurous fiction and unmatched, empirical perception. Indeed, between 1880 and 1895, he wrote nine books on outdoor pursuits. In March of 1881 he published his first book, entitled *Flirtation Camp,* or *The Rifle, Rod, and Gun in California,* which described in a technical way California's wild game—afoot, afloat and on the wing. This technical description was placed in the context of a sporting romance with just enough lovemaking woven together with the wildlife adventures to give it additional zest. His popular treatise on still hunting came out in the following year. In 1886 another fascinating outdoor book appeared; entitled *Southern California,* it gives us a great variety of information on southern California's mountains, valleys and streams, its animals, birds and fish, as well as hunting, fishing and camping in this area.

In 1902 he published *The Deer Family,* one of several books for The American Sportsman's Library which he co-authored with Theodore Roosevelt and others. The book soon emerged as a standard work in the field. It consisted of an instructive collection of essays about the natural history of deer, as well as an interesting aggregation of stories about the adventures of deer hunters. After reading the book, John Spears rightly observed in *The New York Times* that "Van Dyke is always intensely amused when he thinks of the tenderfoot, with his brand-new, shiny outfit and his obtrusive helpless imbecility, and yet he is the tenderfoot's best friend. The backwoodsman 'snorts' when told that books can teach a tenderfoot anything, but Van Dyke's writings have made sportsmen of some of the most helpless tenderfeet that ever hit the trail." In 1903 he also co-authored several other volumes for The American Sportsman's Library on the waterfowl of the Pacific Coast and on the hunting of upland gamebirds.

During the first decade of this century, he continued to write many articles on small and big game hunting that appeared in such popular magazines as *Outing* and *Collier's.* He also frequently contributed articles to *The American Field* and *Forest and Stream,* two of the most prominent hunting journals at the turn of the century. To accompany these articles on hunting, he created his own wildlife illustrations and pen sketches. Although he first went to southern California in poor health at the tender age of 34, he soon found a perfect cure in turning his un-

divided attention to outdoor pursuits, especially still hunting for deer, and writing about his outdoor adventures.

In addition to writing books and articles on hunting and various aspects of natural history, Van Dyke continued to practice law in the courts of California, and wrote many articles and several publications promoting San Diego County. He also established himself as an irrigation specialist. Indeed, Van Dyke became the first American to give substance to the idea that the importation of water was essential to the early prosperity of San Diego. By the 1890s he emerged as one of the prime movers in the construction of the great Flume Company that first brought decent water to San Diego from Lake Cuyamaca. This technical experience as an irrigation engineer led him to a systematic study not only of the water requirements of human endeavor, but of mammals and water's relationship to movement patterns of wildlife.

After a thorough study of the basic element of water, Van Dyke formulated some perceptive remarks about hunting deer at waterholes in wooded terrain. First of all, he observed that deer will frequently go a day or more without water even in the hottest and driest weather. Actually, they can dispense with water altogether when browse is succulent. When deer approach waterholes, however, they are quick drinkers, generally wasting little or no time—especially if heavily hunted. Secondly, Van Dyke noticed that in counties where water is scarce and the season especially dry and hot, deer will generally seek water right at daybreak. But he hastened to add that "how a deer will act in going to water or leaving it, as well as his time of watering, are things that cannot be reduced to a rule." Thirdly,

Van Dyke discovered that deer frequently postpone drinking water until after feeding, and when going to water at this time they generally walk quickly and stop infrequently. After many years of watching whitetails at a small waterhole in the North, I found this particular observation quite true. Yet Van Dyke continually reminds us not to place too much reliance on the whitetail's daily water requirements.

Van Dyke left San Diego in 1900, and lived in Los Angeles until 1903, when he purchased a 1200-acre estate near Barstow. On this estate in the Mohave Desert he again put his specialized knowledge of water to use and became a pioneer desert alfalfa grower. At the age of 67 he worked out of doors six or seven hours a day, paying no attention to the temperature. "I was not in any way obliged to do this, but I found my health better always for exercise, and I learned many years ago that the best way to endure heat is the same as enduring cold—to keep yourself strong with exercise and a good appetite." He also served as a local justice of the peace for the small community of Daggett. San Diego never forgot Van Dyke. The family name still applies to streets in East San Diego and Del Mar. American deer hunters never forgot Van Dyke either. His classic text on still hunting stands as a giant on the American sportsmen's bookshelf, a text one returns to with great delight. Theodore Strong Van Dyke, keen and observant naturalist, pioneer American still hunter, engineer, farmer, writer and lawyer, died on June 26, 1923.

During his lifetime, Van Dyke was often referred to as "one of the first authorities in the sporting world" and as "that prince of a sportsman." Indeed, he exhibited all of the qualities of the true sportsman, and these qualities are vividly revealed in his book *The Still Hunter*. First of these was his passionate love of nature in every form and phase, which continually prompted him to study her patiently and faithfully. Consequently, he knew every tree and flower in the regions he hunted and fished, not only by their names, but by their minutest features. He had the same familiar acquaintance with the animals he pursued. "In the saddle at four o'clock and miles into the hills by the time it was light enough to shoot—such were the requirements," of the deer hunter Van Dyke believed, if he were ever to learn the habits of this unique animal.

Second of these sportsman-like qualities was his esthetic appreciation of the woods. After searching for deer in the woods of the East Coast, and after pursuing them in the old hardwood timber of Minnesota and Wisconsin, as well as in the wild forests of Oregon, Mexico and California, Van Dyke gradually formulated a spiritual statement on what the woods meant for the deer hunter. The woods, he maintained, give scope and deeper satisfaction to the hunter who values game more for the skill required to bag it, than as a thing to eat or boast of. In 1907 he wrote, "no wonder Bryant called the woods God's first temple. For nowhere else can you feel the mysterious power that rules all. Not upon the prairie, though there are few places where you feel smaller than on its vast sweep of loneliness. Nor on the sea with its still more certain proof that there is no fellow man within many miles. Nor yet on the mountain top where you can see even more plainly what a trifling link you are in the mighty chain of being." Like his contemporary Aldo Leopold, Van Dyke

"The still-hunter's dream. Yet with whatever proficiency in still-hunting any mortal ever reaches, with all the advantages of snow, ground, wind, and sun in his favor, many a deer will, in the very climax of triumphant assurance, slip through your fingers like the tread of a beautiful dream."—T. S. Van Dyke *Photo credit Leonard Lee Rue III*

viewed man as one of the smallest minorities in the whole superstructure of life's many forms.

This idea is no more evident than in his conception of the final stage of deer hunting, the ultimate stage he hoped all deer hunters would reach—sooner or later. In this stage the mere act of killing, though it requires the highest skill, merely becomes an inferior factor in the pleasure of those who really love the woods and hills. "In this stage there is more real enjoyment than in any other. I never saw the time when I cared a cent for records or anything of the sort and have always despised the 'trophy' business which too often means beastly murder. I never had an Indian or a guide hunt any game for me to pull the trigger on, and would far rather do the hunting and let the Indian pull the trigger. What I wanted from a deer hunt was not that particular bit of meat or that head of horns, but to know whether I could get that buck or he get me. The pleasure in resolving this problem begins with the very first attempt to play your wits against the wits of the game.'' The number of hunters who reach this stage, Van Dyke acknowledged, is greater than many suppose, and many reach it early.

In *The Deer Family,* which he co-authored with President Roosevelt, he described this final stage of deer hunting in his own personal context. It bears repeating. ''From 1875 to 1885 I lived where deer were so plentiful that going out to find fresh tracks was like going to the corner grocery. In the greater part of the section there were no hunters but myself, and deer so abundant that I made my own game laws, with no one to protest. Compelled to spend most of my time in the hills to regain lost health, I had little to do but study nature; and many a deer have I tracked up without a gun, and many a one have I let go unshot at simply because I did not want it, enjoying the hunt just about the same. In this way I knew many a deer nearly as well as if he were hanging under the tree at the house, for I rarely troubled those nearby, but kept them for emergencies, short hunts, and hunts without a gun.'' Shooting deer with the aid of today's excessive technological gadgetry would have disgusted Van Dyke, as it did Aldo Leopold.

As a deer hunter, Van Dyke always believed that he belonged to a hunting fraternity with a well-defined code of conduct and thinking. In order to obtain membership in this ideal order of true sportsmanship, he believed, one had to practice proper etiquette in the field, give game a sporting chance and possess an esthetic appreciation of the whole context of the sport, which included a commitment to its perpetuation. He also encouraged deer hunters above all to improve their ''mental furniture,'' to avoid drawing hasty conclusions from an insufficient number of instances, and to avoid inaccuracy of statement. As he put it in *The Still Hunter,* ''it's always and eternally that 'old buck' or 'big buck' that a writer kills (with his quill), until in the interest of philosophy one is almost tempted to offer a reward for any reliable information about the killing of a small doe or fawn.'' He also came down hard on the braggart, on the man who talks of placing a bullet wherever he wishes to place it in a running deer and at any distance, or at one standing beyond 150 yards. This type of fellow deer hunter Van Dyke labeled as ''an ignoramus who takes his listener for a bigger fool than he is himself.'' Yes, as deer hunters we have a lot to learn from his lofty ideals of true sportsmanship.

In 1882 the *New York Spirit of the Times* recognized these qualities of true sportsmanship, and called his book on still hunting ''the best, the very best work on deer hunting.'' *The New York Evening Post* agreed: ''Altogether the best and most complete American book we have yet seen on any branch of the field sports.'' Sir Henry Halford, one of England's foremost hunters and anglers, characterized it as ''by far the best book on the subject I have seen—in fact, the only really good one.'' *Forest and Stream,* the most prominent outdoor journal of the time, categorized it ''as a well written primer on still hunting, a valuable book which gives us a general theory of deer hunting. It serves to impress upon the student who is venturing into this new and difficult field of research, the importance of the three cardinal principles by which success may be attained, viz., caution, patience, and deliberation. It deserves high praise.'' In 1904 the *New York Times* observed that "lovers of paradox, still hunters of subtleties in the expression of truth, will rejoice by the manner in which the author conveys instruction" in the art of deer hunting.

In my own opinion the book represents a very successful attempt to combine the interest of a deer hunting novel, which is all too rare in our time, with the more practical features of an authoritative work on deer hunting methodology. Even with the passage of time, one can hardly dispute the above-mentioned evaluations. Indeed, Van Dyke's basic philosophy of still hunting as formulated in 1882 remains pretty much intact today. Even after 100 years of intensive deer hunting in America, and after a tremendous amount of theorizing on this subject, the principles of still hunting according to Van Dyke have received little or no embellishment.

It would be difficult to adequately summarize his basic principles within the scope of this chapter; it took Van Dyke himself one volume or nearly 400 pages to do so. I would like to recall some of the highlights of his theory, however. To begin with, Van Dyke points out that still hunting is an extremely puzzling and mystifying affair. The intensity of concentration demanded by this type of hunting produces a total commitment and awareness to the natural environment around you. For many deer hunters it's almost like a mystical experience. "When you have mastered it, you will say it is the deepest and most enduring of all the charms the land beyond the pavement has to offer." Van Dyke attributed its popularity to this mystifying aspect and to the fact that you tend to see more deer while still hunting as opposed to stand hunting. My own data indicates he was correct in this assessment. Based on an analysis of Stump Sitter Data Sheets for

1978 and 1979, I found that on the average, stand hunters saw 433 deer per 1000 hours of hunting, whereas still hunters saw 554 deer per 1000 hours, or an increase of 28.2 percent.

Van Dyke's list of basic precepts that all still hunters should follow is long indeed. Here are a select few.

1. "Avoid noise while walking by selecting trails, easing off brush with your hands, going around it, crawling through it, etc.
2. Avoid going down wind.
3. Keep on high ground as is consistent with quiet walking and wind direction.
4. Keep the sun on your back.
5. Beware of short-cuts in still hunting.
6. Positively no hurrying, for in still hunting, Hurry is the parent of Flurry.
7. In still hunting you never have an advantage to spare.
8. If patience ever brings reward, it is to the still hunter.
9. You can scarcely have too strong a pair of binoculars or use them too thoroughly—though you should not use them until you have first given a careful and extensive sweep of the area with the naked eye.
10. When greatly pursued by hunters, whitetails drift into a state of chronic suspicion of their back track.
11. Everyone who still hunts should get his feet accustomed to buckskin moccasins.
12. A fair percentage of failures in still hunting come from leaving in your net a few loose knots to tighten which could have cost you only a trifle more of work, care, and time.
13. The simpler and lighter you dress the better—the most valuable knowledge in the world is to know what we can dispense with.
14. In scarcely any branch of life is one

more apt to draw wrong conclusions from hasty observation than in still hunting white-tailed deer.

15. In no other branch of the field sports is there such an array of exceptions to nearly every rule.''

Interwoven amidst these basic precepts, we find two major themes running throughout the book: learned ignorance and the necessity of seeing deer before they see you. ''We are never so wise,'' Van Dyke once wrote, ''as when we know what it is that we do not know.'' For example, there are many movement patterns of whitetails that remain impossible to reduce to rules, since the animal is frequently governed by the caprice of the passing moment. But just as there are doctors who will never admit ignorance on any complication, so too do we encounter a host of deer hunters who ''have ever on their tongue's end an exact explanation of every movement of a deer.'' As an editor of a specialized magazine on deer and deer hunting, I agree with what Sir William Hamilton once said: ''Contented ignorance is better than presumptuous wisdom.'' This axiom certainly applies to the field sport of still hunting whitetails, whether with bow, gun or camera.

Van Dyke lived according to this axiom, throughout his hunting career, and continually studied errors committed while in the field. No matter how many years of experience you have in still hunting, ''make it your custom whenever you lose a deer to study how you lost him. This may occupy a little time at first, but in the end it will repay you. Few things are so fatal to ultimate success as an early germination of the idea that you are a pretty smart chap on deer. The teachers you need are disappointment and humiliation. If these cure you of still hunting,

it is well; for it proves you were not born for that, and the sooner you quit the better. But if there is any of the true spirit in you, defeat will only inspire you. You will learn more from your failures than many do from success, and they will arouse you to double care, double energy, double keeness and double hope. The analysis of error is a far better source of instruction than the analysis of truth. For this reason you should at first study failures more than successes. And this will be rendered all the more easy by the fact that at first you will probably have little beside error to study.'' It is safe to say that during his deer hunting career Van Dyke studied errors in a prodigious manner in which not one in 1000 hunters has either the humility of soul or the patience to do.

Even at the risk of being tedious, Van Dyke continually emphasized the idea of seeing deer before they see you, and the extreme difficulty, in the majority of cases, of doing so. This theme runs throughout his book and his hunting adventures, and remains a basic principle the still hunter must never forget. ''The advantage that one of two persons or animals at rest has over the other one moving, is immense.'' Once a whitetail gets this advantage, you will rarely get him. ''Nothing in the whole line of hunting is so important as to see the deer before he sees you; and there is scarcely anything else so hard to do. In this more than in almost any other one thing lies the secret of the old and practical still hunter's success.''

Van Dyke's classic text contains much valuable information not only on the secrets of still hunting, but on all phases of deer and deer hunting, on everything from the ''myth of the waiting game'' after you hit a deer, to the mythology of solunar theory—all given in an engaging and en-

tertaining manner. At times the passages
are so inspiring with their charming descriptions that they will send you to your
deer shack at any time of the year, even
if only in an imaginary sense. Indeed, the
book frequently assumes a tinge of poetry. In an unpublished letter dated March
19, 1952, his son, Dix, tells us that his
father always cherished a desire to be a
poet, and even wrote a book of poetry
that apparently remained unpublished.
Consider, for example, the following poem
that Van Dyke aptly entitled *A Dilettante
Sportsman:*

'Twas on a clear and frosty morn,
When loudly on the air were borne
Those weird and deeply thrilling sounds,
The clanging tones of clamorous hounds.
"How sweet," said he, "that music floats
And rolls in wild tumultuous notes;
Now ringing up the mountain's side,
Now waxing, waning, like the tide,
Or swinging loud across the dell
Like Pandemonium's carnival."

Hot bounds his blood in swift career,
When bursts the uproar still more near,
And hope and fear alternate play
With bounding joy and dark dismay.

As louder, nearer, bays the pack,
Cold shivers dance along his back;
From tip to toe his nerves all tingle,
His knee-pans seem almost to jingle,
All o'er his skin hot flashes amble,
And on his head each hair doth scramble;
He feels his heart erratic beat,
He nearly melts with inward heat,
And grasps with quivering hand the gun
As nears the pack in rapid run.

And now there comes an ominous sound
Of hoofs that fiercely spurn the ground,
Close followed by a sudden crash,
As through the brush with headlong dash
There bursts in view a lordly buck.
"Ye gods!" he chattered, "oh, what luck!
But oh! ain't he a splendid sight!
Those spirit-eyes! How wildly bright!

What graceful form! What glossy vest!
What massive neck! What brawny chest!
What proud defiance seem to shed
Those antlers o'er his shapely head!
How in the sun they flash and shine
From rugged base to polished tine!"

"Phew!" said the buck, with lofty bound
That scattered dirt and leaves around;
Then skipped across the field of view,
Waved with his flag a fond adieu
To his admirer's ravished eye,
Just as the hounds came foaming by.

"But where's my gun? He's gone! Oh,
thunder!
How could I ever make such blunder!
It looked so fine to see him run
I quite forgot I had a gun."

In the final analysis still hunting, more
than any other type of deer hunting, requires a great deal of field experience before the tyro reaches a practical realization of the simplest principles. Van Dyke
frequently compared this type of hunting
with the game of chess; both games keep
you at your wit's end. Still hunting, he
rightly argued, is both an art and a science. After 35 years of deer hunting and
20 years after the publication of his book,
Van Dyke wrote a fascinating article entitled *Hunting the Virginia Deer* for *The
Outing Magazine*. In this article he again
addressed himself to the subject: "This
subject is so vast that I can give but sam-
ples of what one must learn to realize the
highest pleasure that can be drawn from
still hunting. With the wild Virginia deer
it is the farthest from murder of all that
is done with rifle or gun, the finest game
of skill man ever plays, finer even than
he plays against his fellow man. In *The
Still Hunter* I thought I had treated the
subject too fully, but in looking it over
twenty years after publication it seems

as if I had not said enough. The vast range of the subject, the many ways in which you may be left alone, the intense care, eyesight and knowledge of the game and the woods necessary for much success, make still hunting the Virginia deer a joy to thousands who would not touch a gun for any other purpose, for beside it all other hunting is tame and even the pursuit of the blacktail and the mule deer often ridiculous in simplicity.''

The book will certainly not fail to awaken your enthusiasm, for Van Dyke uses the pen as skillfully as the gun. The work is crisp and readable throughout. His powers of observation and ability to picture graphically what he experienced while afield, remain unsurpassed. The book is written as though the author were talking to some fellow deer hunter, recounting, as such never tire of doing, exciting incidents afield which have their date in history, but which renew their life in vivid recollections. I think that no better praise can be bestowed upon it than to say that the sportsman who reads it will vividly relive his own days afield. In short, its spirited and lifelike descriptions will make every deer hunter who has ever found enjoyment in still hunting whitetails, tingle with the delight of pleasant recollections. A classic!

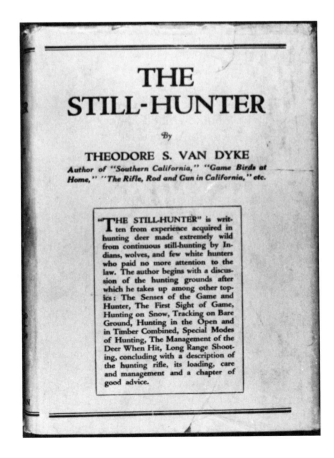

The deer hunter who reads this book will vividly relive his own days afield. The book's spirited and lifelike descriptions will make every deer hunter, who has ever found enjoyment in still hunting whitetails, tingle with the delight of pleasant recollections. An unsurpassed classic! *Photo credit Robert Wegner*

Chapter *5*

The Professor
of Game Management

In a letter to Roy Case, a prominent American bow hunter, dated January 11, 1935, Aldo Leopold acknowledged his profound enthusiasm for deer hunting when he observed that there is simply no sport superior to bow-and-arrow deer hunting. In the same letter, however, he referred to the frustration bow hunters sometimes encounter while pursuing whitetails with their bow: "Killing a white-tailed buck with a bow and arrow means going through a series of unexpected mishaps and keeping it up until one of the haps fails to miss." Who would disagree with this jestful lament?

In this chapter I describe Leopold's deer hunting adventures, and examine his attitude toward deer hunting. It will be argued that in Leopold's life and writings we find the most eloquent justification for deer hunting in this century. His defense justifies the sport ethically, ecologically and esthetically. In his famous *Sand County Almanac,* Lepold confessed that he discovered ecology by having been a hunter. By his own admission, he had "congenital hunting fever" throughout his life. Unfortunately, few contemporary ecologists who read this patron saint of the ecology movement realize or understand his true passion for the hunt.

Though Aldo Leopold (1887–1948) was unquestionably a distinguished wildlife manager, scientist, educator, public policy-maker and environmental philosopher, he was first and foremost an enthusiastic deer hunter, as his letter to Roy Case indicates. Born in 1886, in Burlington, Iowa, Leopold grew up in a family of outdoor-loving Germans. From his early childhood days, when he roamed the woods and fields along the banks of the

A beautiful, heartwarming book. A classic on the ethics of hunting and woodsmanship. A must for all deer hunters! *Photo credit Robert Wegner*

Mississippi with his father and brother, Leopold acquired a life-long, pronounced passion for hunting.

Early family hunting occurred at the Crystal Lake Hunting Club and at the Lone Tree Hunting Club across the Mississippi River in Illinois. While hunting along the banks of the Mississippi during the early decades of this century, the young Leopold used a single-barrel shotgun for which he paid $7. According to Edwin A. Hunger, an early hunting partner of Leopold's, Leopold shot gamebirds with great finesse, and proudly boasted that his single-barrel did the business just as well as the expensive guns

his sportsman father possessed. Deer hunting, however, gradually captured Leopold's attention—at first with the rifle and later with his bow and arrow. As one of his hunting partners once remarked, "Aldo became a hunter, under the tutelage of his father, from whom he learned the credo of the sportsman. Hunting was his first love, never to be relinquished—though in later years he gave up the gun for the less destructive bow and arrow."

His passion for the hunt we find recorded on almost every page of his hunting journals. According to these journals, we learn that Leopold was making his own archery equipment for hunting as early as 1924, for on a long canoe trip in Canada in the summer of that year, Leopold mentions making a bow of white cedar for his son, Starker. Yet it wasn't until the fall of 1926 that Leopold became extremely interested in hunting big game with the bow and arrow—undoubtedly the direct result of his reading of Saxton Pope's 1925 edition of *Hunting with the Bow and Arrow*. From this point forward he read and collected many of the famous books on the history and theory of archery and bow hunting. His personal library on this subject included many of the classic titles—everything from Ascham's *Toxophilus* to Thompson's *The Witchery of Archery*. During this time he also read and studied in great depth William Monypeny Newsom's *White-tailed Deer* and T. S. Van Dyke's *The Deer Family*— making extensive notes on both of these classic texts on deer hunting methodology.

One of his first deer hunting trips with the bow occurred in 1927, when Leopold and Howard Weiss, treasurer of the C.F. Burgess Laboratories, hunted whitetails and blacktails in the Gila National Forest

While Aldo Leopold (1886–1948) was unquestionably a distinguished wildlife manager, scientist, educator, public policy-maker and environmental philosopher, he was first and foremost an enthusiastic deer hunter. *Photo credit Wisconsin Department of Natural Resources*

After setting up camp under two large pines near a spring covered with watercress in the Mogollon Mountains, they soon found themselves stalking deer in an endless maze of box canyons. After several days of diligent hunting and heartbreaking misses, their enthusiasm gradually began to wane, for like Pope and Young, these early-vintage bow hunters were shooters of the long range. Leopold gives us an example: "One large whitetail looked at me at seventy yards. He jumped at the flash of the bow. My

"To the deer-hunter or the outdoorsman, deer are the (inner meaning of forested terrain). Their presence or absence does not affect the outward appearance of (the forest), but does mightily affect our reaction toward it. Without deer tracks in the trail and the potential presence of deer at each new dip and bend of the trail, the forest would be, to the outdoorsman, an empty shell, a spiritual vacuum."
—Aldo Leopold
Photo credit Robert A. McCabe

of New Mexico, an area that Leopold had thoroughly studied as a forester. The day they left for the hunt, *The Chicago Daily Tribune* announced rather optimistically that they were expected to bring home at least a deer apiece due to their considerable experience and expertise with bows and arrows. Indeed, their deer hunting enthusiasm ran high. As Leopold wrote in his journal, "we're going to rimrock those bucks on the battleground of New Mexico!"

arrow stuck in his second jump, so that if he had stood still I would have hit him fairly in the neck." Their initial enthusiasm suffered another stunning blow when Leopold hit a large buck, but failed in his three-day effort to recover it. In his journal he noted that they experienced several blue evenings in camp as a result. Their confidence and ambition returned, however, with clean underwear and warm sunshine.

Although Leopold was unsuccessful in his efforts to get a deer while on this trip, he formulated some prudent proverbs for deer camp discussion: "(1) Some whitetails stay in oaks regardless of nuts; (2) Bucks do not necessarily bed on the same side of a canyon they feed on; (3) Only does water before dark, but both bucks and does feed before dark; (4) When you stop to look, stop in the shade; (5) Deer cannot be stalked in dry country except in a heavy wind or early morning. North slopes stay quiet longest; (6) A startled deer will tend to go (a) uphill, (b) into the wind, (c) around a point, (d) toward cover or rough ground. When he is startled by sight, (letter b) is the strongest tendency, when by scent any of the others may be."

After Leopold returned to Madison, Wisconsin, on Thanksgiving Day, an article in *The Capital Times* appeared entitled *Bow-n-Arrow Hunter Back, Empty-Handed*. Yet, the article pointed out that Leopold "returned with the conviction that hunting with a bow and arrow and getting no game affords more enjoyment than hunting with a gun and bringing home a deer." He remained determined to return to the Gila National Forest to continue the chase. Indeed, in 1929 the chase resumed in earnest when Leopold, together with his son, Starker, and his brother, Carl, again returned to the wilderness hunting grounds of the Gila National Forest. They again found deer wonderfully abundant. In fact, his brother, Carl, got an 11-point buck with his rifle on opening day. On this deer hunt, however, Leopold preferred to use his bow, and armed himself with a 60-pound Osage bow and six dozen Alaska Cedar arrows. (The quantity of arrows reminds us of the adventures of Pope and Young, the founding fathers of bow hunting.)

According to Leopold's hunting journals, we get the impression that mealtime ceremonies on these deer hunting trips were always special occasions. For example, on the first day of their arrival Leopold recalled, "we dined on a pot of beans and cornbread in a fall of snow which started in the middle of the afternoon and by bedtime was two inches deep. Had music in our snug dry camp after dinner while all the rest of the world outside was white and cold." The following evening they dined on a prized dinner of ham, hominy and sourdough biscuits. Their menu during this trip included everything from venison liver, heart and kidney stew to turkey legs, quail and venison ribs roasted over oak coals. "What one can cook on oak coals is almost unbelievable," Leopold once remarked.

The ultimate in deer camp cuisine reveals itself in one of Leopold's special treats for the deer camp boys. His recipe reads as follows: "Kill a mast-fed buck, not earlier than November, not later than January. Hang him in a live-oak tree for seven frosts and seven suns. Then cut out the half-frozen 'straps' from their bed of tallow under the saddle, and slice them transversely into steaks. Rub each steak with salt, pepper and flour. Throw into a Dutch oven containing deep smoking-hot bear fat and standing on live-oak coals.

Leopold cooking venison tenderloins on oak coals in front of his deer shack. *Photo credit University of Wisconsin Archives*

Fish out the steaks at the first sign of browning. Throw a little flour into the fat, then ice-cold water, then milk. Lay a steak on the summit of a steaming sourdough biscuit and drown both in gravy." After suppers with menus such as this, the Leopolds generally spent their evenings planning the morning's campaign. Later the "glee club" usually tuned up and got a workout before they all had a final belt of cherry bounce and retired for the night to dream of oak thickets alive with bounding bucks.

Several years ago, Starker Leopold described the "Leopold Hunter's Lunch."

His description characterizes a universal situation between the adolescent deer hunter and his stern, old German father— which many deer hunters will surely recognize. His humorous description bears repeating in full:

"On one-day forays we took a standard lunch—a bread and butter sandwich and a pork chop apiece. As noon approached Dad signified the lunch stop by gathering wood for a fire. In the game pocket of his hunting coat he carried a kettle about the shape and size of a brick, open at one end with a wire bale to hang it over the flame. The kettle was filled with water (or snow as the case might be), and when boiling a cylinder of 'erbs-wurst' was dropped in to create a thin pea soup. While this was transpiring, each of us cut forked sticks and grilled our pork chops over the fire. The soup was served in the kettle lid, which was passed around, sandwiches and chops were consumed in short order, the fire was extinguished and the hunt resumed.

"As a teenager I seemed to live in the land of famine, and these hunting lunches served more to stimulate my appetite than to satiate it. But this was the established order of things, and it never occurred to me to question it. In point of fact, Dad often made fun of hunters who indulged in big lunches. One of his favorite jokes was about an old German uncle in Burlington who set out for a day's deer hunt with a bulging basket, containing sandwiches, cheese, pickles and other goodies, covered over with a tea towel which hid the food but not the emerging necks of wine bottles. This picture created great mirth as we broiled our pork chops over the fire. Secretly I was a bit envious of my great-uncle, but that fact was never mentioned.

"After I left home for college our fall hunting trips were few. But when I occasionally made it home I specifically noticed that the hunting lunches were more ample, and that we returned to the car to eat rather than carrying the food in our pockets. The last year Dad and I hunted together, lunch as it emerged from the car consisted of a bulging basket containing sandwiches, cheese, pickles and other goodies, covered over with a tea towel which hid the food but not the emerging necks of wine bottles.

"When I reminded Dad of our old uncle in Burlington he laughed slyly

Giving the bucks a rest while enjoying the typical "Leopold Hunter's Lunch"—a bread and butter sandwich and a pork chop apiece. *Photo credit University of Wisconsin Archives*

and admitted that tastes change, even among Leopolds."

The daily campaign of the Leopolds generally consisted of two men driving and one man standing. Success with this method obviously depended upon knowing which particular areas were susceptible to driving. As Leopold once acknowledged, "we frequently wasted half of our time trying to drive undrivable layouts. An indefinite amount of time could be well invested in advance in finding the lay-outs which actually work." Small drives for deer, Leopold believed, were useless unless they proceeded slowly enough for each man to sit down half the time.

After two weeks of chasing deer in the mountainous terrain of New Mexico in 1929, Leopold formulated the following maxims of an unsuccessful deer hunter: "(1) A deer never follows anything; (2) A deer will not jump from scent except close by, but he will sneak out as far as the scent will carry; (3) The opposite hillside is always less brushy than the side you are on; (4) Clean your binoculars daily, and never hunt without them. Good illumination and clean lenses are necessary to discern antlers in the shadows. Examine every doe twice; (5) Don't be too cautious. You can run up on a trotting or jumping deer, where you couldn't move a foot on a standing or sneaking deer without detection.''

His frequent misses during this trip prodded Leopold to work harder to develop his proficiency with the long bow. Thus, during the early 1930s, he shot at the indoor range at the University of Wisconsin's gymnasium on most Tuesday evenings. Theory followed practice as he gathered scientific studies on many aspects of the aerodynamics of bow and arrow shooting, and as he sought out the advice of such archery pros as Cassius Styles. He even began to write articles for national sportsmen's magazines on such subjects as Turkish bows and making your own glue. His personal correspondence during these years indicates an intimate acquaintanceship with many prominent archery retailers of the day.

During the early 30s the entire family began to attend championship tournaments with remarkable results. In 1931, for example, Leopold won the Silver Cup of the Wisconsin Archery Association. Mrs. Leopold, an archery instructor at the University of Wisconsin, won the Gold Medal the following year, and held the Wisconsin women's archery championship for several years. She also won honors at the National Archery Association's championships in Chicago. Leopold's son, Starker, also emerged as one of Wisconsin's leading archers during this time.

In 1934, a major event of historic importance took place in Wisconsin when the Wisconsin Conservation Commission revised its hunting laws, as a result of Leopold's initiative, to include the bow as a legal hunting weapon for deer. Thus, in 1934 Wisconsin became the first state to establish a special bow hunting season for deer when the Legislature declared a five-day ''open season'' for deer in Sauk and Columbia counties. On opening day *The Chicago Daily News* announced, that ''the whizz of iron-pointed, feather tipped shafts replaced the roar of shotguns in two counties of central Wisconsin, where for the first time since white men borrowed the country from the Indians archers are pursuing deer to the exclusion of men with firearms.'' *The Daily News* went on to point out that the 66 registered participants were led by ''Lady Diana''— Mrs. Aldo Leopold. In an interview with *The Daily News,* both Leopold and his wife, Estella, reminded archers ''that the stealthiness of the aborigine and all his instinctive lore of the woodland must be mastered by the archer in order to get close enough to deer to bring them down.''

Not only did Leopold and Estella shoot target archery together, but they also bow hunted together. Indeed, their relationship attained the ideal. In an unpublished letter, Leopold once mentioned that while deer hunting Estella matched the fellows in physical endurance, and generally had a better time than anybody. Actually, few men have made any contributions to humanity without the assistance of a sympathetic and understanding wife—and in this case a renowned target archer and bow hunter of the ''Lady Diana'' vintage. As A. W. Schorger, a friend and colleague of Leopold's, once remarked, ''Whenever I saw them departing for the country with their archery tackle, the lines of Longfellow seemed especially fitting: 'As unto the bow the cord is / So unto the man is woman / Though she bends him, she obeys him / Though she draws him, yet she follows / Useless each without the other.' " Estella's abiding faith in Leopold's ability, in his objectives and in his deer hunting adventures . . . stood the test of time.

Leopold's 1934 deer hunting adventures took place on the sandy Wisconsin River bottomlands near Baraboo, Wisconsin. Eight archers were in attendance at Leopold's deer camp, including four members of the family and several of Leopold's colleagues from the University of Wisconsin. All of them slept in Leopold's army tent despite the heavy rain. During the first two days of the hunt they tried to locate deer in the lowlands, which were full of tracks. Unfortunately, rabbit hunters, had driven the whitetails from this domain. On the third day they discovered that the deer were bedding on the uplands several miles away. They then began to drive the upland country with instant results. They soon spotted 40 deer, including a high number of bucks. They learned one lesson immediately: "We found that the does and young deer could be driven with some accuracy and precision, but the bucks were unpredictable. When jumped they were just as likely to take out across the open fields or sand dunes as through the woods."

The Leopold party got five shots, two of which came to Leopold. Leopold's first chance was a running shot at a medium-sized buck at about 40 yards in rather dense timber. Apparently his elevation was right, but he shot just in front of him—thus giving us the usual alibi. It is best, however, that we let Leopold describe his second shot for us himself: "My second shot was one of which I will never see the equal. The drivers had just entered a piece of bottomland timber surrounded by open fields. Starker and I were on a point of timber projecting into one of these fields at a crossing. We had not yet got set because of an unfavorable wind and because of lack of time. A huge buck and a doe broke cover almost before the drivers entered the timber, and came across an open rye field straight at us. The buck was so large that the doe looked like a fawn. They entered our point of timber on the run and on the opposite corner from where we stood. The buck then circled into the timber behind us and came out on a little ridge silhouetted against the skyline and stood there. Apparently they always stop and look around both before crossing an opening and after crossing it. It was a dark rainy day, and I estimated the distance to the buck as seventy-five yards, *which is point blank for my outfit*. I shot, and the arrow went just over his shoulder. Upon later pacing the distance, I found it to be sixty yards. The lack of an automatically correct distance estimate cost me this deer, since everything else was done right. This was the biggest whitetail buck I have ever seen, and he had a magnificent head." Apparently, magnificent heads always fascinated Leopold, for as an associate member of the Boone and Crockett Club he closely followed the records of trophy deer as they were taken throughout America.

In 1935, Leopold acquired an abandoned, worn-out shack near Baraboo, Wisconsin, in part to serve as a base of operation for deer hunts with his bow and arrow. While on vacation at this antique chicken coop, Leopold made a yew bow for his friend and colleague Herbert Stoddard, a specialist in quail research. In a letter to Stoddard in January of 1935, Leopold again revealed his deep-rooted enthusiasm for deer hunting when he wrote that "one cannot fashion a stave without indulging in fond hopes of its future. On many a thirsty noon I hope you lean it against a mossy bank by cool springs. In fall I hope its shafts will sing in sunny glades where turkeys dwell, and that one day some wily buck will have just long enough to startle at the twang of its speeding string."

One of the last deer hunts recorded in Leopold's hunting journals took place during the Christmas holidays of 1937–1938. This trip consisted of a pack-trip along the Rio Gavilan in the Chihuahua sierra of northern Mexico. This deer hunt provided Leopold with a satisfying experience, for he found himself in the presence of a deer herd in balance with the carrying capacity of the land, unlike the situation in Wisconsin where deer habitat was being over-browsed and damaged by an excessively large herd. "It was here," he later reflected, "that I first clearly realized that land is an organism, that all my life I had seen only sick land, whereas here was a biota still in perfect arboriginal health. The term 'unspoiled wilderness' took on a new meaning." Indeed, Leopold took great delight in deer hunting in an area that retained the virgin stability of its soils and the beauty and integrity of its flora and fauna. Deer were abundant, but were not found in excessive numbers.

One day, with the aid of a strong wind, Leopold stalked a buck bedded down in the shade of a great oak tree. Despite his frequent target practice, he overshot the buck and his arrow splintered on a nearby rock. "As the buck bounded down the mountain with a goodbye wave of his snowy flag," Leopold wrote, "I realized that he and I were actors in an allegory.

Leopold's shack, which served as a base of operations for deer hunts with his bow and arrow. Located on the Wisconsin River bottomlands near Baraboo, Wisconsin. "It is here," Leopold wrote, "that we seek—and still find—our meat from God." *Photo credit State Historical Society of Wisconsin*

Dust to dust, stone age to stone age, *but always the eternal chase!* It was appropriate that I missed, for when a great oak grows in what is now my garden, I hope there will be bucks to bed in its fallen leaves, and hunters to stalk and miss." Although Leopold, his son and his brother missed many deer, they managed to hang three deer on the meat pole with the aid of the rifle. Many deer, however, evaded their arrows on this trip. As Leopold's son recalls, "We took time as we rode home to try and analyze why we had failed with the bow and what to do next time. It's a great game."

Leopold's deer hunting trip to the Sierra Madre of Mexico marked his first realization that deer and predators could coexist in relative equilibrium in an uncontrolled environment; that wolves and mountain lions added to the *diversity* of wildlife, and ought not to be exterminated. According to Leopold's biographer, Susan Flader, this 1937/38 deer hunting trip to Mexico represented not only a shift in his thinking on predators, but a significant shift in his attitude toward deer and deer hunting. During this trip, Flader writes, "Leopold shifted from an emphasis on environmental management in order to increase deer populations for sport hunting, to an emphasis on environmental management in order to provide a safe margin between the carrying capacity of the environment and deer population, with controlled recreational hunting as a management tool for maintaining appropriate deer populations. The important point was not so much to increase productivity of or carrying capacity for a single species as to rebuild a *diverse,* healthy environment."

Based on an analysis of his published and unpublished hunting journals, we learn

"Moss paved deer trails are handy for the hunter to follow, and for the ruffed grouse to cross—in a split second. The question is whether the bird and the gun agree on how a second should be split. If they do not, the next deer that passes finds a pair of empty shells to sniff at, but no feathers."

—Aldo Leopold
Photo credit University of Wisconsin Archives

that Leopold's deer hunting experiences were generally family-oriented affairs done in the company of his brother, Carl, and his son, Starker. As a family the Leopolds all preferred to backpack while deer hunting—reflecting no doubt Aldo's cherished ideal of the wilderness hunter. For Leopold believed that packtrips kept the wilderness free of roads, artificial trails, cottages and other works of man, and provided an experience important in the development of national character. Furthermore, he always feared that the expansion of transportation, without a corresponding growth of ecological thinking, would destroy the quality of both the land and the recreational sport of deer hunting as well. In an essay entitled *Conservation Esthetic,* he once wrote that "recreational development (i.e., providing the sportsman with deer hunting opportunities), is a job not of building roads into lovely country, but of building receptivity into the still unlovely human mind." This statement reflects Leopold's deep-seated belief that deer hunters should travel on foot as much as possible, rather than tear up the beautiful terrain with their four-wheel, motorized madness.

One gains the impression from interviewing his friends that deer hunting represented more of a hobby than a professional pursuit for Leopold. According to

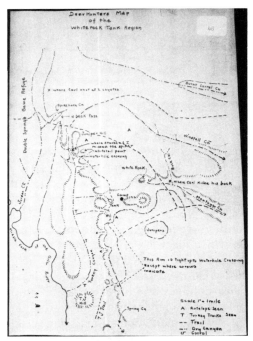

Studying soil maps and topographical maps for hunting purposes became a basic procedure in Leopold's deer camp. He also drew up his own detailed and intricate maps of deer hunting terrain and kept accurate reports on the type of deer browse indigenous to the area in which he hunted. *Photo credit University of Wisconsin Archives*

Professor Robert McCabe, one of Leopold's hunting partners and a successor to the Chair of Game Management at the University of Wisconsin, Leopold would never reorient his academic schedule around his hunting time. Nevertheless, when in the field he hunted with great passion and determination. Studying soil maps and topographical maps for hunting purposes became a basic procedure in Leopold's deer camp. He also drew up his own detailed and intricate maps of deer hunting terrain, and kept accurate reports on the type of deer browse indigenous to the area in which he hunted. Carbon copies of such technical reports on habitat and browse were distributed to his colleagues. Like many deer hunters, he, too, photographed not only the quarry, but his daily hunting activities as well. The photographs were later affixed to the pages of his hunting diaries. At the end of each day, he summarized the daily adventures in his hunting log. His journal entries take on the specificity of Stump Sitter Data Sheets—the original pages of both have the pungency of birch smoke and show evidence of slapped mosquitoes and coffee stains.

Indeed, deer hunting was Leopold's perfect hobby, a hobby that not only entailed making his own bows and arrows, but even his own glue. The pastime actually infected his entire family. He once described his hobby as "a defiance of the contemporary." In an essay on man's leisure, he characterized the art of making long bows for deer hunting as a superb way of spending one's leisure time. Actually, making archery tackle for hunting purposes had the added benefit of giving Leopold "an effective alibi (an alibi he never needed) for being late at the office and for failing to carry out the trashcan on Thursdays."

As with many of us, deer hunting with the bow and arrow provided Leopold with a consuming interest in the technical problems of archery. Consequently, he remained throughout his life a master craftsman—making his own quivers, broadheads, field points, bows, arrows, arm guards, finger tabs, glues and wooden cases for storing arrows. Leopold's deer hunting equipment was unrelated to mail-order catalogs; the handmade bow and arrow remained the proper weapon for stalking whitetails.

Leopold's deer hunting trips were not search-and-destroy expeditions. Deer hunting was a "ceremony, complete with ritual and incantation," as Leopold played the role of the whitetail's substitute predator. With profound respect he matched the instincts of the whitetail against his own homemade weaponry—rejecting factory-made gadgets and "where-to-go" management mentality. He abhorred the conduct of slob hunters, and inveighed against them. He denounced their abominable ethics, which are still currently destroying the personal and cultural values of deer hunting. When he harvested a deer, he reverently dissected the animal in his continuing study of food habits, whitetail diseases and population dynamics. In his hunting journals, he kept accurate observations and precise measurements on every aspect of the anatomy of the deer he harvested. The entrails were weighed, and estimates were made of the liver and kidneys and the head and the hide. He also measured the antler spread and the length of the ears and the hooves.

With respect to his attitude toward deer hunting, Leopold was a man ahead of his time. As early as 1930, he envisaged a time when deer hunting would be a profitable private enterprise, and hence insisted on compensation to the landholder in the form of hunting fees or club memberships. In thinly forested deer country, where stray bullets become particularly dangerous, Leopold prophesied that hunting in the future would be confined to bows and arrows, or to short-range projectiles yet to be revived (one thinks of the muzzleloader). In the future, Leopold argued, public policy would attempt to regulate the crowd in an effort to keep deer hunting safe and enjoyable. Fifty years ago he aimed for quality deer hunting over a long season in an attempt to ensure a proper distribution of kill. It's not surprising that the Variable Quota Idea, which Wisconsin initiated in 1963, was an idea Leopold had proposed as early as 1918. Indeed, it seems that Leopold was about 50 years ahead of his time.

This is not to suggest, however, that all of Leopold's ideas on deer management were without error, for he spent a lifetime correcting errors in his own approach to game management. (His complete turnaround on predator control comes to mind.) One of the great lessons implicit in his attitude toward deer and deer hunting should not escape our attention: A man can learn from experience and can recognize when his ways or ideas are in error. He can thus change and adjust them as he grows in wisdom and knowledge.

At his deer shack in Sauk County, Leopold grew in wisdom and knowledge as he studied the interrelationships between animals, birds, plants, grasses, shrubs and trees. While at the shack he also penned some of the greatest essays ever written on ecology and conservation. One of these essays, entitled *The Land Ethic,* contains a crystal-clear attitude toward deer hunting that eloquently defends the sport ethically, ecologically and esthetically. One basic ethical precept underlies his attitude: "A thing is right when it tends to preserve the integrity, stability, and beauty of the biotic community. It is wrong when it tends otherwise." In other words, deer hunting is right when it preserves the integrity, stability and beauty of the land. It is wrong if it tends otherwise.

When deer are allowed to increase *without* increasing their natural food supply, calamity occurs to the timber, the flora, the birds and the deer themselves. It can require from 10 to 50 years to restore the damage excess deer can inflict upon the forest's vegetation. The elimi-

nation of various plant species as a result of deer overbrowsing their range, Leopold argued, must not be permitted. Instead, deer herds must be regulated and adjusted to land use. Deer hunting must be viewed as an instrument of control in maintaining a desirable relationship between deer populations and farming and forestry. We need to think about deer and the integrity of the land.

It is within this ecological context that we must view deer hunting. Herd reduction is not merely an issue of state economics or personal recreation. It is, more

"In October my trees tell me, by their rubbed-off bark, when the bucks are beginning to feel their oats. A tree about eight feet high, and standing alone, seems especially to incite in a buck the idea that the world needs prodding. Such a tree must perforce turn the other cheek also, and emerges much the worse for wear. The only element of justice in such combats is that the more the tree is punished, the more pitch the buck carries away on his not-so shiny antlers."

—Aldo Leopold
Photo credit Leonard Lee Rue III

important, a means to a larger end, namely, ecological integrity and environmental health. Deer hunting allows game managers to adjust the deer herd in line with the requirements of land health, so that deer do not damage natural plant reproduction, or change the composition and undermine the diversity of plant life. This is Leopold's legacy for the modern American deer hunter.

Like T.S. Van Dyke, Aldo Leopold was a great American deer hunter, not because he hung up many trophies, but because he expressed the cultural values of the sport and defended it as a great tradition with roots deep in our past. His eloquent defense of deer hunting ranks second to none. His thoughts on the philosophy of hunting stand with those of Xenophon, Jose Ortega y Gasset, T.S. Van Dyke and Theodore Roosevelt.

Chapter 6

An Affair with Deer

"I find it infinitely more rewarding to observe the small secrets that enable a deer to survive than to visit a huge metropolis to see what man has wrought. I spend more of my time with wildlife than with people, and I do so by choice." This quote reflects the philosophy of Leonard Lee Rue III, who believes that in order to film, hunt, lecture or write about deer, one must spend considerable time living with them and learning to know them from first-hand experience.

Indeed, Leonard Lee Rue III prefers the quiet solitude of nature to the concrete jungle of plastic fantastic. He lives among deer; he watches them, studies them and photographs them. He writes books about them and lectures about them. He hunts them, feeds them and eats them. He crisscrosses the continent, east to west, north to south, to learn more about them. Fascinated by all things in nature for as long as he can remember, Rue has made the study of deer in particular a never-ending quest.

After spending several days with Lennie at his secluded home in the wooded hills of Blairstown, in Warren County—in what is probably the most rugged and unspoiled corner of New Jersey—I almost concluded that this tall, lean, white-bearded woodsman lives so close to deer that he actually communicates with these critters. In fact, Rue has been a neighbor of the white-tailed deer for most of his life, for he has always lived on the very fringe of the deer forest. His lifetime study of deer seems unavoidable; their paths crossed too frequently for it to have been otherwise.

This chapter presents a portrait of an enthusiastic man, a driven man, an intense man with flair and gusto; a man utterly obsessed with photographing, lecturing and writing about deer. His zest for learning more about these graceful and spirited creatures is contagious and infectious; his life without them would be impossible to conceive.

Rue's roots lie deep in the rural landscape of northwestern New Jersey. Although born in Paterson, New Jersey on February 20, 1926, he grew to manhood on a farm atop Manunkachunk Mountain near the Delaware Water Gap. His father, Leonard Lee II, was a marine engineer who always wanted to farm; he consequently bought one, although he continued to work on ships. His mother, Mae (Sellner) Rue, instilled in the young boy a love for pictures and book learning. One of the first books he remembers reading as a youngster was entitled *Birds Worth Knowing* (1928), by Neltje Blanchan, which he received for his eighth birthday from his Uncle Ed. The book remains on his library shelf to this day. By the tender age of 8 the young Rue had already recorded his natural observations of a yellow-shafted flicker excavating a hole in a dead tree.

Born into a family of world travelers and book readers, Lennie as a youth read books whenever he was not studying birds, plucking chickens or butchering venison for the table. Ernest Thompson Seton, a naturalist whom Lennie resembles in many ways, became one of his earliest heroes. Indeed, he lived with the tales of Ernest Thompson Seton; he read every Seton book he could get his hands on, devouring the stories and committing their lessons to memory. Even today, the entire Seton collection stands on the shelf near his desk. One tale in particular, *The Trail of the Sandhill Stag* (1899), influenced the young boy in a profound manner. This thought-provoking sensitive and moving tale of the long, endless pursuit of a black-tailed stag, with its realistic paintings and imaginative illustrations of deer, called out to Rue's heightened sense of adventure in the wild, and further stimulated his awakening love for deer.

Actually, Rue has been following the trail of the sandhill stag in one way or another for the past 50 years. Whereas Seton drew realistic paintings of deer, Rue, the portraitist, photographs them in a highly esthetic, yet realistic manner. Both men became popularizers of scientific and technical information about animals in general, and deer in particular.

Like Seton, young Lennie Rue grew up on a farm and tramped the wooded hills from an early age with little or no formal education ever rubbing off on him. In his Preface to *The Deer of North America* (1978), he recalls those early years on the farm near the Delaware Water Gap:

"Times were rough on the farm during the last years of the Depression, and the work was hard. The life was a good one, though, and if I had my early life to live over I wouldn't change it at all. I'm thankful that I haven't forgotten how to do hard manual work, although I'm equally thankful I don't have to work that hard physically today. Every moment that I could spare from my work (and some that I couldn't) I roamed the wooded hills and valleys and along the streams and rivers. I lived for the hours I could spend in such surroundings, and I still do. Not much formal education ever rubbed off on me, but my thirst for knowledge about everything in the outdoors was unquenchable. It remains so today."

While roaming the wooded hills of New Jersey to quench that thirst for knowledge, the boy lived with the gun. In fact, he even toted the gun to school with him,

An early tramp to North Carolina, 1935. The hand-carved knife would later be replaced by the ever-present Randall knife. *Photo credit Leonard Lee Rue III*

hiding it in a hollow log during school hours. After school he would retrieve his special 22 and shoot game animals for the pot enroute to the farm. He is, today, an expert rifleman and a certified rifle instructor.

During his earliest years, he also stalked, but never shot, catbirds with his own homemade bows and arrows. Even back then he had a respect for the creatures with which he shared the world, and did not kill for the sake of killing. Rather, he killed only for the sake of eating.

As a young man, he ran a trapline in and around Belvidere. One season, while trapping part-time, he caught 93 foxes in six weeks. To this day he makes no apology for the fact that most of his knowledge of wildlife stems from what he learned as a hunter and fox trapper. In that sense, he follows in the tradition of Aldo Leopold. Reflecting on his boyhood years, he tells us that "trapping was one of the few sources of extra money available to me. I spent every minute that I could spare, winter or summer, in the woods, the fields or on the river. The knowledge of wildlife that I gained all year long was put to use during the hunting and trapping season. And because of this knowledge, I was successful."

As a result of his roaming the hills, hunting and fox trapping, school to him became little more than an institutional barracks for sleeping. And it's no wonder he slept in school, for he would get up at 5 o'clock, milk 12 cows, feed the horses and pigs, get the milk ready to be picked up for the creamery, and then go up the mountains and down into the rich valley of the Delaware River to check his trapline. Then he walked three quarters of a mile to catch the old, ramshackle, heaterless bus driven by Mr. Frye, arriving at school frozen to the point of having to hobble into the old White Township School at Bridgeville. The combination of early rising, fresh air and strenuous activity often resulted in his falling asleep in class, undoubtedly a major and contributing factor to his failing English. He never quite understood the meaning of a preposition. A proposition he understood. A preposition . . . no.

Today, after publishing 18 books with total sales approaching 2½ million copies, he still doesn't see the need for learning more about prepositions. Abandoning the study of grammar, he turned his attention to more imaginative pursuits such as throwing 22 bullets into the school's potbelly stove to see if he could lift the stovepipe up off the foundation; he couldn't. Few of his elders appreciated such pranks, although his fellow students probably gave vociferous approval.

In any event, Rue did acquire a fascination for stovepipes. In fact, he always became excited and greatly enjoyed watching old Roy Erie, a neighboring farmer, light his kitchen wood stove: "After opening the damper, he would throw several handfuls of fine split kindling or dry corncobs into the firebox. A can of kerosene—'coal oil,' Roy called it—always sat in the corner behind the stove. After pouring a liberal application of kerosene on the kindling, he would put the center stove span and rear lid back in place and toss a lighted wooden kitchen match into the front stove hole. The resultant *KA-FOOOOOM* would shake the stove, rattle the lids and threaten to tear the stovepipe loose from the chimney. But the fire was going.

"This was all pretty exciting fare for a boy 9 years old who had been born in the city and raised there until his folks bought a farm, near Belvidere, up on the hill above Roy's place. But then many things about Roy were exciting. I must call our neighbor 'Mr. Erie,' my folks insisted, but Roy would have none of that. His father had been Mr. Erie, he said, but Roy was his name and that was what I should use. I think he was the first adult I ever called by his first name.

"Roy always knew what would interest a boy, and on different occasions he would open the wall cupboard and bring out a cardboard box that to me was a treasure chest. There were pieces of arrowheads and even a few whole ones, long curving incisor teeth from woodchucks, penis bones from exceptionally large raccoons, walnuts that had been cut open by squirrels, and a few feathers, birds's eggs and other knickknacks. He also had the first tails of ruffed grouse that I had ever seen, spread out like fans, and deer hoofs as well."

Those deer hoofs impressed the boy. But he learned from old Roy Erie that the "good old days" of the late 1930s in Warren County, New Jersey, were not so good when it came to deer and deer hunting. Indeed, a full game pole rarely existed. Nevertheless, in 1938, at the age of 12, young Rue encountered his first deer track, for deer were gradually expanding their range in northwestern New Jersey and eastern Pennsylvania. During those years, deer were so scarce that just the sighting of a deer track often made headlines in the local newspapers. By 1942, however, whitetails had become so numerous that they browsed Rue's soybean patch to the very roots. Rue now encountered deer on a daily basis as he roamed the wooded hillsides with his box camera in hand.

Rue's first photographs of deer were rudimentary and occasionally a little out of focus—decidedly not up to his present-day standards—but with time, effort and patience they gradually improved in composition and crispness. Today, Rue's photographs are the standard of excellence, and Lennie is now the most published wildlife photographer in the nation, perhaps the world, with his photographs acclaimed as "masterpieces of color and clarity." The "Rue quality of needlepoint sharpness" is constantly guarded with every negative checked through a 10x eyeloup.

During the 1950s, Rue guided Boy Scouts of America on canoe trips of 1000 miles or longer through the wilds of Canada. Working as a trail director for an outfit called "Adventure Unlimited," which he founded with Homer Hicks, a long-time friend from Belvidere, he took boys far into the wilds of Quebec, where they camped, canoed and ate the fish they caught. As always, he took pictures of animals while on these trips—thousands and thousands of pictures—and always jotted down field notes, for he was constantly learning.

While tramping the Canadian wilderness, this strong but gentle man profoundly influenced and inspired count-

Taking notes while working as the trail director for Adventure Unlimited in the Canadian wilderness. Lac Farbus, 1960. *Photo credit Leonard Lee Rue III*

less young boys in their attitudes toward animals, hunting, fishing and conservation. A letter to Rue dated January 17, 1974, from a scuba instructor at the University of California, dramatizes that influence:

"A long time ago . . . it must have been fifteen years ago you did me one of the best things ever to happen in my youth . . . you gave me an ideal to shoot for . . . not an unreasonable ideal but rather one that was a person. I thought in my youth that if I ever wanted to be like somebody I wanted to be like Lennie Rue. Events stick in my mind, like the time you tore the bus apart when you thought somebody within the group lifted another scout's personal property . . . and just your general philosophy of conservation and harmony among the living . . . lots of little things made what you stood for a really neat goal for a growing boy to look toward.

"Throughout all of these years I have thought of you and often wonder what you have been doing. When I met Lennie Rue IV sometime ago in Monterey, I was just beside myself with emotion. Here at last was a way that I could indirectly show my sincere gratitude for all the things you did for me as a youth. The problem was that as soon as I got to talking to Lennie IV, I realized that it wasn't as important to treat him well because he was your boy, but more because he was the same kind of man that you are. The kind of guy that I hope I have turned out to be . . . the kind of guy that is the only kind to share a lasting friendship with. Well Lennie IV 'did me good' . . . he accepted my hospitality and accepted my friendship. I know he appreciated what I did for him. I knew it even without words.

"I am still proud of our friendship . . .

Thanks Lennie . . . thanks a lot. I only wish I could teach you to scuba dive like you taught me to paddle a canoe and catch a fish . . . and live a life worth living."

Hank Garrity, the camp manager who was instrumental in hiring Lennie for the job of Boy Scout Camp Ranger, had the same impression. Quoted in *American Forests* magazine, Garrity said that "I could wish for nothing better for my own sons than to have them sit around a campfire and learn to know Lennie and the principles for which he stands. On his journeys into Canada, Lennie was always exceedingly proud of the fact that the boys in his charge left the wilderness just as they found it wherever they camped—except for a little charcoal from their campfire and a covered stack of firewood for the next party that came along. And some of these boys had been tough kids fresh from gang rumbles in the city. Lennie changed them by just being himself."

During the 1950s and through the 1970s, Rue worked as the chief gamekeeper for the Coventry Hunt Club, one of the largest sportsmen's clubs in New Jersey. His job of managing 6500 acres of wooded terrain provided him with the opportunity of living with deer on a daily basis and photographing their social and seasonal activities. With camera in hand, he stalked his prey with all the daring, patience and cunning of the best of hunters, believing that all white-tailed bucks are born with Ph.Ds in evasion. As a result, his beautiful photographs of deer embrace the dreams of many of us. The images are sharp; the pose is right; the action is implied. They clearly possess a sensitivity and an awareness of the essence of the animal that is frequently lacking in the works of others. As an ed-

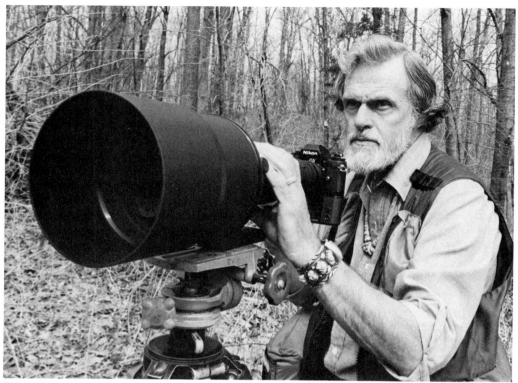

The portraitist at work with the 600-1200mm telephoto lens and "Lash-Lee-Rue" intensity. *Photo credit Leonard Lee Rue III*

itor, I receive countless requests from readers calling for more of his remarkable photographs of the white-tailed deer.

Although he has taken more than 100,000 pictures of deer from every conceivable angle, Rue still gets just as excited when he sees his next deer. He literally saturates the market with his deer photos. Indeed, *saturation* serves as the keynote of his work ethic. As he once told Susan Rayfield, a well-known nature picture editor, "Everything I've done in my life has been with a shotgun approach rather than a fine point. When I used to trap, my friend Joe Taylor, who's a better trapper than I'll ever be, would set just

30 traps in an area because he could pretty much tell exactly where the animals would come in. I had to set 60 traps, and work twice as hard as he did, to cover the same ground. This is the way I've always worked—by saturation. My philosophy in selling photographs has been to take care of the little guys because there are a lot more little guys than big ones. I take care of them and they take care of me."

Lennie also takes care of deer. When it is bitterly cold and the snow lies deep, he snowshoes into the winter deer yards to cut trees for hungry, browsing whitetails. When not engaged in deer projects in the field during the snowy months of

Action in the deer forest. *Photo credit Leonard Lee Rue III*

January through March, he writes about deer. In fact, he wrote his first deer book during the severe winter of 1961. Entitled *The World of the White-Tailed Deer,* the book takes the reader through a full 12 months of a whitetail's life in its natural surroundings. The J.B. Lippincott Company published the book in 1962, and it soon became a classic of its kind. It remains in print to this day, having undergone 11 editions and selling more than 200,000 copies.

Initial reviews of the book launched it on the road to success. *The New Yorker* magazine heralded the book as "absolutely first-rate!" Hal Borland, the distinguished naturalist, wrote in *The New York Times,* "I find it the best book on the subject I ever saw. The pictures are unique and the text excellent. I would call it the definitive book on the white-tailed deer." *The Atlantic Naturalist* labeled it as "scientific, authoritative, readable and convincing." One reviewer in the *Los Angeles Herald Examiner* considered it "exceptionally well-illustrated and amply supplied with some of the best photographs of deer to be reproduced anywhere." Robert L. Downing, of the Georgia Game and Fish Commission, noted in *The Journal of Wildlife Management* that Rue "knows the layman's viewpoint well and his enthusiasm for wildlife is evident throughout the work . . . The book fills a definite need as a readable, interest-holding book for the layman."

Indeed, you will find Rue's remarkable enthusiasm for the white-tailed deer revealed on every page of this book, for this book represents the culmination of many years of field observations of deer. As Rue writes in the Introduction, "Deer are my closest neighbors and about ten-

I've had enough of this Rue feller! Plus, I don't want my picture in any book on deer hunting anyway! *Photo credit Leonard Lee Rue III*

fold more numerous than their human counterparts." Whether quoting the great deer books of the past, all of which Rue has read, or discussing deer problems with C. W. Severinghaus of New York or Joe Taylor, a New Jersey predator-control man, the book moves along with great speed and reaches the inevitable conclusion that when man finally destroys this planet, the whitetail will probably be the last animal to inhabit it:

"It has often been said that the last creature to survive on this earth will probably be an insect. However, the white-tailed deer, which has outlived such early predators as the saber-toothed tiger, disease, starvation, hunting, and mismanagement, seems a likely possibility as a chief competitor for the last remaining herbage on earth."

Writing books on deer has always been a labor of love for Leonard Lee Rue. Even before he finished *The World of the White-tailed Deer,* for which he received the coveted Golden Award for literary excellence from the New Jersey Association of Teachers of English, he knew that he wanted to write another one, one on a grander and more magnificent scale. *The Deer of North America* (1978) is just such a book; a grand, magnificent work; his *magnum opus;* a book that took a lifetime to produce; a work that ultimately symbolizes his love affair with deer. No book on the subject has ever achieved such brilliancy in deer photography.

The instant, critical acclaim for the book overwhelmed both publisher and author alike. Jim Bashline, a noted outdoor writer for the *Philadephia Inquirer,* called it "the best book on the subject I've seen in twenty years." A reviewer for *California Wildlife* remarked that "no one but an extraordinary naturalist, photographer, and writer could have done this book, which is surely destined to become the standard reference on North American deer." *Field & Stream* wrote that "Rue has done a superb job of discussing the natural history of the deer of this continent. We can wholeheartedly recommend this book to hunter and non-hunter alike." Writing in the Allentown *Call-Chronicle,* Tom Fegely, an outdoor writer, observed that "classics are not cranked off the presses every day and when one appears its future is predictable. This one will stand for a long time as the classic about the nation's deer clan."

Even after going through three editions and 150,000 copies, praise for the book continued from every part of the country. *The Milwaukee Journal* labeled it as "one of the best animal books ever written for the interested layman." Writing in *Camping Journal,* Jacquelyn Brown wrote

Measuring the shoulder heights of deer with the ever-present Stanley 10-foot tape. Rue measures every critter he can get his hands on. *Photo credit Leonard Lee Rue III*

that "the book will enable many people to see much more the next time they catch sight of a doe grazing at dusk or a buck bounding gracefully into the shadow of the woods." The *Outdoor News Bulletin* of the Wildlife Management Institute referred to the book as "compelling reading and a masterpiece in photography." Lowell K. Halls, writing in *The Journal of Wildlife Management,* noted that the book was certainly "one of the best illustrated texts available on deer with nearly every aspect of the deer's life and habits superbly displayed. I recommend the book to anyone interested in wildlife. And who isn't?" Gratifying words from

Rescuing deer from the winter deer yards. "Although I kept this little buck in a sheltered pen, offered him various types of native browse, grains, commercial feed, and even tried to give him warm milk concentrates, he would not eat. He died five days later. Starvation was too far advanced for him to recover. I did not know then, as no one else did, that when a deer loses thirty-two to thirty-three percent of its body weight it cannot be saved." *Photo credit Leonard Lee Rue III*

the scientific community for the author . . . a high school dropout.

Letters of praise and more photocopies of reviews poured into Rue's secluded retreat in Blairstown, New Jersey. Gil Whitton, a county extension director, acknowledged in the *St. Petersburg Independent* that "there are so many interesting facts contained in this book that it is difficult to stop reading." While discussing the excellent quality of the book, one reviewer in the *New York Conser-*

vationist exclaimed that "for people who enjoy interesting nature writing, for those interested in deer or those who react positively to excellent pictures of wildlife this book is for them." In a similar vein, Jay Heinrichs wrote in *American Forests* that Rue's "zeal for his subject has produced a book loaded with the most intimate details of the year-round life of deer. If that zeal carries over into strident politicking for scientific management, it is only because of his concern for the individual deer." One critic for the Maryland Center for Public Broadcasting perhaps summarized it best, when he said on Baltimore's Channel 67 that "no one will ever think of Bambi as a real deer again after reading this book."

Rue's latest deer book, entitled *After Your Deer is Down,* published by Wincester Press, appeared in 1981. He co-authored the book with Josef Fischl, a professional meat cutter from Germany. The book provides the American deer hunter with a step-by-step pictorial manual showing everything he needs to know for dressing out deer, including caping, skinning, quartering, boning and cutting up the venison. The book reflects Rue's farm background, when preparing venison was a necessary part of his life. The book emphasizes one basic maxim: "Waste not, want not. That is a maxim on which I was brought up. Being a farm boy, I was used to cutting up and preparing for the table various types of livestock. Venison was done the same way as a matter of course. Doing all of your own meat preparation was a matter of pride, and you knew that everything was done properly, under sanitary conditions, and the portions were just as you wanted them." His methods of venison preparation appear in dozens of national magazines and books, with untold thousands of satisfied deer hunters following his methods. His own homemade venison jerky is still a standard staple for Rue, no matter if he is in his country kitchen or out in the field on a photographic expedition.

When it comes to deer, Rue knows his subject intimately; I believe that he knows more about deer than any other man, and many deer do also. His library of 10,000 volumes spills over with books on deer; technical bulletins, reprints and scientific reports on deer protrude from his filing cabinets to the point where the cabinets can no longer be closed. More than 100,000 photographs of deer involved in every conceivable activity remain on file in the fireproof, atmospherically-controlled vault of Rue Enterprises. His informal narratives, dynamic lectures and beautiful photographs, taken as a whole, present the life of the deer of North America in an entertaining, factual and instructive manner.

When chatting about his love affair with deer, Rue's mannerisms exude a heightened sense of excitement and enthusiasm that stirs one to the very foundation. He speaks about deer with such sureness and sensitivity, with such Billy Graham-like gusto, that his popular deer lectures take on an iron and subjective cast. His deer seminars sweep people off their chairs. When he speaks . . . people listen! His deer lectures are fast-moving, hard-hitting, informative and tremendously exciting. Watching him present a deer seminar at the 1983 Dixie Deer Classic in Raleigh, North Carolina, I noticed that after two and a half hours of solid talking, not one deer hunter out of 4000 listeners had left the hall. Alden Stahr, a friend of Rue's and a writer-in-residence at the Joe

The deer hunter's bible. A grand, magnificent work. A book which took a lifetime to produce; a work which ultimately symbolizes Leonard Lee Rue's love affair with deer. *Photo credit Robert Wegner*

Taylor Campground, likened his speaking ability to "standing in the generating room of a great power plant, with its vibrant hum and the air charged with electricity."

His deer seminar delivers on its promise of telling you more about the white-tailed deer than you ever thought of asking. Indeed, it often answers all your questions about deer before you ever ask them. It explains why deer are their own worst enemies and why they must be managed. It is filled with facts . . . facts . . . and more facts on the natural history of deer. It describes the deer from head to tail, from shoulder height to hoof. It tells you what the deer is capable of doing physically. It discusses what a deer eats

I believe that Leonard Lee Rue III knows more about deer than any other man. *Photo credit Leonard Lee Rue III*

and what it should not eat, as well as the impracticality of artificially feeding deer. It follows the deer not only through its antler growth, body growth and herd growth, but through the four seasons in all their magnificent color. It relates to you where the deer population came from, where it stands today, the outlook for the future, and how you personally affect that future.

Rue impresses you straight out with his integrity, enthusiasm for his work, easy-going manner, willingness to answer questions *ad infinitum,* and forthrightness. He is the most enthusiastic man I have ever met—no exceptions. While attending the Dixie Deer Classic in Raleigh, with Rue, we stayed at the home of Dr.

Carroll Mann, a prominent neurosurgeon and noted big-game hunter. We attended a cocktail party the evening before the Classic. After visiting with Fred Bear that evening until 1:00 a.m., Lennie knocked on my door at 6:00 a.m. and exclaimed: "Get up, Rob, I don't want you to waste your life away!" That statement sounded like it came right out of Robert Ruark's *The Old Man and the Boy.* While I was still in my pajamas at 6:15, Lennie, already dressed, was driving a tough proposition into my brain about me paying him an incredible amount of money for his forthcoming column in *Deer & Deer Hunting* magazine, entitled *Rue's Views.* He got every dime! And I am back to $50 a week and all the road kills I can eat!

I recently traveled to Blairstown to visit with Lennie. Before I awoke at 7:00 a.m., intending to interview him for this portrait, he was already at work *doing my work for me* by recording his life story on my tape recorder. Now there's enthusiasm! Or maybe he just feels bad about the road kills?

But is Leonard Lee Rue really a patient man? I have some doubts. In my discussions with some of his employees, they hinted about revolution in the darkroom and mentioned his nickname "Lash Lee Rue." The graffiti on the walls, such as "Patience, my ass! I'm gonna kill somebody!" or "Keep Calm, Dammit!", raises some doubts. One thing is certain: He loves his work and would never dream of taking a vacation. Disciplined since boyhood by his rural environment, he drives himself in the never-ending search for perfection. "I have all the patience in the world," he tells us, "I just don't have time to use it. I have lectures to give, books to write, places to be. Wildlife has forever, you know. We don't."

Rue, the man, is best understood by a quotation from his controversial book entitled *New Jersey Out-Of-Doors* (1964): "I have often said that I wished I had been born several hundred years ago when I could have seen the real wilderness and its multitudes of creatures. However, I am thankful that at least I was born into the present time to be able to see the remnants of our wildlife and to have the opportunity to photograph them. I often feel that my mission in life is to record the wildlife on film and in words so that future generations will have some knowledge of the creatures that we are fortunate to still have with us."

Rue intends to spend the rest of his life photographing, watching, studying, living with, reading and writing about wildlife in general, and about deer in particular. Through him, we will all surely benefit, for he captures in pictures what most people only talk about.

Leonard Lee Rue III—what more can be said than to say—an imposing name . . . an imposing man . . . spiritual guru of the American deer hunter.

Rue skinning a white-tailed deer. *Photo credit Leonard Lee Rue III*

It is 6:30 p.m. on a Friday evening in early June. A muskrat with a load of grass swims across the quiet pond in front of Rue's house and heads toward the water lilies. I am sitting on a bench in front of a wooden table framed by a long series of picture windows overlooking the small pond, which is surrounded by woods. Camouflage curtains, compliments of the publisher of *Deer & Deer Hunting*, complete the decor. Peacocks meander around the house. Red and gray squirrels scamper to and from the bird feeders on the deck. Cottontails scurry about. The bird feeder in front of the study window draws in a steady stream of purple finches, red-bellied woodpeckers ("woodpeekers," as the 8-year-old Rue once called them), brown-headed cowbirds and rose-breasted grosbeaks. How John Burroughs would have enjoyed the view from the window of Lennie's study!

Lennie hurries into the house after "feeding the critters": after feeding the raccoon, deer, turkeys, quail and God only knows what other animals. On his way to the shower Rue passes through the living room, which houses a vast array of original wildlife art. Caribou antlers hang from the ceiling above his favorite reading chair. Intriguing treasures from his many worldwide expeditions fill the house. The aroma of venison drifts through the house; once again, it's Joe Taylor's favorite recipe for venison sausage.

Rue returns shortly, dressed in jeans and a gray, faded workshirt. He wears a turquoise necklace and wristwatch band, artifacts he obtained from Indians while journeying through the Southwest. Strapped to his belt is his ever-present Randall knife. In his pocket is a Stanley 10-foot tape, ready for measuring every creature—be it bird, beast or insect—that Rue can get his hands on. These trademarks are as traditional for Lennie Rue as the Borsalino hat is for Fred Bear. The trademarks create the image of a mountain man of many years ago. Indeed, in his rugged individualism and charismatic presence, Leonard Lee Rue III seems to walk right out of the pages of James Fenimore Cooper's novel, *The Deerslayer* (1841).

The sun casts its darkening shadows over the pond. During this day, as usual, Rue managed to consume his favorite liverwurst sandwiched between thick slabs of locally baked whole grain brown bread, as well as his daily dosage of vitamins. He read the latest issue of *Prevention:*

The Magazine for Better Health, cover to cover. The Bible was consulted; Paul Harvey was heard from. He photographed deer, talked with his young lady friend, and received several checks in the mail—three basic ingredients for a successful day. And he even managed to read several more chapters of a new book entitled *Program for Living Longer,* by Dr. Carlton Fredericks, one of America's leading nutritional experts. Perhaps he is reading this volume because deep down he realizes that he is consuming himself with work.

At precisely 8:00 p.m. we leave his hillside abode in his VW Rabbit for the historic Millbrook Church, where he will present a program entitled "Alaska's Wildlife" to a group of young students participating in an outdoor education program sponsored by a New Jersey public school. He stares into the distance. His restless, no-nonsense blue eyes mirror the memories of Alaskan adventures with his son, Tim, who, along with Lennie's third son, Jim, and their wives we will meet later in the evening. "I can't stop loving you, I've made up my mind," he sings, sounding and looking a little like Kenny Rogers. . . .

PART II
DEER-HUNTING LORE AND NATURAL HISTORY

Chapter *7*

Deer Droppings

Ever since man first began to hunt deer, he undoubtedly used deer droppings as an indication of where to concentrate his efforts of pursuit. Indeed, no subject in the annals of American deer hunting elicits more jibber-jabber in deer shacks and more stale and tedious calculation in scientific circles than does the subject of deer droppings.

One can almost still hear T.S. Van Dyke delivering one of his famous orations on the subject in his deer shack in the wilderness of southern California in the late 1800s: "Having reached the ridges, pass on from ridge to ridge, noting carefully the quantity of deer droppings, and especially the size of them. It is a common mistake, into which deer hunters of some experience often fall, to count, unconsciously often, a deer to every sign of droppings or two. The beginner is almost certain to estimate the number of deer from six to ten times too high. The age of the droppings is quite as important and should be noted as well. As it is nearly impossible to describe the difference between a stale dropping and a fresh one, this point must be left to your common-sense aided by experience. Staleness is, however, as easy to detect with the eye as it is hard to capture with the pen."

Nonetheless, ever since 1940, when deer researchers in Pennsylvania first introduced the idea of using deer pellets as an index to deer populations, scientists have tried relentlessly to capture the importance of them with the pen. Try this stale equation, for example:

$$\frac{\text{Deer}}{\text{Per}} = \frac{\text{Pellet groups per plot} \times 50 \times 640}{\text{Days since leaf-fall} \times 12.7}$$

The factors 50, 640 and 12.7 respectively represent the number of 1/50-acre plots per acre, acres per square mile and average pellet groups per deer per day.

WOW! This grandiose equation is about as diverse as the number of terms used to describe the droppings themselves: deer beans, deer berries, deer pellets, deer dung, deer manure, deer excrement, deer feces, deer scats and even deer scatology. Thank God that Ernest Thompson Seton, that brilliant naturalist who wrote so eloquently about deer, once made it clear that scatology—i.e., the study of dung pellets—never received formal recognition as a definite department of zoology. Otherwise, I am afraid that many of us would never have gotten past Zoology 101.

Regardless of whether one got past Zoology 101 or not, most deer hunters and field naturalists know that aside from the deer itself, deer droppings afford us the most definitive information of the deer's habits, food and whereabouts. It's not surprising that letters with regard to deer droppings frequently cross my desk. One such letter from a barber in Pittsfield, Massachusetts, reads as follows: "I have a question for you. I would like to know all I can about deer droppings. For instance, how much time elapses between eating and dropping? When does the biggest percentage of droppings occur? In the morning or in the evening? Does the color of the droppings indicate anything special? I know these questions might be impossible to answer, but I would appreciate any effort."

Other questions could be asked as well: How many pellet groups do deer drop per day? How many pellets constitute a group? How long do deer pellets last before deterioration? Do other animals or birds consume them? Can we determine the size of the deer from the size of the droppings? Can we determine the sex of the deer by the shape of the pellet? Can we determine the length of time a deer remained in a particular bed by studying the amount of droppings on the edge of the bed, as backwoodsmen would lead us to believe? Do more droppings accompany nighttime beds or daytime beds? Do they undergo seasonal variation in shape? Can we distinguish the droppings from the various species of deer? Can scientists determine the age of the deer by chemical analysis of the enzymes in the droppings? Do they provide scientists with an adequate clue to diseases? Do deer pellets still represent an adequate index to deer populations?

Since deer droppings frequently represent the only record or principal sign we have of the presence of deer, this chapter pictures and discusses these interesting and material records of a deer's whereabouts. The chapter addresses itself to several of the questions formulated above.

While tracking deer with radio equipment this past winter, I noticed that bedding areas furnish the student of the whitetail with a high concentration of deer droppings to study and observe, for most defecation apparently occurs shortly after a deer rises from its bed. That is what one old-time deerslayer told me while discoursing on the subject:

"Deer stretch, and stick out their hind legs," Old Julian mumbled while firing up his pipe. "They grunt, wiggle their tails and leave some droppings usually before leaving their beds, if they are not driven out. They take plenty of time to get up and stretch themselves before starting from their beds if undisturbed. The amount of droppings on the edge of a bed will indicate to a certain extent the length of time that the deer remained in that particular bed. When a deer gets up, if he leaves no droppings in the bed, he will be pretty sure to leave some so near the edge of the bed that some of them will roll into the bed.''

In checking out Old Julian's story, I found many beds with droppings in them as well as numerous pellet groups near the beds themselves. In reading the scientific literature on the subject, I discovered that more droppings accompany nighttime beds than daytime beds. But whether the amount of droppings actually indicates to a certain extent the length of time the deer remained in its bed, as Old Julian insisted, remains uncertain—bordering perhaps on the line of plausible quackery. In any event, the idea that most defecation occurs shortly after an animal rises from its bed seems certain and coincides with scientific fact. Deer, however, also defecate while changing activities; while grazing, for example, and moving in an almost random manner. Actually, defecation, unlike urination, rarely disrupts ongoing activities.

Deer droppings vary a great deal in shape, color and form at different times of the year and under different food conditions. During the winter months, when deer feed on browse, the pellets are hard and become harder as the winter advances; they are various shades of brown and about three quarters of an inch long. During the summer months, when deer feed on soft vegetation, the droppings consist of clusters of pellets that are more or less stuck together in one mass—linked one to another in bead fashion, although they occasionally remain separate at this

Tracking deer with radio equipment during the winter months allowed the author to locate bedding areas that furnished a high concentration of deer droppings to study and observe. *Photo credit Maren Lea Wegner*

time of the year as well. Fresh pellets during the summer acquire a greenish hue; they tend to glisten and are quite soft inside.

In other words, the form of deer dung depends upon the relative succulence of the seasonal food: when deer are on green succulent feed, they are amorphous and often congealed; on winter dry feed they are dark, hard and oblong. The form also depends upon the length of time the material remains in the colon. As Olaus Murie, a foremost field biologist of his time, once observed: ''The longer it is held the more consolidated and the more elongated the pellet. The type of forage used

During the winter months, when deer feed on browse, the pellets are hard and become harder as the winter advances; they are various shades of brown and about three quarters of an inch long. *Photo credit Irene Vandermolen*

may determine the length of this period, undigested dry browse doubtless being retained longer than the unused parts of succulent food.''

Whitetails regularly void waste from their bodies at any time of the day or night. They may even expel a few pellets while in their bed, but they never urinate when lying down. They defecate approximately 12.7 times a day. The number of pellets per defecation varies from 42 to 320. Recent investigations indicate that the frequency of defecations varies with the kind, quantity and succulence of the

forage. A lubricating mucous coating surrounds the pellet and allows it to drop cleanly to the ground without adhesion to the body hair, thus avoiding strong, pungent odors. I frequently find deer pellets in scrapes. But whether defecating in scrapes has a significant social function, as is the case in many bovids and in the pronghorn, remains an unanswered question in whitetail biology.

Fresh whitetail pellets take on a sort of bronze hue, a moist varnished appearance, and they mash easily. Old pellets lose this luster and mash with more

Whitetail pellets when browsing, upper left. Whitetail pellets when eating grass, lower left. Rabbit pellets, upper right. Porcupine pellets, lower right. Deer pellets at times are not readily distinguishable from those of other mammals such as the porcupine and the rabbit. Their pellets, however, are of a more fibrous, woody texture. Porcupine pellets are somewhat cylindrical and reach an inch and a quarter, while rabbit pellets are smaller and circular or disk-shaped. *Photo credit Leonard Lee Rue III*

difficulty. Deer pellets dry from the outside in; thus the thicker the outside dry layer, the older the pellet. When trying to estimate the age of deer droppings while still hunting, you need to consider the effect of weather. Obviously, they dry more quickly in the sunlight than in the shade, and in dry weather faster than in damp conditions. They also dry more quickly in windy weather than on still days. Remember that all droppings appear at first glance to be fresh immediately following a rain, but many are not.

Pellets deposited under dry conditions harden and persist in an unchanged condition for as long as two to five years. Two-year-old pellets, however, tend to crack and exhibit a rough outer surface;

During the summer months, when deer feed on soft vegetation, the droppings consist of clusters of pellets that are more or less stuck together in one mass. *Photo credit Richard P. Smith*

they appear dull and lusterless. They tend to become embedded in the soil and are grayish-brown in color. One-year-old pellets, on the other hand, have a smooth and shiny outer surface; they are brown to black in color and are not embedded in the soil. Dung beetles *(Canthon simplex)* may ultimately be responsible for destroying the whitetail's "calling card." Whether other animals or birds consume or destroy deer pellets remains an unanswered question, although one deer biologist with the New Zealand Forest Ser-

vice reports that mountain parrots *(Nestor notabilis)* do eat deer droppings.

Common sense would lead us to believe that larger deer excrete larger pellets than smaller deer. In fact, deer researchers at the Institute of Ecology in Mexico believe that a correlation exists between deer age and pellet size. They hasten to add, however, that estimating the age of deer by the pellet size of droppings is subject to many errors. Actually, this idea goes beyond the border of exact science, for other deer biologists suggest

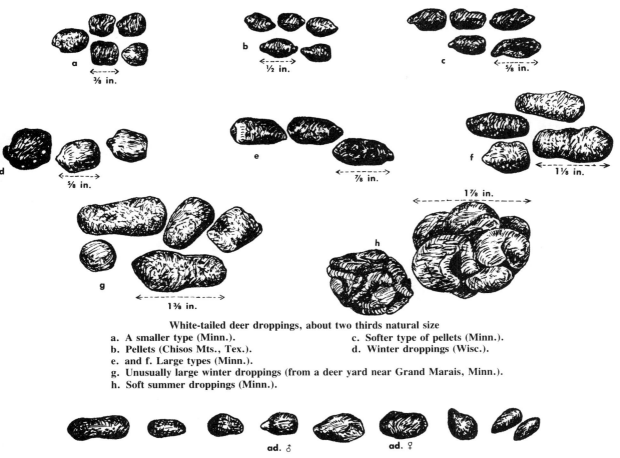

White-tailed deer droppings, about two thirds natural size

a. A smaller type (Minn.).   c. Softer type of pellets (Minn.).
b. Pellets (Chisos Mts., Tex.).   d. Winter droppings (Wisc.).
e. and f. Large types (Minn.).
g. Unusually large winter droppings (from a deer yard near Grand Marais, Minn.).
h. Soft summer droppings (Minn.).

Mule deer droppings, about two thirds the natural size.

that the type of food ingested affects the size of the pellet rather than the physical size or age of the deer. In a study of the defecation rates of mule deer in Utah, Arthur Smith, a professor of Range Management at the University of Utah, discovered that yearlings voided smaller pellets than fawns and that one fawn voided larger pellets than the adult deer. Smith concluded that pellet size has little utility for inferring age. Still, the myth that the size of droppings increases with age persists among many deer hunters, a myth perpetuated no doubt by Van Dyke's insistence that we carefully study the size of all deer droppings.

The external appearance of deer droppings often provides the careful observer with a clue to their origin. But physical appearance is by no means accurate because of the wide range of sizes and shapes that occur, especially in areas where the home range of several species of deer and other ruminants overlap. In such areas, deer biologists identify the origins of the dropping by analyzing their pH values or levels of acidity. Since the pH values of the pellets of the species vary, scientists can reliably identify the maker of the droppings with the aid of a Hach DR Colorimeter, graduated pH paper and a 605 HT Comparator—not exactly standard equipment for the deer hunter's backpack, to be sure.

In 1954, Olaus Murie hinted in an illustration in his classic book, *A Field Guide to Animal Tracks,* that we could determine the sex of the deer from analyzing the shape of the pellet. His illustrations for mule deer pellets contained the familiar male/female symbols. But he made no further mention of this striking new idea in the text of his book. In the same year, Randolph Peterson, a mammalogist at the Royal Ontario Museum, also suggested that the shapes of moose pellets differ for the sexes, with those of the bull being more spherical than the more elongate or ovoid droppings of the cow. He cautiously insisted, however, that the consistency of these sexual differences required additional study to be confirmed. Unfortunately, no further mention of this fascinating idea ever appeared in the literature. Like a promising spark from a campfire, the idea flashed and then died instantly.

The story of man's preoccupation with deer droppings in this century starts with the flashes of insight of Ernest Thompson Seton and his classic deer scatology illustrations. By the late 1930s deer researchers began to use droppings as an index to deer populations, thus going well beyond Seton's descriptions and illustrations. By the 1960s scientists refined their survey method to the point where they could determine the species of the drop-

pings by pH analysis. Rather than removing old pellets from sampling plots, scientists now sprayed the droppings with yellow paint to identify the pellet groups at the beginning of each survey. By the mid-1970s they were baking the droppings at 60°C in forced-air ovens and measuring their weights to determine the food habits of their makers via microscopic identification. Today's statistical and computerized analyses of deer droppings, with their complex mathematical equations, simply overwhelm the mind of the deer hunter—if not the mind of the deer biologist as well. In central Utah researchers now statistically analyze deer droppings with range area data extracted from Landsat satellite imagery.

Do you suppose this is what Van Dyke had in mind in 1883, when he told us in *The Still Hunter* to carefully examine deer droppings?

Deer droppings probably represent a better barometer of deer abundance and activity than any other sign. Yet, few deer hunters really study this sign with great detail. Actually, the almighty deer bean might just be the best scouting tool the hunter has, being especially useful for spring scouting because pellets deposited since leaf-fall can be identified as such, giving the hunter some idea of bedding areas, feeding areas and forage preferences. Deer droppings represent basic clues to other signs and present an excellent guide to a deer's whereabouts and habits. As an example, they can verify whether a bedding area is being used. They make tracks easier to follow. They give you an idea of what the maker was doing. When an animal stands still, his pellets will be found in piles; when deer move, the pellets will be strung out. They frequently indicate the time which elapsed

Deer droppings probably are a better indicator of deer abundance and activity than any other sign. Yet, few deer hunters really study this sign in great detail. *Photo credit Leonard Lee Rue III*

since the other signs were made. If you find fresh cold pellets in the morning, you may assume the deer fed at night. If they are warm, the maker is probably a short distance from you.

Systematic observation of the whitetail's "calling card" in your hunting area can consequently furnish you with the following basic information: (1) a general idea of how many deer are present in your area and whether or not they have been there recently—be careful not to base your evaluation on areas where deer yard; (2) where they are bedding and their forage preference, for not only do droppings indicate where deer spend most of

their time, but the amount of dung present directly relates to the number of pounds of forage removed; and (3) their movement patterns or the amount of traffic on deer trails, for droppings remain while tracks frequently vanish due to weather conditions.

Before concluding this discussion on rectal output, let me just add that it's a good practice to pick these deer beans up as you tramp the deer forest. Squeeze them! If they're wet, warm, quite soft and somewhat greenish in color, especially during the spring and summer, you can bet they have not laid long on the forest floor and that the deer that dropped them is not far ahead. "If they're hot and steaming," as Ernest Thompson Seton once remarked, "the deer is within range."

Collect these chocolate-drop-shaped pellets and throw them in your scent box; they will help eliminate human odor. When collecting them during the springtime, one thing is certain: you will only compete with the dung beetles for these soft, congealed beans of the season.

Chapter 8

Deer Beds

Despite the vast domain of scientific literature on deer, little information exists on deer beds and bedding habits, other than general observations made by scientists and deer hunters alike. Actually, scientific information on beds and bedding habits for any species of wild ruminants remains sparse. Consequently, I refer from time to time in this chapter to more than just one species of deer. Regardless of the species, however, a great deal of mystery surrounds the whole question of deer beds, and innumerable questions come to mind when thinking about the bedding habits of deer.

How much time, for example, do deer actually spend in their beds? Where do they bed? Do they prefer hardwoods or conifers? How do they bed? Are deer beds directly related to wind direction? Can you determine what direction a deer

was watching by studying a bed? Do deer bed facing their backtrails, as many woodsmen think? How long do deer actually sleep while in their beds? Do different beds serve different purposes? Do deer return to a precise bedding location time after time? Is the same bed used more than once? Can deer beds be used as a method for censusing deer? Do changing weather conditions affect bedding habits? Do deer beds contain deer dung? Does a buck's bed differ from a doe's? Do deer generally urinate in their beds when rising (if not startled out of the bed)? Can you determine the sex of the deer by studying urine sign in the bed?

Even more questions come to mind the more one thinks of deer beds and bedding habits. For example, can the general age of a deer be determined from the size of

The location of a deer bed varies considerably with different individuals. Such spots are distributed widely throughout the home range of the animal. *Photo credit Leonard Lee Rue III*

the bed? Do bucks bed in different areas than does? Do various sexes bed together? How close are deer beds to feeding areas? Do deer bed in fields during the daylight hours? Do deer bed in water? Are bedding habits directly related to the various phases of the moon? Do deer cooperate in assuring their security while bedding? What terminates a bedding period? Can you determine how long a bed has been vacated? Does the condition of the bed serve as an index to the deer's state of mind when he left it? Does the amount of droppings on the edge of a bed indicate to a certain extent the length of time that the deer remained in that particular bed? Why study deer beds? How are they related to hunting technique?

These are just a few of the questions we could ask with regard to deer beds.

This chapter addresses itself to some of these questions in particular and to one basic question in general: How much do we really know about deer beds and bedding habits?

In examining a bedding area one day, I startled a buck near to a logging trail. He was bedded down in the confined area of a cut-down oak crown. After I carelessly stepped on a dry branch, he literally exploded from the leafy oak crown and disappeared through the hardwoods like wood smoke. With respect to the speed with which he left his bed, I can well appreciate William Monypeny Newsom's remark that "deer can get out of bed on the dead run. It looks as if there must be a spring in the bed that helps them out." Indeed, deer leave their beds with great haste when disturbed. All four legs catapult them upward and they are instantly running at full speed.

Under normal circumstances, however, the routine rise from a bed consists in the animal shifting its weight forward and rising up on its front knees. In this same motion, as Leonard Lee Rue III observes in his *Deer of North America* (1979), "the animal raises its hindquarters and extends its hind legs. Then the deer extends one front leg, which raises the forepart of the body so that the other foreleg can be extended. Usually the deer then takes a long, leisurely stretch before walking off." When lying down, a deer lowers itself to both knees of its front legs, and then lowers its hindquarters to the ground below. Deer generally lie down with one side of their body touching the ground and with the legs on that side tucked underneath. As Rue observes, "only rarely will a deer lie down with all four legs beneath the body. In fact, this position usually indicates that the deer suspects danger and is ready to jump up fast."

The bedding positions of different deer vary from time to time. Some deer bed with their neck extended full length along the ground and with their eyelids closed. Other deer bed with their noses tucked into the groin. Others frequently bed with their heads erect, ears folded back over the neck and eyelids partially closed. Deer occasionally stand up, change position and lie down again, or even browse for a few moments before bedding again. In their study of mule deer on the Hastings Natural History Reservation, Linsdale and Tomich, two well-known deer researchers, provide us with an excellent description of deer at rest: "In the time of resting deer assume a variety of positions by shifting the ears, head, and forelegs, or,

less commonly, the entire body. Resting deer are not purposefully alert to their surroundings, but they rely on the involuntary function of the senses for information. A deer at rest in the daytime may occasionally lay its head back on a flank or hind leg and doze. The eyes are not fully open; the lids droop more or less, but sometimes suddenly open wide and then gradually close again. This is apparently as close to sleep as deer ever come."

Deer hunters and scientists alike frequently debate the question of whether deer actually sleep. The answer to this question seems fairly clear if we avoid the problem of semantics. If we consider sleep to be a resting mode with a significant reduction in alertness, then deer "sleep." I base this conclusion on my own field observations in which whitetails place their heads alongside their bodies and seemingly remain unalert. Actually, scientific measurements by radio telemetry indicate deer do indeed become unalert and sleep, especially in cold weather. In his *Elk of North America* (1951), Olaus J. Murie recalls an instance in which he walked up on a male Alaskan caribou quietly resting in his bed. He soon noticed that the animal's head drooped lower and lower until his antlers rested on the ground. On another occasion Murie actually captured and restrained with a rope a sleeping female caribou. Murie did not observe sleep in elk, but suggests that it probably occurs.

In his *Year of the Red Deer* (1975), Lea MacNally, a prominent British wildlife photographer, records that he occasionally found red deer lying sound asleep curled up like dogs, nose to rump with not even the twitch of an ear. He hastens to add, however, that only when deer feel *absolutely* secure will they sleep in such a manner.

In commenting on sleeping habits in his *Pronghorn Antelope* (1948), Arthur Einarsen states that antelope often sleep, but without continuity or regularity and only for short periods of time. "Although asleep, these animals will respond to a strange scent. Often when a sleeping buck is observed at close range, he will leap into action when his nose tells him of the observer's presence."

I still wonder, however, whether trophy bucks *ever* sleep, besides the eternal repose we sometimes grant them by hanging them on the meat pole? In any event, one thing seems certain: we might well question the practical importance of a deer's sleeping pattern at least with regard to the hunter. For as T. S. Van Dyke correctly observes, "the times when a deer thus loses himself in the daytime are very rare, and nearly all his sleeping is done at night. And even if he were sound asleep in the daytime, it would not allow for any carelessness in approaching him. His senses are not to be trifled with under any circumstances. So that the question of a deer's sleeping by day is of no practical importance."

If deer do not spend a great deal of time sleeping while in their beds, what are they doing to preoccupy themselves? Obviously, they're placidly chewing "Apple-Jack" and dreaming of avoiding your stinky body. Deer hunters tell us as much. Scientists, on the other hand, tell us that one of the primary reasons why deer bed in the first place is to chew their cud. Deer are herbivorous cud-chewing animals related to cattle and sheep. They need to eat large amounts of food and as quickly as possible so that they can re-

turn to the safety of thick cover. Cud chewing is a process that enables them to do this. They bite off vegetation and swallow it quickly. This allows them to gather a lot of food in a short time. Once they have regained the safety of their bed, they are able to regurgitate small packages of food, re-chew it and then swallow and digest it in a leisurely manner.

Deer biologists have studied the cud-chewing process with great specificity. Arthur Bentley, an Australian deer biologist, reports that red deer and fallow deer on a grass/hay diet chew each cud approximately 51.4 times. Leonard Lee Rue III, after observing hundreds of deer in the cud-chewing process, believes that "they masticate each piece of their cud with an average of 40 chews. The largest number of chews I ever witnessed was 52, the smallest 23. The average 40 chews take 45 seconds." Deer actually spend from six to seven hours a day chewing their cud, although they rarely occupy more than 20 minutes consecutively in the cud-chewing process. The actual length of time spent in cudding varies with the quality of the diet.

The best summary of the cud-chewing process comes from the pen of Raymond E. Chaplin, a well-known British deer biologist. In his book entitled *Deer* (1977), he points out that "ingested food is not chewed to any extent and is normally swallowed and stored in a special compartment of the stomach, the rumen/reticulum. From there it is regurgitated as a bolus and this cud is then chewed and swallowed again, this time into a separate compartment (the omasum) and thence into the fourth chamber (the abomasum). Cudding is done at leisure in the security of the bedding area." Cud

Deer masticate each piece of their cud with an average of 40 chews. The average 40 chews take about 45 seconds.
Photo credit Leonard Lee Rue III

chewing is thus one basic reason why deer bed down, although they also bed down to conserve energy.

All wild ruminants, especially deer, exhibit what Aaron Moen of Cornell University calls "thermoregulatory behavior." This process allows deer to conserve energy or to dissipate energy by altering their bedding posture. During periods of high temperature, for example, deer will frequently bed down in a stretched-out position with all four legs extended outward from the body so as to maximize the radiating surface. During periods of very cold temperature, deer avoid this sprawling posture and tend to close their bedding position in an attempt to conserve more solar radiation. In the closed position, at least 20 percent of their body participates in conductive heat transfer to the ground.

Deer can also secure insulation and reduce the effective wind velocity past their bodies by bedding in deep snow. During heavy snowstorms, deer frequently lie down and stay down, if undisturbed, until the storm passes, even if it lasts for several days. As Rue observes, "they literally become buried in the snow. The insulating qualities of their coats are so

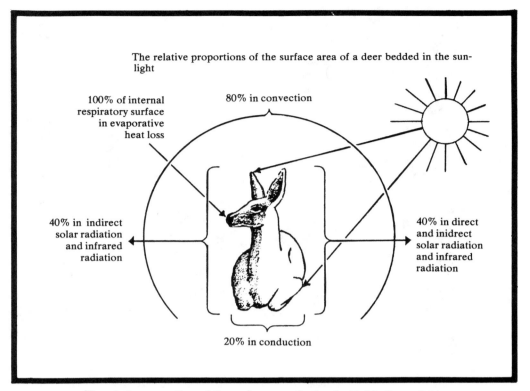

The relative proportions of the surface area of a deer bedded in the sun-light

100% of internal respiratory surface in evaporative heat loss

80% in convection

40% in indirect solar radiation and infrared radiation

40% in direct and inidrect solar radiation and infrared radiation

20% in conduction

The relative proportions of the surface area of a deer bedded in the sunlight.

efficient that the snow doesn't even melt. The covering of snow itself also acts as insulation, giving the deer additional protection from the cold.''

Deer also seek protection from extreme heat and pesty insects by lying in water. A shake or two after rising dispels most of the water from a deer's coat. Personally, I have not seen deer lying in water, but in his unique record of the year's life cycle of the Highland red deer, Lea MacNally brilliantly photographs this type of behavior. In noting how deer lie in water to achieve coolness, MacNally writes that ''I have watched deer subside, as with a sigh of relief, into the placid dark water of a pool, only head, neck and line of back visible, this last awash in the gently flowing current; then rise when completely satiated, and saturated, and expel, with one vigorous shake, the soothing wetness in an enshrouding nimbus of silvery droplets.''

Few systematic observations exist on the actual proportions of the day in which deer spend bedding. In his classic book, *Fallow Deer* (1975), Donald Chapman records that fallow deer during mid-May to September spend 7 to 21 percent of daylight hours in bedding and ruminating and 5 to 31 percent of daylight hours in bedding without ruminating. Even though

Deer secure insulation and reduce the effective wind velocity past their bodies by bedding in deep snow. During heavy snowstorms, deer frequently lie down and stay down, if undisturbed, until the storm passes, even if it lasts for several days. *Photo credit Leonard Lee Rue III*

deer of all species are restless animals, they do in fact spend a great deal of time resting. Indeed, when conscious of man's presence, deer are capable of long periods of bedding and immobility. In addressing himself to this question of how many hours deer actually spend in bedding, A. B. Bubenik, a French deer biologist, concluded that during the spring and summer roe deer spend approximately six hours in bedding and during the autumn and winter bed for at least five hours.

Deer bed down quite commonly for as long as an hour and a half at a time. After 300 observations of completed rest intervals for mule deer, Linsdale and Tomich noted that the average length of bedding time was 47 minutes. Approximately 94 percent of the rest periods were from one to 90 minutes long. They also ob-

served a tendency for rest periods to become longer from January to midsummer and then steadily decline until autumn. The longest time any deer remained continuously in its bed was 234 minutes. Natural disturbances such as driving rain and gusty wind, bothersome insects, the warmth of the sun and aggressive companions frequently terminated the bedding period.

In studying the nocturnal movements and activity rhythms of whitetails in Pennsylvania, G. G. Montgomery of Penn State reached a similar conclusion with regard to the duration of whitetail bedding: whitetails bedded for about an hour and a half each time they bedded. Montgomery also reached the following interesting conclusions with regard to whitetails and bedding: (1) Nighttime bedding usually occurred in fields near the lower

Duration of Various Bedding Activities		
	Spring/Summer	Autumn/Winter
Feeding	6 Hours	7 Hours
Cudding	6 Hours	7 Hours
Bedding	6 Hours	5 Hours
Sleeping	4 Hours	2 Hours
Movement	2 Hours	3 Hours

Reprinted from Richard Prior, **The Roe Deer of Cranborne Chase** (London, 1968)

Duration of various bedding activities.

limits of their ranges. (2) During the summer months, the peak of bedding occurred seven to eight hours after sunset or just before dawn, and nearly all deer were active at dawn. During the autumn the first peak of bedding occurred about five hours after sunset, and in the winter time about four hours after sunset. (3) Undisturbed deer frequently bedded near their food supply.

When preparing to lie down, deer frequently circle and often scrape with the forefoot on the selected spot. The spot is generally an oval-shaped area that measures about three feet in length by two feet in width. A day or two after the deer has departed, the grass and leaves that were flattened down by the body of the resting deer straighten out and little indication exists that a deer even rested there. Quite frequently, only the freshest beds remain as evidence.

In most cases the terrain greatly influences a deer's selection of a bedding place. Weather conditions also strongly affect the choice. In general, whitetails prefer high ground—ridges, hillsides and knolls where they can be sure of detecting the approach of danger well in advance of its arrival. They frequently bed just under the crest of hills rather than on the top where the wind is less steady. They rely heavily on sound and smell, rather than sight, to herald the approach of a hunter. Actually, they use their bedding cover as a blind to slip out of existence.

Each family group tends to have its own special spot for bedding. Indeed, groups of deer often bed down within a few feet of one another. Presumably, does, yearlings and fawns bed in this manner for safety's sake, for each deer's alertness helps to protect the group. During the spring and summer months, deer often

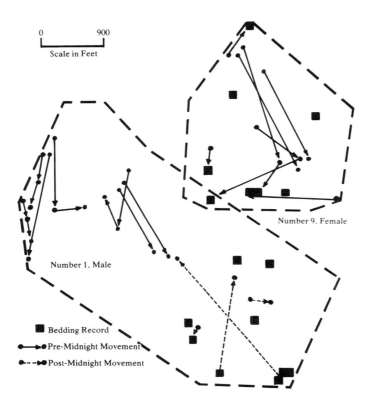

0
900

Scale in Feet

Number 9, Female

Number 1, Male

■ Bedding Record

●——▶● Pre-Midnight Movement

●- -▶● Post-Midnight Movement

Nocturnal movements and bedding sites of two adult deer that showed movements typical of those deer which moved down the slope each evening. The mountaintop was above the upper points of the ranges. The lines connecting dots or squares indicate sequential sightings of the animals during the same nights. Outlines represent maximum observed limits of the ranges. *Credit* Journal of Wildlife Management *(1963)*

bed down in the fields where they feed, especially if the grass provides some protection. Antlerless deer, in particular, seldom go any farther from their feeding area than absolutely necessary. As autumn approaches, deer move deeper into the woods and search for heavy cover in remote areas.

Mature bucks frequently bed in small pieces of cover, little hideaways that are overlooked by many deer hunters. Indeed, deer get used to outwitting hunters by bedding in cover that looks less than ideal. Habitat which appears to be the last place a mature buck would choose for bedding security never receives any hunting pressure. Clever bucks master this lesson. Never overlook those little

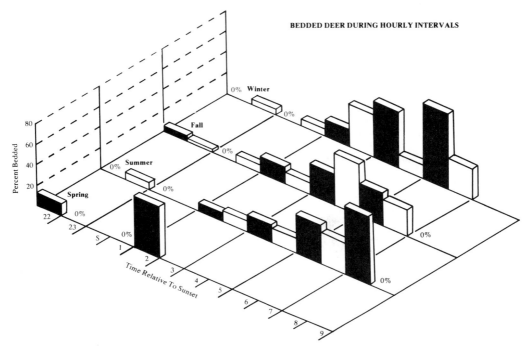

BEDDED DEER DURING HOURLY INTERVALS

Percentages of all deer seen that were bedded during hourly intervals before and after sunset. The data recorded during each of the four seasons were combined after clock times were adjusted to read as if each day began at sunset. *Credit* Journal of Wildlife Management *(1963)*

islands of trees near fields and woodlots, those little patches of cover, those small isolated thickets; bucks frequently bed in just such places. Large bucks will also lie very close to you without bolting, especially if they suspect they will be passed over.

Trophy bucks with beautiful racks generally maintain solitary bedding habits before and after the rut. They seem to bed down in places that have at least two escape routes, and tend to select bedding areas where everything they need is nearby. If they bed within the area of other deer, they select the most inaccessible part. To down one of these mature bucks, you must know their bedding habits.

Whitetails show a strong preference in bedding habits for coniferous forest types during the winter months. After studying 86 deer beds, Hosley and Ziebarth, two deer researchers from Massachusetts, noted that 39 beds, or nearly one half, were found in white pine stands 15 to 70 years of age. Eighteen beds, or slightly less than one fourth, were located under Scotch pines. Deer placed only seven beds of the total in hardwood stands or in the open.

In this Massachusetts study, deer frequently bedded on the north side of openings in the pines where the sun reached the ground. They placed their beds most commonly where the lowest coniferous limbs were from five to 10 feet above the ground. According to Hosley and Ziebarth, there appeared to be no attempt on the part of the deer to locate beds with any particular degree of visibility in mind. Apparently they used their ears and nose rather than their eyes to warn them of danger. In this study the deer showed no marked preference for bedding on a particular slope. They usually bedded on knolls, however, rather than in depressions.

After studying the bedding behavior of white-tailed deer in an Adirondack forest during the winter months, Donald Behrend of New York reached similar conclusions: hardwood types were nearly avoided for bedding. Deer bedded extensively in conifer and conifer-hardwood types. Eighty-seven percent of all beds counted (347) during the months of January, February and March for 1964 indicated a marked preference for bedding in conifers, an obvious tendency for deer to bed on rises, and a tendency of deer to bed where the snow was the shallowest. By marking deer beds in the snow with diagonal cuts made by the blade of an axe, Behrend also observed that 32 percent of the beds marked in January were known to be reused. Four percent of the beds were reused three different times. Both studies in this regard ultimately indicated that deer prefer coniferous shelter for bedding, so they can avoid wind chill, and that deer bed in shallow snow.

Most deer biologists would probably agree that the bedding area represents one of the most significant habitats in the life of an adult deer. It contributes to the well-being of the animal by providing shelter from the elements, by increasing its chances of escape from enemies, and by fostering a sense of security. Yet, few

The author collected this 11-point farmland buck in the 1981 bow hunting season as a result of continually moving his tree stand closer and closer to this buck's favorite bedding spot. After field-dressing this three-and-a-half-year-old cornfed whitetail, the author found that the buck weighed 245 pounds. Hornaday's formula for determining live weight showed that he weighed approximately 300 pounds on the hoof. The rack measured 17 inches on the inside spread. *Photo credit Maren Lea Wegner*

detailed scientific studies examine beds and bedding habits. Nonetheless, the following generalizations can be made based on the available scientific evidence.

(1) Whether or not deer drop dung on their beds remains a highly debated issue. Some scientists argue that deer defecate at the ends of their beds while resting, other researchers maintain that they do not.

(2) Tallying deer beds as a method for measuring deer populations fails since we do not know how many beds each deer makes per day. Indeed, bed counts have little potential as a measurement for censusing deer, although they can be used to identify cover-type preference.

(3) While deer do not necessarily use the same bed twice, they do tend to bed down in the same approximate area. These areas vary with the seasons.

(4) Adult bucks are frequently the first to bed down in the morning, although bedding activity can be initiated by any member of a group.

(5) The pattern formed by a group of deer when bedding is random except as governed by the variations in site locations.

(6) Deer examine a site quite thoroughly before bedding down. They frequently lower their nose to smell the ground and search the site with their eyes. They also paw the ground to scrape away loose debris or snow.

(7) Deer seek sunny spots to bed down and change their locations as the shadows change, especially during cold weather.

(8) Strong winds cause deer to pick

Why study deer beds? Because they represent the secret to the successful placing of tree stands, which need to be positioned near bedding areas in order to provide more shooting-light potential. *Photo credit Irene Vandermolen*

sheltered bedding sites. They also change beds as the winds change.

(9) Deer maintain a major rest period during the middle of the day.

(10) The frequent interchange of beds by young deer might have a direct bearing on the transfer of ticks from one deer to another.

(11) At least one scientist concluded that moonlight affects the choice of bedding sites at night: deer are inclined to bed in open, grassy meadows during dark nights but stay back in the trees during moonlit nights.

(12) Deer commonly change their positions at least once during a three- or four-hour rest period.

(13) Bucks apparently urinate in their beds immediately after rising.

(14) Bedding activity increases during the winter months and occurs during the greater part of the night. Three long bedding periods interspersed with shorter feeding periods frequently characterize nighttime activity during the winter months. The first period is generally longer than the other two.

(15) Bedding habits are not uniformly regular, for many characteristics of the deer's physiology, as well as atmospheric and other external conditions, continuously modify the bedding habits of deer.

Why study deer beds? Why acquire a woodland knowledge of them? Because they represent the secret to the successful location of stands that need to be positioned near bedding areas. Why? Because deer frequently leave their bedding areas and move toward feeding areas sometime within the last hour before dark. Conversely, deer leave feeding areas on a schedule enabling them to arrive at their bedding areas shortly after dawn. Thus a stand near a bedding area provides much

Mature white-tailed bucks often hold tight to their beds and let the deer hunter pass. But more often than not, they sneak out of their bed without a sound, especially if they believe that they have not been spotted. *Photo credit Leonard Lee Rue III*

more shooting light potential than a stand placed in or near a feeding area.

A knowledge of deer beds and bedding habits can also increase your success while still hunting. There is no sense in still hunting an area which does not contain deer. Know where the bedding areas are and then still hunt them. When you still hunt a bedding area, try to determine which trails deer use to reach the bedding area. Travel these same trails in an upwind direction. Always consider the weather factor. On windy days deer frequently lie on the lee or most protected side of their bedding areas. If it is extremely cold but sunny, hunt the southern exposure of ridges and slopes. If the weather is hot, still hunt thickets offering shade. Remember, whitetails often hold tight to their beds and let the hunter pass. But more often than not, they sneak out of their bed without a sound, especially if they believe that they have not been spotted. White-tailed bucks literally hold their heads down and all but get on their knees at times to sneak out of their beds.

In the final analysis, then, how much do we really know about deer beds and bedding habits? Not very much! Let's be modest. As one professor of wildlife ecology exclaimed the other day, "deer still bed down where and when they damn well please." Perhaps we find the most eloquent summary of our ignorance with regard to deer beds and bedding habits in that masterful treatise entitled *The Still Hunter* (1882) by T. S. Van Dyke: "Just when and where a deer may be expected to lie down it is, of course, impossible to say. Like many other kinds of game, they are provokingly irregular in their habits, and do not appreciate your kindness in picking out nice lying-places for them, but prefer to make their own selection."

Chapter 9

Whitetails and Alfalfa

At an annual meeting of the American Society of Agronomy, an old deer hunter and distinguished professor of agronomy whom many referred to as "Mister Alfalfa" once remarked that "unlike gold, alfalfa did not make history by motivating men to conquer and to exploit, or to search and to seize. It was, and is, a crop for the peaceful pursuits of man. Its part in human affairs was not meant for the adventurer or the buccaneer; yet it followed in their wake to become one of the greatest forages of the new hemisphere and also one of its principal sources of renewable wealth."

Indeed, as one of the principal forages of American agriculture, alfalfa *(Medicago sativa L.)* not only plays a very important part in the pursuits of man, but in the diet of the white-tailed deer as well.

Depending upon the field's location, deer can be seen bedding and feeding in alfalfa fields at almost any time of the day or night regardless of the state in which you live.

After hanging around alfalfa fields for many years and after studying the relationship between this herbaceous perennial plant and the white-tailed deer, I conclude that whitetails, like man, see alfalfa as the "queen of the forages." Unfortunately, much of the deer nutrition literature focuses on the winter diet, with relatively little or no analysis of the preference, composition, and digestibility of such summer and fall foods as alfalfa. This chapter describes the relationship between whitetails, deer hunters, and alfalfa fields, and suggests that the successful pursuit of whitetails frequently

When most deer hunters think of alfalfa and its importance to the white-tailed deer, they usually think of the emergency delivery of alfalfa to the winter deer yards. *Photo credit Leonard Lee Rue III*

depends upon understanding the relationship between alfalfa fields and deer movement.

The name alfalfa comes from the Arabic language; it means best fodder. Historically, it is the only forage to have been cultivated before the era of recorded history. Historians generally agree that it originated in Iran. Today it grows wild from China to Spain and from Sweden to North Africa. It has become widely acclimatized in South Africa, New Zealand, Australia and North and South America. The world's total acreage of alfalfa reaches an excess of well over 85 million acres. The United States alone has more than 30 million acres. Small wonder that deer are seen feeding and bedding in alfalfa fields throughout this country.

When most deer hunters think of alfalfa and its importance to the white-tailed deer, they usually think of the emergency delivery of alfalfa and the problems of artificial feeding. But the importance of alfalfa goes well beyond supplemental feeding for starving deer. In emphasizing the importance of alfalfa for deer, deer biologists from California, for example, tell us that alfalfa is not only the most palatable plant deer can eat, but that it has a high level of crude protein and digestibility. It is also high in mineral content, containing at least 10 different vitamins. It has long been considered an important source of vitamin A.

Today alfalfa is a widely grown and very important forage crop in Pennsylvania. It is produced on approximately 19 percent of the total acreage harvested for field crops in the Keystone state. Pennsylvania ranks 14th in the United States in alfalfa production. Wisconsin, California, Minnesota, Iowa and Nebraska lead the nation. The results of a 1979 mail questionnaire survey regarding deer damage to alfalfa fields indicates that Pennsylvania farmers perceive considerable losses. Of 2426 respondents, 21 percent reported deer damage to alfalfa and estimated their average loss to be $592.

A recent study by scientists at Pennsylvania State University verifies the farmer's claims of severe deer damage to alfalfa, demonstrating statistically and economically significant losses. The study concludes that alfalfa loss to deer approximates 20 percent of the crop, and that "in areas of the fields where heavy deer damage occurs, there is a thinning of the alfalfa stand which results in an increased growth of grasses, thus lowering the value of the crop, both as a foodstuff and a cash crop."

Despite the fact that we have yet to discover a reliable method for quantifying the yield reduction of alfalfa as a result of deer grazing, deer researchers at the University of Wisconsin estimate the daily consumption of alfalfa by deer to be well over three pounds per deer. They also tell us that the longevity of an alfalfa field may be shortened as a result of excessive deer grazing, for as alfalfa plants are injured or killed, associated grasses and weeds naturally gain a competitive edge and increase their proportions until the yield of the field is no longer economical.

After studying the rumens of 246 whitetailed deer, the Wisconsin Department of Natural Resources reached the conclusion that one deer consumes 92 pounds of alfalfa per year (five pounds per day during the summer and spring), and that the average farm annually loses between 0.2 to 0.7 tons of alfalfa as a result of deer damage. If a whitetail ate only alfalfa throughout the spring and summer months, he would consume 920 pounds. Yes, deer are in the alfalfa fields; it used to cost Wisconsin taxpayers more than $7000 a year in deer damage claims for alfalfa loss alone. (Note: The state of Wisconsin no longer reimburses farmers for deer crop damage.)

In Dane County, where I hunt, alfalfa accounts for 14.6 percent of the land use. The average alfalfa acreage per deer for farms in deer range in my area reaches 4.5 acres. According to the Wisconsin Department of Natural Resources, alfalfa is found in deer rumens in Dane County for every month except January. From April through December the percentage of occurrence varies from 27 percent to 71 percent.

During the springtime, alfalfa represents 13 percent of the food deer consume; the greatest volume of consumption occurs in April. The dramatic increase in occurrence from March to April suggests that deer prefer plants with a high level of nutrition, for the protein level of the alfalfa plant is exceedingly high in the early growth stages. The low volume of 2 percent in June results from the first cutting. After the mechanized beasts leave the field, the lush, leafy, green alfalfa plant remains little more than brown stubble. The increased use in July indicates a renewal of feeding on the alfalfa regrowth. According to the Wisconsin Department of Natural Resources, "alfalfa averages 10 percent of the entire fall volume consumed in the southern counties, and comprises 18 percent of the October volume. If freezing lowers the palatability of alfalfa, it could explain the decline in occurrence from October to November.''

Herbaceous plants such as alfalfa are not chemically stable over time. Seasonal differences in their chemical compositions occur in relation to the development of the plant. In other words, physiological changes take place as the plant progresses from dormancy to leaf production, flower production and seed production. As a crop of alfalfa matures the percentage of protein, for example,

decreases rather regularly. From the bud stage to seed production the protein content declines more than 20 percent. Some alfalfa experts suggest that the protein content of alfalfa drops even more dramatically, from 24.5 percent in the immature stage to 15.9 percent in the full bloom stage. Others calculate the loss in protein to be around 17 percent. As the plant matures its digestibility, mineral and soluble carbohydrate content decreases as well.

The rapid decline in the protein content

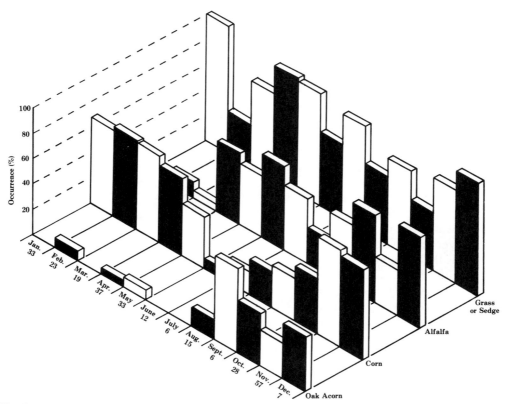

Monthly use of alfalfa in southern Wisconsin as determined by rumen analysis. The sample sizes are listed below the months. *Credit Charles M. Pils*, et al., *"Foods of Deer in Southern Wisconsin," Department of Natural Resources, Report #12, December, 1981.*

Alfalfa use by season and month.

Month	By Season[1]		By Month	
	Vol. (%)	Occ. (%)	Vol. (%)	Occ. (%)
January	1	12	0	0
February			1	13
March			1	5
April	13	52	46	54
May			12	52
June			2	58
July	7	43	11	66
August			8	27
September			3	50
October	10	46	18	68
November			8	35
December			6	71

[1]Winter (22 December - 20 March), Spring (21 March - 20 June), Summer (21 June - 22 September), and Fall (23 September - 21 December).

—Charles M. Pils, *et al*, "Foods of Deer in Southern Wisconsin," Department of Natural Resources, Report #112, December, 1981.

Alfalfa use by season and month. *Credit Charles M. Pils,* et al., *"Foods of Deer in Southern Wisconsin," Department of Natural Resources, Report #12, December, 1981.*

of alfalfa is of great ecological significance for the white-tailed deer. According to Aaron Moen of Cornell University, "the timing of these changes in relation to the timing of the birth of deer fawns is of interest because fawns begin nibbling leaves shortly after birth. If the fawns are born at a time when both the protein content and the protein digestibility is high, considerably more nutritive value can be derived from the plants. A month later the same forage species might have only half as much useful protein, resulting in a subtle deterioration in the range quality unless the fawn can compensate by selecting later-maturing species."

These observations raise the interesting question of whether deer can, in fact, choose forage of higher nutritive value. The literature on deer nutrition and for-

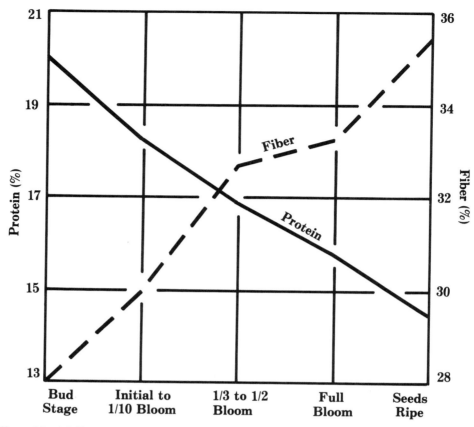

Alfalfa protein and fiber content at different growth stages. *Credit John H. Martin,* Principles of Field Production *(1967)*

age selection contains innumerable references indicating that deer not only make definitive selections of forage plants, but likewise choose those species which are particularly nutritious. The scientific evidence indicates that the most preferred plants such as alfalfa are high in protein and various carbohydrates such as starches and sugars.

Critical observations of deer in alfalfa fields show that they use olfaction to make their initial selection of forage. If they like the smell of the alfalfa plant, then they taste it; and if they like the taste, they proceed to feed on it. Deer biologists agree that once whitetails are familiar with a particular plant, they learn to recognize it by sight and do not hesitate to feed upon it without going through the procedure of first smelling and then tasting. It still remains somewhat doubtful, however, as to whether deer can detect the presence of nutrients or digestive inhibitors in plants through olfaction; it may depend upon other unknown factors.

Observing deer in alfalfa fields during July and August should become an annual event in the life of the serious deer hunter. Bucks not only hang around alfalfa fields to feast on gourmet alfalfa, but to confront, challenge and spar with one another. They generally travel in groups at this time and frequently enter the field during daylight hours—in the order of social dominance, with the superior bucks coming last. I once saw 14 bucks standing together in the same alfalfa field with the sun in the sky. These bucks were observing one another's racks—a unique occurrence I refer to as "the lull before the storm."

Observing deer in the alfalfa field before the opening of bow season can be a marvelous experience and can present quite a fashion show. My diary entry for July 16, 1982 makes the point:

Partly cloudy, hot and humid. Left for the island woodlot in the alfalfa field dressed in safari pants. Wind from the south/southeast. After taking my perch on top of my Ambusher Tree Stand, I began to read Sigurd Olson's The Singing Wilderness *to preserve the flavor of the passing moment. Like Olson, I come to the deer forest to seek peace and quiet, to find a place where thoughts are long and undisturbed. An eastern meadowlark suddenly disturbs my reading as he lands in the elm tree in front of me. This gregarious songster floats in the breeze on a small elm branch; he sails off as abruptly as he arrived.*

At around 8:15 p.m., the fashion show begins. First a 4-pointer and then a large 8-pointer. Undoubtedly the same two bucks who violently sparred beneath my tree stand the night before. I can still recall the swishing sounds of their bodies passing through the bromegrass and alfalfa beneath me, the desperate sense of their power. Their vigorous sparring match questions the idea that deer re-main docile while in the velvet. Little do they know that I observed their sparring match from as close as eight feet above them last night. I shall never forget how the 8-pointer pushed the younger buck into the bottom of my pole stand and almost knocked me out of the tree stand. How that youngster continually antagonized that dominant 8-pointer—like a featherweight sparring with Larry Holmes.

A 6-pointer soon joins them in the alfalfa field. They all remain in the shade close to the woodlot, with alfalfa hanging from their mouths. Two 4-pointers suddenly come out of the triangle, pass the island woodlot, run toward the hog forest and join the others. Unlike the previous evenings, this group of bucks soon returns to the deer forest.

I now observe a doe—antlerless deer are rare in this area. While she feeds on alfalfa, another buck walks along the fenceline and disappears under the apple trees. Her fox-red color makes the green alfalfa even greener. Where are her fawns? I wonder to myself. As it gets darker the morning doves somberly coo in the distance. The firebugs alight. Finally the whip-poor-will strikes up. What a rude intrusion upon the serenity and harmony of the moment. I now know it is time to leave the deer forest.

As I take my leave, the doe snorts at least a dozen times and waves the familiar flag. Before leaving the alfalfa field I see three more bucks; two 4-pointers and one with a massive velvety rack that's too far in the distance to distinguish points. The last buck snorts out a final adieu—a rather noisy ending to a July evening.

I return to the farm for a glass of red wine and some flute music by James Galway. Ten deer seen: nine bucks, one doe.

What an incredible buck/doe ratio! In July and August, bucks in velvet remain in the uplands near alfalfa fields where they try to fight off mosquitoes, flies and other bugs while establishing social dominance by sparring with one another.

When observing deer for research, I position myself at the edge or border of alfalfa fields because that spot affords a panoramic view. Many bow hunters are attracted to these border stands because of the long view. Using stands along the edge of the field would seem to suggest a chance at more deer. Rarely does it work that way, however. As the bow season progresses, whitetails become nervous and suspicious at the end of the day, and seldom appear in the alfalfa field until after dark. Actually, the hourly trend in deer using an alfalfa field reaches a peak several hours before midnight.

To see deer close enough for killing shots, I follow well-worn trails into the surrounding woodlots. The farther back from the field the better. If you keep yourself deep within the deer forest near the bedding area, the zone of shelter and seclusion deer depend on, you will more likely have them meander by close and unaware. Gene Wensel summarizes the point in his book entitled *Bowhunting Rutting Whitetails:* "The stand should be placed about a hundred yards upwind and twenty-five yards parallel to the woodline from where you expect the main herd to enter the field. This will give you the best opportunity at the trophy buck as he approaches the field on his subordinate trail just at last shooting light. Don't listen to the people that tell you to watch the edges to see deer. They'll keep on seeing and taking the does and immature bucks while you'll see fewer but bigger deer."

Deer will continue to eat alfalfa when available until the first killing frost, which usually occurs around mid-October in my area. Then, as the maples blaze with scarlet red and as the cornfields take on the somber hue of smoky gold, deer gradually abandon their normal movement patterns to and from the alfalfa fields. They now begin to feed on corn and bed in the cornfields as well. When this shift in food preference takes place, be prepared to change your stand location and hunting tactics, for you now confront the difficult problem of hunting whitetails that frequently feed *and* bed in standing cornfields.

The next time you cross an alfalfa field during the summer, try eating a handful of leafy, green alfalfa. It's not comparable to high-grade whiskey or Red Fox chewing tobacco, but you will enjoy its beautiful aroma and succulent taste. There are only two things finer in the life of the deer hunter: the sight and smell of fresh hanging venison next to alfalfa bales in the barn, and the taste of venison roast served on a bed of alfalfa sprouts during the cold wintery nights of January and February. I have been eating alfalfa sprouts for years. What a fantastic treat! Their fine, threadlike appearance also adds a visual plus to salads served with venison tenderloins.

Indeed, alfalfa has a deservedly high reputation as a food, but its use has been largely confined to consumers with hoofs, horns and antlers. That alfalfa may someday serve its purpose with the genus *Homo Deer Hunter* is no new idea. Since the early 1920s flour, tea, coffee, syrup, extracts and candies have all been made from alfalfa. During the 1930s, South African biologists discovered that alfalfa makes an excellent and palatable vege-

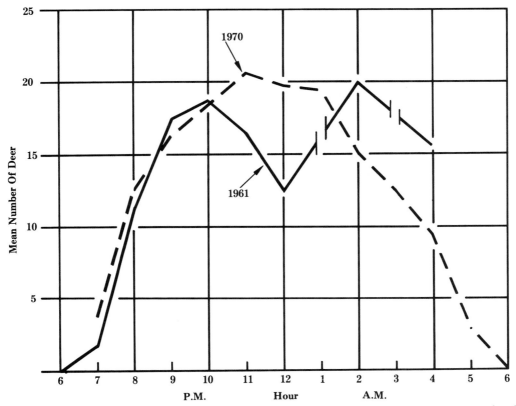

The hourly trend in deer using an alfalfa field during late summer in western part of Colorado. *Credit Al Hofacker*

table for human consumption—eaten either raw or cooked as a spinach.

Use the very word "alfalfa" at a cocktail party with city slickers and you will almost always get a laugh or two. Apparently those three syllables roll off the tongue in such a way that makes city people think of haystacks and manure. Making fun of alfalfa is extraordinarily foolish, however, for if anything qualifies as a miracle plant it is surely *Medicago sativa,* to use the Latin name.

Why? For many reasons: (1) It minimizes pollution by reducing water runoff and soil erosion; (2) It is one of the most powerful nitrogen-fixers of all legumes. A good stand of alfalfa pulls 250 pounds of nitrogen per acre from the air each year. That figure compares to an average of only 80 pounds of nitrogen fixed by other leguminous plants; (3) It is a highly significant source of 10 different vitamins, being especially rich in vitamins A, C, D, B_2 and E. And with a protein content ranging from 15 to well over 20 percent (depending on its geographical location), alfalfa is far better than wheat, which only averages about 13.8 percent protein. It also scores better with regard to calcium and iron than does wheat. In

The author harvested this 8-point, farmland buck as a result of studying alfalfa fields and deer movement patterns. *Photo credit Maren Lea Wegner*

short, it's a perfect food to make into natural food supplements for people; (4) It adapts well to a wide variety of growing conditions and will thrive and produce excellent hay in every state of the union; (5) It serves as an excellent compost stimulant; and (6) Scientists have discovered a remarkable cholesterol-lowering agent in alfalfa. Small wonder that venison is low in cholesterol. The chemical substance called "saponin" somehow manages to bind cholesterol into insoluble complexes that the body cannot absorb. If further scientific studies confirm alfalfa's protective effect against cholesterol, human consumption of this overlooked food will undoubtedly increase.

Finally, with regard to using alfalfa for human consumption, the American Society of Agronomy reports in a monograph entitled *Alfalfa Science and Technology* (1972) "that the prospect of using processed alfalfa as a major source of protein for direct human consumption provides an attractive weapon in meeting world food needs. The arguments are familiar; sooner or later, population growth will force us to abandon livestock production on the basis of efficiency and cost. Humans will be forced to survive on cereal grains supplemented with either vegetable protein, or fish meal, or both. Alfalfa is a prime candidate as a source of vegetable protein for human use because of its high yield of protein per acre."

Why study alfalfa? The reasons are obvious: it's a super food for man and deer. Why study alfalfa fields and their relationship to white-tailed deer movement? Why spend so much time studying one preferred deer food? Deer hunter and naturalist John Madson, from the prairie land of Illinois, answered this question the other day when he told me that "somewhere out there under the eaves of the forest, and in the predawn mists of old neglected alfalfa fields, is a huge and solitary buck that no deer hunter has ever seen except in half-remembered dreams. It's just as well—for one glimpse of that great stag would drive a hunter to neglect home, family and job, blinding him to love and duty. Beware, Rob! Hunt that stag in the alfalfa field at your peril, because one look at him will ruin you for all ordinary deer and all the humdrum, ordinary duties that society demands of us! Oh, he's out there—lurking and watching. Beware!"

Chapter 10

Acorns and Whitetails

In my childhood, the horse chestnut never seemed to go out of style. Indeed, the horse chestnut still remains an eternal trophy of childhood. The acorn, on the other hand, which is so much more useful, seems to be completely neglected by the modern generation. Perhaps the chestnut dazzles us with its beauty—with its color and luster of mahogany? True, the sleek brown acorn is surely less aristocratic in appearance, but it can be eaten by hunter and whitetail alike. With the coming of autumn, the acorns, with their pointed noses and stout caps, will soon lie on the ground again in great profusion—tempting whitetail and hunter alike to search out the whereabouts of certain oak trees.

While splitting oak one day at the deer shack, I began to realize how much we depend upon this remarkable tree, with its massive trunk, its thick, rugged bark and its large, deep roots. Not only does it house my tree stand and provide sturdy pillars for the meat pole, but it furnishes oak coals for venison tenderloins, acorns for sourdough acorn bread and plentiful firewood for the potbelly stove. As Aldo Leopold once wrote in *A Sand County Almanac* (1949), "if one has cut, split, hauled, and piled his own good oak, and let his mind work the while, he will remember much about where the heat comes from (as he sits in his deer shack on a cold wintry day), and with a wealth of detail denied to those who spend the weekend in town astride a radiator." More important, however, the oak tree nurtures the whitetail, and aids me in locating him.

This chapter examines the symbiotic relationship between acorns, whitetails

Deer and squirrels directly compete for the acorn crop. Large deer herds may definitely be a controlling element in the number of squirrels that can live in any given area. Unlike the whitetail, which can feed on plant browse and other foods, the squirrel depends mainly upon acorns and nuts. *Credit David Constantine*

and deer hunters. The story, naturally enough, takes us through the traditional forest food chain: from acorn to deer to hunter. Historically, if we examine the whole sweep of human existence, it seems likely that man has actually consumed many millions of tons more of acorns than he has of the cereal grains. Indeed, acorns were often the very "staff of life" for the early America deer stalker who, like the whitetail, usually preferred the sweet acorns when he could get them. Both deer hunter and whitetail in early America, however, never refused to gather and use even the bitterest kinds, although both preferred the white oak acorns because of their low amount of tannic acid.

The American Indians, who gathered and stored great quantities of acorns for making bread, developed several simple methods of washing out tannin and bitter taste with water. The Indians of the Great Lakes region usually boiled the acorns into a mush that they combined with maple sugar and venison. Modern-day experiments indicate that an edible salad oil similar to olive oil can be obtained from the fatty acorns of the California live oak and other black oaks. Because of the acorn's high oil and starch content, it is very nutritious, and is reported to be easily digested.

In a superb article on the acorn in the August 1918 issue of *National Geographic,* C. Hart Merriam, founder of the United States Fish and Wildlife Service, tells us that "acorn flour makes a rich glutinous food and contains a surprisingly large quantity (eighteen to twenty-five percent) of nut oil of obvious nutritive value. It is also easy to work with, being what cooks call a 'good binder,' which means that it holds together well even when mixed with several times its

bulk of corn meal or other coarse or granular materials." Merriam goes on to point out "that a food of such genuine worth should be disregarded by our people is one of many illustrations of the reluctance of the white man to avail himself of sources of subsistence long utilized by the aborigines. We seem to prefer crops that require laborious preparation of the soil, followed by costly planting and cultivation, rather than those provided without price by bountiful nature."

It's a pity that this ancient food that nourished the childhood of our race, and which continually nourishes deer all across America, should today be virtually neglected and despised. Yet, I sense that the acorn is coming back into its own, at least with regard to the wild palate. People are again beginning to appreciate the dark wholesome breads of our ancestors, and are rediscovering that they can be prepared with acorn meal. Actually, many deer-shack chefs use white oak acorns in making acorn bread, cake and muffins. Famed naturalist John Muir, during his numerous and arduous tramps through the California wilderness, often carried the hard, dry acorn bread, and considered it the most compact and strength-giving food he had ever eaten. Undoubtedly, some deer hunter with dietetic ingenuity will soon discover a new method of preparing venison with acorns—maybe even a delicacy? Whether or not acorns have become standard materials for wildlife cookery at your deer camp, one thing seems certain: unlike the hunter, the whitetail has never lost its voracious appetite for these nuggets of nourishment.

Scientists tell us that more than 186 different kinds of birds and animals utilize oak in one way or another as a primary source of food, and that with the possible exception of *Rubus* (raspberries, dewberries, blackberries), this number exceeds that recorded for any other genus of woody plants. In fact, the real importance of acorns for whitetails can hardly be exaggerated. Deer will eat approximately 1.5 pounds of acorns per day per 100 pounds of weight, when they are available. The availability of this rich carbohydrate and consequent fat accretion frequently makes the difference between death and survival for many deer during severe winters. According to rumen content analyses, acorns during good mast years was up as high as 62.4 percent of the whitetail's total food in fall and early winter.

As Leonard Lee Rue III pointed out in his *The World of the White-tailed Deer,* "when there is a good crop the deer forsake all other types of food, even apples,

ACORN USAGE BY 440 DEER IN MISSOURI, 1948-1953

Month	Number of Stomachs	Percentage of Total Diet
January	8	32.4
February	23	32.0
March	23	16.4
April	17	16.0
May	6	14.3
June	4	0.0
July	8	7.5
August	10	0.1
September	11	31.4
October	16	62.4
November	131	43.8
December	183	45.7

(Reprinted from the *Twentieth North American Wildlife Conference,* p. 345. "Acorn Yields And Wildlife Usage In Missouri" by Donald M. Christisen and Leroy J. Korschgen.)

Not only do whitetails eat the acorns but they also browse the oak twigs. *Photo credit Leonard Lee Rue III*

to stay in the forest and glut themselves on acorns. . . . Time after time, people who used to see deer feeding in old orchards on the dropped apples, or in corn fields, asked me where the deer disappeared to. They had not disappeared; they were just concentrating on acorns. When deer feed in the orchards or fields they are easily seen but they are not usually seen while feeding in the woodlands. When the acorns drop, deer stay in the woods and up on the hilltops. They need not travel because the acorns are in their bedding areas."

Nutritionally, the acorn represents a highly desirable food for whitetails; relatively high in fat and carbohydrates, it contains protein, vitamins (the A and B-Complex), calcium and phosphorus. Consequently, acorns provide much-needed energy and nutrients for deer during the winter months. Deer generally eat them in a preferred order: white oak acorns are usually eaten first, followed by the acorns of the pin oak, the red oak, the black oak and the scrub oak, at least in my area. This preference, however, obviously varies from area to area. H. R. Gilbert and G. H. Hart, for example,

Live-oak trees overbrowsed by black-tailed deer. *Photo credit Leonard Lee Rue III*

COMPARISON OF CHEMICAL VALUES OF DIFFERENT KINDS OF WESTERN ACORNS

Species	Crude Protein (percent)	Fat (percent)	Tannin (percent)
Black oak	4.3	14.7	1.9
Scrub oak	2.6	4.3	4.1
Blue oak	3.5	5.8	2.6
Water oak	3.1	5.5	3.2
Interior live oak	3.5	17.8	5.0

(Reprinted from William Dasmann, *If Deer are to Survive* [Stackpole, 1971], p. 64.)

tested the chemistry of different kinds of western acorns, and found that the Columbian blacktail preferred the California black oak, which has only 1.9 percent tannin, while having 4.3 percent protein and 14.7 percent fat.

Despite the fact that whitetails, like some of the other herbivores, do not have gall bladders to assist them in neutralizing acids and emulsifying fats, their body chemistry readily assimilates the carbohydrate content of acorns. As Leonard Lee Rue III points out, "without loosening a deer's bowels, acorns are processed and passed through the body in a very short time. This allows the deer to consume greater quantities of acorns per day than it would of other foods, which raises the daily protein intake. Conversion of the fats and starches to the deer's body fat is very rapid. You can almost see the deer putting on weight." Actually, the acorn crop so profoundly affects the body of the whitetail that deer biologists, in their determination of the relationship of live weight to dressed weight, devised two equations—one for

ACORN AVAILABILITY FOR DEER

Quality of acorn crop	Average number of pounds of acorns per tree	Availability to deer
Poor	0-5	Few acorns early in the fall; none thereafter.
Fair	6-10	Acorns in the fall; few or none throughout the winter.
Medium	11-20	Acorns through the fall and part of the winter. None left by spring breakup.
Good	21-30	Acorns through the fall and winter; some left in the spring.
Excellent	Over 30	More acorns throughout the fall, winter, and spring than all mast eaters combined, at high population levels, can consume.

(Reprinted from Jerry P. Duvendeck, "The Value and Prediction of Acorn Crops for Deer," University of Michigan Dissertation, 1964, p. 71.)

Acorn availability for deer. *Credit Jerry P. Duvendeck, "The Value and Prediction of Acorn Crops for Deer," University of Michigan Dissertation, 1964, p. 71.*

an "acorn year" and a second for a year without a heavy mast crop.

Oaks on the average produce good crops of acorns once in three or four years. What causes a "bumper crop" of acorns, deer hunters frequently ask? Nobody seems to know for sure. But climate and other environmental factors may have their effect. A similar question arises: Do older oak trees produce more acorns? Scientists tell us it's difficult to generalize about the relationship of acorn production to the age of the tree. Comparatively low acorn production, however, occurs on oaks with diameters of less than 14 inches breast high. There also seems to be a great difference in acorn yield between trees of comparable size and age and similar site. Some trees are traditionally heavy producers and others light producers. "A stand of twenty-seven oaks per acre averaging ten inches in trunk diameter," William Dasmann tells us in his *If Deer are to Survive* (1971), "will produce an average yield of nearly 150 pounds of acorns. This can double or triple in good production years." Generally, acorn yields increase as the trees mature. Few trees below the age of 20 years produce much of a crop. Acorn production directly relates to tree diameter at breast height and crown size, with crowns exposed to sunlight being the best producers.

Scientific studies indicate that deer harvests are directly related to acorn yields, and that large numbers of deer are annually taken in oak stands. It would probably not be an exaggeration to say that the acorn is a barometer of deer reproductive success, hunting success and total deer harvest. In game management, the size of a future acorn crop frequently becomes a factor in determining deer hunting regulations in some areas. Study acorn availability in your area, and you might just discover the key to a successful deer season. Few deer hunters are well enough versed in their knowledge of oak trees to know which oaks are bearing acorns and which varieties will produce the greatest crop, however. Study your tree identification guides and scout the oak stands with great diligence. Remember, there are at least five different criteria for oak identification: (1) the leaves; (2) the tree's physical shape; (3) the bark; (4) the buds; and (5) the acorns.

I have often seen whitetails flock to a particular huge white oak for its acorns, while literally passing up dozens of other oak trees in the area. Learn not only to distinguish the different members of the *Quercus* family, but study their crowns in early autumn to ascertain the volume of acorn productivity. Open the acorns to be sure that they have not been ruined by insect parasites. Weevils frequently ravage as much as 90 percent of the acorn crop.

With regard to the acorn crop and whitetailed deer hunting, we would do well to read and follow the advice of Byron Dalrymple, one of the great masters of the sport: "I know a good bit about deer and acorns. I watch deer in my front yard each fall when we have a crop on our live oaks. They practically live on acorns and hardly move out of the way when we drive out the driveway. But hunting isn't quite that simple. During a year of a heavy crop, when every tree is dropping forage, the deer don't have to move around much. Only in the years of spotty production do they go beeline to the trees with the heavy mast crops. That, incidently, is a hot tip. Find the full-bearing trees during a scattered crop, and you can even kill a deer moving bed to tree, if indeed not under it, they go that straight and regular."

Deer hunters who buy land for hunting purposes frequently ask themselves how they can improve their deer habitat, how they can harvest their oaks in such a manner as to bring about the maximum benefit for the whitetail. This is a very difficult question to try to answer within the confines of this one chapter. Several generalizations emerge from my talking with foresters and game managers, however. First, because some oaks inherently produce larger crops of acorns than others, foresters recommend that you distinguish the better producers at the time of fruiting in good seed years, and mark them as *leave* trees, since they will serve

White, red and chestnut oak acorns nurture the whitetail and aid the hunter in locating deer. *Photo credit Leonard Lee Rue III*

better as both a food source for wildlife and a seed for replacements. In the absence of records on acorn productivity or observations on seed yield by individual oak trees, oaks with large crowns should be left to produce seed.

Secondly, according to two Missouri foresters, you "should attempt to maintain a variety of oak species, so that complete failures will be unlikely. It is advisable to include oaks from the black group in the variety. Acorns from these oaks do not germinate until spring, and therefore are available to wildlife throughout the winter when other foods are scarce. A variety of oaks tends to stabilize the supply of food and likewise the populations of wildlife which are dependent upon it."

Finally, according to Jerry Duvendeck, a specialist in the value and prediction of acorn crops for deer, leave a total of 20 mature full-crowned oaks over 40 years of age and 12 inches at breast height for each deer using the area. Remember, the larger oaks are the best mast producers. If these trees are removed, it may take 20 to 75 years to replace them.

The deer hunter stands in awe of large oaks and a "bumper crop" of acorns because he knows well that the whitetail will greatly benefit, as will all wildlife. He realizes, too, that behind that pointed tip of each acorn lies the minuscule embryo of a potential oak tree. Yet for all the promise of a "bumper crop" of acorns, life is sparingly given; for fewer than one in 10,000 acorns ever develops into an oak tree. The United States Department of Agriculture estimates that at least 30 percent of all acorns are destroyed or eaten while still on the tree by insects, birds and squirrels. Heavy deer populations literally scour the forest floor for the rest of them. As a result, squirrels, grouse, turkeys and raccoons are frequently deprived of a basic food source vital to their winter survival. Deer hunting, in this regard, helps to keep the numbers of deer in balance with the mast crop and with the needs of other forms of wildlife.

It is interesting to note that the availability of acorns actually determines the amount of browse whitetails consume: browse consumption is highest when acorns are scarce and lowest when acorns are abundant. In Missouri, for example, game managers report increased damage to agricultural crops and forest plantations by deer in years of low acorn yields.

The deer hunter stands in awe of large oaks and a bumper crop of acorns because he knows that the whitetail will greatly benefit. *Photo credit Leonard Lee Rue III*

Like the whitetail, the deer hunter maintains a special reverence for a grove of stately white oaks. While the white oak is obviously only one member of the diverse forest community, only one of the existing 50 species of the *Quercus* family in North America, it is found in more geographic locations and exists in greater supply than any of its peers; it also clings more tenaciously to life than any of the rest of the trees. Similarly, the whitetail is only one member of the deer family, only one of 40 species. Despite this fact, the whitetail covers more geographic locations and exists in greater supply than any of its peers; its ability to adapt to civilized madness surpasses human imagination. If the powers of the evolutionary process were to create a nobler tree or a nobler animal, the white oak and the whitetail would indeed be worthy prototypes! Both represent nature's symbols of strength and endurance, of beauty, grace and splendor.

Chapter 11

At the Waterhole

For more than 10 years I have maintained a steady, vigilant communion with the cosmos and the gods of good cheer at a small waterhole in the North Country. A time-worn, stately and noble white oak tree overlooking this waterhole provides me with my observation point. I frequently return from this autumn post to my study in search of source material on the whitetail's watering habits to no avail, for little has been written on this subject.

This chapter examines the basic water requirements of the white-tailed deer and the whitetail's relationship to water in general. My purpose will be to reach some conclusions about deer hunting over a small waterhole or spring in heavily wooded terrain, particularly during the early months of the autumn bow season.

The quality of any deer range is clearly influenced by a vast variety of factors besides the activities of man, the hunter. When examining the basic elements of deer range, we generally consider the topography of the land, the condition of the soil, the variation of plants and other animals, as well as the supply of natural water. Traditionally, game managers portray the basic elements necessary for deer survival as a triangle, with the three points representing food, cover and water. Water, of course, occurs most conspicuously in ponds, streams or springs; it is found less conspicuously, however, in the grasses, leaves and browse that deer consume. While some kinds of animals, including many rodents, can produce their own metabolic water from the food they eat and never require drinking water, the whitetail cannot; like other ruminants, the whitetail must have water, and cannot convert carbohydrates eaten as food into water. Thus, adequate water in some arrangement or another is one of the basic essentials of deer survival. It is generally agreed that prolonged droughts decrease the deer population in a direct ratio to the decline of free standing water.

But the exact amount of water needed on a daily basis by the whitetail still remains somewhat of a controversial question, receiving as many diverse answers as the diverse number of locations at which deer can water. In analyzing the optimum and minimum water requirements of the whitetail, Aldo Leopold summarized the standard literature on the subject in a way that epitomizes the diversity of opinion: "M.P. Skinner says of whitetail deer in the Yellowstone: They seemed to need water regularly, and presumably drank at least once or twice a day. Archibald Rutledge says of the eastern states: Deer will troop out of their regular haunts in very dry weather, if the water supply fails, going to larger streams and rivers. J.B. Burnham says: Next to moose and caribou as water-loving animals, I should place the whitetail. I think the whitetail requires water every day. Even in the arid country they do not get far from streams. William M. Newsom says: While a deer enjoys playing around water and must have it, he can do quite well with a little. D.E. Lantz says of whitetails in enclosures: A good supply of running water must be provided. E.T. Seton says the nursing whitetail doe waters daily, usually at noon. J.S. Ligon writes me that in the sandhills east of the Pecos River in New Mexico, and on both sides of the Pecos in West Texas, the local race of whitetails are or were found on range totally devoid of drinking water, and offering succulence alone."

Leopold's most important observation

for the autumn bow hunter, however, manifests itself in the following conclusion: Nursing white-tailed does require water daily. This observation explains why does, at least at the waterhole that I frequently watch, water as often as three times a day (morning, midday and evening), and will use the waterhole as the center of their orbit. Throughout the years I have noticed that a doe's cruising radius from water while nursing fawns seems to have a set maximum length. That is to say, I have consistently seen does and fawns stay within a half-mile radius of my observation point throughout the spring, summer and autumn. Bucks, on the other hand—and based on my own observation—will maintain a larger cruising radius from their watering spot and will become primarily nocturnal in their watering habits except for the rut. During the rut they will frequently return to water at any time of day, particularly midday. Indeed, I have missed more bucks during the rut at midday while at the waterhole than I care to admit. The accompanying photo of a white-tailed buck drinking water at high noon suggests that this buck just came from a scrape: if you study the photo closely, you will notice that this buck still has pine needles and a small pine branch hanging from his antlers.

In his text, *Deer of North America*, Rue concludes that deer generally have a daily requirement of about one and a half quarts (or 1.4 liters) of water per 100 pounds (or 45.4 kg) of body weight in winter, and about two or three quarts (or 1.9 to 2.8 liters) of water per 100 pounds of body weight in summer. Rue's figures are apparently based on A. A. Nichol's early experimental feeding of mule deer. But they seem to represent a consensus

This white-tailed buck drinking water at high noon apparently just came from a scrape: If you study the photo carefully, you will notice that he still has pine needles and a small pine branch hanging from his antlers. *Photo credit Leonard Lee Rue III*

of opinion among deer researchers. The problem with these kinds of figures, however, is that they generally represent empirical research based on the experimental feeding of penned deer and not on deer in the wild.

The evidence on this whole question of the whitetail's water requirements still remains somewhat scanty. Our understanding of the optimum and minimum water requirements, Leopold notes, is limited at the very outset by our deficient understanding of the physiology of wild animals. This much seems certain: When succulent vegetation exceeds the availability of dry or dormant plants, deer need

far less water. But in addition to the water content of the whitetail's primary food source, factors such as the extent of exercise, air temperatures, evaporation rates, amount of dew and the availability of salt and snow also influence the daily amount of water that a deer consumes.

On the other hand, our knowledge of the whitetail's daily drinking habits is more precise than our knowledge of the exact amount of water that whitetails consume. The most detailed and useful study in this regard, particularly for the autumn bow hunter, remains E. D. Michael's essay entitled *Drinking Habits of White-tailed Deer in South Texas.* This two-year study, based on data for deer in the wild instead of in captivity, reached the following conclusions:

(1) Peak times of drinking activity were at 7:00 a.m., 11:00 a.m. and 4:00-6:00 p.m.;

(2) No definite pattern of drinking water before or after feeding emerged;

(3) Does accompanied by fawns appeared more wary and cautious than other deer in their approach to water;

(4) Lactating does drank more frequently than other deer;

(5) The watering site frequently emerged as the center of the whitetail's home range;

(6) Water consumption increased directly with the increase of air temperature;

(7) Deer ceased feeding as far as 200 yards away and walked directly to the water's edge;

(8) Once there, they drank quickly and left the area, almost never feeding around the periphery of the water hole;

(9) All deer seemed nervous while

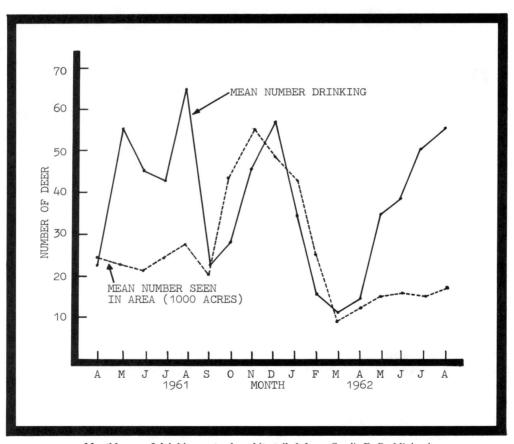

Monthly use of drinking water by white-tailed deer. *Credit E. D. Michael*

drinking and continually raised their heads in search of danger. Does raised their heads an average of 2.3 times per minute while bucks raised their heads an average of 1.7 times per minute;

(10) Following periods of rain, whitetails preferred to drink at temporary ditches and pools of water rather than at their traditional watering site;

(11) Most whitetails drank two to three times a day during summer and only once a day during winter;

(12) Checking the time spent drinking with a stopwatch does not provide a good indicator of the basic water requirements;

(13) Wind and cloud cover had some effect on the daily drinking habits, but no noticeable consistency appeared in the relationship.

Professor Michael summarized his findings in the following three graphs which are reprinted from the *Proceedings of the 21st Annual Conference of the Southeastern Association of Game and Fish Commissioners.* They represent the most accurate information to date on the watering habits of the white-tailed deer. The adjusted values on graph number two and three represent nighttime observations with the aid of a spotlight. The spotlight was turned on only once every half hour for about 10 minutes, thus representing a 20-minute period for each nighttime hour. To compare the daytime and nighttime counts, Michael made the adjustment by multiplying the nighttime count by three.

Whitetails also come to water for reasons other than drinking. While they seldom spend much time near rapid-moving streams and rivers, they do like to eat the lush vegetation in such places. As one

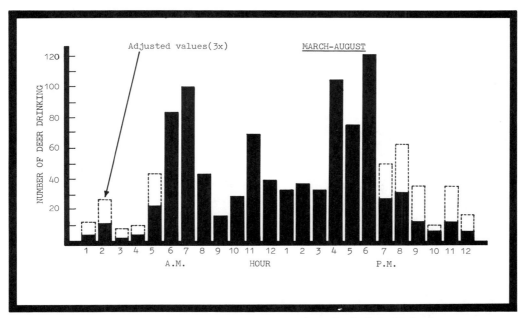

Hourly use of drinking water by white-tailed deer. *Credit E. D. Michael*

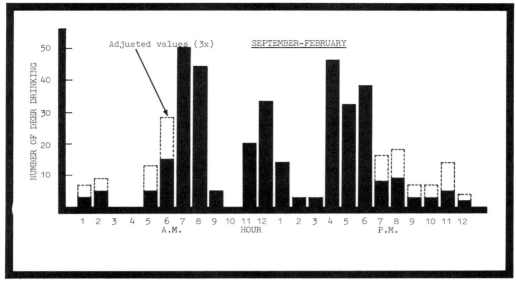

Hourly use of drinking water by white-tailed deer. *Credit E. D. Michael*

Whitetails come to water for reasons other than drinking. They do, for example, like to eat the lush vegetation in such places. *Photo credit Leonard Lee Rue III*

old-time deer hunter observes, "They will feed and bed near placid or slow-moving water, but the louder the drone the less time they spend in the area and the progressively farther away they will bed." As a result of the whitetail's tendency to feed along streams and rivers, hunting guides such as Norman Strung recommend the tactic of float hunting, or "the tactic that's all wet." Since whitetails do not expect danger from the river, and since riverbanks provide whitetails with succulent leafy and woody plants, float hunting for deer has become a common style of deer hunting in some states. This tactic, as Strung points out, takes the hunter into areas which are otherwise inaccessible and provides the hunter with an excellent field of fire as whitetails approach their water site. Drifting in a canoe on a quiet, narrow stream is surely an excellent technique for bow hunting and the ultimate in esthetic relaxation. As one fellow deer hunter recently put it, ''Paddling a canoe on a river or stream is a perfect way to still hunt, especially when the conditions for hunting on foot are noisy.'' But remember to check your big game rules and regulations relative to float hunting in your home state before employing this tactic. The major problem with such a tactic is trespassing on private lands while in pursuit of fallen game.

In his *Deer of North America,* Rue writes that deer frequently feed in water. According to Rue, ''They eat a great many types of water plants, such as eel grass, but they particularly like the algae—the pond scum. I have often watched deer eating long strings of this green ooze. The algae is very nutritious, for it is high in protein.'' But whitetails will also take to water to evade pursuit. Indeed, using water to escape man and predator is one of the basics in every whitetail's bag of tricks. Wounded bucks, in particular, will seek out water and will generally remain near its edge. Deer are excellent swimmers and may simply get to safety by swimming to an island or by crossing a river. Whitetails thus seem to like water! The innumerable instances of their being sighted in open water can perhaps be explained by swimming for the fun of swimming. They have been sighted three to four miles from land in both fresh water and salt water, swimming at speeds of 10 to 15 knots. The longest swim on record is reported by C. Sheldon, who once saw a buck and a doe crossing the 12-mile channel of Frederick Sound. Whitetails apparently like to leap, romp and splash in water, and exhibit every evidence of joyful enthusiasm while swimming.

While many observers believe that deer will also seek out water to get relief from

Deer are excellent swimmers and may get to safety by swimming to an island or by crossing a river. One buck and a doe crossed the 12-mile channel of Frederick Sound, Alaska—undoubtedly the longest swim on record. *Photo credit Leonard Lee Rue III*

stinging, biting insects, which can turn the forest into a living nightmare, others believe this idea is merely a myth. William Monypeny Newsom, for example, argues quite convincingly that the annoyance of insects does not drive deer to water. These pests, he points out, are far more numerous near water than elsewhere, especially in the evenings. Thus Newsom asks, "Why would an intelligent animal like the deer deliberately walk into a paradise of pests if trying to avoid them? This is one of the superstitions of the hunter and closet naturalist that has been repeated so many times it is accepted without thought as a fact." I tend to agree with Newsom that whitetails are not nearly so sensitive to insects and pests as we human observers think.

No discussion dealing with the relationship between whitetails and water would be complete without a few words on the controversial question of using water in the process of field dressing. Many hunters and guides suggest flushing the body cavity with clean water to remove blood, hair and any other foreign substances that might have accumulated during the drag or dressing process, and then quickly drying the cavity with a clean piece of dry cloth. Others violently object and insist on not washing the cavity with water unless you plan on processing the deer immediately. Even then, however, I would tend to disagree. Simply put, water and meat are not compatible substances. The only venison that should ever come in contact with water are the liver and heart. Water in the tissues of meat, many believe, will cause venison to sour. If the viscera has been accidentally cut while cleaning, or if the deer has been shot in the abdominal area, there seems to be a consensus of opinion that the cavity should

be thoroughly flushed with water so that the digestive juices will not spoil the meat. The meat, however, should then be rubbed dry as quickly as possible.

Wisconsin Indian legends handed down from various tribes show the importance of whitetails in the naming of certain bodies of water. The Ojibwa word for lake, for example, was *Mitchigan,* which meant a wooden fence to catch whitetails near the lake shore. The white man translated this word, of course, into Michigan. Nebagamon Lake in Douglas County was originally named *Nee-bay-gomoh-win* by the Chippewas, referring to a place to hunt deer by fire and water. Another Chippewa legend associated whitetails with the formation of the Apostle Islands. "The legend," according to Otis Bersing, "tells of Winneboujou, the giant deity who lived on the Brule River during the summer months. While hunting in the Brule Valley and looking over the treetops, he spotted a deer. Hunting the deer all day, he shot away all of his arrows and threw away his quiver. He then followed the whitetail to the shores of Lake Superior. Disgusted with his failure, he threw rocks at the deer far out in the water. The rocks falling into the water became the Apostle Islands as we see them today."

One of the traditional axioms of wildlife lore, as Byron Dalrymple maintains, is that danger lurks at the waterhole; that game animals, through long years of experience, expect danger at watering places because of the high concentration of so many creatures at one spot. Certainly whitetails approach waterholes with a great deal of caution, drink and leave as quickly as possible. Apparently, some hunters believe a certain stigma is attached to taking whitetails at their source of water. Presumably these hunters be-

Leaving the waterhole with great haste. *Photo credit Leonard Lee Rue III*

lieve that you may be keeping many animals from drinking. This argument, however, does not seem to make much sense. When you think about it, you could make the same case for hunting the whitetail at his source of food. Regardless, some states do not permit shooting whitetails at watering sites. Check your state's big-game rules and regulations.

To summarize, successful deer hunting at a waterhole in heavily wooded terrain will greatly depend upon one basic variable: the abundance of surface water in the square mile in which you are concentrating your efforts. If many watering sites are available, concentrating your efforts at one particular hole will generally prove to be unproductive. Conversely, the scarcer the watering sites in your area, the more use the one you watch will probably get and the more distinct the trails leading to it will be.

Keep in mind, of course, that whitetails have a more detailed knowledge of where water is on their home range than the hunter. It is difficult to pinpoint one specific drinking spot that is utilized daily by one specific white-tailed buck. What you might consider a waterless area may well prove to have several secret watering holes. In other words, it is best to choose a waterhole in a region that is rather arid and in an area where at least six or more main runways come together.

Waterholes are excellent places to hunt, but this is generally true due to elements other than the water itself. That is to say, choice waterholes for deer hunting also need heavily wooded terrain around them and preferred food within the immediate area. If you find such a choice watering site or bubbling spring, become an oak tree and you may well get a whitetail; if not, you will at least have the chance to commune with the cosmos and the gods of good cheer.

Chapter 12

The White-Tailed Fawn

While on a summer photo mission, I once observed a young whitetail approach my tree stand at the edge of a woodlot. Ordinarily, young whitetails are like inquisitive children always searching and getting into mischief, and expressing curiosity about the environment around them. But this young buck fawn approached the edge of the field with a sensitized degree of caution matched only by that of a super buck. As I watched this buck fawn approach, I recalled a passage from John Wootters' *Hunting Trophy Deer* (1977): "Buck fawns reveal a different personality almost as soon as they're big enough to follow their mothers. The word is spooky; they seem to come into the world more alert and wary, and they become continually more so as time goes by."

Suddenly, I heard loud, penetrating callings that were repeated frequently. At first, I thought the sounds might be coming from a catbird or a nuthatch. This sharp *mnah* or bleating noise continued for some time. The doe, already feeding in the alfalfa field, merely looked in the direction of the fawn's calling, and returned to browsing. As the fawn began to search for its dam, it cautiously entered the corner of the alfalfa field. At the same time a ruffed grouse began walking along—flicking its tail and clucking as it approached. The soft *puk-puk-puk* sounds of the grouse were at first inaudible to the fawn. Suddenly, however, it was "high noon in old Dodge City," as these two animals confronted one another. The appearance of the fawn startled the grouse, and the thundering sound of the flushing grouse's wings sent the young buck fawn back into the thick woodlot like a wisp of smoke.

White-tailed fawns are usually born in May and June, after a gestation period of about 205 to 218 days, though the climate may increase or decrease these figures somewhat. *Photo credit Leonard Lee Rue III*

I could hear its tiny hoofs pattering through the leaves and the swish of oak branches as it brushed by long after it melted from view. For a moment I stared in the direction of its flight, charmed first by its appearance and then equally astonished by its sudden departure. As long as I hunt whitetails, I will probably never forget that dramatic meeting of a startled buck fawn and an excited ruffed grouse.

White-tailed fawns are usually born in May and June, after a gestation period of about 205 to 218 days, though the climate may increase or decrease these figures somewhat. Fawns generally weigh about four to five pounds at birth. For the first month fawns spend a great deal of time hiding, sleeping and resting in thick cover. As William Newsom observes, "Either fawns are born knowing the art of skulking, or the doe teaches them at once: for it is certain they know their safety lies in being absolutely motionless when danger threatens. They never forget this lesson, using it in later years to elude the deer hunter."

The entire process of the whitetail's birth is rapid and apparently bloodless. The doe immediately eats the placental sac, and eliminates all other traces of waste that might attract predators. Her prompt eating and licking up of waste tissues and fluids epitomizes one of the ultimate survival values of the whitetail. During parturition and shortly thereafter, the hair on her metatarsal glands stands erect, thus emitting an odor. Consequently, she can dash off to lead a predator away from her fawns, and thereby save them. "All of the romantic drama of the mating or rutting season," as noted deer biologist Bill Severinghaus of New York once observed, "particularly manifest in the behavior of the bucks, leads, through a series of truly climactic events, to the fertilization of the deer eggs, to the beginning of new living deer—deer to continue populating the forest edges, meadows, the stony slopes, and yes, even the crop and range lands of agricultural areas."

During the first few days following birth, fawns remain isolated and bedded, seldom moving more than one to two meters. Arthur Carhart in his *Hunting North American Deer* (1946) tells us that "In the very early days, fawns are helpless even in flight; they are too tender and unsteady to go far or fast. So their protection lies in hiding. They do this instinctively, nestling down, flattening to the ground, remaining still even though a man and a dog may pass within a few yards of their hideout." The duration of

The entire process of the whitetail's birth is rapid and apparently bloodless. The doe immediately eats the placental sac and eliminates all other traces of waste that might attract predators. *Photo credit Leonard Lee Rue III*

the hiding periods varies with individual deer. During their first month, however, fawns do not wander far. Many whitetail researchers believe that the doe stays with them during the nighttime hours, but wanders away during the day to forage and find water—returning only at frequent intervals for nursing.

At birth, fawns have a light tan coat covered with cream-colored spots (250 to 350 in number). These spots create the illusion of small patches of sunlight penetrating the foliage, and provide them with perfect camouflage. They command the admiration of all who see them, and average between one quarter and one half inch in diameter.

The number of fawns produced varies somewhat, but the general rule dictates that a young doe having her first birth will have one fawn. After that she will usually produce two fawns. In rare cases, especially in prime habitat, there may be three, although I have never experienced this situation. Historically, there are several recorded instances of four fawns being found in a doe. Not being a prolific milk producer, the doe experiences a tough time nursing more than two fawns. Deer milk, however, has approximately three times as much protein and butterfat than our finest Grade A cow's milk. While an average Jersey cow has about 5 to 6 percent butterfat in her milk, the milk of the white-tailed doe consists of 11 to 12 percent butterfat.

The sex ratio among fawns is approximately 1:1, with a few more buck fawns

At birth fawns inherit a light tan coat covered with cream-colored spots (250 to 350 in number). These spots create the illusion of small patches of sunlight penetrating the foliage, and provide them with perfect camouflage. *Photo credit Leonard Lee Rue III*

than doe fawns. A considerable body of scientific evidence suggests that more males are produced when mature females are undernourished, whereas well-fed and well-nourished does are likely to produce more female fawns than buck fawns. Mammalogists do not know why more buck fawns are produced in times of poor forage. The sex ratio changes rapidly, however, because postnatal mortality is higher among males than females. Thus, within a week after fawning time begins, there are more females than males. This ratio continues to widen with age.

Fawn mortality is high among both sexes. Scientific studies indicate that 6 to 7 percent of all white-tailed fawns born in the wild die within the first 48 hours.

Whitetails living on a 16 to 18 percent protein diet, however, show a significant decline in postnatal mortality. Habitat shortages, particularly food deficiencies and a low, stagnant water supply, greatly reduce fawn production and fawn survival. On the other hand, an abundance of high-quality summer foods for lactating does enhances the survival of their fawns. If high conception rates are combined with low summer fawn survival, game managers generally know that a winter-spring food problem is causing an absorption of embryos, slinking of fetuses and births of weak, short-lived fawns.

Adequate nutrition during conception, gestation and lactation is obviously of the utmost importance for whitetails. Yet, some of the greatest deer ranges of America carry an overabundance of deer in relation to available nourishing food. As a result, whitetails are unable to secure an adequate diet. This unfortunately is the environment in which many does are forced to live while their unborn progenies grow into the form and shape of white-tailed deer.

The degree of fawn mortality depends upon several variables: (1) the abundance of predators, i.e., coyotes; (2) the abundance of parasite populations; and (3) the degree of nutritional deficiency encountered by the pregnant and nursing doe. Ultimately, however, the fawn's fate depends upon the weather, for fawns are the principal sufferers in severe winters. Being smaller than mature deer, they simply cannot reach as high for browse, and consequently are the first to succumb to winter starvation. Natural accidents also cause additional minor losses. Among the various diseases that commonly plague the whitetail, salmonellosis, a diarrhea of unknown etiology, represents another additional factor involved with fawn mortality.

The weaning period lasts for about four months. Fawns, we must remember, are not ruminants at birth, and cannot digest grass or twigs even if they could ingest them. They must have bacteria in their rumen to start the digestive process. They ingest bacteria from the doe's mouth as she licks them, as well as from the water they drink. If the doe is indulgent, they may nurse until the breeding season begins in November. While male fawns follow their mother for the first year only, female fawns will follow the doe for two years or more after birth.

Mammalogists and wildlife ecologists are not certain whether a special fawning place is chosen or not. It seems likely that fawns are dropped wherever the doe happens to be at the time. One thing is certain: White-tailed deer are enormously productive. One New York doe, we are told, dropped 33 fawns in a 15-year period; at the age of 17, she still produced twin fawns. We have a similar record of a Wisconsin doe that reached the ripe old age of 19½ years; she bore twin fawns through her 18th year. Theoretically, one mature buck and one doe could increase to 22 animals in five years. In 10 years they could increase to 189 animals. It is rare, however, for a herd in the wild to approach this potential.

In 1963, the New Hampshire Fish and Game Department recorded a rare instance of fertility in a white-tailed buck fawn. No conclusions were reached, however, as to the reasons for this unusual precocity. It seems likely that fertility in buck fawns relates directly to a high nutritional diet. Buck fawns on high nutritional diets show indications of rut behavior at 5 months, while those maintained at reduced levels of nutrition show no signs of rutting behavior. In general, however, bucks are about one and a half years old at the time of their first participation in the rut. Does can also breed when six to seven months old, but most breed for the first time at one and a half years of age. In other words, the initial breeding age usually depends upon the health of the animal.

One question which inevitably arises when discussing fawns is whether or not a nursing doe will adopt strange fawns. "Should a doe die, leaving fawns," D.E. Lantz reports in a biological survey dated 1910, "one of the other does attends to the fawns as well as if they were her own."

Modern-day biologists have their doubts about that, however. Observations of fawns and nursing females were made on four occasions when wet does were given a chance to adopt strange fawns at the Wildlife Research Laboratory in Delmar, New York. The first two attempts were failures, while the last two attempts were successful.

Game biologists reached the following conclusions in the Delmar experiment:

(1) What factors stimulate adoption in some cases and discourage it in others are unknown;

(2) Sex may be of some importance in the willingness to adopt;

(3) Age difference did not prevent adoption;

(4) Personality factors of doe and fawn may be very important;

(5) Whether adoption occurs in the wild is not known;

(6) The interesting fact was that adoption did occur in two out of four attempts made under pen conditions.

Another often-asked question deals with the determination of the age of young fawns. Three criteria can be applied directly to fawns with respect to age determination: (1) The condition and/or growth of the hoofs; (2) The degree of healing of the umbilicus; and (3) Characteristic habits. According to Arnold Haugen, a professor of zoology and prominent leader of organized archery, fawns at birth "have hoofs the bottoms of which are covered with a soft semi-gelatinous sulphur yellow pad about one-eighth inch thick. Pointed appendages of the same material are found on the tips of the dew claws. This soft material is abraded and worn away from the hoofs within the first day, with the tips of the dew claws drying to a withered and blackish-looking material within 24 hours. By the eighth day, the withered dew claw tips are indistinct or gone."

Other physical characteristics offer additional means for determining the age of fawns. During the first day, the fawn's umbilicus remains wet and fresh looking. By the second day the umbilici on some fawns are scabbed over, while some are still moist. By the third day, however, apparently all are scabbed over. Behavior also offers some clue as to the age of a white-tailed fawn. Up through the first four days, most fawns lie still when approached, and will allow humans to handle them. During the fifth and sixth days, most fawns will make a desperate attempt to avoid any approaching human.

Deer hunters also ask how fawns and does regroup after being dispersed. The answer to this question lies in understanding the function of the interdigital gland. This gland, which is located between the deer's hoofs, secretes a waxy, telltale substance that is peculiar to each family. This substance leaves a scent on the ground, thus allowing the doe to track her fawn if it wanders off. Fawns are odorless at birth, however. This characteristic, coupled with their protective coloration, serves as a very efficient protection. In about a month the fawn's interdigital gland begins to function, and odors are now produced. Numerous reports indicate that dogs, coming within a few feet of newborn fawns lying in tall grass, are unable to detect them.

Game biologists frequently tell us that it is the youngest age classes about which we know the least. The white-tailed fawn represents no exception in this regard. This problem becomes more acute when we realize that these youngsters represent the most important age class for determining whitetail population dynamics. Although the literature on the white-tailed deer is replete with information on the life history of the animal *in enclosures,* substantive records of the process of parturition and the early reactions of young white-tailed fawns *in the wild* are rare. Since life at this stage hangs in a critical balance for both fawn and doe, we would do well to continue our study of the movement patterns and motions of this creature.

The white-tailed fawn epitomizes the highest perfection of *graceful motion* ever achieved by any animal. One of the finest literary characterizations of the fawn's graceful movement comes from John Dean Caton's *The Antelope and Deer of America* (1877):

"Ordinarily it will stand with its head elevated to the utmost; its ears erect and projecting somewhat forward; its eyes flashing, and raise one forefoot and suspend it for a few moments, and then trot off and around at a safe distance with a measured pace, which is not flight, and with a grace and elasticity which must be seen to be appreciated, for it quite defies verbal description. A foot is raised from the ground so quickly that you hardly see it, it seems poised in the air for an instant and is then so quietly and even tenderly dropped, and again so instantly raised that you are in doubt whether it even touched the ground, and, if it did, you are sure it would not crush the violet on which it fell. The bound, also, is exceedingly graceful and light. Indeed, the step of the fawn of the Virginia Deer is so light that it seems almost worthy of the hyperbole of one referring to another subject when he said, 'It was as light as the down of a feather plucked from the wing of a moment.' If, as it grows up, it loses something of this lightness and elasticity of step, it is only because of the increased size of the animal, which enables one the more readily to individualize the graceful motions which, in the little fawn, seem blended together with a charm like the blending of harmonious sounds."

If you have never seen this graceful motion of the white-tailed fawn, study the deer range you know best during fawning time. If you miss seeing the graceful and harmonious motions of white-tailed fawns, there is one substitute experience you can have: listen to a stereo recording of Debussy's *Afternoon of a Fawn,* one of the most expressive marvels of our time. You will then know what Judge Caton meant when he linked the graceful motion of the white-tailed fawn with the blending of harmonious sounds.

Chapter 13

Deer Play

On October 13, 1980, I recorded the following entry in my deer hunting journal: "After returning to the deer shack this evening, I observed seven extremely active, antlerless deer in the alfalfa field in front of the shack. The fawns, in particular, were extremely playful; they chased around together at high speed, suddenly stopping, changing direction and then rushing off again. One fawn, after encountering a fallen log at the edge of the field, leaped over it into the air, back arched, head shaking and legs a-kicking rather like a bucking bronco. The adult does and young yearlings joined in as well. This playful activity lasted for about two to three minutes and then suddenly stopped. The sight of these graceful little fellows frisking and chasing each other was ample reward for the many hours of watchful waiting."

After rereading this journal entry not long ago and after seeing playful behavior of deer in a cornfield this spring, I began to ask myself several questions: What does this form of activity ultimately tell us about the animal? About its environment? About man? How is deer play related to deer hunting? Does the element of play represent the ultimate bond between man and deer? After all, what was I doing in the deer forest that day? Were my hunting experiences and adventures that day really different from what they were doing as I watched them from the dim light of the deer shack that evening?

In thinking about these questions, one soon realizes that deer play is more easily described than explained. In fact, many famous and historical descriptions of deer play come to mind when one thinks of this seldom observed type of behavior regardless of the species.

Judge Caton, for example, that ardent

deer hunter and prominent judge from Illinois, tells us in his *Antelope and Deer of America* (1877), "that mule deer are the only members of the deer family I have ever seen manifest a clear and decided disposition to play. This they do something after the manner of lambs, by running courses and gamboling about and running up and down the bluffs manifestly for amusement only. I have only once noticed something like this in the white-tailed deer, but at best it was the faintest sort of a play, if indeed that was its meaning." Apparently, Caton thought that whitetails take life a bit more seriously than do mule deer.

With due apology to Judge Caton, some observers (myself included) have seen whitetails exhibit the very behavior Caton ascribes only to mule deer. After studying whitetails in Yellowstone Park, M.P. Skinner, for example, writes that on July 8, 1917, he observed "a three-week-old fawn in a very playful mood, dashing about in high spirits and cutting capers like a colt. In spring, particularly in early June, white-tailed deer, yearlings and adults alike, are often very sprightly and playful. At such times, I have seen one yearling chase another about, and even jump over it repeatedly."

Like Skinner, Townsend and Smith in their valuable *White-tailed Deer of the Adirondacks* (1933) insist that whitetails frequently show a tendency toward playfulness. "This is, as might be expected, most noticeable in the fawns. The young animal is given to more or less running about, dodging bushes and frisking this way and that, apparently overflowing with energy. Playfulness is especially noticeable where there happens to be two fawns in the family. Among the older animals, too, playfulness is sometimes exhibited. A good example of this was seen on the

The white-tailed fawn epitomizes the highest perfection of graceful motion ever achieved by an animal. Even when alone, they will engage in play sessions such as jumping, bucking and running. *Photo credit Leonard Lee Rue III*

morning of 15 June 1927. At 5:30 a.m., three bucks with well-started antlers, apparently young adults, were sighted, quietly feeding in the grass. Presently one of them began to chase one of his companions about the meadow, both of them running or rather bounding in a rather stiff-legged fashion. Soon the third joined in, and the frolic continued for some minutes, one chasing another while the third looked on. Then two of them entered the woods and were lost to sight. The third stood for a time looking for them to reappear, then went on feeding.''

In the summer of 1929, Townsend and Smith also observed two does exhibit a playful mood. "In the afternoon of July 22, on the shore of a lake, we heard a commotion and looked up to see a doe chasing another into the water, about a hundred yards away. The pursued one stopped and looked back from the shallows, trotted on a little ways, and then turned and gave chase to its pursuer. It also struck out with its foot, the other dodging. A large fawn followed closely but took no part in the play. One of the does was smaller than the other and may have been a yearling or a two-year old. It was extremely frisky and presently began to jump up and down on all fours, in the shallow water. Its behavior in part reminded one of a kitten with a ball. It finally dashed away after the other doe, which meantime had gone into the woods. For some moments the sound of snapping twigs and movements indicated that the play continued in the forest whence they had come.''

Deer of other species exhibit such playfulness as well. In an intensive two-year study of red deer behavior in northwestern Scotland, F.F. Darling concludes that deer play tag, engage in mock combat, race and play king-of-the-castle. King-of-the-castle, perhaps the most fascinating example of deer play, revolves around a hillock that is used as an objective, with each member of the deer group trying to attain and occupy the summit. In his charmingly written book entitled *A Herd of Red Deer* (1937), Darling recalls how ''king-of-the-castle would start by one calf mounting the hillock and occasionally rising on its hind legs. This would seem to serve as an invitation, for others would look up, leave their mothers, and run towards the hillock. The hillock was worn by the impress of many tiny feet, and it was obvious that this had become a traditional playing-place. When I say 'traditional' I admit that association of the hillock with previous fun may influence their behavior towards a repetition of the experience when they pass near it again. For I have seen red deer calves come from a distance of fifty yards to their chosen hillock to begin playing, as if their play were premeditated.''

American elk, a species closely related to red deer, also demonstrate a spirit of play by running, kicking up their heels and splashing in water. In his field notes for June 23, 1944, Olaus Murie, a foremost field biologist of his time, describes one instance of elk play in the following manner: ''The sun was low, and the elk obviously felt the exhilaration in the air that comes with a lowering sun in spring. They milled around, ran off in sudden stampedes, all pouring across the meadow into the woods, then suddenly reversing and all coming back again. Some of the cows would run in a crazy fashion, shaking their heads and leaping in a zig-zag manner, just feeling good. Occasionally two cows would leap over each other or chase each other in mock hostility. When some of them came upon a pool of water, they jumped into the water, pranced around, and pawed the water vigorously with their front hooves.'' Indeed, when the snow melts and people speak of spring in the air, deer exude a playful behavior regardless of the species.

The roe deer is one species in particular that demonstrates a unique form of deer play, commonly known as the roe rings. In this form of deer play, roe deer make rings around some natural center such as a bush or clump of grass. These rings consist of circular or oval tracks trodden into the ground by repeated use. Sometimes two rings adjoin and form a figure eight. British deer biologists find roe rings in use during July and August. In his study of *The Roe Deer of Cranborne Chase* (1968), Richard Prior, a professional game biologist, suggests ''that roe deer use them as exercise grounds for the fawns, or to wean them; to brush flies away; and as centers for courtship ritual. Both adults and fawns have been seen running round them by too many observers to leave the dual purpose in doubt. Play and exercise have their part,

Play activity such as jumping over logs increases survival among deer by speeding up their reaction to fear stimuli and by developing an awareness of their surroundings. *Photo credit Leonard Lee Rue III*

A fawn mounts its feeding dam. This type of deer play is generally tolerated by the doe at least for a brief time.
Photo credit Valerius Geist

but the fact that rings are instantly abandoned after the rut points to the greater significance of a reproductive function."

Prior concludes that roe deer indulge in antics that give every appearance of high-spirited play. They participate in mock battles, consisting mainly of butting, unsteady runs and four-footed jumps. Play becomes less frequent with age. In April of 1964, Prior observed the following splendid, high-spirited display: "Seven roe, two bucks and five does, were engaged in communal games on a hillside at Wardour. Besides a form of tag, which covered perhaps three acres with racing figures, two or three deer would break

off to circle a tree at dizzy speed, before rejoining the chase. The whole performance lasted 10 minutes, when it subsided as if by mutual agreement. Although it is dangerous to try to guess the motives behind such behavior, my feeling is that it was pure fun."

While it is maybe dangerous to guess the motives behind this type of behavior, the following generalizations can be made with regard to deer play. They are based on personal observations and scientific literature on the subject.

First of all, since very little analysis of animal play has been done, no simple definition of deer play is possible. Indeed,

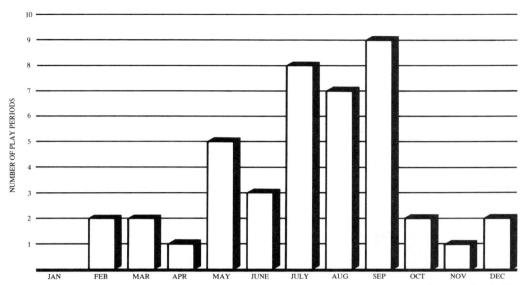

Play periods by month of the year at the Cedar Creek Deer Study Area in northwestern Oregon. *Credit The Canadian Field-Naturalist*, 1975

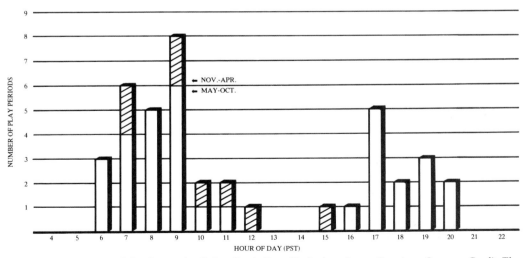

Play periods by hour of the day at the Cedar Creek Deer Study Area in northwestern Oregon. *Credit The Canadian Field-Naturalist*, 1975

Gamboling represents a special form of deer play. Gamboling is a gait in which the hind legs are kicked backward in unison, and, as they are brought forward, the forelegs are kicked forward. The sequence is repeated several times in rapid succession, giving the deer a bucking appearance. *Photo credit Leonard Lee Rue III*

play is one of the least understood categories of deer behavior. In my own opinion, deer play is best described as an activity without an immediate and evident object, an activity that seems to afford great pleasure to those partaking in it. It consists of head jerks, butting, pushing, head shaking, mounting, gamboling and kicking, leaping, running, neck craning and twisting.

Secondly, personal observation and the scientific literature tell me that deer play serves a useful purpose. It is a conditioning for later life. Running races, jumping over one another, dashing around in circles, dodging one another and buck-

ing all help to stretch, stimulate and build muscles, to increase lung capacity, and to stimulate the heart. All of these playful maneuvers will be used later for escaping from predators and hunters alike. The important point to remember, as Lennie Rue once told me, "is that it's done with the exuberance and joy of living that accompany youth and well-being."

Thirdly, deer play indicates an excess amount of energy and reflects the physical well-being of the animal itself. In critical forage years and when deer density is at its peak, deer play remains at a minimum. On the other hand, playful activity appears to be more intense in areas of high-quality habitat and when deer density is lower. In other words, deer play is directly related to habitat conditions and population density. Some deer biologists even view deer play as a useful indicator of environmental conditions.

Fourthly, play periods seem to occur most frequently during the summer months when the deer's "energy budget" is at an all-time high. After studying 42 playful occurrences of black-tailed deer at the Cedar Creek Deer Study Area in northwestern Oregon, Frank L. Miller, a wildlife researcher for the Oregon Game Commission, concluded that "the energy demands of play activities are considered to be such that only animals with an abundance of food can play." The pattern of occurrence of play periods by hour of the day seems to follow the overall activity pattern for deer in general.

Finally, several miscellaneous observations come to mind when reflecting on deer play:

(1) Individuals play progressively less as they mature—adult bucks ordinarily do not play.

(2) There appears to be a complete

breakdown in the dominance-hierarchy while deer are at play.

(3) At times, playfulness becomes so vivacious, especially in young deer, that they frequently look like they are trying to do a handstand.

(4) Considerable playing is done in shallow ponds and streams with an enthusiastic splashing of water.

(5) According to one deer biologist, deer appear to spend more time playing on nights after cloudy or rainy weather.

(6) Deer play usually lasts from one to three minutes, and then stops suddenly and abruptly.

(7) The patterns, duration and intensity of play varies with the species; in other words, deer play is species specific. Why this should be the case remains one of the unanswered mysteries in the realm of deer behavior.

Perhaps the inexhaustible spirit of deer play and the human playfulness of the hunt are best captured for us in classical music. Listen, for example, to the *Presto Finale* of "The Hunt Symphony" by Haydn, or try the highly spirited orchestral piece entitled "Auf der Jagd" by Johann Strauss, and you will know what I mean. Whether you listen to classical music or not, if these two pieces don't put you in the deer forest in hot pursuit of bounding bucks, nothing will! The thundering sounds of guns, the exultation of the chase, the joyous metallic notes of the hunting horns and the baying of the pack symbolize with such power the image of bounding bucks leaping over windfalls and fences, with the deer hunter in hot pursuit, that they literally transform your physical presence from your cozy den to the somber November deer forest.

If this music doesn't incite your imagination with playfulness and deer hunting

"I think the deer, if asked, would rather have a playful scamper through field and stream than spend all his life shut up in a small pen."—Walter Winnans, *Deer Breeding for Fine Heads, 1913.*
Photo credit Leonard Lee Rue III

fever, try reading Maurice Genevoix' epic novel *The Last Hunt* (1940), a charming, nostalgic and unforgettable novel of deer hunting in a French forest that beautifully evokes the emotions, feelings and play element of the deer hunt—ultimately capturing the mystical affinity of play between hunter and hunted, between man and his quarry.

Yes . . . the deer hunt and deer play are related. Indeed, one of the main bonds of interest between man and deer is that both of them enjoy playing in an atmosphere of freedom. Both are players in life's drama. Both of them show their zest for life by chasing objects. Man chases the deer, and deer are known to chase birds, butterflies and themselves. And both have a thoroughly good time doing it. As Walter Winans, a rather bizarre figure in the history of deer hunting, once remarked: "I think the deer, if asked, would rather have a playful scamper through the fields occasionally than spend all his life shut up in a small pen in a menagerie. People who do not take exercise think it a shame to make an animal gallop till it is tired, not understanding the pleasure inherent in becoming healthily and playfully tired out and hungry. When a healthy man has been shut up in a room for some days, it is the greatest pleasure possible to have a hard walk or gallop and come home all of a glow, and if there is likewise some risk, as in big game shooting or hunting, the pleasure will have been so much greater."

In its broadest sense, we can best express the whole process of deer hunting in terms of play, for deer hunting is a

One of the main similarities between man and deer is that both of them enjoy playing in an atmosphere of freedom. *Photo credit Charlie Heidecker*

game to be played according to the rules. In his *Deer of California* (1933), H. H. Sheldon, a well-known naturalist, aptly compared deer hunting to the game of football: "Just as a knowledge of the rules of football, and an acquaintance with the players, increases the interest and the pleasure of those who watch the game, so an intelligent understanding of game laws, and intimacy with the characteristics and habits of the quarry adds zest to the deer hunt." The ethical deer hunter would sooner fail in the hunt than succeed by breaking the rules of the game.

What does the human mind tell us about deer hunting? First and foremost, deer hunting is a game man plays in which he pits his intellect and experience against the instincts of the quarry. It's a game of intense concentration for the mature, others not being equipped to ultimately appreciate its many subtleties. It's an esthetic pursuit with the joy in hunting coming *before* hunting for joy. It's companionship with family members or valued partners. It's the shared experience of the esthetic qualities of a fine autumn day. As a game, it allows us to get away from everyday problems and grants us relaxation. Indeed, 60 percent of all deer hunters, according to Tom Heberlein, a rural sociologist at the University of Wisconsin, cannot find anything in their lives that would be an adequate substitute for this form of play.

This play world has its own codes, rules and language. As one psychologist once told me, "Part of the obsession for deer hunting comes from the fact that it is a game played in a special world artificially created and set apart from everyday life. This play world has its own special rules, costumes and language. As in gambling, players become addicted not so much to winning, as to trying to win. At the same time, however, the common emphasis among hunters upon competition, success and payoff shows how closely man's play resembles his work in American culture. The beauty and perhaps the appeal of deer hunting is that it raises play to ritual.'' One only needs to visit the American deer camp to realize that the ritual and tradition of deer hunting elevate the event from mere play to a satisfying and meaningful lifetime activity.

Deer play just like men. We have only to watch fawns and yearlings to see that all the essentials of human play are present in their merry gambols. They encourage one another to play by what we might call a certain ceremoniousness of gesture. But what is most important in all their playful doings is that they plainly experience tremendous fun and enjoyment, as do we in chasing them. Genuine, pure play in an atmosphere of freedom represents the connecting link between man and deer. Yes . . . deer play and deer hunting are intimately interwoven with one another, although the connection is seldom observed or expressed.

Chapter 14

In Velvet

The extent of my earthly domain, according to the Iowa County Register of Deeds, consists of 20 acres. But the Register of Deeds fails to understand how much acreage I tramp over in July and August in search of white-tailed bucks in velvet, bucks with furry skin that covers their antlers and makes them look like Spanish moss on tree branches. Indeed, every July for as long as I can remember, I have prowled the oak woodlots in search of just one more glimpse of a massive velvety rack disappearing over the next ridge—an occurrence that mesmerizes so many deer hunters and stirs the foundation of anticipation. This July was no exception, for summer wouldn't be summer without deer in velvet.

July is the month of the Buck Moon, as we learn from the Indian lunar calendar. But why the Indians traditionally hunted bucks in velvet is a practice I fail to understand. Perhaps it was because bucks in velvet were fat and the venison could be quickly dried in the hot July sun. Or maybe the Indians pursued deer in velvet because they believed, like many people from the Far East, that the velvet has some aphrodisiac value.

In any event, what is this strange velvety substance that so captures the imagination of the hunter and so strongly resembles Staghorn Sumac, a furry and velvety shrub which bucks sometimes use to rub off their velvet? What is its function? Why is it shed? What myths and mysteries are associated with this magnificent and intricate device of nature?

Velvet, in simple terms, is a modified extension of normal skin in the area of the head and pedicles which envelopes the growing antler. It consists of a pig-

Six stages of velvet and antler growth. *Credit David Constantine*

mented epidermis with fine hairs, a dermal layer including hair follicles and sebaceous glands, and an underlying vascular layer containing the major blood vessels which transport and deposit the materials that build the antler. It bruises readily, bleeds freely on abrasion and suffers frostbite if retained throughout the winter, as is the case with castrated animals.

The velvet stage of antler development represents an absorbing study, and few events in nature rival the unique mechanisms by which the annual renewal of

Velvet, in simple terms, is a modified extension of normal skin in the area of the head and pedicles which envelopes the growing antler. It consists of a pigmented epidermis with fine hairs, a dermal layer including hair follicles and sebaceous glands, and an underlying vascular layer containing the major blood vessels that transport and deposit the materials that build the antler. *Photo credit Leonard Lee Rue III*

deer antlers takes place. The best description I have read of this process is in Sir William Macewen's *The Growth and Shedding of the Antler of the Deer* (1920), a scientific work and blue chip deer book from which I cull the following basic facts:

"The deer's antler is deciduous, a new one being formed every year. The enormous growth of bone forming the antler is produced in three or four months. This growth of the antler proceeds from a single comparatively small centre of ossification situated in the frontal bone. The

regeneration of the myriads of cells and the rapidity of cellular proliferation necessary for the growth of the antler is much greater than that in any other normal process of single bone formation within deer or any other animal.

"In the first year an outgrowth rises from the frontal bone which, when the outgrowth is completed, forms the pedicle. The pedicle not only springs from the frontal bone of the skull, but it is identical with it in structure, having the same blood supply. The pedicle at the beginning of the growing period is highly vascular (containing vessels or ducts for conveying blood) and pulpy, and is covered with cartilage which ossifies from the base upwards. The pedicle once formed is a permanent structure growing in circumference during subsequent years.

"The blood supply of the pedicle comes from the vessels of the skull and frontal bone. The pedicle itself is highly vascular especially towards the centre from which active osseous proliferation is proceeding. The new growth pours out from the whole interior of the pedicle and overlaps it circumferentially, laying thereby the foundation of the future corona.

"A thin layer of cutis (the velvet) spreads with great rapidity over the bone and cartilage of the antler, and keeps pace with the subsequent growth of the latter. The velvet is nourished by numerous big blood vessels which run vertically on the antler. The velvet covers the whole antler from the base to the tip not only with skin, but with glands and hair follicles. Branches of the trigeminal nerve ascend in the velvet in line with the blood vessels and supply the acute sensitivity of the

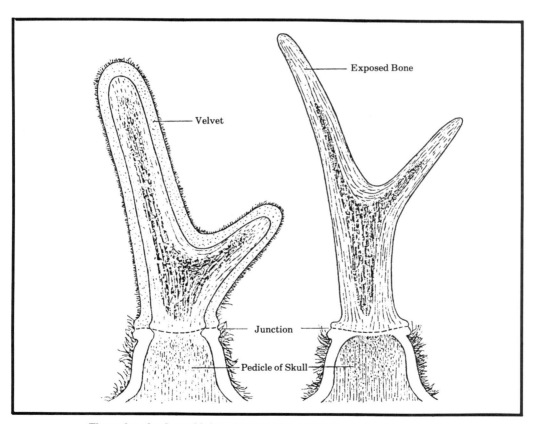

The antler of a deer with its velvet covering and the bony structure exposed.

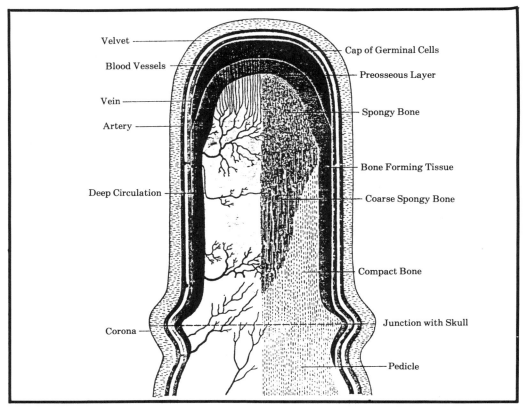

Velvet
Blood Vessels
Vein
Artery
Deep Circulation
Corona

Cap of Germinal Cells
Preosseous Layer
Spongy Bone
Bone Forming Tissue
Coarse Spongy Bone
Compact Bone
Junction with Skull
Pedicle

The blood supply of the growing antler in velvet is provided through the elaborate structure of arterioles and veins depicted on the left side of the illustration. The major structural zones of the antler are shown on the right.

velvet which thus protects the growing antler during its softened state.''

While carrying this soft and sensitive velvet, bucks remain rather docile and carefully shield this velvety membrane by hiding in quiet spots. As one old-time deer hunter exclaimed, ''The instinct that prompts them to avoid painful knocks at this period serves to promote regularity in growth, for any injury to the velvet is liable to be followed by a permanent scar or deformity in the corresponding part of the antler for that year.''

Actually, malformations resulting from injuries during the velvet stage of antler growth may be repeated in many subsequent antler cycles. In relating the lore of antlers to wildlife biology, A. B. Bubenik, a research scientist from Ontario who has made a lifelong study of antlers and produced the definitive work on the subject, makes an interesting observation in this regard: ''Sometimes, when part of a velvet antler is broken and is held to the beam by a piece of velvet, the two pieces grow together. Otherwise, a cartilagenous tissue, or callus, is built up, and the broken piece swings when the callus gets wet."

Research scientists recognize antler velvet as one of the fastest growing tissues known to man. Antler growth may exceed 0.39 inches per day, a growth rate unequaled elsewhere in the animal kingdom. This phenomenal growth rate has prompted medical investigators to study antler growth in an attempt to find more effective methods for the treatment of fractures, neoplasms and neurological disorders.

Since antlers grow afresh each year, and since deer frequently graze on upland pastures which contain high levels of radioactive fallout that metabolically concentrates itself in the calcium of the antlers, antlers provide biomedical researchers with a convenient collector of radioactive fallout. In 1957, for example, British analysis of deer antlers indicated a tenfold increase in radioactivity since 1952 in the Scottish Isles. Similar tests on deer antlers in the United States, Canada and Alaska also found high levels of radioactivity in deer antlers. In detecting environmental contamination, antlers, interestingly enough, can provide man with a good warning signal of possible danger.

As a living tissue, antler velvet is very warm to man's touch. After measuring the heat loss by antlers in velvet, Bernard Stonehouse, a zoologist at the University of Canterbury, concluded that the velvet antler functions as a radiator, with a great deal of heat dissipating itself through the velvet. During the hot summer months, this radiator cooling effect might well be a welcome asset to the animal. But the hypothesis that antler velvet functions as a thermoregulatory mechanism with a ca-

An unusual white-tailed buck with two beams on his left antler and with tatters of dry velvet hanging from his rack. *Photo credit Leonard Lee Rue III*

pacity for cooling large volumes of blood remains highly controversial. Surely the antler velvet cannot be absolutely necessary for thermoregulation; otherwise, both males and females of all species would have antlers.

During August, the deer forest literally bursts forth with so many forms and species of life that it seems almost impossible for the forest to contain them all. After a warm August rain, the deer forest all but steams with tropical beauty. "There is a feeling of unlimited life," Sigurd Olson once said in describing it, "an awareness of forms growing everywhere in places which a short time before seemed barren."

When I walk through the forest, no form of life stops me more quickly than the sudden appearance of a fox-red deer with tatters of velvet hanging from his rack. At this time, they look untidy, a bit comical, somewhat like cervine scarecrows as they stand knee-high in the garden of their delight with their velvety crowns frayed to ribbons. They do not, however, remain in this condition for long.

As I walk along, I wonder to myself: What triggers the shedding of velvet? What does it signify? Is it related to the breeding cycle? Does the blood from the shedding velvet color the antlers, or is it the stain from bucks shadowboxing with bushes that give the antlers their coloration?

The mechanics of velvet-shedding have fascinated people for years. Only in recent times, however, has the importance of light and hormones been appreciated with regard to the shedding of velvet, for nature holds her secrets closely. During the 1940s and 50s, George B. Wislocki, a professor of anatomy at the Harvard Medical School, demonstrated that the shedding of velvet is controlled by increased daylight and the interaction of hormones derived from the testes and the pituitary gland located near the base of the brain.

Increased sunlight during the spring is transmitted from the eye of the deer to the pituitary gland, which either stimulates the start of antler growth directly, or releases testosterone, the male hormone, which in turn stimulates the start of the cycle in early May. As the breeding season approaches in early fall, the level of testosterone increases in the buck's arterial system, which causes the antlers to mature and the velvet to shed—signifying the beginning of the rut. The specific causal mechanisms of this intricate process are still not entirely known.

A consensus of opinion seems to suggest that nutritional levels of deer may be associated with the timing of velvet shedding. Time estimates for velvet shedding vary considerably, though. The reason for this variability in the date of velvet shedding is unknown. Some researchers have seen the process completed in three hours; others record the duration to be from several days to several weeks. One mule deer living in captivity, for example, shed his antler velvet slightly later each successive year and failed to shed it completely during the last few years of his 18-year life. Sick and wounded deer also retain their velvet for indefinite periods of time.

One of the most notable instances of the removal of velvet took place in Yosemite Valley in 1927, and was recorded by Joseph S. Dixon, a former biologist of the National Park Service. His fascinating story needs to be reproduced in its entirety:

"On September 14, I found a very tame buck with large antlers still in the velvet. At this date he was all shed out into the short 'blue' (really gray) winter coat. He was fat and in excellent condition, with large well-balanced antlers that carried three tines on each side. I watched him for some time at a distance of ten feet as he fed on goldenrod stalks which were just ready to bud. As far as I could see, even with binoculars, the velvet was as solidly attached as ever to the antlers, and there was no break or tear in it at any point. I left him at six p.m., still chewing peacefully on the goldenrod.

"Twelve hours later, at six o'clock on the morning of September 15, I met this same buck coming out of a thicket of western chokecherry where I later found evidence that he had been 'horning' the brush to free his antlers of velvet. The velvet which the day before had covered his antlers now hung in long limp ribbons from the base of his antlers, to which support the shreds remained firmly attached. The shreds of velvet caused the buck considerable worry in that every time he lowered his head to graze on the grass they dangled in front of his eyes and obscured his vision. The buck kept shaking his head vigorously and twice I saw him take the offending strands in his mouth and chew them off as high up as he could grasp them. The velvet thus obtained was not dropped or thrown away but was *chewed up and swallowed with evident relish.*

"By seven o'clock all of the velvet had been 'bobbed' by being chewed off to the level of the buck's mouth. The buck then went out and after bedding down in the center of the meadow began chewing his cud. Half an hour later this buck was down near our camp horning some smooth willow saplings in an effort to get rid of the remaining velvet. He no longer rubbed the tips of his antlers which were then hard and polished and a beautiful brown in color, but spent most of his energy in trying to remove the velvet where it was still tightly attached at the base of his antlers. By nine o'clock the wet, stringy strips of velvet had begun to dry and to shrivel up into narrow 'shoestrings' which, two days later, resembled strips of dried up, twisted rawhide that remained tightly attached to the antlers. The bony burr at the base of the antler, however, stuck out and protected the velvet so that even repeated rubbings of the antlers against willow saplings failed to remove it.

"I was much interested in finding out just how the strips of dried-up velvet would finally be gotten rid of, so I continued to keep close watch on this particular buck and, on the morning of September 18, I watched him lower his head, then reach forward with his right hind leg and using the sharp points of the hoof as a chisel, he neatly pried off and dislodged the remaining shreds of dry, stiff velvet."

Deer biologists believe that old bucks shed their velvet earlier than young ones. The question as to why the biggest, best-conditioned, dominant bucks shed their velvet earlier than young deer remains one of the unanswered mysteries of deer behavior. While studying deer behavior at the Rob and Bessie Welder Wildlife Refuge in Sinton, Texas, David Hirth, a well-known deer researcher, closely observed 293 white-tailed bucks during the period of velvet loss. He concluded that the loss of velvet clearly started with the oldest and largest individuals and proceeded to progressively younger and

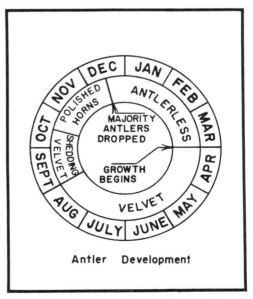

Circle graph showing antler development through the year.

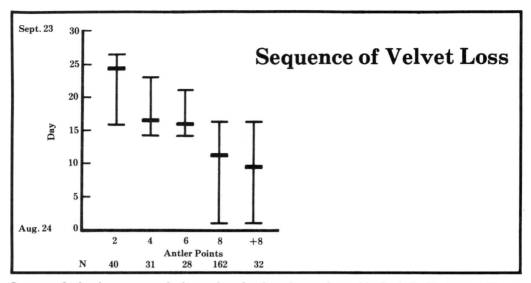

Sequence of velvet loss among males by number of antler points as observed by David H. Hirth on the Welder Wildlife Refuge. N is the number of males of each antler class examined during the shedding season. Vertical lines indicate range of velvet loss dates and the horizontal bars show the mean velvet loss dates. *Credit The Southwestern Naturalist,* 1977

smaller bucks. According to Hirth, "Freshly cleaned antlers were almost white, but they soon became stained reddish-brown from the sap of huisache and mesquite trees debarked by the males."

The coloration of antlers arouses a good deal of controversy amongst hunters and biologists alike. We know that the color of the velvet itself varies slightly from one species of deer to another. We also know that the color of the fully developed antlers varies considerably. Some are dark black, dark brown, nut-brown, yellowish brown and mouse-gray. Controversy abounds as to the origin of the brown color of antlers. Some wildlife observers regard the dried blood of the velvet to be the principal source of color. But this point of view overlooks the pure white color of the newly exposed antlers. Others believe that stains from shrubs and trees against which bucks rub their antlers are

the primary source. I am inclined to agree with this view.

After many hours of searching for bucks in velvet and after studying the scientific literature on the subject, I jotted down the following notes in my deer shack diary:

(1) Antlers in velvet take on a more massive dimension than they actually possess while in the polished state. As they develop, their porous and almost spongy texture is consolidated to form a harder and more compact surface, shrinking a little in the process.

(2) Bucks in velvet, F. F. Darling tells us in his delightful book on red deer, frequently use their hind feet to remove the velvet. Personally, I have never seen this form of behavior.

(3) Raymond Chaplin, an English deer biologist, tells us in his book entitled *Deer* (1977) that the growing velvet possesses secretory cells which produce an odori-

ferous substance. The significance of such secretions by the velvet is unknown. They may act as "sunburn oil to protect the skin or even as an insect repellent against the many blood-sucking insects that would feed on the velvet. I have never seen, for example, ticks on the velvet."

(4) While deer hunters cannot eat antlers, antlers, like Easter bonnets, are here to stay and deer hunters are glad of it. Fortunately for both deer hunters and whitetails, whitetails will probably never develop antlers so large that they doom themselves to extinction, as did the Irish elk in prehistoric times.

(5) In the Eastern medicine trade, high prices are paid for antlers in velvet. The Academy of Science in Moscow, for example, "reports that clinical tests have been run on people using chemicals from dried antlers in velvet. They find that antlers do indeed contain hormones and other chemicals which can be used to heal wounds and to help relieve certain symptoms of old age." Commercially, the Russians produce a tonic elixir called "Pontocrin" from antler velvet, a substance they believe heals all ailments. Maybe the American Indians collected antlers in velvet for medicinal value.

(6) Deer hunters seem to prefer to kill bucks with regal tine tips polished to old ivory, rather than bucks in velvet. If you do shoot a buck in velvet, the velvet will be added to the mounted rack by the taxidermist before you place the antlers on the wall of your den. In the event that you do shoot such an unusual trophy during the early bow season, precautionary measures should be taken to preserve it. Robert E. Donovan, the author of *Hunting Whitetail Deer* (1978), gives us the following advice in this regard:

"The problem with velvet antlers is that the antler is still growing, the interior is soft, and it is full of liquids and blood that will turn rancid if not quickly treated. The velvet itself is delicate and should be protected from physical damage. Velvet antlers should not be grasped roughly nor used as handles for moving or dragging the carcass. The hunter who anticipates encountering velvet racks should take a pint of formaldehyde and a hypodermic needle along with him. As soon as possible after the kill, fill the hypodermic needle with formaldehyde, push it into one of the soft antler tips, and slowly inject the fluid. In an ideal case, the formaldehyde will eventually start to trickle out near the base of the antler telling you that complete penetration has been achieved. Repeat the process at each antler tip and in the soft areas around the forks. It's also a good idea to soak velvet antlers overnight in a solution of one part formaldehyde to thirty parts of water. Take the antlers out of the solution the next day and allow them to dry in a cool place."

This year's full Buck Moon seems brighter, rounder and cooler than ever before. Maybe that's because we are already dreaming of the Harvest Moon of September and the beginning of the bow season. The bow season is, after all, one important reason why we take to the field in July and August. We also tramp the deer forest as the summer ends, because studying deer in the velvet enhances our overall ability to locate deer at will; it adds immensely to our knowledge of the quarry. And if our wives are lucky, we might even return with a bucket full of blackberries, for the blackberries are ripening now. It is time to make jelly, and what fantastic jelly it is!

July days are long, dusk comes late,

and the nights bring on a sense of leisure. While others concern themselves with Independence Day festivities, traditional picnics and fireworks, we roam the hills looking for blackberries and deer in velvet, because we know the larder from last year now looks thin.

Despite the fact that summer days can be hot, the sun soon drops toward the horizon and a cool northerly breeze drifts in across the cornfield. Green acorns hang heavy in the oaks. The aroma of alfalfa is in the air, for the silos are being filled.

A white-tailed buck in velvet. Note the flies that torment bucks while their antlers are covered by the living tissue known as velvet. Flies are especially attracted by the smell of drying blood and tissue as the velvet dries and sheds. Consequently, bucks seek escape in the thickets and shade of high hilltops which, being cooler and windier, are less fly-infested than the lower land. *Photo credit Leonard Lee Rue III*

The fragrance of clover and milkweed take possession of the land. The nocturnal and lonesome *whip-poor-will* echoes out its cry.

Many of my July days end with me in front of the old brick fireplace, preparing venison tenderloins. As the savory smoky odor ascends the oak hillside, I lay my Game Getter 2117's into the target. For a brief time in July and August, I forget the turmoil and tension of the world and dream of bucks in velvet entering alfalfa fields in the peaceful shadows of the evening. After a few glasses of Cabernet Sauvignon, a well-balanced, dry red wine that never seems to lose its velvet, I return to my deer books to escape the insatiable mosquitoes and to read further under the category of deer antlers.

Deer antlers are, after all, of great interest to laymen as trophies and to game biologists as indicators of the condition of the range. They have intrigued and mystified naturalists since ancient times. One thing seems certain: antlers, whether polished or in the velvet, are the very reason for the existence of many deer hunters. Consequently, antlers adorn the walls and halls of studies, dens and country cottages.

Who would deny the idea that the beauty of a stag lies largely in its antlers, especially when they are in velvet! From the buck's point of view, they are his pride and glory. As noted naturalist John Madson once remarked, "with them he is a lusty warrior, without them he's a meek nonentity." I know of no greater thrill in July and August than to see majestic bucks in their reddish summery coats and velvety antlers pass beneath my oak tree, jump the wooden gate, and slip silently into the warm velvet darkness of the night.

Chapter 15

In the Orchard

The image of the lone buck in the abandoned apple orchard strikes a universal chord in the mind of the deer hunter and naturalist. As John Burroughs, that famous backwoodsman from Woodchuck Lodge, once remarked: "There are few places on the farm where there is so much live natural history to be gathered as in the orchard." Indeed, the trees not only bear a crop of apples, but bring deer in from miles away to rub off the bark, break the limbs, browse the buds, browse the leaves and ultimately eat the fruit. This chapter highlights the special yet problematic relationship between apples, man and whitetails.

Apples (*Malus pumila*) rank unquestionably as one of the whitetail's most preferred and best-liked foods. They are grown throughout America, but we find their principal areas of production in the Northeast and the Far West. Naturally, the greatest use of apples by deer occurs in these two regions. Actually, deer browsing in apple orchards in this country represents one of the most common forms of wildlife depredation in America. Damage to orchards by deer ranks second only to grain crop damage. Not only do they eat the apples that drop off the tree, but they will stand up on their hind legs to reach high for this noble fruit, whether ripe or green.

Whitetails also seem especially fond of rundown, abandoned orchards. In fact, some of the largest deer I have shot throughout the years have come from under the apple boughs of abandoned orchards—one while standing on his hind feet reaching high for the cherished fruit of paradise!

Mature whitetails eat apples by either

Apple trees not only bear a crop of apples, but also bring deer in from miles away to rub the bark off, break the limbs, browse the buds, browse the leaves and ultimately eat the fruit. *Photo credit Leonard Lee Rue III*

to bloat themselves and soon suffer from indigestion, or rumenitis. When this takes place, their droppings acquire the texture of apple sauce. Given the fact that deer will eat one to one and a half pounds of acorns a day and from three to five pounds of alfalfa, it seems likely that they might consume as much as five to six pounds of apples a day, given the water content of apples. An exact measurement in this regard has never been made, at least to my knowledge.

When apples fall to the ground, they frequently bruise quite badly. Some old-time deer hunters believe that when the air gets into the fruit while it lays in the sun, the apples begin to ferment and can

biting them in half between their incisors and upper jaw, or by taking the whole apple in their mouth and crushing it with their rear molars. "While doing this," as Lennie Rue once observed, "the deer appears to be eating soapsuds, as the apple juice and saliva pour out of its mouth in long sticky strings. Fawns, being unable to open their mouths that wide, are forced to eat apples in a daintier manner and must take many small bites from the apple. To prevent the apple from rolling away from it, the fawn backs the apple up against its two front feet and holds it there with its mouth as it eats."

When high winds force apples to the ground by the bushel baskets, deer tend

Young deer, being unable to open their mouths wide enough, are forced to eat apples by taking small bites at a time. To prevent the apple from rolling away, young deer back the apple up against their front feet and hold it there with their mouth as they eat. *Photo credit Richard P. Smith*

Eating apples in the orchard. Deer may consume as many as five to six pounds of apples a day. An exact measurement in this regard has never been made. *Photo credit Leonard Lee Rue III*

thus make deer intoxicated. While birds seem to intoxicate themselves with berries, I have never personally seen an intoxicated deer, nor have I ever read about such an occurrence in scientific literature. Intoxicated deer hunters from too much Applejack or hard cider . . . yes. Intoxicated deer . . . no. This idea, as is so often the case with deer hunting tales in general, goes beyond the realm of science into apple sauce itself.

Deer not only show a decided preference for apples, as opposed to other cultivated fruits, but they actually discriminate between the different varieties of apples. In New England orchards, for example, deer apparently relish the McIntosh more than the Delicious; in other orchards, according to E.M. Mills, a former biologist with the United States Biological Survey, they like the Alexander better than the Northern Spy.

We know that certain apple species differ in taste and texture. As one apple enthusiast declared, "Some are tender and delicately crisp; some are so firm you can hardly get your tooth through them. Some are tart with sweet aftertaste; some present the opposite sequence. Some suggest spiciness or wininess; some are mild but subtle; some are so intense in effect that they are like small explosions of flavor. Some have thin, almost flavorless skins; in others, an astringent skin is part of the whole effect. There are apples so juicy you almost need a bib to eat them, and equally good ones that will barely exude a drop."

But do deer really select and prefer one variety of apples over another? It seems safe to conclude that while palatability might be a factor in some cases, the varieties of apple trees that suffer the most extensive damage are those which are grown extensively within the range of the deer. In other words, crop distribution rather than preferred palatability dictates which apples whitetails actually consume.

Not only do whitetails consume apples, but they eat other fruit as well. Orchardists in Tuolumne County, California, for example, report that deer eat peaches and spit out the pits. In some cases they find the ground literally covered with the peach pits after a nighttime raid by deer. Deer also eat prunes, apricots, cherries and pears. Apples, however, still remain one of their best-liked fruits.

In Ohio, the wild crab apple (*Pyrus coronaria*) ranks first in the frequency of the food eaten by whitetails and second in the percentage of dry weight found in their rumens. Since crab apples rot very slowly, they remain available as deer food for several months after falling to the ground. Whitetails eat them in quantity during all seasons of the year, even in summer, but utilize them most heavily in the fall. Likewise, whitetails in New Brunswick, Canada, utilize early-ripening apples as soon as they become available. Rumen analysis of whitetails in this area indicates that 64.5 percent of their diet during July to September consists of fruit, mainly in the form of apples.

Yes, deer feed in the orchard; not only do they eat the apples, but they browse the leaves, buds and twigs of the trees themselves. One orchardist in New York, for example, reported that 87 two-year-old trees were destroyed in three nights by one deer, as shown by the deer's easily followed tracks. In the same orchard, six deer destroyed 175 apple trees in one night. One orchardist in Michigan exclaimed, "Deer have browsed in the lower branches of my old bearing trees, eliminating fruit production as high as the deer can reach. They have nibbled leaves and buds from my half-grown orchards and have browsed and killed many young trees set out one or two years before." In sampling 45 young trees in the two outside rows of an orchard in southeastern Minnesota, deer biologists found that 66 percent of the trees were severely injured and 33 percent of the trees were dead as a direct result of heavy and continuous deer browsing.

When browsing on apple trees, deer eat the lateral and terminal growth twigs in winter and large quantities of fruit buds in late winter and early spring. Continuous browsing on the buds and terminal twigs injures young apple trees to the point where many cannot survive. Deer browsing on apple leaves causes serious damage as well, as young trees need all their leaves for supplying growth substances to their shoots and fully developed trees need them for proper fruit production. Deer browsing in its worst form inhibits the growth of lateral buds and causes wide crotch angles, which in turn produce an unwanted spreading type of bushy growth rather than the development of strong, well-formed branches. Deer also strip bark from the apple trees with their mouths.

One thing is certain: Deer damage in the apple orchard is real. The intensity of this serious problem continues to grow because of the increasing size of the American deer herd and the escalation of the dwarf and semi-dwarf apple tree plantings in various parts of the country, which makes deer damage even more likely since dwarf trees give deer greater exposure to their leaves, buds and twigs. After browsing their buds and twigs, deer stunt and misshape these young trees and make them useless for future production.

New York wildlife biologists and extension specialists at Cornell University report that orchardists currently lose as much as 10 percent of their total crop value to deer. The extent and seriousness of deer damage becomes clear when one realizes that New York alone produces an apple crop valued at almost $60 million a year. In some areas, researchers estimate deer damage to small apple trees at 50 cents a tree. In one extreme case, an orchardist conducted an independent appraisal of his total deer damage; the loss approximated $10,000. Researchers at Cornell University demonstrate that deer can virtually eat up a grower's profits if no steps are taken to control them. Understandably, many apple growers consider deer to be a "nuisance they could do without." As a deer hunter, I am frequently a welcome guest after asking for permission to hunt deer in an orchard.

Orchardists in this country employ every conceivable method to keep deer out of the orchard. They spray their trees with repellents, using everything from lime-sulfur to nicotine dust, from whale oil soap and liquor cresolis compound to Naphthalene flakes. They try to scare deer from their orchards by hanging old clothes saturated with human scent on their trees. They fence their orchards with barbed wire and electricity. They hang automatic flashguns on tripods four to five feet above the ground which explode loudly, while at the same time a pilot burner throws a beam of light in different directions. They remove deer by trapping and translocating them to other areas. They use dogs to scare them from the orchard, as well as electric bells and horns, kerosene flares, sundry noisemakers, explosive rockets and other concoctions.

Several deer researchers in Maryland not only entertained the idea of laying out a minefield for the protection of apple orchards, but actually surrounded orchards with booby traps. Whenever a deer pushed against a string, a large firecracker exploded and punished the deer with a deafening report. In waging war against deer in the orchard, biologists in Virginia encircled orchards with M-80 Salutes—firecrackers exploded by Japanese booby traps. One orchardist in Maine swears by tar paper cones hung in trees, as well as blood meal from meat packers placed on the ground.

All of these methods have been tried with varying degrees of success. Despite everything, regulated sport hunting still remains the best and cheapest method of controlling deer damage to orchards. It is not the complete solution by any means. Indeed, proper deer herd control by managed hunting as well as deerproof fences and chemical repellents must all be employed if America's multi-million dollar fruit industry is to escape serious and widespread damage by deer.

While deer damage to commercial orchards causes great problems for fruit growers, damage to wild orchards remains less of a concern for the farmer and landowner. During the rut, I frequently find main breeding areas with active scrapes in abandoned orchards of old farmsteads. Consequently, each fall I try to locate at least one stand in or around a wild orchard.

One of my favorite tree stands overlooks a misshapen crab apple tree complete with scrape and licking branch. Almost every buck that passes through this old orchard tends to stop under this tree and lick the overhanging branch in a vigorous manner, regardless of the season! The social significance of this licking activity during summer remains another mystery of whitetail behavior. I once saw a buck pawing in the scrape beneath this crab apple tree in the middle of July. On one occasion I had six bucks standing under this apple tree at the same time.

The author shot this buck while it slowly passed through an abandoned apple orchard located less than 100 yards behind a farmer's barn. The orchard served as a main breeding area for this buck. In fact, he rubbed apple trees in this orchard so vigorously that a pronounced blister formed beneath his preorbital gland, as seen in the photo. I frequently watched this old-time farmlander feed under his favorite crab apple tree for 30 to 40 minutes at a time. *Photo credit Maren Lea Wegner*

The scrape beneath this particular crab apple tree has remained an active scrape during the rut for the past five years. I find that the most vigorous rutting activity in the area in which I hunt frequently takes place in this abandoned orchard.

One apple-fed buck that I shot from this tree stand rubbed apple trees in this orchard so vigorously that a pronounced blister formed beneath his preorbital gland. Such damage to apple trees as a result of antler rubbing, while not as common as browsing, is frequently more severe. Indeed, what this type of damage lacks in frequency it makes up for in severity, as indicated in the remarks of one wildlife biologist from Colorado: ''Bucks are a menace to young apple trees. Their rough, bony antlers scar young trees. Not only do they rub them, but they twist and break young trees to the extent that they require replacement.'' Scientists in Ohio report that white-tailed bucks rubbed 1145 nursery trees with a wholesale value of at least $30,000 during 1978 and 1979 in one nursery in Carroll County, Ohio. Would you believe that orchardists frequently support liberal deer harvests and grant deer hunters permission to enter their orchards?

Professor John D. Harder, a zoologist at Ohio State University, once measured the detrimental effect of antler rubbing on apple trees. He found that antler rubbing removed bark and cambium and exposed the xylem to drying winter weather. Since most rubbing occurs in late fall and early winter, little sap flows to heal the wound. Trees from one to three years old, averaging 4.0 centimeters in trunk diameter, sustain the most damage. Of 3282 apple trees inspected for antler rubbing in 1967, Harder found that 220 or

6.7 percent were rubbed; 9.1 percent of them died. Twenty-eight percent represented the highest incidence of antler rubbing in any one apple orchard.

Most deer activity occurs in orchards interspersed within good deer range, especially orchards surrounded by alfalfa fields, cornfields and woodlots containing oak trees. Whether you hunt deer in the orchards of California or Pennsylvania, you will find that deer prefer to feed in the orchard between 5:00 a.m. and 9:00 a.m. and from late afternoon until midnight. During September and October, however, I often encounter deer feeding in the orchard during the middle of the day. During severe winters you will find them in the orchard at every hour of the day. Old, well-established orchards receive the heaviest use, especially orchards with an abundant supply of cull apples on the ground.

Apples usually drop in an orchard during the months of September and October. When an apple falls, the deer hunter hears the sudden rustle amid the branches, leaves and twigs, and then the mellow thump on the forest floor. There the apple lies in the grass, no longer dependent upon the tree. Now it mellows, making itself a tempting treat for man and deer alike. When the early American Indians saw the apples ripening on the forest floor, they knew that sooner or later they would find deer under the apple boughs. So they waited patiently and concealed themselves for easy shots at their favorite game. That image of deer in the orchard still lurks in the mind of the modern-day deer hunter; just another historical link connecting the apple of today with the romance of our bow hunting past.

Whether we use a commercial apple scent, apples in our scent box, or whether we just like to eat apples while in the deer forest, many of us know that old, abandoned orchards, when we find them, represent excellent places to hunt deer, to breathe crisp, clean air and to listen to the marvelous sounds of all wildlife. Hunting whitetails in the orchard, as novelist William Faulkner once observed, represents "the best game of all, the best of all breathing, and forever the best of all listening."

Many deer hunters surely agree. Byron Dalrymple, that old master deer hunter from Texas, underscores the idea of hunting whitetails in the orchard when he recalls that, "One fall I was cruising around in the Pigeon River State Forest in northern Michigan just prior to deer season . . . In a little clearing beside a cedar and alder swale, six or eight scrub apple trees had branches that bent low. The grass was beaten down flat. There were deer droppings and bedding spots everywhere. As fast as apples fell, the deer got them. Deer of the entire locality might be browsing far and wide on a great variety of fare. But these apples were simply irresistible for dessert. This little windfall had tied a number of deer to this specific place. As it happened, I couldn't get to that wild orchard on opening day, but I sent a friend. With one shot he corroborated my thinking that invariably the quickest way to a buck's steaks is through his stomach!"

Surely, the quickest way to venison steak served with apples is through the whitetail's stomach. Find apple orchards and you will more than likely find deer. It might take time to locate apple trees in the wild that bear fruit, but the time will be well spent. Remember, it is easier to find wild apple trees in thick forests during the springtime when they are in blossom. Some deer hunters I know not only plant apples trees to enhance the deer habitat in their hunting area, but combine their springtime roaming for apple blossoms and possible tree stand locations with autumn apple picking and bow hunting for the ultimate in the American outdoor experience.

Deer hunters often plant apple trees to enhance the deer habitat for future years in their hunting area. *Photo credit Richard P. Smith*

PART III
THE DEER-HUNTING MYSTIQUE

Chapter 16

The November Deer Hunt

For uncounted centuries man has been a hunter in endless pursuit of food. These centuries have left an indelible mark on us all, and when we go on our November pursuit of the whitetail, ancient reactions surge out of our subconscious. Even the thought of the November deer hunt—when bucks paw the ground—brings a feeling of ultimate excitement, and inevitably leads to Havilah Babcock's observation that "my health is better in November," a statement that countless deer hunting widows have heard since time immemorial. This chapter examines the philosophical meaning of some of the basic ingredients of a successful November deer hunt: (1) the deer shack in the popple; (2) the esthetics of nature; (3) deer hunting camaraderie; (4) our ethical behavior while in the field; (5) autumn solitude; and (6) buckskin and venison. It will be argued

that a rich blend of these essential ingredients, when taken into conjunction with one another, provide us with a basic philosophy of deer hunting, and constitute what we know of as THE WHITETAIL EXPERIENCE—renewal, reaffirmation and self-realization.

When wood smoke from a copper-wired stovepipe of a secluded deer hunting cabin curls above the vast expanse of pines and oaks, redshirts tend to reflect on the ultimate meaning of deer hunting. No concept, I believe, receives more attention in the mind of the deer hunter than the deer hunters' camp itself. Inherent in this concept is the idea (which goes without saying, or should at least), that a deer hunters' camp is a community effort; that each man should have a job to do and should carry it through to completion.

Whether one chooses the job of cook-

"My health is better in November."
—Havilah Babcock.
Photo credit Irene Vandermolen

ing or gathering wood, tending the fire or washing dishes, the chores obviously need to be done and need to be divided to avoid bickering and argument. The proof of a man's worth in this regard, as Larry Koller once observed in his classic *Shots at Whitetails,* "might not be highly apparent on the trip itself, but in retrospect his cooperative qualities and good common sense, his willingness to share equally in labors and discomfort, will shine in the golden light of memory when the next fall season finds Jack Frost painting his landscapes."

Every fall, when the deer hunting fever stirs in our blood, we drop everything and head for the deer shack with a persistence matched only by Jack Frost himself. Many deer hunting widows seem mystified and awed by this November ritual. But I contend that if they were to carefully examine the scenic and unspoiled territory, the sweet smell of decaying acorns and leaves, the smell of gun oil and rubber boots, of charcoal-cooked venison and birch smoke from Grandpa Fred's potbelly stove, as well as the feel of woolen socks and flannel shirts . . . not to mention the distant sounds from a transistor radio of Bing Crosby singing "When the Blue of the Night Meets the Gold of the Day," they too might understand this inevitable exodus to deer camp and may even excuse the late return of their tired and bewhiskered mates for Thanksgiving Day dinner?

Indeed, half the fun of deer hunting undoubtedly lies in missing Thanksgiving Day dinner, of camping out and roughing it, so to speak—of getting away from the madness of modern civilization. While many hunters prefer the luxurious comfort of motels, the tar-paper deer shack way back in the popple will perhaps afford you the greatest opportunity of harvesting a trophy whitetail. For one thing, you limit your competition in remote areas, as rank-and-file deer hunters frequently stick close to public roads. There's also something quite romantic and magical about relaxing around a campfire, roasting last season's venison under a sky ablaze with stars, as well as reliving the day's hunt, exchanging stories of past hunts and simply taking life easy with your hand-picked hunting companion far away from the noise of any public roads.

Modern-day luxuries of public motels are thus immaterial to sportsmen, as many North Woods deer hunting shacks attest. "It matters not," Olive Glasgow writes in the *Wisconsin Sportsman,* "that spiders have curtained the windows with webs, that mice must be dislodged from matresses, that the outside pump freezes up and has to be primed, that the cooking is rudimentary or that the fire will die out in the woodstove before dawn leaving you to wake in a deep freeze." Then what does matter, one might well ask?

What does matter is that this November ritual offers a temporary respite from occupational schedules, employment tensions and pressures, and provides freedom from family restrictions. It means a time to unwind with like-minded comrades in an atmosphere of oil-burning lamps, an atmosphere infamously noted for its absence of pretention, especially after everyone has truly enjoyed Aunt Dinny's rich blend of chile concarni and prune pie. It means hitting the hay with a sigh of contentment, knowing that neither traffic nor telephones will disturb your dreams; it means being lulled asleep by the murmur of wind-lashed pines as tracking snow gently falls outside the cabin window.

The November deer hunt also means tall tales in the evening over a game of two-card draw. One only needs to quote the November 25, 1917, entry of *The Bucks Camp Log* to grasp the ultimate height of these tales: "The bunch drove the vicinity of the Poise stump this afternoon. A lead mine could be started with the bullets we left down there. We had five deer surrounded. The bombardment sounded like an English barrage. Deer were running everywhere. They were so thick around Mr. Hill, Sr. that he had to push them away beyond the end of his gun so he could shoot them. He got buck fever so bad that he was shooting in a circle. Mr. True said the air was so thick around Mr. Hill, Sr. that he could not shoot through it." And so it goes. . .

Ultimately, the deer shack at this time of the year reverberates with the emotional excitement of the primitive chase through the snow-bound forests of November. For the chase is a healthful and invigorating form of recreation that deeply affects the character of the sportsman, a recreation which infuses hardy, physical habits, quickness of eye and hand, and instills courage and self-reliance. These crucial habits of mind surely comprise in no small way the very mental constitution of a people. Yes, life at the deer shack has a different flavor. It is reduced to simpler terms; life's complex equations all but disappear. It need be only one room, just large enough for a couple of bunks, a fireplace and a table; but it must be, above all, as close to the primitive as possible. Such a cabin tucked back in the popple provides a convenient place for the deer hunter to observe whitetails at any time and on a moment's notice, without having to bother with a lot of equipment; a simple shelter where you can just move in, spend a few hours, a night or two, or even a week if the mood dictates. But it must be an outpost away from the telephone and interruptions, an outpost where you become part of the natural environment itself.

Becoming part of the natural environment itself is, after all, what deer hunting is really all about. Sure it's nice to bring home a many-tined trophy, but that isn't the end-all of the November deer hunt. Deer hunting means more than that! I think hunting camps and deer shacks represent at least half the reason why deer hunters go into the woods in November. But the other reason deals with the esthetics of nature, with wood smoke and moonlight, with the sweet respiration of the earth itself.

Sure, the deer hunter vigorously hunts the whitetail, but he is also there to feel

Becoming part of the natural environment itself is a major element in deer hunting. Sure, it is nice to bring home a many-tined trophy, but that isn't the end-all of the November deer hunt. *Photo credit Richard P. Smith*

the icy snow blowing in his face and to hear the sharp sound of buck hooves in the crisp autumn leaves of November. He also goes to the field to observe geese riding the crest of storm clouds and to taste the exquisite flavor of fresh deer liver and home-grown onions brewed in an open-faced skillet. He also takes to the field to experience the orange glow of the harvest moon hanging over the deer shack and the ghostly rise of wood smoke into the starry night. He hunts because the forest absorbs him and transforms him into the natural environment. He hunts

whitetails not necessarily to bring home venison, but consciously or unconsciously, to become a part of the spirituality of the earth, once an integral part of him, but now largely isolated by concrete and asphalt.

Deer hunting is, moreover, a marvelous form of happiness, as the great Spanish philosopher Jose Ortega y Gasset once pointed out. I know one of my happiest moments is watching the moon rise over the cabin, seeing its first glimmer over the ridge and its slow, majestic emergence until finally the huge orange ball of fire is free from the horizon—casting its enchantment on the deer shack and on my thoughts of trophy whitetails. Immersing oneself in moonlight, in the countryside and in the healthful exercise is the true joy of the whitetail experience. Deer hunting submerges us in the mysteries of nature, and in a sense constitutes a religious rite in which homage is paid to what is divine and transcendent in the wilds.

Deer hunting is one of those few activities that grants us "a vacation from the human condition," as Ortega observed. When pursuing whitetails we divert and distract ourselves from industrial madness and its laborious occupations. When we leave the city of Degeneration and go to the woods, it is astounding how naturally and quickly we free ourselves from worry, tension and temper. A fresh and fragrant atmosphere once again circulates through our blood as we become submerged in nature. It's almost like returning to the old homeland.

To enjoy the intensity and pure happiness of nature, we seek the company of whitetails. We descend to their level. We feel emulation toward them. We pursue them. We imitate and behave like them. This mystical union between hunter and whitetail is what it means to become one with nature. Of all those writers who have waxed most eloquently on this subject, Ortega best summarizes the point when he writes in his *Meditations* that in hunting we "instinctively shrink from being seen; we will avoid all noise while traveling; we will perceive all surroundings from the point of view of the animal, with the animal's peculiar attention to detail . . . Wind, light, temperature, ground contour, minerals, vegetation, all play a part; they are not simply there, but rather they *function,* they act . . . they intervene in the drama of the hunt from within itself, with concrete and full being."

Our deer hunting companions also serve important functions in the drama of the deer hunt. All deer hunters know this and recognize the ultimate importance of selecting good hunting companions. For in wilderness hunting, where the deer camp is isolated, group unity becomes essential. Just as one bad apple can spoil a bushel, the poor behavior of one individual can make or break the pleasure of a deer hunting trip. Indeed, our hunting partner represents perhaps one of the most significant elements of any successful deer hunt.

Throughout the years I have hunted in large groups where success ran very high in regard to the number of deer harvested, yet the pleasure of the hunt was greatly reduced by one or two individuals. I have also hunted with other groups where no deer were harvested, yet the experience remained a memorable one because of the pleasant character of the individual hunters. In choosing our hunting partners, we need to exercise a great deal of care: They should usually be close friends whose natural virtues are well

We hunt whitetails not necessarily to bring home venison, but consciously or unconsciously, to become a part of the spirituality of the earth, once part of us, but now largely isolated by concrete and asphalt. *Photo credit Erwin A. Bauer*

known in advance, and whose depth of interest in the sport closely matches that of our own. Under no circumstances should deer hunting ever become a competitive and selfish endeavor between individuals. The only place for selfishness on a November deer hunt, John Madson once wrote, "is in taking more than

The day after the close of the season. *Photo credit Erwin A. Bauer*

your share of work, discomfort, or disappointment."

The good deer hunting partner accepts adversity and the unchangeable with grace and a grin. The worst partner is undoubtedly the so-called "claimer," the individual who shoots and grabs, and eternally denies ever missing a shot. Ethical circumstances dictate that when you are uncertain as to who killed a deer, waive your claim and say you missed. No whitetail, not even a many-tined trophy,

is worth risking a friendship, particularly a long-standing friendship between landowner and invited guest.

The best definition of a true deer hunting partner is that formulated by John Madson in a booklet entitled *For the Young Hunter*. It applies to the veteran deer stalker as well. It reads as follows: "A real hunting partner is one who shares without asking a share in return, who gives without thinking, who places your well-being and pleasure above his own. Such

A long-ago deer hunter, doing it in style! *Photo credit Minnesota Historical Society*

a man may be rich and well-born, or a smelly old gaffer in bib overalls. But mark him well, wherever you find him. He is a gentleman, and a proper man to share your fire with.'' I am extremely fortunate in having found such a deer hunting companion; they seem to be remarkably rare in the course of one's lifetime.

The existence of deer hunting as we have known it for the past 50 years comes under daily attack from many quarters. One bitter attack appears in *Audubon* magazine, the magazine of the National Audubon Society, in a five-part series entitled *Bitter Harvest,* which began its publication in the May 1979 issue. While this misleading and somewhat confusing series of articles is definitely slanted against the deer hunter's behavior, it is

not exactly an authentic antihunting piece either. Yet, it certainly provoked a tremendous outburst of antihunting sentiment in this country. Consider, for example, an excerpt from a letter from one reader of *Audubon:* ''The only way to be fair to hunters is to give them their own medicine: gang up on them, one thousand to one; pursue, terrorize, trap, torture and shoot them with their own bullets and arrows. Then leave them to hobble wounded until they die.'' It is most unfortunate that *Audubon* should perpetuate such unwarranted emotionalism. Articles of this kind, however, illustrate the force and impetus of the antihunting movement in this country, a point that many deer hunters still overlook.

While we do not need to defend the sport of deer hunting, we do need to defend our deer hunting ethics. For if our sport is to exist in the future, we must work hard at improving our ethical behavior while in the field. Without delving deeply into the abstract dimension of hunting ethics, I should like to briefly examine a five-stage growth process which Professors Robert Jackson and Robert Norton of the University of Wisconsin—La Crosse recently conceptualized with regard to the waterfowl hunter. These five stages can apply to the deer hunter as well.

Jackson and Norton call the first stage of this developmental schemata *the shooter stage,* in which the novice seemingly needs to pull the trigger to test out his weapon's capabilities. Unfortunately, everything under the sun is shot at during this stage, including tin cans, signs, insulators, and worse, blackbirds and even hawks. Once this primitive need is satisfied, however, the hunter moves to stage two, *the limiting-out stage,* where bag-

"A real deer hunting partner is one who shares without asking a share in return, who gives without thinking, who places your well-being and pleasure above his own. Such a man may be rich and well-born, or a smelly old gaffer in bib overalls. But mark him well, wherever you find him. He is a gentleman, and a proper man to share your fire with."
—John Madson
Photo credit Minnesota Historical Society

ging game becomes the major objective. At this stage the hunter generally measures his success exclusively in terms of the number of birds or animals harvested. From this development level, the hunter moves to stage three, or *the trophy stage.* Here the deer hunter shoots bucks and trophy bucks only. Selectivity has finally manifested itself at this level.

From here the hunter graduates to *the methods stage,* a stage characterized by great intensity. At this stage the hunter is obsessed with methodology; countless volumes of how-to-books line the walls of his hunting den. At this stage the deer hunter acquires all of the most sophisticated equipment in the vast technological repertoire. Hunting at this stage becomes the most important dimension of this person's life. As Jackson and Norton observe, "It's what they do best, and they live for the opportunity to practice their expertise . . . Unfortunately many of these dedicated and experienced hunters have not yet accepted those self-imposed and voluntary controls which Aldo Leopold felt marked the ethical hunter."

Finally, after many years of hunting and at about the age of 40, *a mellowing out stage* appears in which the hunter finds satisfaction in the total hunting experience, in the camaraderie of the hunt, in the esthetics of nature, in the social life of the deer camp, and in the sublime solitude of the November woods. Harvesting whitetails now seems more symbolic than essential to the actual process of hunting itself. At this stage our knowl-edge and appreciation of all aspects of wildlife management and the environmental system which we share with all wildlife makes us as much a philosopher as a hunter—Aldo Leopold's dream come true! Hopefully, we will all reach this fifth and final stage of deer hunting well before the age of 40. Helping the beginning deer hunter to move through these stages as quickly as possible and without ethical violations represents the greatest challenge hunter education faces today.

Getting game at this fifth and final stage of deer hunting becomes only incidental

The author's father, with one of his many-tined trophies. The date was November 29, 1932. *Photo credit Robert Wegner*

to the lasting enjoyments of the mind. While deer hunting we harvest whitetails, but in participating in this sport we also become one with the wild and all its sights and sounds—a far greater consideration. For the November deer hunt means being alone in the forest, being able to realize more clearly one's hopes and aspirations; it means being able to reaffirm the road one has already taken on life's many journeys, and being able to renew oneself for the long, uncertain journey over the next ridge. When I am deer hunting, alone in the snow-clad hills of the North, the sense of stress and hurry is gone and time seems endless and remote.

The clearest way into autumn solitude is through a forest wilderness filled with whitetails. Only by going alone in silence, without a lot of civilized baggage, can one truly penetrate into the heart of the wild and the world of the whitetail. All other travel is mere dust and chatter. While traveling alone, nature's peace flows into every vein and civilized cares drop like autumn leaves. Solitude, tranquility and silence, a sense of oneness with all living things, and the awe with which we observe the whitetail . . . this is what deer hunting really means.

Being alone in the November woods sharpens one's sensibilities and makes one more alive to the ways of the wild. It awakens ideas and thoughts generally lost due to interruptions and occupational responsibilities. Autumn solitude allows you time to mull over such ideas, to penetrate their meaning, and to translate them in your mind. It brings back a sense of perspective and timelessness, a sense of being engulfed by something greater than yourself. Solitude is surely one of the most important aspects of the November deer hunt. When I reluctantly return from the

deer shack in late November, it is always a dramatic shock to again encounter the decadent sounds of civilization.

Another one of the real bonuses of the November deer hunt is the eating of venison, sweet and prime, over a wood-burning stove or a campfire, especially after a long day afield. My own preference with regard to this gourmet delight is simply to cut small butterfly steaks from the tenderloins, and place them on an open fire with a touch of lemon pepper. Of course, one also needs a glass or two of a fine Cabernet Sauvignon or Beaujolais to accompany such a festive occasion. When properly field-dressed and prepared, venison easily surpasses the taste of top-grade beef; it is also healthier than beef due to its lack of high levels of fat and cholesterol. Such rich protein, uncontaminated by chemicals or food preservatives, is fit for a king. One can understand why royalty in medieval times tried to claim possession of these animals.

For most deer hunters, the only animal's hide deemed of permanent value is one that retains its softness, toughness, pliability and warmth after being exposed to the natural elements. Such is the case with buckskin, which not only played a vital role in the economy of the woodland Indian tribes of early America, but made up a sizable element as a medium of exchange in the early American economic structure of the 19th century. While it takes a lot of deer hunting to make a full-length buckskin jacket, the effort is worth the investment. The leather is soft and immensely durable. One can hardly imagine better vests, gloves, bags or slippers than those made from buckskin. Buckskin has one disadvantage, however: When it gets wet, it soaks up water like a sponge and quickly sags and

This picture epitomizes the ideal deer camp that is seldom, if ever, achieved in reality. The average American deer camp, infinite in variety, falls somewhat short of this nostalgic ideal. Deer camps, like whitetail antlers, come in all sizes and shapes. Following are a few versions of what it looked like in the past . . .

One of the earliest deer camps on record existed in northern Michigan, near the banks of the famous Au Sable River, whose waters were the color of dark-brown sherry. During the height of the lumbering era, this deer camp consisted of a rickety barn, a broken-down blacksmith shop and a well-ventilated house of log construction. Just how well-ventilated Deer Camp Erwin actually was, we learn from the memoirs of one of its camp residents: "The ventilation of the deer shack was generous in the extreme. The roof was tight, but all around one found open chinks between the logs; through these the stars could be seen by anybody that had nothing better to do than look at them. Up through the middle of the floor and out through a big hole at the ridge-pole went the stove pipe, always hot enough to worry an insurance man." The residents of this deer camp slept on ticks filled with straw, and laid upon the floor. Since their consciences were always clear (a normal situation for most deer hunters), they slept with exceeding soundness. Some dreamt of giant bucks, others of rifles that wouldn't go off.

During the gun season of 1877, and ever since Michigan initiated her first regulated deer season in 1859, mighty hunters of the wilderness lived there, ate vast quantities of venison and bedewed the deer shack floor, pleasantly and copi-

ously, with strong infusions of Virginia plug. At 4:30 each morning the deer hunters were awakened by boss man Erwin's shout of "Breakfast, you lazy laggards," which was followed with the inevitable cry of "Daylight in the swamp!" The hunters slowly arose from their straw-filled mattresses and made their way to the first floor, where they found frying pans filled with sizzling rashers of bacon and pots of hot coffee in full blast—the aroma doing justice to famed Delmonico's. After a short trip to the "schmidt-haus," they sat down to a hearty meal of bacon, venison liver, boiled potatoes, fried onions and bread and butter.

"Coats were then buttoned up, rubber blankets and ammunition belts slung over shoulders, cartridge magazines filled, hatchets stuck into belts, rifles shouldered, and out we sallied into the darkness through which the faintest glimmer of gray was just showing in the East."

Thus, with high hopes the hale and hearty woodsmen of Deer Camp Erwin headed for their early morning stands in the deep thickets of Cedar Swamp. Nowhere on earth, at least for the first few hours, did hope bloom so eternal. Then a steadily falling, freezing rain soon changed the picture to a somewhat uncomfortable state of mind, where hands became numb and teeth chattered like "miniature castanets." Still, they refused to put on their heavy gloves for fear that they would hamper their shooting ability. As the day passed they stamped their feet and did the "London Cabman's exercise" with hands and arms to keep warm. Distant shots frequently reverberated throughout the forest. At camp that night, the lucky hunters had to tell again and again how they shot their big bucks of the 250-pound variety. For the

With the meat pole hanging heavy, the deer camp boys of yesteryear gather around the campfire to exchange tall tales and to tell again and again how they shot their big buck of the 250-pound variety. Deer Camp Erwin was clearly well planned and fitted out for comfort. Note the beer bottles on the table and the tin cup of elixir in the hand of the gentleman on the right. Note also the mirror and straight-edge razor nailed to the tree supporting the meat pole. *Photo credit State Historical Society of Wisconsin*

unsuccessful sportsmen, it was "wait until tomorrow." Their disappointment was quickly lessened by a superb meal of roasted venison, baked beans, fried onions and potatoes.

All deer camps need a boss man in residence, and Deer Camp Erwin was no exception in this regard. John Erwin of Cleveland, a gentleman at whose door lay the death of a grievous quantity of big-racked bucks, fit the bill to a tee. From one account we learn that his 70 years "imparted rigor and activity to his stalwart and symmetrical frame. Hale, hearty, capable of enduring all manner of fatigue, unerring with his rifle, full of the craft of the woods, and an inexhaustible fund of kindly humor, he was the soul of our deer camp." All 12 hunters were under his orders, and remained so until the deer hunt was over. According to one visiting

deer hunter from upstate New York, "He was implicitly obeyed; none of his orders were unpleasant; they simply implied the necessary discipline of successful deer camp hunting."

By the time these 12 deer hunters broke camp, 23 deer hung on the meat pole. It had been a successful outing in more ways than one. No one got lost. No visitor left camp hungry—or thirsty. The hunters paid well for local services, and treated the local people with courtesy. Indeed, over the years the deer hunters at Camp Erwin developed a long-lasting friendship with local loggers and farmers. After a rough ride aboard horse-drawn wagons, the hunters boarded a train for Detroit. En route they enjoyed a leisurely meal with cigars and whiskey. They arrived safely in Detroit with a ton and a half of venison or thereabouts. After saying their farewells, they all went their individual ways, thus ending an "expedition with plenty of wholesome recreation to make one's recollection of it wholly pleasant."

In the winter of 1910, a group of Wisconsin deer hunters purchased a 600-acre tract of land on the shores of Lake Laura in Vilas County in an attempt to enjoy excellent deer hunting and wholesome recreation for many years to come. The purchase included several vacated dwellings of an old timber company. In March of the same year, the hunters formed a corporation, the articles of incorporation being filed with the Secretary of State. So far as we know, Deer Foot Lodge was one of the first corporations ever chartered to hunt deer.

An old woodsman by the name of Charlie Anderson was given charge of the property, and agreed to live at Deer Foot throughout the year. "Old Charlie" was apparently quite honest and dependable enough, except in one respect. Three or four times a year he was given to spells of intense intoxication that generally lasted as long as his money lasted. This strange and somewhat quaint character was never known to touch liquor when deer camp was in session, however. Actually, according to the camp record, "it was Charlie who made Deer Foot Lodge possible, for as caretaker and quasi-host, any member of the Lodge could go there at any time of the year, and find a warm shelter, food, and a hearty welcome."

The annual hunt at Deer Foot began on the 10th of November and ended on November 30. Twenty-two men from all walks of life generally filled the camp's four buildings to the utmost capacity. Ac-

After a rough ride aboard horse-drawn wagons, these hunters boarded a train for Detroit. En route, they enjoyed a leisurely meal followed by cigars and whiskey. They arrived safely in Detroit with venison weighing a ton and a half, or thereabouts. *Photo credit State Historical Society of Wisconsin*

cording to the camp's log, there was no formality about breakfast. "Some were on time, some were late, some were very late." But all hunters in residence were on their stands long before they could even see the sights on their rifles—Rule Number One.

Like many modern deer camps, Deer Foot Lodge had a well-articulated set of rules. Some of them even contained the added dimension of humor. Consider, for example, the following rules from the camp's record: "Don't hold mass meetings in the woods any more than you can help. At such meetings there is only a slight attendance of deer. If you have to get together for confab, do it silently like red Indians or shadows. After you have killed a deer, look on those that are left dispassionately, not avidly or voraciously; consider the claims of the amateurs who haven't killed a deer and give them a chance. Don't rub it into them by killing more and thus deprive them of their right. Tub in the nearby lake every two or three days, first breaking the ice. Nothing is more conducive to good feeling than this."

Deer Foot Lodge also exercised very explicit rules with regard to the care and handling of guns. "No one under any circumstances was to bring a loaded gun indoors. No one cleaned or even handled guns in camp except the guides, who carefully examined every gun before cleaning so as to be certain that there were no cartridges remaining in the barrel or the magazine. No one was to shoot at any object until he was certain that it was a deer." Deer Foot Lodge never experienced a single hunting accident in its entire 25-year history.

Throughout its history Deer Foot Lodge tended to be a family-oriented affair, con-

sisting of several close-knit families which tended to socialize with one another throughout the year, not just during the deer hunting season. Because the members of the lodge and their sons took up most of the available room, outside guests were only invited on rare occasions.

The present-day deer camp hasn't changed much in this regard. According to two University of Wisconsin sociologists, it seems apparent that strong family ties not only represent one of the key factors in developing and sustaining an interest in deer hunting, but also strongly influence the establishment of certain deer camp traditions. One deer hunter, for example, summarized this point quite well when he exclaimed that "My father not only taught us to be hunters, but also my cousins. Together we make a party of seven that all hunt the same way, think the same way, and wait all year to be together for the deer hunt."

This profound sense of togetherness and camaraderie remains an essential ingredient of the American deer camp, and reveals itself in the following entry of the camp's log, which was written in response to the death of one of the camp's members—a certain M. C. Ewing, a judge from Wausau, Wisconsin: "In the death of M. C. Ewing, Deer Foot Lodge suffered an irreparable loss and there is left a vacancy which can never be filled. Perhaps there is no better test of genuineness of character than the trials and hardships of deer camp and no place where men more freely and unreservedly disclose their true character. In the field and around the campfire, he contributed his full share of all that goes to make friendship and companionship really worthwhile. His solicitude for the welfare of others, and his vast knowledge of the habits and ways of the wild, all found full scope for exercise and made him in deer camp as everywhere a leader.''

The liquidation of Deer Foot Lodge occurred in the fall of 1935. The last nostalgic entry in the camp's log reveals in a vivid way what deer camp really means for the American hunter: "There probably will never be another Deer Foot Lodge, or anything like it for our crowd, and it does hurt to have it pass out of our lives. Of course, we cannot be deprived of our deer camp memories and we can treasure them for the balance of the time we are permitted to strive for existence and struggle with the Depression. Deer Foot Lodge really made a record and brought everyone of us closer together.''

Sometime around 1916, another group of deer hunters from Ladysmith, Wisconsin, banded together and formed the Bucks Club. These deer hunters, like those of Deer Foot Lodge and Deer Camp Erwin, loved to chase the whitetail, and prided themselves in their skills of woodsmanship. They too acquired an old log cabin that had formerly been part of an old abandoned lumber camp. This particular camp was located in the Blue Hills of northern Rusk County. Every fall, when the deer hunting fever stirred in their blood, they dropped everything and headed for their deer shack in the hills with a persistence matched only by Jack Frost himself.

The daughter of one of these hunters describes the scene with great eloquence: "As a youngster I was always greatly mystified and awed by this November ritual of deer hunting and the inevitable exodus to Bucks Camp. Several weeks before the event took place, my father began to acquire a kind of glow, and the smell

of gun oil and rubber boots hung in the air. An object referred to as a pack sack was brought forth and filled with wool socks, flannel shirts, and more to the point, I thought, a big bar of German sweet chocolate for quick energy in case he got lost in the woods. I knew what happened on the home front while the men were off on this hunting foray. My mother locked more doors than usual; we got to sleep later, and all the neighborhood women and children gathered for a manless Thanksgiving dinner.''

Like the members of Deer Foot Lodge, the hunters of the Bucks Camp were compatible by nature and quite willing to share work loads. The right kind of human chemistry in this regard is what makes a deer camp function properly, and the Bucks Camp was a classic example. Their camaraderie was not only evident in the field, but at the card table as well. For aside from their guns, knives, hunting licenses and red clothing, the most important requirement of their camp was a pocketful of nickels. Their deer camp card games—whether smear, sheepshead or poker—were played in earnest, as we learn from the following entry of their diary: "Le Blanc got us up at 5:30 a.m. for pancakes. Everybody sat down just as though they were real deer hunters and the pancakes disappeared. Then most of the bunch calmly received the report of some hardy soul that the day outside was a little unpleasant and decided not to venture out into the inclement weather, but got their exercise playing smear.''

While this entry in the camp's log contains more humor than fact, it seems evident that many smear games transpired, and that while playing smear a great deal of sundry libations were passed around the table. Their policy with respect to wine-n-whitetails was summarized in one word, however: MODERATION. With regard to drinking in deer camp, the members of the Bucks Camp wholeheartedly agreed on one proposition: "A man may drink wine, even carry a little with him on an expedition, and be both a gentleman and a sportsman, provided he has force of character sufficient to stop when he has partaken moderately."

All agreed that those deer hunters who need three shots of whiskey for every shot at a buck deserve to be chastised in a way that delicacy forbids mentioning in print. That the whiskey flask should be rigidly excluded from deer hunting, where victory in the field is the hard-earned result of clearheadedness and steady nerves, is a fact that all American deer camps should consider.

Many similarities existed between the Bucks Camp and Deer Foot Lodge, and I am sure that many of us recognize some of their characteristics in our own deer camps. Both camps were located on the shores of a lake that provided the be-whiskered deerslayers with the opportunity to "tub in the lake" despite the weather. Both camps provided year-round recreation for their members, including bird hunting, fishing, skiing and other camp activities. Both camps produced literary records of real merit, which inspire all deer camps to faithfully keep a daily log of events. As one deer hunter observed, "It is fun to recount those occurrences years hence in the company of those whose deeds and misadventures have been recorded in the log." In both camps music-making activities enlivened the life of the party, with the hunters themselves writing their own lyrics to well-known tunes. The Bucks Camp even had a Victrola that pumped out jazz sounds

much sweeter and peppier than their musty deer tales of the past. And finally, both camps tended to be family oriented in nature.

BANG! goes a rifle, and like steel springs released from horrendous pressure, deer abound in every direction. BANG! goes another shot. BANG! BANG! BANG! When the gun smoke finally clears after 41 seasons of intensive deer hunting at Buckshot Inc., the record indicates that 230 white-tailed bucks went to the meat pole. When and where did this success story take place?

The Buckshot story had its informal beginnings in 1928, when a group of avid deer hunters began buying land near Cable, Wisconsin, for the expressed purpose of hunting deer. Following the tradition of Deer Foot Lodge, the Buckshot Group eventually purchased more than 400 acres of land, and incorporated under Wisconsin Statutes for the stated purpose of "hunting, fishing and other recreational activities."

Buckshot Inc. was special in one important respect, as we learn from the memoirs of one of its founding members: "It was quite a straight-laced group with great emphasis on hunter safety. Liquor and gambling were not permitted. Also, one of the wives did most of the cooking and someone almost always said 'Grace' at the always big evening meal. I recall one of my fellow faculty members saying that he didn't think there was a deer hunting camp like that in North America." As the years passed, the number of hunters steadily increased until the annual deer hunt became the major event of the year.

Like its predecessors, Buckshot Inc. kept an accurate record of its camp activities. From the record book of this deer camp, a 12- by 14-inch buckskin-bound volume, we learn that the initial group consisted of only eight deer hunters in 1928. But after gathering at the same place each season for more than 41 years, the hunting group eventually included over 144 persons who had attended camp at one time or another.

The group of hunters consisted of 19 different families, which became a very closely knit social group as the years went on. Birthdays and weddings within the Buckshot Group were events to be celebrated and remembered. Featured social event of the year, however, was the annual deer hunters' dinner, held on the last Saturday night before opening day. All of the hunters, past and present, and their families were invited. The menu, besides venison, frequently included bear, moose, antelope and elk. "Hundreds of pictures were shown, stories told and even secrets shared. This annual get-together, the eating together, the sharing of experiences, and just being together was always looked forward to with great expectancy. Without it, the Buckshot story would not have been complete."

While many of the camp's hunters went to their "happy hunting grounds" during the first 40 years of its existence, it seems remarkable that this extraordinary group survived the generation gap, with sons, sons-in-law and grandsons still perpetuating the Buckshot tradition right up to this day. Undoubtedly, the camp log played a significant role in this development. For as each tenderfoot joined the camp, he generally read the log and learned the history of those who came before him.

Like most deer hunters, the Buckshot Group loved to tell stories; and like most deer camps, their stories had the ten-

dency to acquire an extra added inch of fiction with each recitation, bordering at times on pure Irish malarky. Consider, for example, the story of O. B., the great bear hunter from the North who apparently had to negotiate with the Bear Haulers Union to get his bear out of Big Swamp. Actually, it's reported that he was so deeply impressed with his accomplishment in shooting the bear that he mailed a postcard home to his wife which contained the following inscription on it: "God made the mountains and he made the valleys / He made the giant oak and the little blades of grass / He made the oceans and the little drops of water / He made me and he made a Bear Hunter."

Or how about the story of big Al, who fired just one quick shot across the long canyon at a rapidly departing "Harvey Wall Hanger." When one of the younger hunters ran up to him and shouted, "Did you get him?" Al calmly replied, "You heard me shoot boy, didn't you?"

And so it goes . . .

While each of these camps has its own individual history, its own stories and favorite spots, each of them represents a part of the great clan, kin to all other deer camps in American deer country. Each of them teaches us a lesson; from each of them we acquire a better understanding of this American institution. After studying the history of various American deer camps from the past, and after living in various deer camps during the past 20 years, I have reached the following conclusions about this great American institution.

First of all, these four historic deer camps document something which many deer hunters know perfectly well: Deer hunting is a social event and often a fam-

The American deer camp documents something that many of us know perfectly well: Deer hunting is a social event and often a family affair that takes place in a log cabin, a large tent, a trailer on wheels, a quick lean-to of bark or a tar paper shack nestled way back in the woods. *Photo credit State Historical Society of Wisconsin*

ily affair that takes place in a log cabin, a large tent, a trailer on wheels, a quick lean-to of bark or a tar paper shack nestled way back in the woods. And that enduring symbol of deer camp—regardless of its physical nature—is still with the modern deer hunter.

We learn from Tom Heberlein, a rural sociologist, for example, that 60 percent of all deer hunters cannot find anything in their lives that would be an adequate substitute for the joys and experiences of the traditional American deer camp. Eighty-eight percent of them indicate that the social contacts with hunting companions, friends and relatives at specific deer camps in the woods are of the utmost importance. The chase of the elusive whitetail, the deep sense of the November tradition and the camaraderie of camp life apparently fill a niche which nothing else can equal. As one veteran deer hunter from Vermont recently remarked, "If someone asked me where I'd most like

to be if the choice were free as my fancy, I'd say . . . DEER CAMP."

Secondly, nothing feels or smells so good as deer camp on the night before the hunt. Indeed, nothing brings the same warm comfort as thoughts of deer camp camaraderie. No sweeter sleep ever refreshes a tired man or boy as he falls asleep in deer camp. Or does it? Here's one deer hunter's opinion on this question: "There was venison that first night for all of us, and homemade breads and pies too. The venison sizzled and filled the camp with magic smells. We ate by the light of the fireplace, and the men told deer stories. I just listened by the fire, with the shadows of men and boys playing on the walls. Outside, a moon played across cold December hills. In bed, I listened as the embers died, and the old cast-iron stove cooled and snapped. I lay under an old buffalo robe, the legacy of bygone sleigh riders, and felt the cold creep into the shack. I could not sleep but imagined great-racked bucks browsing through leafless hardwoods on the mountain. Then suddenly my father was jogging my shoulder in the dark and I heard a match scratch. Breakfast was in the making.''

Thirdly, deer shacks are not just for the young at heart. I know of many men of 65 and over who long to get into a deer shack to mess about with pots and pans, and who eventually stir up quite a delectable dish. Each deer camp has its chief cook, and many of these cooks tend to be of the senior citizen variety. It would not be an exaggeration to say that many deer camps are built around the chief cook and his potbelly stove. Actually, as one deer hunter recalls, ''Men may not cook a meal all year at home, but let deer camp call and a million gourmet cooks are born overnight. It's a secret kept from women—and don't you dare tell it—but the best meals of a hunter's life are eaten at deer camp.''

If you doubt the veracity of this statement, consider, for example, the menu of Deer Camp Hiawatha, a camp located somewhere in the wilderness of northern Michigan sometime between 1897 and 1903:

DEER CAMP MENU

SUPPER
Venison steak
Fried Bacon   Fried Onions
Potatoes With Jackets On
Cucumber Pickles   Cold Baked Beans
Buckwheat Cakes   Canned Plums
Clover Honey   Crabapple Jelly
Fried Cakes
Hot Coffee—Rich And Black
Spring Water From Silver
Creek

Say, ye deer camp enthusiasts and lovers of dark, red, flavored venison—would

Bringing home "the bacon," one way or another. *Photo credit Minnesota Historical Society*

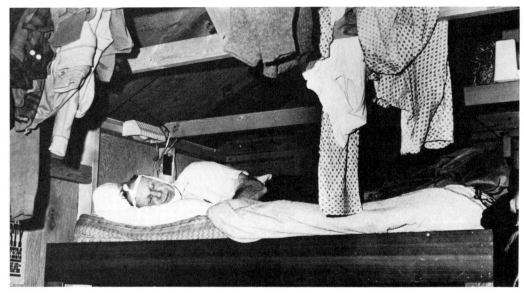

Deer camp headgear, invented to prevent snoring. *Photo credit State Historical Society of Wisconsin*

you have liked that feast? Give most deer hunters such a menu and a whiff of Hoppe's No. 9 and they're off to the deer shack to be sure. Such a meal not only delights the heart of the sportsman, but fills his soul with silent joy. Sipping red wine and smoking pipes around the blazing logs must have been a sheer delight after that glorious feast! Following in that tradition, many Americans at the end of a long day afield still sit before their cozy fire, draining draughts of October ale, puffing at their pipes, spinning out yarns half untold, and watching the fragrant blue smoke ascend toward the rafters in graceful little clouds.

Fourthly, success can be a powerful and motivating factor in determining where deer hunters go to do their hunting. In a sociological study on the role of deer camps in relation to deer hunting success—done in 1972, under the auspices of the New York State Department of Environmental Conservation—we learn that 27 percent of all deer taken for the township which their study focused on were the direct result of camp-related hunting. Simply put, the deer camp generally lends itself well to a concerted plan where individuals are assigned various roles, such as leader, driver and stander. Consequently, these individuals do their task and share in the group success. As one researcher observed, "A deer bagged by an individual is a group accomplishment. The more success, the greater the accomplishment; productivity and group cohesiveness strengthen each other. As the group continues to hunt together the backlog of experience, accomplishment and enjoyment builds."

Hunting success, according to this New York study, remained markedly greater for deer camps whose owners were also residents of the area in which the shack or cabin was located, as one might suspect. Poor success occurred at deer camps whose owners resided elsewhere in New York state than the township under study. Researchers also noted an almost nil rate of success for deer camps of out-of-state owners. The documented illegal kill associated with deer camp-related hunting, however, was extremely high. In 1968, according to this study, 53 percent of the deer taken in deer camp situations were taken illegally. Apparently, deer hunters who hunt in groups still need to work on their deer camp ethics.

In a similarly related study on the group dynamics of deer camp, Professors Jackson and Norton of the University of Wisconsin—La Crosse, conclude that hunting on your own land ranks high as a condition affecting the tendency to violate. While the local people frequently blame outsiders or city slickers for deer hunting violations, this study's findings showed that the "hometowner" and landowner are generally the ones to watch. Sociological studies seem to indicate that many deer camps have not really come to terms with violations and violators.

Fifthly, a deer camp seems to represent a contagious disease that converts comfort-conscious city slickers into bewhiskered woodsmen who can satisfy themselves, at least for a few days, with the most primitive type of existence. Unfortunately, many deer hunters who were never brought up among broken-down deer shacks in the popple will probably fail to understand the ultimate fascination of preparing for the adventurous environment of deer camp, or the thrill of creeping away from a woodland shack on the opening morning as the dim black horizon stretches out in the distance. Deer hunters not acquainted with shacks in the wilderness will simply not feel the fas-

cination of opening up the shutters of a clammy and long shut camp, of starting the fire and arranging their hunting gear with the utmost precision, or of sweeping out the dusty cobwebs and the long-defunct bats from underneath the stove; nor will they experience the immense satisfaction of seeing an isolated shack rapidly acquire the warmth and comfort of a miniature home in the wild. And deer hunters who opt for the modern conveniences of home clearly miss out on some of the interesting surprises, picturesque experiences and memories provided by the deer shack.

Sixthly, deer camp vividly reminds us of our own human sense of insecurity. As I write these lines I can hear the northeastern wind beating the branches of the forest trees until they exude those weird sounds—sounds of a violent storm, with eerie rustlings of scattering leaves, twigs and branches. Suddenly, a dramatic rain and wind storm rages against the deer shack with unabated fury. The rain beats down on my tar paper shack like the noise of roaring muzzleloaders. The moaning sounds and flying spray roll off the shack, and heavy gusts of wind hammer the abandoned grain binder out back. It is a terrible night. I begin to realize how utterly helpless is man in such times of nature's wrath, especially when she threatens to toss her lightning bolts against my shimmed-up abode. How frail and small we seem under these conditions. How insecure is life and all living, animate things. Yet, my deer shack is snug and cozy, a fire snaps and crackles in the potbelly stove, and the savory smell of roasting venison penetrates the air around me. The shack remains aglow with candle power, and the author writes until late into the night.

Clinton County, Pennsylvania, deer hunting camps (circa 1903). *Photo credit Pennsylvania Historical and Museum Commission*

The deer shack boys arrive at District Station #4. *Photo credit State Historical Society of Wisconsin*

Finally, by way of conclusion: some individuals take wine to stimulate them, others take tobacco; but I take the deer shack with all its mystic charms of forest solitude. Deer camp is, after all, not so much a physical thing as a state of mind. Undoubtedly, the enjoyment to be had from a deer shack, log cabin, tent or lean-to in some vast wilderness is due somewhat to temperament, and not every individual will be able to get even a smack of it. As for myself, each trip to deer camp proves my susceptibility to deer camp camaraderie, on the one hand, and to the charm of forest solitude, on the other. Give me a weekend of freedom at the deer shack and I will experience original ideas varying with every cloud of wood smoke. For deer camp represents a time of tall imaginings and grand expectations. While deer camp obviously means many things to many people, for me it means studying the ways of nature and hunting whitetails from dawn to dusk—in a word, experiencing the ultimate in freedom, and thus gaining a new lease on life. Yes, your deer shack in the popple is undoubtedly your greatest possession. Cherish it! As Aldo Leopold once wrote, ''It is here that we seek—and still find—our meat from God.''

Chapter 18

Buckskin

I think most of us would agree that a woodlot without whitetails is like a wall without pictures. I also think we would agree that much of the thrill and charm of deer hunting is influenced by our historical knowledge of the whitetail's role in the romantic days of the Indian and buckskin-clad woodsmen. In this chapter I examine the role of buckskin in history, and elucidate the famous characteristics of genuine deerskin—the aristocrat of leathers.

From the derivation of the word, we learn that "buckskin" has at least several different meanings. First of all, it generally refers to the soft, velvet-like, pliable leather made from the skins of deer— more particularly, to breeches made of buckskin. Historically, in this regard, the old Leatherstocking hunter in his fringed buckskin suit was still a familiar figure on the streets of Lexington, Kentucky, as late as 1797. Given the current interest in the smoke pipe—in muzzleloading, black powder, buckskinning and so on— it would appear that Freddy Frontloader is not merely an artifact of the Old West, but epitomizes a new breed of men and women who are not content to merely read about history, but desire to re-enact it. Indeed, the buckskin-clad muzzleloader is again blossoming forth in full regalia, feeling a spiritual kinship of brotherhood, no doubt, with those dead men of olden days who also knew the exhilaration of deer hunting in more primitive times.

Buckskin also refers to the nickname of the American troops during the Revolutionary War, and is thus synonymous in meaning with "a native American." One of George Washington's biographers stresses this meaning when he writes, "George Washington a buck skin! . . . impossible! he was certainly a European." In the English tradition of tailoring, buckskin also denotes a kind of strong-twilled woolen fabric used for trousers that is highly milled to about 27 inches and then cropped and finished with the pile or nap so shorn as to show the texture through it. In the Western states the word describes horses with a grayish-yellow color. In common usage the word has also become a proper noun. In central Colorado, for example, we find Buckskin Mountain and in Big Timber, Montana, we encounter The Buckskin Press.

A little-known historical fact reveals that American deer hunters donated some 238,262 deer skins in 1943 to make gloves, jackets and mukluks for the armed forces during the Second World War. Similarly, during the Korean War the demand for buckskin gloves for front line soldiers was so great that it completely exhausted the entire national supply. Indeed, buckskin has been used for a variety of purposes throughout history.

Many historians would agree that the white-tailed deer, more than any other animal, played a very important role in the building of our nation. Not only did they sustain and clothe the pioneers and feed the soldiers of the Revolutionary War, but they made it possible for trappers and explorers to survive as they pushed the frontier westward. Venison clearly played a more significant role in the colonial diet of the 16th, 17th and 18th centuries than beef. One can hardly imagine what the exploration and development of America would have been like without the white-tailed deer.

Even before colonial times, the Indian inhabitants of this land depended to a large degree on the whitetail for food, clothing and a great deal of folklore. The entire body of the deer furnished the Indian with so many items of daily use that it would be impossible to mention them all. Henry W. Shoemaker in his *Pennsylvania Deer and their Horns* (1915), summarizes them quite succinctly: "The bowstring was often made of the green deer skin; the shoulder blade was used as a hoe; the prongs of the horns were used as flint-choppers, scrapers, etc.; the heads were used in various ceremonies, and the antlers were symbols of power and so of chieftainship; the teeth and small bones were used as dice in various games; the small bones were made into needles for sewing the hides with thread made out of the sinew, and the bone and horns were carved as ornaments. In fact, there was hardly any part of the deer which was not made use of by the Indian for food, shelter, clothing, arms, agricultural implements, household utensils, decorations, games, fishing tackle, etc."

During the colonial period, deer skin quickly became a major item of trade with European countries. According to records of His Majesty's Custom Service, for example, almost 3 million pounds of buckskin from some 600,000 whitetails were shipped to England from Savannah, Georgia, between 1755 and 1773. By the middle of the 18th century an average of 30,000 to 40,000 deer skins were shipped annually to Europe from several different Southern ports. The same situation occurred far to the North as well. According to Robert Donovan's *Hunting Whitetail Deer* (1978), "Colonial records indicate that in Florida during the 1750s white-tailed deer hides traded for use as leather exceeded the monetary value of all other trade commodities combined.

The annual export of hides from Charles Town during the period of 1739 to 1762 fluctuated between 131,000 and 355,000 pounds depending on hunter luck and the state of local warfare. Deer skins were so widely accepted during the 1760s that they were taken in payment at a standard rate of about eighteen pence per pound in the hair.''

As a medium of exchange, buckskin made up a sizable element in the early American economic structure of the 18th century, particularly when money was scarce. As an example, the citizens of the short-lived State of Franklin (Tennessee as we know it today) in 1784 paid their civil officials a salary in deer skins. The Governor received 1000 deer skins per year and the Chief Justice 500. Lesser officials received a specified number of smaller pelts. In addition to authorizing the payment of salaries in buckskin, the general assembly of the State of Franklin even made it lawful for the payment of all land taxes, as well as for certain other commodities, to be paid in deer skins— one deer skin equaling six shillings.

As market hunting continued throughout the 19th century, an astonishing number of whitetails were killed for the hides alone. In Minnesota, Michigan and Wisconsin (to identify just a few states), tens of thousands of deer were killed, and many of them for their hides only. As Otis Bersing reports in his *A Century of Wisconsin Deer*, ''In dealing with the Indians, the white trader handled thousands of deerskins each year. Skins were classified in the market as buck, doe, and fawn. The early French traders also sold skins by the pound as red skins or summer coat, blue skins or fall coat, and gray skins or winter coat. Light and heavy shaved skins were also sold. In the 1830s at Green Bay,

skins sold for 12 to 18 cents a pound. Thousands were sold . . . In 1804-05, Malhiot, a French clerk with the Northwest Fur Company stationed at Lac du Flambeau, inventoried almost 10,000 deerskins taken by traders in an area now known as Iron, Oneida, and Vilas Counties.''

Around 1803, Michael Curot, a trader, reports exchanging rum for buckskin and tells of similar exchanges of an inferior grade of brandy for deer skins at his port on Yellow Lake in Burnett County.

In various parts of Texas, so many deer skins were baled and transported that it appeared that buckskin was the main commodity produced in that state. An early Texas trader operating in Indian country by the name of George Barnard shipped no less than 75,000 deer skins between 1844 and 1853. At his death he remained one of the wealthiest men in Texas—the foundation of his fortune having been laid in buckskin. As restrictive game laws were passed, these abusive days of market hunting and trafficking in deer hides soon came to a close. These records, however, testify to the importance of the whitetail in the economy and early development of America. Not only did deer skins serve as a medium of exchange between whites, but as the currency *par excellence* between red men and white men alike. Historically, a buckskin became a sort of standard of value; things were sold for so many ''bucks.'' Hence our slang phrase, of which so few people know the origin. Indeed, early American economics might well have been termed ''buck-conomics.'' For any way you look at it, a lot of the bucks involved in deer hunting, both past and present, are of the kind you can spend. When the whitetail is placed in this context, one can understand the desire of many people today to see this unique animal replace the bald eagle as our national symbol. It would seem that early American history provides data to support their sentiment.

For most modern-day deer hunters, the only animal's hide deemed of permanent value is one that retains its softness, toughness, pliability and warmth even after being exposed to the natural elements. Such is the case with butter-soft and butter-colored buckskin. T.S. Van Dyke's statement that "for durability buckskin is as important as it is to the hero of a sporting romance," represents no exaggeration. The leather is soft on the one hand and immensely durable on the other. One can hardly imagine more durable and longer-lasting vests, gloves, bags or moccasins than those made from buckskin. No surprise! Henry Wadsworth Longfellow pointed this out to us as early as 1855, when he wrote in his *Song of Hiawatha*:

"For durability buckskin is as important as it is to the hero of a sporting romance."
—T.S. Van Dyke
Photo credit Leonard Lee Rue III

Hiawatha had mittens, Minjekahwun,
Magic mittens made of deer-skin;
When upon his hands he wore them,
He could smite the rocks asunder,
He could grind them into powder.
He had moccasins enchanted,
Magic moccasins of deer-skin;
When he bound them round his ankles,
When upon his feet he tied them,
At each stride a mile he measured!

From his lodge went Hiawatha,
Dressed for travel, armed for hunting;
Dressed in deer-skin shirt and leggings,
Richly wrought with quills and wampum;
On his head his eagle-feathers,
Round his waste his belt of wampum,
In his hand his bow of ash-wood,
Strung with sinews of the deer;

In his quiver oaken arrows,
Tipped with jasper, winged with feathers;
With his mittens, Minjekahwun,
With his moccasins enchanted.

Buckskin formed the clothing for Indian and roving pioneer alike; it covered the moccasined feet of all who ventured along the woodland trails of early America. Hiawatha's clothes of buckskin were soft, pliable, gentle to the touch and easy to sew. One can understand Hiawatha's love for buckskin. It is warmer than cloth of equal weight. Innumerable tests have proved it to be the warmest of all leathers. It washes like cloth, and is more wind-resistant than any other cloth. With its ability to cut the penetration of cold wind, it is understandable that the famed pony express riders preferred it to any other clothing. Thorns will not pierce it, brush will not rip it, nor will burrs or stick-tights fasten themselves to it. As a result, buckskin retains an eternal and universal appeal. In his *Woodcraft* (1939), Bernard S. Mason characterized this byproduct of the harvested whitetail in eloquent words befitting an American tradition: "Perhaps those who have never spent long evenings beside a little campfire in the woods, or knelt over glowing coals to cook their meals will fail to understand the eternal appeal of buckskin, but to those who have, no word is needed. The magic of woodsmoke is in it, the most stirring of all perfumes is of it! Wherever it goes in the city world it carries with it perpetually and abundantly that matchless aromatic lure of the wilds, to fill the room with a restless urge to *go, go, go away from here*. It is literally steeped with incense of wood smoke."

BUCKSKIN YIELDS

Dressed Deer Weights	Hide Size	Approximate Yield
90–130 lbs.	Small	6–8 sq. ft.
130–175 lbs.	Medium	9–11 sq. ft.
175–200 lbs.	Large	12–15 sq. ft.
Over 200 lbs.	Extra-Large	16–18 sq. ft.

One average-size deerskin yields enough leather for 3 pairs of gloves.
Moccasins require about 3 sq. ft.
Handbags require 4 to 6 sq. ft.
Jackets and coats require 30 to 40 sq. ft.
Purses, wallets, key cases, etc., are made from remaining scrap leather.

The average deer hide weighs between 10 to 12 pounds, and contains about 8 to 10 square feet of usable buckskin, whether used for moccasins or an elegant full-length coat for the deer hunting widow. According to William Monypeny Newsom, buckskin is toughest in the red (referring to the summer coat), thickest in the blue (as the autumn coat is called) and thinnest in the gray (referring to the winter coat). The blue skin, most whitetail-scholars agree, is most valuable—referring, of course, to autumn buckskin. An explanation for this peculiarity lies in the fact that deer hair of the winter coat is larger in diameter than autumn hair, although it grows out of the same follicles. But because it is larger, the grain of leather from a winter-killed deer is coarser than that of the autumn hide.

Even the scars or surface imperfections of deer skin merely represent a natural characteristic of the hide. In fact, they attest to the genuineness of the leather and enhance its natural beauty. In short, genuine deer skin represents the ultimate in esthetic appeal, comfort and durability. While wool wears out, buckskin seems to go on forever. It wears and wears, keeping its good looks, and far outlasting more conventional leathers. It was indeed fortunate for both the Indian and the white man that the whitetail was so extremely plentiful during the early days of our nation. To this day the image of fine leather accessories made from genuine deer skin lingers on in the back of the deer hunter's mind as he stalks whitetails.

After stalking the whitetail, the moment of success eventually comes, when the grand old monarch of the woods lies before you, with all his imposing dignity. No other process deserves more attention, from this vantage point, than that of skinning your deer, especially with regard to buckskin—the exquisite end result of all your deer hunting efforts. For the process of skinning remains something of an art; the art being to remove the skin only, without excess meat attached and without making accidental incisions through the hide. Unfortunately many deer hides are ruined each year during the skinning process because deep knife cuts form weak spots and blemishes in the finished leather. Dragging your trophy long distances over sharp sticks and rocks also causes the same blemishes in the finished leather, and should be avoided at all costs. Remember, as the hide is stretched and buffed during the tanning process, these weak spots eventually form holes in the leather. The hide should be pulled off as much as possible, rather than cut off. Skinning, it is important to note, is made much easier if done while the carcass is still warm; after the animal is chilled or frozen, you almost have to whittle it off. While warm, the hide can almost be pulled off the carcass without the use of a knife.

As soon as the hide has been removed from the deer, lay the skin out flat in a cool, dry place, flesh side up. Remove all flesh from the hide. Leave the remaining tallow on the hide. The tallow helps to keep the hide soft. Apply plenty of salt immediately . . . the kind that is used in water softeners or for livestock . . . and rub it in well with your hand or a stiff-bristled scrubbing brush. Use about three pounds of medium-coarse salt for each hide. If fine table salt is used, apply four to five pounds to each hide. If in doubt, use more than needed. Many tanning experts recommend that you should not use rock salt, since it lacks the sur-

face area that finer salt has. Wait until the hide is cured before you roll or fold it up, so that the salt can draw out the water and blood and work completely through the hide, thus setting the hair and preventing it from slipping. On the following day it is best to shake off the sopping-wet salt, and re-salt the whole hide.

Do not leave the curing hide in the sun, but rather in a shady, well-aired location. After about two or three days the salt will form a crust, indicating that the hide can now be folded (flesh side in), and prepared for shipment. When placed in a solid carton and tied securely with heavy-duty twine, you can be assured that the hide will arrive at the tannery in good condition, without excessive draining of water or blood while en route. Send the hide to the tanner or taxidermist immediately. Don't wait until it smells bad, or until mildew and bugs destroy it. To pay the lowest shipping rates by truck, mark the package and bill of lading "Green Salted Deer Hides." After your hide arrives at the tannery, it is marked with a steel punch. The punch pierces a letter and several numbers in the hide. These numbers coincide with the company's file card on which the record of your hide is kept until the tanning process has been complete.

Frozen or unsalted hides should not be shipped to a tannery. Folding or bending dry, unsalted hides causes grain cracks and breaks the thin outer layer of skin—all of which damages and spoils the appearance of the leather. If for some reason you must ship dried hides, be sure to ship them in a very large and durable container so that they will not be bent or crushed in transit. It is best to avoid this situation if you can. Unfortunately, more leather is spoiled or ruined by neglect on the part of the hunter in preserving the hide than by anything else. Remember, properly preserved deer hides make one of the finest leathers in the world—unexcelled for softness and esthetic appeal! With its rustic spontaneity, buckskin clothing represents the symbol of the American outdoorsman, regardless of his race, color or occupation.

After arriving in America, the Pilgrims soon discovered that the Indians were especially well-versed in the process of tanning deer skins. The Crow tribe, in particular, was especially adept in the process of soft buckskin tanning, which even today has scarcely been improved upon. They used a rather unusual method, as we learn from Charles D. Spotts' *The Story of Leather* (1973): "The Crow-Indians bathed the deer hides in a solution of lye (wood ash) obtained from camp fire ashes. With the hair thus loosened and thereafter removed, the skins were stretched out to dry. The brains of the buffalo or elk were rubbed on the skin and worked into the pores by hand. A hole was then dug in the ground in which a small fire was built of rotten wood. A tent was placed over the hole. The skins were left in the tent for several days until thoroughly penetrated with the smoke. The final product was a leather that would withstand a thorough wetting and return to its original soft and pliable condition when dried." Thus buffalo and elk brains, made into a paste, represent the only ingredients of this recipe, besides wood ash, brute strength and perseverance. This paste imparted to buckskin its chief characteristic: the softness of butter.

During the colonial period, deer tanneries were small family-oriented businesses that secured their hides from the local deerslayers and, in turn, sold the buckskin to the shoemaker, the harness shop, book binders and other leather craftsmen in the area. These small, independent deer tanneries soon became victims of industrial progress as bigger and more mechanized tanneries, specializing in all kinds of leather goods, gradually replaced them. Today, modern commercial tanning facilities almost eliminate the necessity for any deer hunter to tan his own deer hides. Many excellent tanneries exist in all parts of the country, and do a superior job, at a price anyone can afford to pay.

For the energetic diehards of the do-it yourself school, I would like to recall an old Chippewa recipe for making buckskin. It should be noted at the outset that this old Indian art requires time, a great deal of patience and a tremendous amount of elbow grease. Olive Glasgow, a wildlife photographer, adds to these sturdy qualities "a sound stomach or a bad sinus condition to withstand the inevitable stench." For tanning deer hides in this tradition is a fascinating, foul-smelling, rewarding, messy business that takes many years of practice before you ever do it well—assuming you manage to ignore the overwhelming pungency of the process long enough to learn the craft. Your first attempt to undertake this long, arduous and trying operation might just be a failure of the highest order, to say the least. But your second or third attempt should show some measured improvement, if patience wins out. Here's how it works.

There are six basic steps: (1) soaking; (2) dehairing and fleshing; (3) soaking and stretching; (4) treating with brains; (5) soaking and stretching; and (6) smoking. To begin, soak the deer hide in a mixture of wood ashes and water so that the hair can be more easily scraped from the skin. Once the hair has been removed, the hide is "fleshed out." During this process place the skin over a smooth log or fleshing beam, and remove all membranous tissue with a knife. Next, soak the hide and wash it in clear water. Then wring it out and tightly stretch it in every known direction. Prepare the brains by chopping them up into very fine particles, and by putting them into a bag of loosely-woven cloth. Boil them for about an hour. Pour the water into a huge iron kettle, and wait until your hands can bear the temperature. Next, rub the bag between your hands under this slimy solution until the brains are forced through the cloth. This solution softens the hide. Each day thereafter for about a week, remove the hide from the solution and wring it out for a general tug of war between two individuals. If you are alone hook your foot in the bottom of the hide and stretch it in every known direction or until you are thoroughly stretched out of shape yourself. Preferably both! Next, pull and work the hide in this soapy solution, again and again, using plenty of muscle and plenty of time. When the hide has been wrung dry, wet it again and repeat the whole process of wringing, pulling and twisting all over again.

Now tightly stretch the hide on a drying frame. With the aid of a rubbing stick of hardwood, measuring about two feet long and three inches wide at the broad end, scrape and rub the hide *ad infinitum*. Rub, rub and rub some more, using as much muscle as possible without tearing the hide. Continue rubbing until the hide is thoroughly dry, which should take you well beyond the point of wetting your whistle with a little fire water . . . When the hide is dry, it is ready for the final smoking process, which colors and tans the leather. Smoke the buckskin over a slow fire made of decayed wood (well-rotted punk wood, preferably white cedar). Continue the process until the deer skin takes on the color desired, the color ranging from a light yellow to a dark yellowish-brown. The Indians stretched the deer skin over a barrel and directed the smoke to it, or made a tent-like structure of branches over a hole in the ground. Smoke houses used for curing meat were also used. After being smoked, scour the skin in lukewarm water, rinse and dry. You now have buckskin, authentic in every respect, and prepared in the true and ancient Indian tradition. Many Indian tribes recorded their lives, exploits and histories in intriguing pictographs on deer hides soft-tanned in this manner. One can hardly imagine a more appropriate or beautiful wall-hanging, where woodcraft atmosphere is desired, than a painted deer skin in the old Chippewa tradition.

It is with some reluctance that the writer closes this chapter on buckskin. Undoubtedly, a full book could be written about this one special aspect of the deer hunting sport, but space limits such expansion. I have endeavored to recall the cultural and historical significance of this exquisite leather, and to illustrate the satisfaction which lives forever in the mind and heart of the white-tailed deer enthusiast as he or she wears garments made from the hide of this creature.

Yes, the whitetail's precious hide can be made into luxurious, enduring garments that have the special property of drying soft and pliable after being wet; so don't discard your deer hide next fall! Buckskin provides wonderful leather for garments, surpassed by no other for beauty of texture, softness and durability. Buckskin gloves, coats, caps and purses, with their smooth grain finish, are a joy to own and a pleasure to wear. They are velvety to the touch, and yield to every movement of the body. They are quiet in the woods and almost impervious to cold wintery winds. Truly ideal garments for the woodsman and his Mrs.!

Thus, let none of your buck be wasted. As Larry Koller once put it in his classic *Shots at Whitetails*, "Eat the venison, tan the hide, tie bucktail lures from the soft tail hair, make bass fly-rod lures from coarse, hollow body hair. Mount the head for your den, make a hat rack or gun rack from the feet. Make or have made a pair of gloves, a buckskin shirt or a pair of moccasins. Yes, brother, the whitetail deer is a magnificently bountiful creature."

While deer hunting means many things to many people, it surely means, above all, supplying the deer hunting widow with post-season elegance . . . with genuine buckskin . . . the aristocrat of leathers. Adding a beautiful buckskin coat to your wife's wardrobe might just convince her of the legitimacy of spending so much time pursuing whitetails in the autumn woods of the North? Indeed, buckskin goes well with women; it is as traditionally American as apple pie! While a full-length buckskin coat with class and tradition takes many a hunting season to acquire (at least five medium-size deer skins), the effort is well worth the in-

An elegant buckskin coat, cap and gloves designed by the W.B. Place Company, a leader in the tanning and manufacturing of buckskin garments since 1866. *Photo credit Robert Wegner*

vestment. Maybe she'll even listen to your hunting tales? If not, you will at least own an item that is comfortable and personal, and when asked where you bought that beautiful, soft leather coat, you can snort, as John Madson does, "Bought it? Man, I don't buy my clothes, I shoot 'em!"

PART IV
THE DEER HUNTER

Chapter 19

Scientists Stalk
the Deer Stalker

During the past decade, American deer hunters tramped millions of miles of deer trails through deer forests, swamps, swales and frosty fields. Not far behind them came a small army of wildlife managers and social scientists in hot pursuit. Using the same kind of scientific precision and testing that is required of biological data, this group of scientists stalked the American deerslayer in an attempt to learn and understand more about the human dimensions of the deer hunting experience.

With the use of cluster analysis, computer simulation models and ideas having their theoretical base in psychology, these social scientists studied the whim and fancy of the American deer hunter. With an unusually fine degree of technical lingo and academic gun smoke, they measured behavior patterns, attitudes, preferences, experiences, opinions, activity

patterns and ultimate satisfactions. Their studies focused on deer hunters in Ohio, Pennsylvania, Maryland, Arizona, Wisconsin, Colorado, Michigan, Vermont, Washington, Massachusetts, New York, New Jersey, Mississippi and Montana, to name but a few of the states involved. The sheer number of their studies reaches well in excess of several hundred items: they include everything from Masters Theses to Doctoral Dissertations, from Pittman-Robertson reports to short notations in obscure journals; from short essays in the *Wildlife Society Bulletin* and lengthy features in the *Journal of Wildlife Management* to popularized versions of these technical reports in national sportsmen's magazines.

Ultimately, they quantify Aldo Leopold's earlier thesis that deer hunting satisfaction lies in the seeking as well as in

1. Nature
2. Escapism
3. Companionship
4. Shooting
5. Skill
6. Vicariousness
7. Trophy-Display
8. Harvest
9. Equipment
10. Outgroup Verbal Contact } Hunter Density/
11. Outgroup Visual Contact } Crowding

Dimensions of the deer hunting experience. *Photo credit Al Hofacker*

the getting; that the pleasure of deer hunting comes more from the process than the product; that there's more to deer hunting than killing. Or as Gordon MacQuarrie, the one-time, beloved outdoor editor of the *Milwaukee Journal,* once remarked, "that the means are greater than the end and every deer hunter knows it!"

These social scientists, commonly referred to as The Human Dimensions Study Group, quantified this thesis with a great degree of statistical sophistication. There now seems to be a general consensus of opinion among this group that at least 11 basic components constitute deer hunting satisfaction as we now know it. Listed in decreasing order of importance, these components are as follows: nature, escapism, companionship, shooting, skill, vicariousness, trophy display, harvest, equipment, outgroup verbal contact and outgroup visual contact.

The ordering of these factors clearly suggests that there are many satisfactions associated with deer hunting, several of which are more important than the harvesting of game. This chapter describes

and examines these various components of deer hunting satisfaction as originally formulated by Dale Potter, John Hendee and Roger Clark of the USDA Forest Service.

The first of these components revolves around the idea of becoming one with nature. When examined through the eyes of these scientists, the modern-day deerslayer has many characteristics reminiscent of James Fenimore Cooper's ideal man in nature and few of those outrageous characteristics so ineptly portrayed in Michael Cimino's film entitled "The Deer Hunter" (1978).

For example, when surveyed 5540 Washington State deer hunters clearly chose "nature" as the foremost element of their deer hunting experience. While their definitions of the term varied, a common theme emerged nonetheless. Some stated that they just wanted to be close to nature. Others glorified the idea of "just being outdoors." Some maintained that the "smells and sounds of the deer forest and fields" were the ultimate clincher. Others desired to camp out while deer hunting in an attempt to see all forms of wildlife.

In a similar study of 144 central New York State deer hunters using the Arnot Forest, researchers reached the same conclusion: "to get outdoors and enjoy nature" ranked as the primary component of deer hunting satisfaction. In this particular study, Daniel J. Decker and others supported the long-standing claim that there is more to deer hunting than killing. "Getting outdoors to enjoy nature was most important to our hunters." After surveying 234 Wisconsin deer hunters, Tom Heberlein, a rural sociologist from the University of Wisconsin, similarly concluded "that harvest-oriented activities were not the most universally shared motivations for deer hunting, but rather nature appreciation and the opportunity to get outdoors were ranked the highest.''

Regardless of the state, this trend persists. For example, when surveyed 5244 Michigan deer hunters underscored the nature component when they told scientists that getting out of doors and enjoying the beauties of nature ranked highest in the order of their reasons for going deer hunting. Four hundred personal interviews with Colorado deer hunters, which included direct questions, open-ended questions and rank-type responses, also produced similar results: the major reason expressed for deer hunting was love of the outdoors. A survey of 563 New York deer hunters hunting in the northern Catskill Mountains demonstrated the same point in an even more dramatic fashion.

Instead of worrying and thinking about their job, school or family—the everyday concerns of waking consciousness—deer hunters tell social scientists that they focus on the sights, sounds and smells of nature; the patterns of shifting clouds over stands of white oaks; the movement of air currents rippling the surface of ponds; the smell of impending rain or decaying vegetation on a November day; the flash of a whitetail disappearing through the pines.

The most sophisticated and sensitive research on whether or not this characterization represents an accurate portrait of the American deer hunter has been done by Stephen Kellert, a professor of forestry and environmental studies at Yale University. In his national survey for the United States Fish and Wildlife Service, Professor Kellert characterized deer

NATURE—component number one. Social scientists indicate that deer hunters clearly choose nature as the foremost element of their deer hunting experience. *Photo credit Irene Vandermolen*

hunters who hunt for the purpose of obtaining close contact and exposure to nature as ''nature hunters.'' This type of deer hunter desires an active and participatory role in nature; he or she views deer with admiration, respect and with intellectual curiosity. According to Kellert, they seek an intense involvement with deer in their natural habitats throughout the year; they appreciate the deer hunt because it forces them into an awareness of natural phenomena.

In addition to these surveys and interviews, Gene Hill, that master storyteller, best summarizes for us in a literary and philosophical way the nature component of deer hunting satisfaction when he says that ''The thing that cements the love of a man for his carpet of leaves and his ceiling of stars is the knowledge that just being involved is enough. There is no score worth keeping. All we should ever count is hours; never birds, nor length of antler or hits or misses. If we want to do something where we can't lose, then we must accept the proposition that we cannot win. We are not involved in a contest, but a very simple and pure journey that promises each day will be different, unrepeatable, unrecapturable. Each time is unique. If there is anything of value to be entered in the log, let's leave it at a series of impressions. A day without deer is a day spent in delicious solitary thought, a day that might bring you closer to un-

Reason	Times Indicated	Percent
Love of outdoors	313	15.8
Companionship with fellow sportsmen	255	12.8
Challenge with the animal	211	10.6
Outdoor recreational activity	201	10.1
Escape from daily routine	157	7.9
Food	140	7.1
Challenge with environment	127	6.4
Seeking new hunting experiences each year	124	6.2
Companionship with son or another child	113	5.7
Exercise	88	4.4
Thrill of shooting an animal	69	3.5
Other	188	9.5
Total	1,986	100.0

Reasons why Colorado sportsmen hunt deer. *Credit Bernard J. Schole, et al.* "Colorado Hunter Behavior, Attitudes, and Philosophies."

derstanding the infinite mystery of it all." This statement ought to be engraved on every weapon taken into the deer forest.

In viewing what the scientists say about deer hunters, we must realize that like the crafty whitetail, the deerslayer becomes quite elusive himself—i.e., he has learned to tell social scientists what they want to hear. Consequently, what he says he does and his actual behavior in the field are frequently two different things. If all deer hunters were in fact "nature hunters" of the Aldo Leopold caliber, we would not experience opening days that result in traffic jams, shotgun-slug hailstorms and the appearance of search and destroy missions. Hence, in summarizing the scientific literature on the deer hunting experience, we must proceed with the utmost caution.

Escapism, scientists tell us, represents the second most significant component of why men take to the deer forest. Why? To get away from it all . . . to get away from work pressures, daily routine and decadent civilization! To get away from people, to get away from home, to experience solitude and isolation. Indeed, there's much to be said in favor of the solitary way of deer hunting, of being a solo hunter. T.S. Van Dyke and George Mattis, those two distinguished still hunters, have told us that with great eloquence. It lets us get acquainted with ourselves. Surely, we should never feel sorry for the man who goes to his deer stand on his own. In most cases his deer stand has a secret feel about it. "It's a place," Gene Hill once remarked, "where we find ourselves coming back to, time after treasured time. For deer perhaps, but more than likely just because we love the quiet of the place or the music of a nearby brook."

Reason For Hunting	Response Category (%)						
	Very important	Somewhat important	Not very important	Total number	1st most important	2nd most important	3rd most important
Getting out-of-doors and seeing wildlife	78.7	18.8	2.5	517	51.2	19.6	10.3
Challenge and suspense of hunting	61.4	29.5	9.1	485	15.6	26.2	13.0
Association with hunting group or buddy	46.1	32.9	21.0	477	4.5	14.2	16.8
Want venison for food	41.1	33.6	25.3	304	11.5	9.2	7.5
Shooting a deer	28.0	39.4	32.5	289	3.8	5.4	9.0
Getting away from it all	55.8	23.7	20.5	477	8.1	11.1	16.8
Exercise	53.4	26.5	20.1	298	4.3	11.8	23.1
Firing and handling a gun	22.2	22.0	55.7	454	0.9	2.4	3.5
Total Number					443	423	399

Reasons why New York sportsmen hunt deer. *Credit Charles Burt,* "White-tailed Deer Attitudes in East-Central New York."

I have had my share of solitude in the deer forest and it is beautiful. It gives me perspective and a sense of timelessness. It is not surprising that deer hunters inform scientists that escapism and solitude represent the second most important component of the deer hunting experience; that they go into the bush to find silence, freedom and independence; that they come back stronger, better and happier with minds uncluttered with civilized problems. After roaming the snowy hills of November, one old-time deer hunter put it this way: "When you're alone, you have time to do things without thinking of anyone else. If you want to go exploring and climb some high ridge instead of hunting, you may. Many times I've looked at a ridge and wondered how it would seem being way on top of it, feasting my eyes for an hour or two or a whole day, or climbing to some snowy slope where perhaps no man had ever been. If you want to enjoy a bit of shoreline, watch a beaver storing food in the pile beside his lodge, you can do it."

Storing food for thought is surely one of the benefits and satisfactions of deer hunting, whether done alone or in the company of others. Actually, American deer hunting, social scientists reaffirm, generally takes place in the company of others, despite the well-known fact that solo deer hunters tend to be more successful. Regardless of the element of success, companionship, or the desire for social contact with hunters in one's own party, represents the third most impor-

ESCAPISM—component number two. Scientists tell us that most deer hunters dream of escaping to the deer shack. Why? To get away from it all . . . to get away from work pressure, daily routine and decadent civilization! The deer shack is a place where, as one deer hunter from Illinois once exclaimed, "I eat like a bear and sing like a wolf and feel like I'm bull-pine tall." *Photo credit Charles J. Alsheimer*

tant component of the deer hunting experience.

In examining this component, scientists tell us that more than half of all deer hunters surveyed feel that who they hunt with is one of the most important aspects of their deer hunting trip. Seventy-one percent of Maryland hunters, for example, indicate that they have at least one hunting partner with whom they go on *nearly all* of their hunting trips. Eighty-five percent of Ohio hunters hunt with the same companions year after year. These companions are usually family or relatives (83 percent) or friends (64 percent).

In analyzing the behavior of deer hunting groups in Wisconsin, Robert Jackson, a psychologist at the University of Wisconsin-La Crosse, notes that 75 percent of the deer hunters he interviewed stated that they started to deer hunt because of family ties. Fifty-four percent of them indicated that their father was the major influence in their becoming a deer hunter. Brothers, sisters and close relatives were credited by another 21 percent of the hunters. Indeed, strong family ties make up one of the key factors in developing an interest in deer hunting. Seventy-five percent of Wisconsin deer hunters hunt with a party of between three to eight persons. Sixty-eight percent of them insist that their primary satisfaction is social. Such strong social ties to the deer hunt suggest that any future attempts by state departments of natural resources to limit hunter numbers will be perceived as disruptive to the individual's deer hunting group.

The deer hunting group obviously influences hunter behavior. With regard to the group bag, Jackson found a conspicuous gap between rules and regulations and actual hunting practice. "While technically a hunter should quit hunting once he fills his tag (in Wisconsin), it seems relatively few apparently do. Better than eighty percent of the hunters who had filled their tag indicated that they continued to hunt with the party. Many hunters contend that this may be an unenforceable regulation."

Jackson's study also unfortunately reveals that few deer hunting groups formulate clearly defined rules or practices with regard to violators and violations. Apparently the deer hunter in a party behaves in a manner defined and approved by the group. This kind of behavior sometimes conflicts with the hunter's personal values. One deer hunter told Jackson that "I used to hunt with the group but got tired of all the arguing and decisions of how and where we were going to hunt. I've hunted alone now for the last couple of years and like it."

In constructing a portrait of deer hunters using the Pocomoke State Forest in Maryland, James J. Kennedy, a professor of forest resources and outdoor recreation at Utah State University, studied the motivations and rewards of deer hunting in a group versus alone. He sampled three types of deer hunters: forestry-wildlife students, rural Virginia hunters

COMPANIONSHIP—component number three. Scientists reaffirm that American deer hunting generally takes place in the company of others, despite the well-known fact that solo deer hunters tend to be more successful. Indeed, deer hunting is a social event. Sixty percent of all deer hunters cannot find anything in their lives that would be an adequate substitute for this form of recreation. *Photo credit Charles J. Alsheimer*

and hunters largely from the Baltimore metropolitan region. The forestry-wildlife students tended to hunt alone and were primarily concerned with getting a deer. They saw disadvantages in hunting with a group; namely, too much noise, too much dangerous behavior and too many conflicts with solitude and hunting procedure. The rural Virginians, on the other hand, saw advantages in a deer hunting party, such as sharing in group success as well as in sharing expenses. The urban hunters also saw advantages to hunting in a group and greatly appreciated the social and security aspects of the group; they seemed to enjoy the camaraderie as much as actually hunting deer. Kennedy reached the conclusion that because wildlife managers are often sophisticated woodsmen—needing the advantages of the group less than the average hunter—this situation sometimes creates barriers for them in understanding their clients.

Whether we hunt alone or in a group, most of us understand that group hunting demands careful selection of hunting companions. Throughout the history of American deer hunting, countless statements of sound advice have been given with regard to selecting your deer hunting companions. After many years of studying the American deer hunter and after wading through vast dustbins of literature on this subject, I still believe that the best advice in this regard comes from the pen of Charles E. Myers, an ardent deer hunter from the state of Washington. He writes as follows in his marvelous book of deer hunting memoirs, entitled *Memoirs of a Hunter* (1948): "A man who worries or chafes about his business or profession as soon as he is out of the corporate limits of his town is

to be avoided by the members of a wise deer hunting party. The real sportsman wants the men of his party to be first, incapable of purposely breaking the game laws; secondly, to leave every thought and care of his business behind; thirdly, to be lively sensible of the fact that there is hard work to do around the camp like the hewing of wood and the drawing of water and that he must voluntarily do his full part; fourthly, he must refrain from the discussion of subjects or matters that might embarrass or humiliate any member of the party. In the large he must be a fellow with tact, and one who can make the best of an awkward predicament or serious accident; fifthly, he must have a good time whether game is bagged or not and must not complain that the trip was a failure in case he has to return home empty handed."

In thinking about this whole question of whether to hunt alone or with other companions, I must admit I have a strong bias for the profound and witty advice of an old Iowa backwoodsman whom I once met in Bear Swamp. "It's a privilege," he told me, "to tramp the deer forest with a wise hunter; a pleasure to go out with one of equal skill, if he is a friend; and a happy enough responsibility to take a novice along . . . sometimes."

The shooting dimension, component number four, appears to be more important for small game hunters than deer hunters, for deer hunters do not get as many shots, and hence do not seem to value shooting as a major source of satisfaction. That is what deer hunters are telling scientists, at least. Deer hunters using the Arnot Forest, a controlled deer hunting area in central New York, for example, indicate that "to get shots at deer" is of secondary importance.

Still, deer camp stories abound with shooting exploits and the making of difficult shots. One only needs to re-read the November 25th entry of famous *Bucks Camp Log* for 1917 to grasp the ultimate excitement in deer shooting: "The bunch drove the vicinity of the Poise stump this afternoon. A lead mine could be started with the bullets we left down there. We had five deer surrounded. The bombardment sounded like an English barrage. Deer were running everywhere. They were so thick around Mr. Hill, Sr. that he had to push them away beyond the end of his gun so he could shoot them. He got buck fever so bad that he was shooting in a circle. Mr. True said the air was so thick around Mr. Hill, Sr. that he could not shoot through it."

One social psychologist from the University of Wisconsin-La Crosse characterizes shooting as a stage through which all deer hunters travel. In reflecting on what he calls the "shooter stage," Professor Robert Jackson observes that many hunters in interviews relate hunting satisfaction with being able to get shooting. Young hunters often indicate that an excellent day of deer hunting was "excellent" because they got a lot of shooting.

"The beginning hunter," Jackson concludes, "apparently wants to pull the trigger and test out the capability of his weapon. He may shoot at blackbirds, signs, insulators, tin cans and what not." If this is an accurate assessment, one would hope that most deer hunters would go through this state like the flash of a whitetail disappearing in a standing cornfield.

Skill, the fifth component, incorporates one's knowledge of the quarry, physical ability and mental cunning with hunting satisfaction. Most seasoned deer hunters know that bucks in the three- to four-year-old class do not survive to maturity by outrunning danger but by outwitting it. And so too must the hunter outwit his quarry, if he is to succeed. While all kinds of hunters place some importance on the skill factor as a dimension of hunting satisfaction, the deer hunter in particular says skill plays a major part in his satisfaction.

This component consists of many elements beyond making a difficult shot: it entails knowing the everyday habits of the whitetail; knowing the defenses and personality of a particular whitetail; outsmarting that whitetail on his own terrain; stalking him on a one-on-one basis; calling him; reading his sign; tracking him; filming him; dressing, skinning and preparing the venison; and finally teaching someone else these skills.

These kinds of skills can be a source of great personal satisfaction. A deer hunter from Montana once described it this way: "I can find an uncommon pride in carrying a knife I can shave with; in being able to place an effective shot; in knowing how to read signs that lie hidden in wet grass, fall leaves and the rubs on trees, and in being able to put them into meaningful order. And I have never met a deer hunter who didn't share that attitude. When you can do these things on your own, you will discover a unique pleasure—you will become what you do. It's a dimension of deer hunting that makes the experience richer yet, and a hunter wealthy in the bargain."

Deer hunting obviously requires a combination of many skills and knowledge that well exceeds the handling of a weapon, and in the process places a premium upon inventiveness and problem solving. The sport also provides a lasting ecological experience in which participants acquaint themselves with the importance and functioning of natural systems. In this sense, deer hunting becomes a lifelong process of learning and improving skills.

What motivates the deer hunter is not, as the antihunter thinks, a pleasure in killing, but rather a profound pleasure in the learning and optimal performance of various skills . . . in the development of man himself. The idea that hunting produces a pleasure in killing remains an unsubstantiated and a most implausible statement. It is amazing how many antihunters neglect this element of skill in hunting and focus their attention instead on the act of killing. In trying to understand why antihunters choose this interpretation, we need to recall the words of Erich Fromm, one of this century's greatest psychologists: "Their interpretation of the pleasure in hunting as a pleasure in killing rather than skill is characteristic for the impoverished person of our time for whom the only thing that counts is the *result* of an effort, in this case killing rather than the process of hunting itself."

The sixth component of deer hunting satisfaction, according to what deer hunters tell scientists, is called "vicariousness" by researchers. This out-of-town word refers to those elements of the deer hunting experience which are not dependent upon direct participation, such as watching hunting movies or TV programs on hunting, telling deer hunting stories or reading sportsmen's magazines such as *Deer & Deer Hunting.* It refers to those activities that may serve as temporary substitutes for deer hunting or may heighten the expectation of the deer hunt. Scientists maintain that vicariousness or

off-site enjoyment actually heightens as the probability of harvesting deer decreases. In other words, reading magazines on deer and deer hunting becomes a prime supplement to action in the deer forest when the probability of success or of seeing deer declines.

Actually, this component of the deer hunting experience not only refers to studying magazines on deer and deer hunting while relaxing before a fireplace, but to reading deer books and miscellaneous scientific reprints in the deer forest as well. My brush copies of Van Dyke's *The Still Hunter* and Koller's *Shots at Whitetails,* as well as sundry reprints from my cherished black boxes, accompany me to the field as surely as do my Browning Stalker II or my Remington Model 1100.

The importance of this component cannot be overemphasized, for demographic studies indicate that more than 70 percent of all deer hunters read sportsmen's magazines regularly. One wonders what 70 percent of America's 12 million-plus deer hunters are looking for in a magazine on deer hunting. Outdoor editors ponder this question even in their sleep. I have come to the conclusion that many of them want scientific information on deer habits as it relates to hunting methods; solid how-to pieces on bow hunting, gun hunting and camera hunting; profiles of leading deer hunters; historic and nostalgic articles on deer camps; first-person adventure stories; natural history articles on deer based on scientific fact; classic essays on deer hunting written by great outdoor writers (past and present); odd and unusual facts about deer; and editorial essays on broader conservation and environmental issues as they relate to deer and deer hunting.

Deer hunters want to be entertained,

enlightened and informed with *factual* articles of a technical nature that relate deer behavior and habits to hunting methodology. The ideal deer hunting magazine offers a rich blend of science, outdoor literature and personal experience. It is entertaining, educational, enlightening and inspirational. It enhances the image of the American deer hunter. It emphasizes the humanistic and esthetic values of the sport as well as hunter ethics.

The enthusiasm and vigor for this type of material is well known throughout the outdoor publishing industry. Yet, the outdoor publishing industry by and large continues to market a tremendous amount of warmed-over, thinned-out rehash. The dusty shelves of my library are filled with the stuff. One wonders when it's going to stop coming off the presses. As one avid deer hunter exclaimed: "After being cautioned for the 97th time not to hunt with the wind because of the deer's highly developed sense of smell, these instructions begin to lose some of their appeal." Indeed! As an editor of a specialized magazine on the subject of deer and deer hunting, I receive countless letters making the same point.

Many deer hunters not only have their favorite outdoor magazine, but their own favorite trophy whitetail that they pursue throughout the year with bow, gun and camera. For two years I chased a trophy 9-point farmland buck over countless miles of deer trails. While pursuing this 9-pointer, I frequently reflected on the seventh component of the deer hunting experience: what scientists call trophy display. In studying the scientific literature on this component, I found that a significant number of deer hunters told the social scientists that they enjoy showing trophies to friends and relatives,

TROPHY DISPLAY—component number seven. Many deer hunters have a trophy whitetail that they pursue throughout the year with bow, gun and camera. This 9-point farmland buck eluded the editor for two years before the final picture-taking ceremony took place. *Photo credit Maren Lea Wegner*

bringing trophy whitetails home, preserving them, and displaying them on the walls of their dens.

But what is the ultimate meaning underlying this behavior? Aldo Leopold best answers this question, I believe, when he writes in his *Sand County Almanac* (1949) that "hunters outwit their game primarily for one reason—to reduce that beauty to possession." That one phrase, "to reduce that beauty to possession," best captures the meaning of why we chase trophy whitetails and eventually adorn our dens with preserved mounts. Think of that phrase the next time you stare at your trophy whitetail from your easy chair; for the idea of reducing the whitetail's beauty to possession surely means more than any linear measurement of antler tine or beam, whether it be based on the official scoring system of the Pope and Young Club or the Boone and Crockett Club.

Although the components discussed thus far emphasize other aspects of the deer hunt, the harvest, component number eight, constitutes a significant part of a satisfactory deer hunt. In fact, several studies indicate that killing a deer is very important to deer hunting satisfaction. In a study of deer hunters in the Sapphire Mountains of Montana, for example, George Stankey of the USDA Forest Ser-

HARVEST—component number eight. There is always a fine satisfaction in seeing hung up in camp a wily old buck that has been worth your best efforts in defeating, and it is no mean art to be able to hang them to appear at the best advantage. Shortly after 4:00 p.m. this buck was dangling between heaven and earth, with his heels up, adding a most inspiring game-some appearance to our camp. *Photo credit Wisconsin Department of Natural Resources*

vice concludes that harvesting a deer represents a major component of the hunt, and that when designing programs to provide satisfactory deer hunting experiences, game departments need to ensure hunters with some reasonable expectation of success.

Stankey's survey of 402 Montana deer hunters demonstrates that as success ratios decline, other satisfactions dependent on a successful hunt also diminish. Success, as Stankey points out, "might be more accurately characterized as serving a catalytic function in that its presence or absence might influence both the type of additional satisfactions experienced by the hunter and their relative importance to him." While getting an animal is a necessary variable in determining satisfaction, success alone is not sufficient, as the Stankey study demonstrates. Again, deer hunters—in this case from Montana—indicate that the hunter strives for a broad set of satisfactory outcomes rather than one that simply tries to maximize one objective, namely success.

If successfully tagging a deer were of the utmost importance, given the fact that only a very small percentage of deer hunters actually succeed in doing so (17 to 20 percent), the rate of desertion from the sport of deer hunting would probably be quite high. And this is not the case. In fact, the rate of desertion is generally thought to be quite low. As it turns out, lack of leisure time, posting and crowded conditions—and not failure to succeed—appear to be the major reasons expressed for quitting deer hunting. After studying the reasons for quitting, Lowell Klessig of the University of Wisconsin reports that 67 percent of those who quit did so for social and psychological reasons, 18 percent because they became physically unable, and 15 percent because of scarcity or lack of game.

The ninth basic component of the deer hunting experience revolves around equipment—the owning, maintaining, using, comparing and ultimately the collecting of it. Indeed, we never tire of talking about hunting equipment or maintaining it. We even carry it around in our trucks whether we plan on using it or not. On Saturdays we start the day out by cleaning up storm windows, but soon divert our attention to cleaning guns and sharpening broadheads. We dream about equipment. We study catalogs and catalogs of equipment. We can never seem to get enough of the stuff, and our wives agree. We sneak it into the house and hope that the chancellor of the exchequer is preoccupied with her $1000-plus Elna sewing machine that we finally had to buy to placate her objections to our insatiable appetite for buying more deer hunting equipment. While scientists have done little research in measuring and quantifying this component, they seem to agree that it ranks right up there with pipe smoking, top-shelf bourbon, trout fishing and deer shack storytelling.

Components number 10 and 11 scientists label "outgroup verbal contact" and "outgroup visual contact." This gibberish refers to the effect on deer hunting satisfaction of talking with hunters outside one's own party and seeing hunters outside one's own party. Deer hunters clearly distinguish between contact with outsiders and social interaction within their group. It is not surprising that verbal and visual contacts with people outside one's deer hunting party while in the woods remains at the bottom of the list. In fact, at least one third of American deer hunters indicate that outgroup vi-

sual contact detracts from their deer hunting satisfaction.

As deer hunters, we are probably more familiar with these last two components of the deer hunt under the more generic names of hunting pressure, hunter density or crowding. While the pressure of deer hunters outside of one's party is often considered an asset because they move deer and thus increase the chances of success for everyone, they are also seen as competitors for the same resource, especially in areas that receive heavy hunting pressure. In such situations their presence actually detracts considerably from a satisfying deer hunt.

While American deer hunters tend to disagree on the desirable levels of hunting pressure, considerable evidence indicates that seeing more than 10 other deer hunters from outside one's own group on opening day is less than desirable. When levels reach a point, as one sociologist remarked, "where other hunters are directly interfering with hunting procedures, the sport develops a competitive aspect that is common to other consumptive recreational activities, and the cooperative nature of deer hunting is lost." Even though deer hunters indicate that there are presently too many hunters in the deer forest on the one hand, they are unwilling on the other to incur additional costs to reduce deer hunter density, to abide by restrictions of numbers or to be manipulated by way of distribution. And so another one of the eternal paradoxes between deer hunters and game managers seems to remain fixed and in place.

For the past 50 years deer hunters and game managers have been sensitive to public accusations that the kill is the primary attraction of sport hunting. In the past our counter-arguments to these accusations too often revolved around informal and highly impressionistic statements. Before 1970, only a few rare and philosophical articles on hunting quality even existed. One thinks of Aldo Leopold's *Wildlife in American Culture* (1943), for example. But for the most part, discussion of hunting quality was practically ignored in the wildlife management literature or treated as a "mystical phenomenon" escaping the limits of precise measurement.

Since 1970, however, an ever-growing cadre of social scientists in the wildlife human dimension field have been confronting this issue with empirical evidence. Indeed, they have produced a large amount of literature dealing with the human dimensions of the deer hunting experience which supports and documents the long-standing claim that there is more to deer hunting than killing game, that many peripheral satisfactions and values accrue during the deer hunt which are far more important than harvesting game. Their conclusions confirm the idea that few deer hunting experiences fit the traditional Daniel Boone stereotype of the deerslayer who has to return from the deer forest with his quarry in hand, if he is to find ultimate satisfaction.

Their research findings clearly indicate that the numbers of hunters will have to be managed more carefully and perhaps even limited to maintain opportunities for high-quality deer hunting; that management agencies need to institute programs that are more conducive to higher levels of human satisfaction. The implications of their studies encourage a multiple-satisfaction approach to deer hunter management—i.e., an attempt to combine deer hunters seeking similar satisfactions with

hunting areas having the maximum potential for providing those satisfactions.

Their research demonstrates that seeing a very high number of hunters in the deer forest actually decreases satisfaction almost as much as getting a deer increases it. Many of these scientists believe that controlling hunter numbers, as opposed to increasing the probability of success, may be a more effective way of increasing deer hunting satisfaction. Indeed, hunting is changing whether we like it or not. In his book entitled *Hunting in America* (1973), Charles Waterman rightly predicts that "those hunters imbued with the independent spirit of the frontiersman will be unhappy to find themselves subject to increasingly restrictive regulations."

To summarize: While deer hunters presumably go afield in search of venison, they find many associated experiences and satisfactions more important than the harvest itself. It is the total package of these various components that provides a positive rationale for deer hunting and distinguishes it from mere killing. The pleasure of deer hunting comes more from the *process* than from the *product*. The product (successfully shooting a deer) is necessary because it supplies us with the logical end of the process; but it is not sufficient in itself to produce ultimate satisfaction. In his *Meditations on Hunting* (1972), Jose Ortega Y Gasset, Spain's leading philosopher, summarizes the point with provocative insight: "One does not hunt in order to kill; on the contrary, one kills in order to have hunted."

Ultimately, the fate of deer hunting in this country lies not in the hands of these scientific researchers specializing in the human dimensions of the hunt or even in the hands of the deer hunter; it lies in the hands of the general public. Consequently, it behooves all of us to analyze in great detail the various components of the deer hunting experience and to emphasize the qualitative aspects of the deer hunt, for it clearly consists of many more dimensions than just measuring tines, antlers and harvest figures.

A letter that crossed my desk the other day summarizes the point. It was written by James W. Coward, a barber from Battle Creek, Michigan. "The killing of a deer is not, in itself, significant. To hunt fairly, ethically, and to make a kill as humanely as possible is very significant. A true deer hunter is not just a killer. To hunt deer is much more than just the kill. It is an arousal of the primal instincts in man. It is the taking of a role—the predator, the hunter. It is the joy and relief of an unsuccessful stalk as well as the sad, reflective emotions that come from the kill. To me, these mean much more than a Boone and Crockett rack or 100 pounds of venison."

Chapter 20

The American Bow Hunter

Some men cruise the woods with gun or rifle in hand; and some cruise the autumn woods with bow and arrow in hand. It is of these latter individuals that I wish to talk about. This chapter will discuss them, their ways and the object of all their desires. One thing seems certain: They all have an overwhelming passion for those "woodland wearers of kingly crowns." The American bow hunter of the whitetail will usually forego every other pleasure on earth for that rarest one of pursuing and stalking a many-tined trophy whose antlers, as he moves through the brush, are likely to make the novice bow hunter imagine that the entire woodlot has suddenly been set into motion.

We might begin our analysis of the American bow hunter by asking ourselves several questions: Why does one bow hunt in the first place? What does a brief history of regulated bow hunting tell us? Who were the famous individuals of our sport, and what contributions did they make? Who is the American bow hunter? How popular has bow hunting become among women? What does the future of bow hunting look like?

In doing public programs on deer and deer hunting throughout the year, I frequently ask deer hunters why they hunt deer with bow and arrow. This is actually a very difficult and complex question. The answer, in most cases, probably involves heredity, emotion and sentiment, more so than logic. At first glance their answers seem as varied as their backgrounds. But upon closer scrutiny a common theme emerges. Some deer hunters, for example, tell me that they hunt with their bow because they find pleasure in attempting to secure a trophy whitetail under the most challenging conditions—conditions under which their skill and experience must be matched with whitetail wits on a more even basis than in any other form of hunting.

Others explain that they wish to extend their deer hunting season in an attempt to sharpen their woodsmanship and to increase their overall hunting skills. Some answer the question by saying that they derive greater satisfaction in taking deer with such a relatively primitive weapon; in other words, from doing things the hard way. As one young chap declared, "I like primitive things and ways of life. I'm sick of the modern mechanical age!" Others merely wish to shed time clocks and specific destinations at appointed times; to gear themselves down to the pace of the quarry; to become slow, patient and ever more alert. Others announce, more ambitiously, that they bow hunt in an attempt to recapture to a degree some of the perceptive powers of primeval man. Many announce that they do it because they love it! They hasten to add, however, that "this is no reason, but merely an emotion difficult to explain."

One middle-aged gentleman told me that it represented a means for getting more fun out of deer hunting. Furthermore, he exclaimed, "It is good conservation because it allows for additional recreational use of the deer herd, but does so at no significant loss to the deer herd." His deer hunting partner nodded and underscored his idea by saying, "I enjoy the social life in deer camp and the fun of trying to outsmart whitetails. I deer hunt Indian style because you actually have to outsmart the deer in their own backyard—a feat which is rich in sport, but thin in soup. In a word, there is more fun in the chase."

A common thread running through these observations indicates that many deer hunters choose the bow because it provides them with a closer contact with the outdoors, especially during the Indian Summer days of September, October and early November. The challenge of the chase, as their observations reveal, makes each success something special. In surveying deer hunters on this question of why they bow hunt, I found that one phrase constantly re-occurred: "More fun in the chase." Let's examine this phrase for a moment. I think it gets at the very heart of why we bow hunt.

Unlike such predators as the bobcat, cougar and wolf, which all hunt deer to satisfy their hunger, the modern sportsman pursues deer so that he may study and enjoy nature in all her various forms and intricate harmonies; and the better the modern deer hunter is qualified to do this, the higher will be his sense of pleasure. "More fun in the chase" means that you are given the opportunity, because of the prolonged season, to acquire a better understanding of the natural history of the object which you pursue. It is not surprising that many hunters take countless books on deer and deer hunting with them to their deer shacks. "More fun in the chase" refers to a contest with sharp wits where satisfaction merges with admiration for the object that you eventually overcome. The pleasure of the chase is thus measured by the intelligence of the whitetail and by his capacity to elude pursuit, on the one hand, and by the labor involved in his capture, on the other.

I think most of us would agree that in bow hunting the harvesting of whitetails is, after all, only a small part of the whole experience. The chase consists of many things: the adventurous life with its wild surroundings and grand beauty, as well as the opportunity to study and observe the ways and habits of all woodland creatures. Indeed, the chase for the bow hunter is among the best of all national pastimes. Maurice Thompson, an early American deer hunter and foremost authority on sylvan archery at the turn of the century, best characterized the ultimate fun involved in the chase when he wrote in an essay entitled *In the Woods with the Bow,*

Sooner or later, most bow hunters learn the sweet truth of ancient wisdom: Pursuit is more enjoyable than possession. *Photo credit Richard P. Smith*

that "I chase game animals with the bow not with any particular desire to kill, but only to go into the woods, to get away from roads, to go into new, untrodden places, where something indescribable, yet real, lingers, wavers, and shines." Sooner or later most bow hunters learn the sweet truth of ancient wisdom: Pursuit is more enjoyable than possession.

Several years ago the New York State Field Archery Association sent its membership a questionnaire entitled "Why are you a bow hunter?" The following statements represent some of the common answers given to this question by New York bow hunters. They are quoted verbatim:

(1) "I get more thrill out of seeing an arrow winging toward its mark, even if I miss."

(2) "Less hunters in the woods to scare the deer. I ain't scared to death some trigger-happy jerk is goin' to plug me."

(3) "I like the sporting element. Archery is the most sporting of any form of hunting. It more than gives the game an even chance."

(4) "With present numbers of hunters and reduced numbers of game, something like this is necessary if we're to have any hunting left."

(5) "Your ability to kill depends on your skill. Sort of gives the game an even chance."

(6) "The woods are quiet and not crowded during archery season. This enhances the pleasure of being afield and makes hunting worthwhile for me."

(7) "I hunt with a bow because I think honestly and truly it is the one sport that a true sportsman can enjoy."

(8) "I hunt with a bow because it keeps the pace of hunting down. I can observe more, think more and enjoy nature more keenly. I'm 75 years old."

(9) "It is the most sporting type of hunting. You have to beat the thousand guardian angels that each deer has working for him. With a rifle you can just blast them away."

I think these statements aptly summarize the American bow hunter's attitude toward why he hunts.

In the literature on deer and deer hunting we also find a vast array of answers to this question. In his classic *Shots at Whitetails,* for example, Larry Koller formulated an answer to this question which bears repeating: "The archer hunts not for meat, not for the trophy, but for the sheer, pure joy of matching wits and endurance with that clever animal, the whitetail buck."

In answer to this question, Maurice Thompson wrote that "When a man shoots with a bow, it is his own vigor of body that drives the arrows, and his own mind that controls the missile's flight. Not so with gun shooting. The modern weapon is charged with a power acting independently of muscular operations, and will shoot just as powerfully for the schoolboy or the weakling as it will for the athlete."

Dr. Saxton Pope, one of the fathers of

"The archer hunts not for meat, not for the trophy alone, but for the sheer, pure joy of matching wits and endurance with that clever animal, the white-tailed buck."

—**Larry Koller**
Photo credit Irene Vandermolen

America bow hunting, agreed with this assessment when he wrote in his *Study of Bows and Arrows* (1923) that "The bow is a more sportsmanlike implement than a gun because it requires more skill and personal strength, and in hunting it places the man and his quarry on a more equal footing. It fosters the preservation of game." Pope aptly elaborated his answer by saying that "the beauty of woods, valleys, mountains and skies feeds the soul of the sportsman where the quest of game only whets his appetite. After all, it is not

"The beauty of woods, valleys, mountains and skies feeds the soul of the sportsman where the quest of game only whets his appetite. After all, it is not the killing that brings satisfaction, it is the contest of skill and cunning. The true hunter counts his achievements in proportion to the effort involved and the fairness of the sport."
—**Dr. Saxton Pope, 1923**
Photo credit The Pope and Young Club

the killing that brings satisfaction, it is the contest of skill and cunning. The true hunter counts his achievements in proportion to the effort involved and the fairness of the sport."

Following in the footsteps of Saxton Pope, Fred Bear underscored the same idea. "You don't go hunting to kill, you go hunting to hunt . . . There are hunters and there are killers. To the true sportsman, the kill is an anti-climax."

I bow hunt because fewer deer hunters are in the field than during the gun season, and because the whitetail is also less wary at this time. This means, as John Cartier notes in *The Modern Deer Hunter* (1976), "that you can hunt at your leisure, hunt the way you want, and have little fear that other hunters will spoil your chances."

Who would not want to be afield under these ideal conditions and during the most beautiful and picturesque part of the fall? Who would want to forgo the continuous learning process that is involved in bow hunting? For the instrument we have chosen to hunt with dictates that we sharpen and refine our "woodsmanship," in the best sense of that word. On the other hand it demands a higher degree of patience, stealth, self-restraint, woodsmanship and all-round whitetail savvy; and on the other, it also provides us with that rare opportunity of observing the peak rutting frenzy of the whitetail. Furthermore, bow hunting represents a form of hunting that gives us plenty of fun in the chase, but with very few deer in the bag. Aldo Leopold, one of America's early bow hunting enthusiasts and prime initiator of the first specialized archery season for bow hunters, considered it the perfect hobby, if for no other reason than that the making of archery tackle for hunting purposes provides us with an "effective alibi for being late at the office, or for failing to carry out the trash can on Thursdays."

The development of the bow and arrow represents a significant factor in the survival and cultural development of Western civilization. From the Paleolithic Period, when the bow first appeared, to the dawn of the modern age, man has relied on archery as a means for acquiring food. Archery played a paramount role in human affairs up until the 16th century, when the bow was eventually superceded by the firearm. Today, the theory and practice of archery constitute one of the most ancient and noble traditions of the human race. When man abandoned the bow in 1595, as a weapon of war and as an instrument of the chase, archery lost much of its popular appeal, and was merely kept alive by a small handful of ardent enthusiasts called toxophilites. This was its status in America during the closing years of the 19th century. The popularity of archery gradually began to increase during the early years of the 20th century, however, and in the later half of the century experienced a sudden and almost incredible upswing. To understand its current popularity, we need to examine several events that took place around the turn of the century.

The first of these occurred in 1878, when the first book on shooting game with a bow appeared. Entitled *The Witchery of Archery*, this complete manual of archery consisted of lively chapters on bow hunting adventures afield and afloat. It also contained practical directions for the manufacture and use of archery implements in hunting. Within two years of its publication the Patent Office in Washington was flooded with applications re-

lating to the manufacture of archery goods. Apparently the excitement and enthusiasm engendered by this book took hold of an America saddened by the guns of the Civil War, for archery was off and running. Archery clubs soon sprang up all over the country. Indeed, this unique and stimulating book—more than any other—set the stage for the furor for bow hunting that was to spread over the entire country some 50 years later.

Once you have read *The Witchery of Archery* by Maurice Thompson, you will never escape from the romantic allurement and the picturesque hallucination of hunting in the wild with bow and arrow. It would not be an exaggeration to say that the sport of bow hunting as we know it today practically owes its existence to this book. As a result of the interest stimulated by it, the National Archery Association was established and held its first tournament at Chicago in 1879. It's not surprising that this association, which has ever since nurtured the sport and furthered competitive enthusiasm, chose for its first president the author of *The Witchery of Archery*.

This book soon became standard reading for such individuals as Dr. Saxton Pope, Art Young, Howard Hill, Ben Pearson and Fred Bear—all outstanding leaders of the sport. All of these individuals heard, as Dr. Saxton Pope once wrote, "the low whistle of the flying arrow and the sweet hum of the bowstring singing in the book, *The Witchery of Archery* by Maurice Thompson."

J. Maurice Thompson (1844–1901), who wrote this lyric of exquisite purity, and his brother, Will (1846–1918), who wrote less but shot more, were so intimately bound up with the beginnings of American interest in bow hunting that I think a few words about them would be in order. As Pope rightly observed, "We who shoot the bow today are children of their fantasy, offspring of their magic. As the parents of American archery, we offer them homage and honor."

The Thompson brothers were born in Indiana, and began to play with bows and arrows, probably associating the idea with Indians, while in their childhood. In their early life their parents moved to Georgia, and when the Civil War broke out their Irish blood and southern environment made them respond to the call to arms: They enlisted in the Confederate Army, and fought in the ranks until the surrender of Lee at Appomattox. Returning home, they found their father's plantation destroyed and the family destitute. Consequently, they took to the woods for several years—living exclusively on wild game that they shot with their beloved bow and arrow. They eventually went north to Indiana. After working as field laborers by day, they studied law by the fireplace during the evenings. By the 1890s they were both practicing law. Indeed, they were inseparable companions: they enjoyed the same sports, the same books and the same work. They even married sisters. During their lifetimes they both maintained a passionate and inconquerable love for the woods and fields, and both were consequently ardent sportsmen—hating the degeneration of city life. As experts with the long bow as well as with the rifle, both acquitted themselves brilliantly at public tournaments.

Their humorous public exploits of wing-shooting and other "fancy work" with the bow will surely bring a smile to your face. While shooting golden-winged woodpeckers at 80 yards with 75-pound straight bows currently exceeds the laws of conservation, you will delight in Maurice Thompson's descriptions of such fantastic bird shooting with bow and arrow. After shooting 98 arrows, we are told, Maurice once landed 16 ducks on the wing. On the other hand, 77 arrows were lost to posterity. Will once shot 121 arrows; 46 went to posterity, while 19 birds died on the wing.

Occasionally, this type of shooting resulted more in accident than in admirable skill, as the Thompsons were the first to point out: "To be sure, a goose at 30 yards is not difficult to bring to a stop, but it is only the rarest chance that one gets such an opportunity. Occasionally, when we started a raft of ducks from some weed-circled pool, an arrow slung at random through the thickest of the flock would send back to our ears the short, sudden sound of a hit." Still, we can appreciate the skill involved when we learn that Maurice, while shooting hunting arrows, could break 37 out of 50 Bogardus glass balls thrown into the air toward him at 12 yards. At 10 yards he could hit a lead pencil five times in succession. While Maurice was clearly the better teller of tales, Will was the better archer; he was a five-time U.S. Archery Champion for the years 1879, 1884, 1888, 1901 and 1908. There are not many sports in which an individual may count 30 years between championships.

As a team, the Thompsons almost single-handedly brought one of the world's oldest weapons into a new age of popularity. In doing so, not only did they devote much of their time to hunting with this ancient weapon, but they also studied the life of their quarry—believing that an archer must always study animate nature and learn its ways, if he is to capture it. The mass archery fever created by these two brothers, which appeared later in the century, was nothing less than phenomenal. Their philosophy of bow hunting encourages us all. Maurice summarizes his thinking when he writes that "The demand which this old implement makes upon one's patience, wariness, stealth, and skill is of itself an endless fascination; and when, at last, the successful shot is delivered, something strangely and inexplicably thrilling comes out of it. Moreover, the simple fact that shots are many and killings few may account for the greater part of bow hunting's fascination. The archer shoots for the joy of shooting, not for the bag's weight."

Brother Will underscores this same idea when he asserts, "How many I have missed to the one I have killed!" While these words were written over a century ago, we would have a difficult time saying it any better.

The next significant development in the history of American bow hunting occurred in 1912, when Dr. Saxton Pope (1875–1926), a professor at the University of California's medical school, befriended Ishi, the last wild Indian of the Yana Tribe. From Ishi, Pope learned the technique and the folklore of archery, pursued not as a pastime but as a way of life. So began Pope's mastery of the art of hunting big game with the bow and arrow. The results of Pope's careful study of Ishi's ways and his intimate details of bow hunting were published in his *Hunting with the Bow and Arrow* (1923), a classic that has inspired bow hunters ever since. When the book first appeared, however, bow hunting was little more than a curiosity with no mass appeal or any significant following.

In this book Pope expressed a philosophy of bow hunting which was very sim-

HON. MAURICE THOMPSON,

"The demand which this old implement makes upon one's patience, wariness, stealth, and skill is of itself an endless fascination; and when at last, the successful shot is delivered, something strangely and inexplicably thrilling comes out of it. Moreover, the simple fact that shots are many and killings few may account for the greater part of bow hunting's fascination."

—Maurice Thompson, 1878
Photo credit Emory University

ilar to that of the Thompson's. Satisfaction was not wholly centered in merely a shot well-placed or a trophy quickly come by; nor was the joy found primarily in the size of the bag or even in the certainty of the bag. But rather, the emphasis was placed on woodcraft, on outsmarting wild animals, and on the world of little things one must master to get near enough for a shot. Like the Thompsons, Pope believed that woodcraft was probably the most important and most difficult part of every bow hunter's training. Every woodlot represented a textbook in

Art Young (1883–1935), who was one of the founding fathers of American bow hunting and Saxton Pope's hunting partner. *Photo credit The Pope and Young Club*

wildlife ecology; woodcraft was the translation of that textbook. Actually, every woodlot provides us not only with a textbook on wildlife ecology, but with an entire liberal education. Unfortunately, this crop of wisdom, which never fails to appear each year—is not always harvested.

In reading Pope's books, one finds it hard to dispute his idea that the bow rather than the shotgun or rifle demands a closer understanding of nature. One also tends to sympathize with his belief that it gave him more pleasure to shoot at a deer and miss it with an arrow, than to kill all the deer he ever had before him with the gun. It's also hard to contradict his analogy between hunting and golf. Who would disagree with him, for example, when he

writes in *The American Bowmen* (1926) that "one hurries on to that *next time,* when he is going to do *everything known to science.* Then his foot slips, or he plucks the bow string, and the whole day is spoiled." The humor in Pope's writing is undeniable. Consider, for example, Ishi's opinion of white men: "Ishi always said that a white man smells like a horse, and in hunting makes a noise like one, but apparently lacks any horse sense."

When Ishi died of tuberculosis in 1916, Pope had enlarged his interest in hunting with the bow. Like Will Thompson, he also wrote about his findings and hunting adventures in *Forest and Stream.* To the astonishment of many sportsmen and naturalists, Dr. Pope soon began to take grizzly bears, cougars and elk with his six-foot straight bow made of yew wood. On many of his hunting adventures he was accompanied by his sportsman-friend Art Young (1883–1935), who had also mastered the outdoor sports at an early age. Together Pope and Young shot most species of big and small game in the United States, and went on many successful bow hunts to Alaska and Africa. In 1926 Young made a film entitled "Alaskan Adventure," which captured the essence of their hunting exploits, and which was to profoundly influence Fred Bear. Throughout history the hunting adventures of Pope and Young have generated much fireside discussion, and today almost reach legendary proportions. Just the thought of going deer hunting with two or three 80-pound straight bows and six dozen arrows excites one's mind with romantic adventure.

In 1957 the prestigious Pope and Young Club was founded as a lasting tribute to these two bow hunting pioneers. The club dedicates itself to promoting conserva-

The hunting adventures of Pope and Young generate fireside stories that today seem legendary. Most of their tales are true, however, and you can relive them by reading Dr. Saxton Pope's book entitled *Hunting with the Bow and Arrow. Photo credit The Pope and Young Club*

tion projects and high ethical standards in bow hunting. It advocates quality rather than quantity in big game harvest, and strives to maintain the wildlife heritage so dear to us all. In a recent memo from the club, the president summarized its underlying philosophy: "As hunters we find more satisfaction in the quest than in the quarry brought to bag. We believe bowhunting allows the maximum in hunter participation for a given game harvest and having chosen to hunt trophy class animals, we have assured ourselves of many pleasurable hours afield."

As we have seen, several individuals played major roles in the development of modern-day bow hunting—some by their hunting exploits and remarkable shooting, others by their dedication and promotion. The next major event of historic importance took place in Wisconsin during the late 1920s, when individuals such as Roy Case and Aldo Leopold successfully petitioned the Wisconsin Conservation Commission to revise its hunting laws to include the bow as a legal hunting weapon. As a result Roy Case, as early as 1930, shot the first deer with his bow

In 1930 Roy Case shot the first deer with a bow and arrow in Wisconsin under a special permit. The spike buck, which weighed approximately 112 pounds, was taken during the gun season with a 54-pound straight bow at 20 yards. One can only image the difficulties this pioneering bow hunter had as he tried to bow hunt whitetails during the regular gun season! *Photo credit Roy Case*

and arrow under a special permit—a spike buck weighing approximately 112 pounds. The deer was taken during the gun season with a 54-pound straight bow at 20 yards. One can only imagine the difficulties this pioneering bow hunter of untiring efforts had, as he tried to bow hunt whitetails during the regular gun season! In 1934, however, Wisconsin established America's first special bow hunting season— thanks to the enthusiastic efforts of Case and Leopold.

Both of these individuals, it should be noted, first became interested in bow hunting after reading Saxton Pope's *Hunting with the Bow and Arrow;* both of them also won the Silver Cup Cham-

pionship Trophies of the Wisconsin Archery Association during the early 30s. Both subscribed to a similar philosophy of bow hunting. "We hunt," Case once wrote in an eloquent defense of bow hunting, "for the sport of it, not for the results alone. A trout fisherman could get plenty trout with worms but it would not be half the fun as with his rod and flies. Thus with the archer." Leopold agreed, and rejoiced upon hearing the news of Case taking the first legal buck with his bow and arrow.

The popularity of modern bow hunting as a field sport was also enhanced by Fred Bear, whose greatest contribution to the sport lies in his personal philosophy of hunting. Bow hunters, he once told the editor of *Bowhunter Magazine,* have a success ratio of only about 6 percent. Consequently, they experience all the basic thrills of hunting, but with very little killing involved. Being in the woods stalking animals and enjoying the social camaraderie of camp, Bear always maintained, are the greatest thrills of bow hunting. The kill is always last.

Reflecting on his philosophy of hunting in his *Field Notes,* he wrote that "Trophies are not really important and have a low priority on my list. A downed animal is most certainly the object of a hunting trip, but it becomes an anti-climax when compared to the many other pleasures of the hunt. I like to think that an expedition be looked upon, whether it be an evening hunt nearby or a prolonged trip to some far-off place, as a venture into an unspoiled area. With time to commune with your inner soul, you share the outdoors with the birds, animals, and fish that live there."

I think this statement sums up the feeling of many modern-day bow hunters, and eptomizes one important lesson that we learn from a brief history of American bow-n-arrow hunting: There is some intangible quality in going afield with a bow which encourages the archer to accept a philosophy of hunting that emphasizes the chase rather than the kill—a philosophy of hunting which is hardly understandable to those whose sole purpose in hunting is merely to fill the pot.

The American bow hunter may well be a bricklayer, a surgeon, a corporation president, a housewife, salesman, mechanic, teacher, preacher, rancher, writer, actor, soldier, assembly man, plumber, electrician, *ad infinitum.* One thing is certain: There is no such thing as the stereotyped American bow hunter. We do know, though, that the average age of this special breed of hunter is 30. Seventy percent of them are married, and 96 percent of them are males. Thirty-nine percent of them experienced some college training, while 18 percent of them are college grads. Forty percent of them belong to local archery clubs, and 80 percent of them also hunt big game with their rifles.

The American bow hunter is sometimes a she—a mother, a wife or perhaps a girlfriend. More frequently, she's a woman "on her own and of her own," drawn to the sport for many of the same reasons listed earlier. According to Cheri Elliott, managing editor of *Bow and Arrow,* there are approximately 80,000 female bow hunters in America today, representing 4 percent of the total number. Many of them are not only champion target archers but also editors of the nation's leading archery and bow hunting magazines. Before the mid-60s, though, women for the most part remained "unsung heroes" in the history of the sport. As one leader of organized archery correctly notes, "Men were so busy promoting, hunting and reporting on their archery prowess that they overlooked the contributions and accomplishments of the fairer sex—the Lady Diana."

Why women should be attracted to bow hunting is not a difficult question to understand. Sheila Link, a consultant to the National Rifle Association, gives us an immediate answer: "Not only do gals enjoy archery, they also know that the experience involved in drawing a bow and in hunting is very beneficial for one's figure."

As early as 1878 Maurice Thompson strongly recommended bow hunting for women who were "adverse to the gayeties and fashionable dissipations of the watering-places,'' and who wanted to have well-rounded and beautiful forms. In *The Witchery of Archery* he wrote that ''Ladies who wish to have rounded and beautiful forms must learn that exercise in the open air and free light of outdoors is the one thing they need. As soon as they have learned the use of bows and arrows, they may roam the green fields and shady woods, shooting at tufts of grass, or the slender stems of the young trees; nor need they have any fear of tramps or robbers, for a drawn bow, in the hands of a resolute woman, will bring the boldest villian to a halt, or to his death, if necessary.''

Today, many women are switching from gun hunting to bow hunting. Lady Diana— the huntress pursuing the stags of old— is again becoming a popular sight in the woods of America. As Sheila Link puts it, ''Becoming a bowhunter will certainly help anyone—man or woman—become a better firearm hunter. But there's one danger in taking up archery: you may become so addicted to hunting with a bow that you'll find rifle hunting a comparatively tame game.''

Up until a few decades ago, when many people heard the very words ''bow hunting,'' they merely thought of Robin Hood and the Sherwood Forest gang or of the American Indians and their tales of wild buffalo hunts. I can recall how people laughed at me during the 1950s, as I stalked whitetails in camouflage with bow and arrow. They probably wondered to themselves how this ''modern Robin Hood'' would ever harvest a whitetail with such a primitive instrument. Little did they know how hard we studied our quarry, and how hard we practiced our shooting skills. In more recent years, however, thanks to the efforts of such individuals

as the Thompson brothers, Dr. Saxton Pope, Art Young and Fred Bear (to name but a few), bow hunting has become one of America's fastest-growing field sports. It has even entered the hallowed halls of ivy. The University of Wisconsin—Stevens Point campus, for example, now has Bow Hunting 101 listed on its timetable of semester course offerings.

According to a United States Fish and Wildlife Service report, the number of persons who purchased hunting licenses decreased in 1979, yet the number of bow hunters continued to grow, partly because of the long-term hunting opportunities provided by many states. The average state allows approximately 117 days of bow hunting annually. Five states even allow bow hunting for some species or other every day of the year. Today there are more than 1.3 million Americans who bow hunt for deer alone. During the past 40 years the sport has seen tremendous growth. Michigan's first bow season in 1937, for example, only drew 193 participants, as compared to more than 211,700 residents and non-residents who now hunt deer with their bow and arrow in that state. While Wisconsin registered only 40 bow hunters in 1937, today there are well over 170,000 bow hunters in the autumn woods of Wisconsin. Indeed, bow hunting in Wisconsin has become ''big business.'' Between 1967 and 1971 a total of $2.5 million was spent by bow hunters in license fees alone. According to an economic survey conducted by the Wisconsin Department of Natural Resources, an estimated number of more than 2 million man-days of recreation in one year were derived from Wisconsin bow hunting.

When one realizes that the thrills of matching reason against instinct are more important than putting meat in the freezer or antlers on the wall, one begins to acquire a philosophy of bow hunting. When one realizes that the kill isn't what is important, one begins to acquire a *mature* philosophy of bow hunting. When one realizes that the appeal of the sport lies in the demanding challenge involved, one begins to acquire a mature philosophy of bow hunting in the *best tradition* of Dr. Saxton Pope and Fred Bear. As Bear tirelessly reminds us, bow hunting emphasizes the pursuit and the chase, rather than the kill. One of the most significant features of bow hunting is its tendency to bring the mind into contact with the ultimate reality of nature. In the act of hunting, as Erich Fromm once observed, "Man achieves a certain though transitory unity with Nature."

In the ultimate stage of deer hunting, the bow hunter and the quarry no longer oppose one another as individual objects, but merge together as one reality. The bow hunter ceases to be conscious of himself as one who is engaged in pursuing his quarry. This heightened state of spiritual consciousness is realized only when completely empty and rid of the self. When this happens the bow hunter becomes one with his quarry and one with perfecting his technical skills of archery and woodsmanship. If this sounds like a religious ritual, you're right—it is. Dick Lattimer's description of Fred Bear's world gives us a vivid impression of the natural religiosity of the American bow hunter: "Fred Bear's world is one of woodsmoke, pawed acorns, the sweet smell of decaying leaves, the twitch of a deer's tail, and ragged birch bark blowing in the wind."

Although the dramatic increase in bow hunting license sales in America has leveled off in the past few years, it is not hard to understand the popularity of bow hunting and why bow hunters continually increase in numbers each year. We only need to read the following stimulating passage from Dr. Saxton Pope, one of the founding fathers of bow hunting, for an obvious explanation: "If you can smell the dank forest incense and your hand itches to draw a cloth yard shaft across a sturdy bow, then you are one of the immortals. In you we have the heart of the true archer. To you, I hereby bequeath . . . the long delicious trails and mountain paths. The ecstasy of cool running streams I give you freely when athirst, and last of all I leave to you the thrill of life and the joy of youth that throbs a moment in a well bent bow, then leaps forth in the flight of an arrow . . . May the gods grant you all space to carry a sturdy bow and wander through the forest glades to seek the bounding deer; to lie in the deep meadow grasses; to watch the flight of birds; to smell the fragrance of burning leaves; to cast an upward glance at the unobserved beauty of the moon. May they give you strength to draw the string to the cheek, the arrow to the barb and loose the flying shaft, so long as life may last."

Far from being an endangered species or a mere survivor from our historic past, the highly specialized sport of bow hunting is thriving as never before. One reason for its growth and stability lies in the fact that the American bow hunters' concern for preserving and enhancing the environment is exemplified not only in his hunting methods and in the primitiveness of his weapon, but in his entire philosophical approach to the sport. The strength of our sport in the future, however, clearly lies in organizational development and in hunter education. You cannot overemphasize the importance of the educational work of such national organizations as the National Field Archery Association, the Pope and Young Club, the Fred Bear Sports Club, the Professional Bow Hunters' Society, Bowhunters Who Care, the National Bow-hunter Education Foundation, as well as many state and local bow hunting organizations. They all need our help to continue their endeavors. Join them and become active! Help to establish the deer hunting archer as the most conservation-minded sportsman of all.

Fred Bear returns to the deer shack after a successful stalk of yesteryear. *Photo credit Fred Bear*

Chapter 21

Crippling Losses and the Future of American Deer Hunting

The problem of crippling losses is without doubt the most serious and most controversial problem in the entire field of deer and deer hunting. Unfortunately, not enough deer hunters or state game officials recognize it as such. Too often game agencies and deer hunters alike fail to understand the magnitude of the problem, and fail to realize that unrecovered game represents a serious threat to American sport hunting. This chapter describes in a dispassionate and systematic way the nature of the problem as it's revealed in the scientific literature, and as it's reflected in the words of the leading figures of the deer hunting fraternity.

Before we can solve this critical problem, we must first recognize that it is in fact a problem; we must face the issue with factual data before we can negate the losses. TO REITERATE: A SUB-STANTIAL RECOGNITION OF THE PROBLEM HAS NOT YET OCCURRED. Too frequently the subject of crippling losses merely remains a lively topic of non-conclusive discussion at DNR meetings, in barbershops and sporting-goods stores, and worse, around deer camp fireplaces. The scientists, however, portray a different state of affairs, a shocking and dismaying state of affairs to say the least. They tell us, for example, that on the average 30 percent of the legal harvest remains in the woods. The bleached bones of these deer carcasses (probably more than 200,000 nationwide) greatly tarnish the image of the American deer hunter, and could foreshadow the end of American deer hunting as we currently know it.

When I speak of "crippling losses" in this chapter, I refer to animals that were

A forked-horn blacktail wounded and lost by hunters on the University of California Hopland Field Station in Mendocino County, California. During 1957–1974, wounding loss in this area amounted to at least 20 percent of the recorded buck harvest. *Photo credit Guy Connolly*

wounded in the field and never retrieved by the hunter—whether done so intentionally or unintentionally, whether legally or illegally. In other words, I use the term to refer to all deer shot during a hunt and left dead on the range for whatever reason. For the most part, the very term "crippling losses" is unfamiliar to many deer hunters. Those hunters who have heard of it probably have given it but little thought. Their curiosity toward deer hunting statistics is usually satisfied when they know the harvest figures for their hunting area, or the census figures of winter deer losses. Whatever our personal knowledge or opinions on this subject might be, one thing seems

certain: Most of us will be radically astonished when we study the results from the scientific literature.

Between 1916 and 1980 more than 50 scientific studies on crippling losses took place all across America.

While it is hard to generalize from all these studies, since their methods of collecting and analyzing data greatly vary, the following generalizations with regard to crippling losses and deer hunting can nevertheless be made.

First of all, the problem is much more important than generally admitted. Many people totally underestimate the nature of the problem. It is hard to understand this reluctance to recognize the waste!

A COMPREHENSIVE REVIEW OF CRIPPLING LOSSES				
WILDLIFE RESEARCHER (Or Organization)	**YEAR**	**TYPE OF SEASON**	**PLACE & TYPE OF INVESTIGATIONS** (S) Field Search (Q) Questionnaire	**CALCULATED CRIPPLING LOSS** (% of legal harvest left in woods)
Aldo Leopold	1916	Not Known	New Mexico (Q)	30%
Mich. Dept. of Conservation	1928	Not Known	Michigan	23%
U. S. Forest Service	1934	Not Known	Huron National Forest	Above Legal Harvest
Richard J. Costley	1937	Not Known	Utah (Q)	19%
Roy Dale Sanders	1937	Bucks Only	N. W. Wisconsin (S & Q)	68%
Roy Dale Sanders	1938	Bucks Only	Ibid.	60%
Urban C. Nelson	1939	Not Known	Minnesota (Q)	19-20%
Richard J. Costley	1940	Either Sex	Utah (S)	25-42%
Harlan G. Johnson	1940	Not Known	Arizona	10-15%
Gilbert N. Hunter	1945	Not Known	Colorado	15%
W. Leslie Robinette	1939-46	Either Sex	Utah (S)	17-21%
Laurence E. Riordan	1947	Not Known	Colorado (Q)	13.8-39.2%
Wendell Bever	1948	Not Known	South Dakota	19.2%
Ernest Swift	1948	Not Known	Wisconsin	45%
Ralph C. Guettinger	1950	Either Sex	Wisconsin	17-22%
Wyoming Big Game	1952	Not Known	Northern Wyoming	20%
Longhurst, et al.	1952	Bucks Only	California (S)	30%
J. G. Teer, et al.	1953-61	Not Known	Texas	15%
Chester Anderson et al.	1954	Not Known	Wyoming	18%
Whitlock & Eberhardt	1955	Bucks Only	Michigan (S)	79%
Wis. Dept. of Conservation	1956-64	Either	Wisconsin	35-150%
Severinghaus & Cheatum	1956	Either	Nation-Wide Estimates	18% Or More
Dahlberg & Guettinger	1956	Either	Wisconsin	17-22%
Stanley G. DeBoer	1956-57	Bucks Only	Wisconsin (S)	64%
Taber & Dasmann	1957-58	Bucks Only	California (Q)	Over 40%
R. D. Schofield	1958	Either Sex	Michigan	50%
Wendell G. Swank	1958	Not Known	Arizona (S)	32%
Stanley G. DeBoer	1958	Either Sex	Wisconsin (S)	31%
Ray D. Hart	1959	Not Known	South Dakota (Q & S)	8.2%
Raymond D. Schofield	1960	Bucks Only	Michigan	4 Deer Per Sq. Mile
Laurits W. Krefting	1962	Bucks Only	Wisconsin (S)	52%
Laurits W. Krefting	1963	Either Sex	Wisconsin (S)	37%
C. W. Severinghaus	1963	Either Sex	New York	6.19-7.07%
R. Van Etten, et al.	1965	Either Sex	Michigan	10-15%
D. C. Autry	1966	Not Known	Illinois	31%
H. P. Weeks, et al.	1967-69	Either Sex	Indiana	25%
James A. Dechert	1967	Not Known	Kentucky (Q)	25%
J. L. Roseberry, et al.	1969	Either Sex	Illinois (Q & S)	31.6-35%
Robert D. Welch	1970	Either Sex	New Mexico (Q & S)	92%
Robert L. Downing	1971	Either Sex	Georgia	19%
William N. Holsworth	1973	Either Sex	Ontario (Biologists)	5.5%
W. Creed & J. Kubisiak	1973	Either Sex	Wisconsin (S)	2.9-10.9%
Hardin & Roseberry	1974	Either Sex	Illinois (Q & S)	19-24%
Connolly & Longhurst	1975	Bucks Only	California (Q & S)	21%
K. Menzel	1975	Either Sex	Nebraska (Q)	15-20%
C. Kirkpatrick et al.	1976	Either Sex	Indiana	25%
Losch & Samuel	1976		Nation-Wide Compilation	30%
N. J. Papez	1976	Either Sex	Nevada (Q)	35%
Daniel C. Worsham	1977	Either Sex	Tennessee (S)	10.8%
W. L. Robinette, et al.	1977	Either Sex	Utah	45%
Keith Causey, et al.	1978	Either Sex	South Carolina	16%
F. A. Stormer, et al.	1979	Either Sex	Indiana (Q & S)	27%

A comprehensive review of crippling losses. *Credit Robert Wegner*

Some scientists "believe that some of the seeming unconcern officially over this wastage of game is due to a fear that the hunting public may blame the law enforcement officers for not preventing it."

Secondly, the only realistic approach to this problem lies in somehow converting the crippling losses into legal harvest. But as history demonstrates, this is by no means a simple proposition. If we could convert this waste into legal harvest, we would be able to take home much more venison each year without a significant effect on the remaining herd!

Thirdly, the reasons why deer are left in the woods during the hunting season vary, but some of the more common reasons, according to a study done on the Fishlake National Forest in central Utah, are as follow: "(1) The deer was diseased; (2) The deer was of inferior size or in poor condition; (3) The terrain was rough or the place where the deer was killed was a long distance from camp and

The ethical deer hunter carefully examines every arrow, whether he thinks he hit the deer or not. *Photo credit Richard P. Smith*

there were no means of packing it out; (4) Storms forced the hunters out of the mountains before they had an opportunity to bring the deer into camp; (5) More deer were killed by the party than the licenses permitted; (6) The meat had spoiled or the deer was badly shot up; (7) The hunter could not find the deer after returning to pack it out; and (8) The deer escaped from the hunter after it was critically wounded."

Fourthly, additional information from this study in Utah indicates a high recovery by hunters of wounded bucks, but a very low recovery of antlerless deer. This situation unfortunately reflects the premium placed upon the two classes of animals by deer hunters. Geographically, the situation doesn't seem to change. We read, for example, in the *New York Fish and Game News* (Winter, 1952) that "A Game Management crew working the Connecticut Hill area of Tompkins and Schuyler Counties found as many dead does and fawns left lying in the woods as legal bucks removed from that area." But why? Because too many deer hunters, scientists suggest, are "flock-shooting" into the animals during the hectic atmosphere that adheres in gang hunting. Scientists also observe that the cause of the greatest loss of wounded deer revolves around the shooting of deer which are out of range and the inability of the hunter to track the wounded animal. According to one scientific researcher from the Virginia Bureau of Sport Fisheries and Wildlife, "Few hunters have the will power to resist shooting at deer that are beyond the effective killing range of their weapon, or that are moving too fast to be hit consistently in a vital spot."

Fifthly, hunter density plays an important role in determining crippling losses. It appears that a lost deer is more likely to be recovered by another hunter when hunter density is high. In other words, crippling losses are inversely related to hunter density: the higher the hunter density, the lower the crippling losses. In buck-only seasons the crippling loss generally remains higher than in antlerless seasons. In a research manual from the Wildlife Management Institute, entitled *Mule and Black-Tailed Deer of North America* (1981), deer biologists reach the following conclusions: "Crippling losses seem to be higher when only bucks are hunted than when any deer is legal game. Therefore, on ranges where the kill must be restricted, limited numbers of hunters with any-deer permits may be preferable to larger numbers of hunters allowed to take only bucks."

In many states, some form of antlerless deer season has significantly reduced the waste. To repeat: "Hunters' Choice" means less crippling losses. Yet, the American deer hunter generally refuses to support antlerless seasons. Here is how W. Leslie Robinette summarizes the problem in a classic study, entitled *The Oak Creek Mule Deer Herd in Utah* (1977): "Our observation of reduced mortality under the 'any deer' law, suggests that limiting the number of 'any deer' permits for areas requiring reduced kill would be preferable to 'buck only' hunting. We found a gratifying decline in crippling losses among antlerless deer with the 'any deer' law, but their loss rate was nonetheless still three to four times that of bucks. Several approaches to the problem present themselves. Increased warden surveillance of hunters afield and stiffer penalties for offenders are, of course, possibilities, but *the long-term solution would seem to lie in hunter ed-*

ucation. . . . Too many hunters shoot without aiming for a vital spot or shoot when deer are beyond effective range; others expend too little effort at recovering wounded animals; while still others leave dead deer that fail their expectations. Many hunter attitudes must change if the increasing demands for sport hunting are to be met."

Sixthly, the data indicate widely divergent assessments of crippling losses have been reported. This variation reflects definitional problems and different research techniques that scientists employ. Assessments based on hunter questionnaires have been variously characterized as negligible, low or not serious to considerable or fairly large. Quantitative estimates based on field studies, however, have generally ranged from 20 to 30 percent of the legal harvest during any-sex seasons and considerably higher during buck-only seasons. Many scientists agree that crippling losses generally equal 30 percent of the legal harvest. At that percentage level they represent a factor of major consideration in setting desired harvests and determining game populations in the future.

After analyzing the data, we soon learn what Aldo Leopold observed in his *Game Management* in 1933: that the crippling rate is from 10 to 100 percent as large as the kill—with the average crippling loss being at least 30 percent of the legal kill. In surveying the literature on crippling losses in 1976, two scientists from West Virginia University (Losch and Samuel) reached the conclusion that 42 scientific studies indicated a crippling loss of 30.4 percent of reported legal harvests.

Finally, some unrelated generalizations:

(1) Some scientists believe that the use of improved technological devices such

as higher velocity rifles, binoculars and scopes may be instrumental in reducing the crippling rate.

(2) Deer wasted by hunters during the fall hunting season provide foxes with their primary winter food.

(3) Crippling losses for experimental deer hunts are usually less than for normal outside hunting.

(4) Crippling losses depend upon type of weapon, weather conditions, terrain, cover, type of hunt, hunter ego and hunter ability.

(5) Wounding losses increase as deer become more wary, and as hunter success decreases.

(6) Successful gun hunters wound more deer than the unsuccessful group.

(7) Trophy hunting and publicizing the need to reduce large deer herds are probable reasons believed to encourage intentional abandonment.

(8) Some scientific researchers (Dahlberg and Guettinger, for example) are of the opinion that crippling losses are roughly proportional to the size of the deer herd being hunted—believing it logical to assume that with more deer and more hunters in the field, crippling losses will increase.

(9) Scientific data show that many deer are left intentionally.

(10) It is probable that hunters exert less effort to recover wounded antlerless deer than bucks.

(11) Deer hunters are less reluctant to kill and claim a buck crippled by someone else than an antlerless deer.

(12) It appears that many crippled deer do survive, so perhaps the "mercy shooting" as practiced by some American deer hunters should be discouraged.

(13) Since deer hunters are frequently unwilling to admit wounding, estimates based on hunter reports are usually quite conservative.

(14) Road hunting greatly contributes to the problem and must be stopped immediately.

(15) Wildlife professionals must implement policies to negate these losses.

Comparisons of crippling rates for bow hunters and gun hunters are very difficult to make because of various biases and because so few comparative studies have been done on a nationwide basis. While it is virtually impossible to thoroughly evaluate archery versus gun season losses, some general discussion of the factors involved in this regard is merited.

Between 1976 and 1979, a random sample of 9300 Iowa archers were sent questionnaires to determine hunter success, type of bow used, years of hunting experience, number of days hunted and crippling rates. After correlating data, Lee H. Gladfelter of the Iowa Conservation Commission reached the following conclusions: (1) Archers using compound bows had significantly higher success rates than other archers; (2) Between 1976 and 1979 the use of the compound bow increased from 32 percent of the hunters to 73 percent; (3) Crippling rates not only increased but were significantly higher for compound bow users. Apparently compound bow users are taking advantage of the added power, and are over-extending their shooting range. Compound users frequently shoot the arrow completely through the animal—compounding the problems of tracking.

In a study of hunter-inflicted wounding of white-tailed deer in southwestern Indiana, three Purdue University scientists conclude that "During regulated hunts for either antlered or antlerless deer the per capita wounding rate (per 100 hunter days) by archers is 1.5 times that by gun hunters." Evidence from their research also suggests "That bow hunters may wound antlered males in higher proportion than they are represented in the living population." The reason for this situation can probably be attributed to the relative boldness of bucks and their increased rut activity during the bow season. Since bow hunters apparently see more bucks than gun hunters, they tend to harvest and wound proportionately more antlered deer than gun hunters. While bucks still rut when the gun hunt begins, the extreme disturbance caused by the high density of gunners tends to depress rut-related activities of males.

This Purdue University study, entitled *"Hunter-Inflicted Wounding of White-Tailed Deer"* (1979), refuted the popular notion that novice bow hunters wound the most deer. The opposite seems to be the case. The study also supports the interesting idea that bow hunters have a better opportunity than gun hunters of bagging antlered deer. They conclude that bow hunters apparently admit wounding more readily than gun hunters.

It is important to note that most scientists conclude that recovery from wounds frequently occurs more often with archery-related wounding than for gun-related injuries, since an archery-related wound is generally smaller, cleaner and entails less mutilation. In other words, an arrow has a less devastating effect upon impact in comparison to bullets. They also point out that arrows imbedded in muscle have a tendency to work out and that death by hemorrhage is relatively painless. Even though scientists tend to agree that bow hunting results in a greater wounding rate proportionately to gun

hunting, we must remember that the actual impact on the deer herd is offset by the higher rate of recovery that may occur with archery injuries and by the archer's relatively low percentage of the total deer harvest.

Speculation concerning unrecovered losses from bow hunting versus gun hunting has long been a controversy throughout the annals of American deer hunting. Stories of high crippling losses as a result of bow hunting frequently originate from the bow hunters themselves, who often exaggerate hunting experiences in which they allegedly hit a deer (however superficial) and lost it. Many listeners automatically assume that the deer in these hunting tales dies a lingering death. Experience indicates that a high percentage of these deer not only survive, but were entirely missed in the first place. Estimated losses, however, range from those where archery losses considerably exceed gun losses to the exact opposite, with gun losses in greater excess.

In a 746-acre enclosure at Albany, Georgia, Robert L. Downing of the Virginia Bureau of Sport Fisheries and Wildlife reported in 1971 that archers failed to recover 50 percent of the legal harvest. In comparing losses by archery, buckshot and shotgun slugs, Downing wrote that "Archery caused the highest rate of crippling loss; buckshot an intermediate rate; and slugs, the lowest rate." The high loss by archers in his study is probably explained by the small size of the sample. Downing added, however, that data for bow hunters at the Radford Arsenal in Virginia indicated very nearly as high a loss in that area. "Of the 138 deer killed by archers, 43 (31 percent) were not recovered. . . . At both locations archers had frequent opportunities for shots at too great a distance to be sure of making a clean kill. Crippling is likely to be high under these conditions and appeared to be the principal cause of loss. . . . The rate of archery loss is high, and if a large portion of the hunting pressure is by archers, an effort to control this loss may be required.''

In sharp contrast to this high comparative assessment, other scientific studies indicate the opposite situation, with gun losses in greater excess. Stanley G. DeBoer of Wisconsin, for example, reports that crippling losses in the Necedah National Wildlife Refuge for bow hunters in 1957 represented only 10 percent of the legal harvest, whereas the gunners left 31 percent of the harvest in the field or three times that of the archery loss.

In the final analysis, however, the question is not whether bow hunters wound more deer than gun hunters or vice versa, but rather how are we going to curb both kinds of losses? That is the question!

What do we learn, then, from the scientific literature? We learn one undeniable fact: In reality, the crippling loss considerably exceeds the popular conception of it. Unfortunately, the problem will most likely continue. Indeed, the problem should represent a special cause of concern for deer hunters, wildlife managers and game officials; it does for non-hunters and antihunters! They are using this problem as part of their attack against sport hunting.

Leading members of the deer hunting fraternity have frequently voiced their outrage and concern. Unfortunately, their pleas, exhortations and admonitions go unheeded and unobserved. It is high time we read and reread the following statements:

''Too few deer hunters realize that after hours of patient toil, and a shot fired with perfect coolness and accuracy, the glossy prize that you so fondly imagined yours beyond a doubt may be suddenly resolved into the most slippery intangibility on earth, and that the hunt instead of ending has in reality only commenced.''
—T. S. Van Dyke, *The Still Hunter* (1882).

''One shot—no cripples—that should be our aim.''
—William Monypeny Newsom, *White-Tailed Deer* (1926).

''Too many hunters shoot at any part of the animal's body, instead of at a selected point. If a buck jumps up ahead of them, their rifles instantly crack, although the tail and quarters offer but a fleeting target. Hence the bloody trails, the cripples that succumb slowly under the hardships of the following winter, the bleaching bones of fine specimens that wander for miles before lying down to perish with a bullet through the ham or kidneys . . . If you are of the right stamp you will take pains to learn where vital spots are located on a deer's anatomy, instead of blazing away helter-skelter, and maiming several individuals before you happen, through a stroke of graceless luck, to knock one over.''
—Paul Brandreth, *Trails of Enchantment* (1930).

''More wounded deer should be recovered than are taken each year to date; fewer of these fine animals should be wounded to stagger off into swamps and thickets and die slowly and miserably, alone, without comfort, not knowing why; with festering wounds, tongue and throat slowly burning for the water they cannot reach; with fever gradually consuming their great strength and vitality, and their blood slowly flowing to the forest floor, taking with it the final spark of vigor. These whitetail deer are warm-blooded creatures, like ourselves. They must feel pain to much the same degree, perhaps even more, because of their extreme sensitivity. The killing of them must be done quickly and cleanly, without excuses.''
—Larry Koller, *Shots at Whitetails* (1948).

"A common denominator of all sporting codes is not to waste good meat. Yet it is now a demonstrable fact that American deer-hunters, in their pursuit of a legal buck, kill and abandon in the woods at least one doe, fawn, or spike buck for every two legal bucks taken out. In other words, approximately half the hunters shoot any deer until a legal deer is killed. The illegal carcasses are left where they fall. Such deer-hunting is not only without social value, but constitutes actual training for ethical depravity elsewhere."
—Aldo Leopold, *A Sand County Almanac* (1949).

"It has been shown repeatedly that losses in deer wounded and eventually killed by hunters, but never recovered by them, run from 15 to 25 percent of the actual reported take. In some areas, we have good reason to believe that the loss may be considerably higher. . . . Unfortunately, we have considerable evidence that the failure to recover a large percentage of wounded deer can be attributed to the indifference, or to the lack of knowledge, of many of our deer hunters—or to both."
—C. W. Severinghaus, *New York State Conservationist* (1950).

"Too many impossible and long-chance shots are taken by deer hunters. . . . Pass up those long shots so that your conscience need not bother you about the deer you crippled and let get away."
—Frank C. Edminster, *Hunting Whitetails* (1954).

"Texas Game and Fish Commission figures reveal 19 percent of deer shot at are wounded without being recovered. This figure of wasted venison is too low, for a greater number are shot at and wounded without the hunter knowing his shot took effect simply because the hunter did not bother to find out whether or not the target was hit, or because he did not know how to find, or interpret, signs left by the animal at which he shot. The figure of unfound deer which die from wounds inflicted by hunters would approximate twice that figure (or 38 percent of the legal harvest.)"

—Dr. Frederick H. Weston, *Hunting the White-Tailed Deer in Texas* (1954).

"Thousands of deer are wounded and left to spoil in this country every year simply because hunters won't go over to the spot where the animal was and look for blood, cut-off hair, or other signs of a hit. At least 50 percent of all wounded animals can be recovered simply and easily, as in a high proportion of the cases they do not run over 100 yards and leave a trail a child could follow."
—Jack O'Connor, *The Art of Hunting Big Game in North America* (1967).

"The number of animals left in the woods to die of gunshot wounds is not realized by the ordinary man. In the big emphasis to fill the bag, too many hunters refuse to pass up any shot regardless of consequences if it offers the slightest chance for getting their deer. It is unfortunate that these hunters do not linger in the deer country after the hunting season to learn first hand of the misery caused by trigger-happy shooting. And this misery continues until time or the rigors of winter painfully eliminate these maimed animals."
—George Mattis, *Whitetail: Fundamentals and Fine Points for the Hunter* (1969).

"Studies on Utah's Fishlake National Forest turned up considerable deer carcasses with bullet slugs in them. While some of the deer could have been victims of poachers—or even the unclaimed deer of so-called 'sportsmen' seeking bigger bucks—it is not likely. A few would have been worth measuring for the record books. Apparently the only reason they were not tagged was the fact that the hunters couldn't find them."
—Hartt Wixom, *Field & Stream* (1970).

"When I think of the great number of deer left in the woods each year by hunters to suffer and die, I'm appalled as all true sportsmen should be. Extensive long-term studies by conservation departments indicate that 33 percent of all wounded deer are never retrieved. This is the national average—a disheartening statistic indeed."

—Ralph S. Norris, *Science of Hunting the Whitetail Deer* (1972).

"It is estimated that hundreds (of thousands) of deer wastefully die each year of wounds inflicted by hunters who lack either the ability or the sense of responsibility to track them down. These range from the wild 'snap-shot' at a flashing white tail to the fluke hit on a standing or walking animal. It seems incongruous with the basic values behind hunting and sportsmanship, but it continues to happen nonetheless. I have witnessed hunters on several occasions shoot one, two, three or more times at a whitetail bounding in the distance and then assume, without checking, that they have missed."
—Malcolm A. Makin, *Field & Stream Deer Hunting Annual* (1973).

"Trailing a cripple is a sad and depressing task, but it simply must be done. No man who even pretends to claim the honorable title of 'sportsman' will run the slightest risk of leaving a wounded deer in the woods, and, harsh as it may sound, I believe no sportsman has the right to fire at a deer until he has mastered at least the fundamentals of reading sign and trailing."
—John Wootters, *Hunting Trophy Deer* (1977).

"I can recall how distressing it was for me as a youngster in Vermont to go out into the woods and find the remains of cripples that had died after being hit. Some of the deer were antlerless animals that some 'sportsman' had shot without waiting for positive identification. These misidentified animals were then just left to rot in our woods. On at least one occasion, though, I found a buck that the hunter was apparently unable to locate after shooting it. (All this land was, by the way, posted; no one was supposed to be hunting on it.) In my opinion, the second greatest sin that a hunter can commit is taking a careless shot at a deer. The worst thing that he can do is to fail to follow aggressively the trail of a deer that he has wounded whether his shot was careless or not."
—Robert E. Donovan, *Hunting Whitetail Deer* (1978).

"Recent public surveys indicate that people are not so much bothered by the killing of wildlife as by the thought that poorly trained shooters are crippling game."
—George Reiger, *Field & Stream* (1980).

Need we go on? Yes . . . indeed, it's a problem! What are we going to do about it?

The time has come when self-respecting sportsmen must refuse to countenance or even associate with hunters who are careless with guns and indiscriminate in their shooting practices. The future of deer hunting is on the line.

The time has also long passed for high-powered, mandatory hunter education. The time is long overdue for adoption of stringent proficiency testing. Candidates for the deer hunting license ought to pass in-depth examinations dealing with deer anatomy, wounded deer behavior, tracking problems and overall marksmanship. We cannot settle for anything else. Common sense tells us this! And yet it does not happen.

People must pass these examinations or they must not be allowed to enter the deer forest as a hunter. Short and simple! There is no other alternative. Our standards for allowing people to enter the field as hunters are too low. Indeed, they are currently an abomination to human intelligence. Until this problem is met head on, the future of American deer hunting is bleak.

We now successfully manage deer herds. It is high time we successfully manage the "herd" of slob hunters who are turning the sport of deer hunting into an indiscriminate, trigger-happy shooting gallery. It is within the power of sportsmen and game managers to do so. Why are we waiting and doing nothing? It is evident that we must require hunters to take stricter hunting skill tests before they are allowed to hunt. The current system borders on the ludicrous and the absurd. Our standards for the deer hunting license are crude and barbaric; they need to be brought into the 20th century. Until our standards for certification are tightened, the problem of crippling losses will continue.

Are special interest groups dragging their feet because they realize that in stricter certification procedures fewer hunters will pass, and consequently fewer people will buy bows, arrows, guns, shells and sporting equipment? Are money interests exercising a paralyzing effect upon this issue? Everybody talks a good tune, but when the votes are cast, mandatory hunter education and stricter examinations lose out. We must ask ourselves why?

We are long overdue to find an effective solution to this problem. The solution will have to come from both game managers and sportsmen. Unfortunately, we do not see a solution on the horizon.

The picture one gets when examining this subject is ugly. It is being told with the hope that a little shock treatment will jar people out of their indifference toward this useless slaughter. Even though the offending hunters represent a minority, they operate with "deadly efficiency." When are we going to get rid of them? When are we going to test them out of existence? Because whether we like it or not, that is the only way we are going to get rid of them.

"The more I think about it the more I am convinced that crippling-loss figures must be had as a basis for intelligent game management of any kind. While I certainly concede that the sentimentalists will use and probably misuse figures of this sort and thus do some possible harm to sport hunting, I do think such harm would be a drop in the bucket compared with the harm which would result from a policy of unwillingness to face facts as they are."

—Aldo Leopold to Paul L. Errington, **Unpublished Letter,** April, 1933

Chapter 22

The Deer-Hunting Ethic

In surveying the vast domain of literature on hunting the white-tailed deer in America, and in speaking with game managers, rural sociologists and professors of wild-life ecology, one observes with great amazement how little has been written on the proper ethics of this eternal pursuit. While there is surely no dearth of information on this subject in the popular press, much of it remains, unfortunately, mere apologetics that skirt the philosophical issue and reveal little scholarly insight or research. As one environmental scientist recently observed, the extent of the literature on this topic consists merely in emotional attacks and rebuttals and in editorial journalism without much new information or systematic study.

The best study on this subject still remains Jose Ortega y Gasset's *Meditations on Hunting*, which all deer hunters should read and ponder. In this treatise on hunting, originally published in 1942, the great Spanish philosopher argues that hunting, like every human activity, has an ethic which clearly distinguishes virtue from vice. Indeed, the modern deer hunter today must formulate a deer hunting ethic to measure and evaluate his conduct in the field. Such an ethic must deal with at least the following essential components: (1) consideration of hunting as a privilege rather than a right; (2) restriction of modern technological advantages; (3) elimination of road hunting; (4) implementation of mandatory educational course work and subsequent examination prior to licensing; and (5) recognition and consideration of the German attitude of mind toward hunting.

This chapter addresses itself primarily to the first of these components: the question of whether deer hunting should be considered a right or a privilege? This basic question and its resolution, it seems to me, is of the utmost importance, especially considering the badly tarnished image of today's hunter, the frequent problems we encounter between hunter and landowner, and the growing strength and impetus of the antihunting movement in this country.

Traditionally, Americans have considered hunting as an inherent, inalienable right exempt from behavioral control by social policy or social norms. But is it? I think not. Hunting, we must remember, is a social value and not necessarily an inalienable right which every civilized and humane society must unequivocally defend. As one rural sociologist recently observed, "Society has the ability to prohibit hunting behavior with appropriate legislation and enforcement . . . The value of hunting is a value that is socially determined by the attitudes and behavior of (all) people who live in that society. A social decision can be made to prohibit hunting just as a social decision can be made to enhance it with public programs."

Most sociological surveys today show that rural habitation and pro-hunting views have decreased in recent years in favor of urban dwelling and antihunting attitudes. That is to say, demographically, the more urbanized the population becomes, the more addicted it becomes to antihunting sentiments. This trend may well be the number one problem facing both wildlife managers and deer hunters.

Given the fact that the deer hunter is primarily born and raised in rural areas and that increased urbanization suggests a future decrease in the proportion of the population that hunts, we might do well to intellectually defend hunting in the

What American environmental education must build today is an ethical underpinning for hunting, in general, and for deer hunting, in particular; what we need, as Leopold foresaw many years ago, is a new woodcraft of the highest cultural order. *Photo credit Irene Vandermolen*

context of a privilege, following the German tradition. We would thus assume greater responsibility toward developing an ethic that enlightens both the sportsman in his duties and responsibilities, as well as the non-hunting population in deer hunting as a proper instrument of sound game management.

To turn toward Germany for a proper attitude on a deer-hunting ethic is surely not new. Aldo Leopold did so as early as 1936, when he observed that hunting in Germany was properly considered a privilege which entailed an all-day examination, as well as a practical test of whether the hunter knew how to handle and shoot a weapon safely and effectively. German hunters, Leopold re-

One of the greatest books ever written on the ethics and philosophy of hunting. A classic! Based on the correct assumption that human nature is inseparable from the hunting instinct. *Photo credit Pam Riepe*

minded his readers, did not merely stop at the local gun shop and pick up a license.

Before receiving a license today, German hunters attend mandatory hunter education programs that stress the identification of local game and predatory species, as well as their feeding habits and life histories. Game foods, game protection laws and laws governing trespass and arrest also comprise an essential ingredient of the German hunter's educational program, as does the dressing and handling of carcasses and the evaluation procedures of measuring trophies. Before anyone is authorized to purchase a hunting license in Germany, he has studied ballistics, practical shooting, game biology, hunting techniques and ethics, principles of game management, game diseases, and the customs and language of the hunter, *die Jägersprache.*

The course of study involves approximately 100 classroom hours and demands a great deal of *Sitzfleisch,* (homework and sticking to the job). The candidate is then asked to pass a three-hour written examination consisting of about 150 in-depth questions. A three-hour oral examination which deals with practical matters then follows. The candidate then shoots a rifle and a shotgun before a board of judges. Fifty percent of the candidates fail. This whole rigorous process might cost as much as $300, but the license is good for life unless revoked for due cause. No one goes through this procedure, effort and expense unless he has an all-consuming dedication to hunting and wildlife ecology.

When the candidate finally does become a hunter through the granting of a license, one becomes a member of the official *Deutsche Jägerschaft* (German Hunters' Association), a national society which promotes wildlife education for its members, publishes a central journal entitled *Deutsche Jagd,* and conducts ecological research for the benefit of its members.

The amazing thing about this whole procedure is that it is not imposed upon the individual by the government, but by the German hunters themselves and their national hunting association. With increasing industrialization and population and decreasing rural land area, this system of hunting has worked very well. The system has changed little since 1936. Indeed, modern observers still agree with Leopold's final assessment that the German "system of law, administration, ethics, customs, and procedures is incredibly complete and internally harmonious."

The educational requirements for the hunter are concisely contained in one slim volume of 550 pages, entitled *Jägerprüfung* (Hunter Examination). Its length reminds one of Tolstoy's *War and Peace*.

One of the most cherished German traditions, exhibiting a profound respect for the game animal, the Germans call *der letzte Bissen* (The Last Bite). Following the kill of a deer, the hunter places a small branch of a native tree, such as an evergreen branch, crosswise in the mouth of the animal as a token of last respect. He then dips a small branch in the blood of the animal and places it in the right side of his hat band. Standing before the fallen game the German hunter than offers a prayer to Saint Hubertus, Patron of the Hunt, for the game, the fine weather and the camaraderie of the hunt, thus maintaining Saint Hubertus's attitude toward game animals as "beings" rather than just targets to shoot at. The Last Bite signifies a final salute to the animal and symbolizes the return of his soul to our Maker.

In the absence of these kinds of traditions, and in comparing our voluntary hunter-safety program with the sophisticated German system of hunter education, it is not surprising to learn that many Germans think North Americans lack a deep and profound respect for the animal they hunt. One frequently encounters the following German attitudes toward American hunters:

"You are too intent on getting your bag limit in the shortest possible time. The essence of the hunt is thus lost in the process."

"You Americans make good soldiers when you have an Eisenhower to lead you. But good hunters? Never!"

How can our European colleagues think much differently of us, when we are constantly bombarded by American technological gadgetry generally advertised for its instant value for the man who simply does not have the time for long, arduous hours of practice in the field? Take, for example, a typical advertisement for a new shotgun: "Mount it on your gun, slip into the field, get your deer, and be home in time for the cocktail hour!"

Today's deer hunter must not choose to exercise the overabundance of ultimate technological advantages. White-tailed deer only exist and thrive because men hunt under certain self-imposed disadvantages. More than ever we need a new morality which prevents the genuine sportsman from using his technological gadgets to the fullest, if we are ever to justify sport hunting to the non-hunting public. Leopold put the issue this way:

"Our tools for the pursuit of wildlife improve faster than we do, and sportsmanship is a voluntary limitation in the use of these armaments. It is aimed to augment the role of skill and shrink the role of gadgets in the pursuit of wild things . . . The gadgeteer has draped the American outdoorsman with an infinity of contraptions, all offered as aids to self-reliance, hardihood, woodcraft, or marksmanship, but too often functioning as substitutes for them. Gadgets fill the pockets, they dangle from neck and belt. The overflow fills the auto-trunk, and also the trailer. Each item of outdoor equipment grows lighter and often better, but the aggregate poundage becomes tonnage. The traffic in gadgets add up to astronomical sums, which are soberly published as representing 'the economic value of wildlife.' "

One wonders what the founder of wild-life ecology would have thought had he

For a fascinating mix of whitetail facts with profound deer hunting philosophies, read *Deer & Deer Hunting* magazine (P.O. Box 1117, Dept. 5B, Appleton, WI 54912), the leading magazine on the subject. As one reviewer observed: "This highly regarded, first-class publication not only presents the latest scientifically substantiated data on whitetail behavior but also covers all facets of deer hunting. It fills a large void in the conventional outdoor magazine market. It is refined, extremely interesting, useful and highly impressive!" *Photo credit Pam Riepe*

read the following list of problem areas which confront, or should confront, the conscience of all deer hunters. The list was prepared by the 1976 Wisconsin Hunting Ethics Committee and epitomizes the magnitude of the problem. The problems are listed in order of importance:

1.) No required hunting examination (regulations, marksmanship, species identification, landowner rights, vision check).

2.) Not enough wardens to enforce present laws.

3.) Hunters damaging property (buildings, machines, fences).

4.) Lack of knowledge of species and sex difference of game and gamebirds (including waterfowl).

5.) Failure to know laws, species and seasons.

6.) Failure to learn proper weapon handling.

7.) Shooting out of season.

8.) Use of automobiles while hunting to spot game or to shoot from the automobile.

9.) Littering, leaving animal remains along highways.

10.) Hunter concentrations on public hunting grounds on opening days.

11.) Game laws are not always clear and easy to understand.

12.) Not enough effort put on retrieving game.

13.) Chicken-hearted local courts (minor fines).

14.) Lack of hunter education concerning the role of nature and wildlife management principles.

15.) Hunters do not know about safe gun handling or ballistics.

16.) Use of citizen's band radios or walkie-talkies while hunting.

17.) Lack of enforcement.

18.) Lack of knowledge by hunter in field-dressing and care of game.

19.) Backtags still not required for all kinds of hunting.

20.) Deer hunter concentrations along roads and in towns.

21.) Hunters hunting without permission.

22.) Hunters expect the state to provide hunter opportunity in return for license fee.

23.) No identification needed to buy a license.
24.) Failure to secure understanding with property owners.
25.) Hunter concentrations around goose refuges.
26.) Shooting signs, insulators.
27.) Courts are too lenient on violators.
28.) Measurement of success in terms of bag limit.
29.) Better advertisement or education concerning existing laws is needed.
30.) Little or poorly trained supplementary enforcement staff.
31.) Trespassers will not leave land when confronted by landowner.
32.) Hunters cannot identify wildlife.
33.) Not enough hunting land available.
34.) Hunters need to set an example to other hunters through their own conduct.
35.) Failure to respect the rights of other hunters.
36.) Driving on fields and damaging crops.
37.) State trespassing laws and local ordinances not clearly defined (hunters do not know trespass laws).
38.) Indiscriminate shooting of deer before determining sex.
39.) Wardens have too many other duties not related to field enforcement.
40.) Use of off-road vehicles or snowmobiles for hunting.
41.) Shooting protected species.
42.) Shining and shooting animals at night.
43.) Hunting by permission signs do not tell how to find the owner.
44.) Disputes between hunters for game and hunting areas (duck blinds and deer stands too close).
45.) Failure or disinterest of landowners and officials to prosecute.
46.) Lack of appreciation of the esthetic values of hunting.

47.) Shooting too close or too far for hunter's equipment capability, resulting in wasted game.
48.) Concentrations lead to long shots, rapid firing and danger of being shot.
49.) Hunters resort to unfair or illegal practices in order to fill bag.
50.) Lack of awareness of ethical responsibility beyond statutes or regulations.
51.) Regulations not always available at time of license purchase.
52.) Some laws considered impractical and are ignored.
53.) Urban hunters do not inherit hunter savvy.
54.) Hunters hunting too close to buildings or hunting where landowners instructed them not to hunt.
55.) Spooking or shooting livestock.
56.) Failure of hunters to report violations seen.
57.) Lack of knowledge concerning wildlife population dynamics.
58.) Complicated or confusing regulations, people do not understand them or will not read them.
59.) Use of illegal weapons or shot.
60.) Advertising or news releases by equipment manufacturers or game departments creating false impressions about game abundance or accessibility.
61.) Not utilizing game which has been taken (by people who enjoy hunting but not eating game).
62.) Property boundaries poorly marked.
63.) Hunters do not get permission to hunt before season and ''bother'' landowner during the season.
64.) Excessively large hunting parties for drive purposes.
65.) Bird hunting without using a dog.
66.) Unsupervised young hunters.

67.) Hunters damaging trees (blinds) and cutting firewood.

68.) Failure to accept hunting as a privilege and not a right.

69.) Shooting before or after hours.

70.) Shooting of raptors.

71.) No minimum qualifications are necessary (physically handicapped).

72.) Lack of target practice.

73.) Purposely shooting undesirable game.

74.) Department of Natural Resources offices not open when most people can get to them.

75.) A hunter with permission bringing along a carload of friends.

76.) No attempt to get citizen cooperation, no public relations work.

77.) People breaking into shacks and stealing.

78.) Exceeding bag limits.

79.) People must be able to remain anonymous when reporting violations.

80.) Use of dogs to hunt deer or bear.

The items on this list all contribute in one way or another to the bad performance and image of today's sportsman. We should re-read this list if we are to grasp the nature of the problem. There are many things for us to be concerned about, if we are to label ourselves sportsmen.

Leopold would have been most appalled with number 78: exceeding the bag limits. Leopold, like early bow and arrow hunters such as Fred Bear and Saxton Pope, enjoyed hunting the white-tailed deer as a gentleman should enjoy it, and expressed utter disgust with the tawdry meat hunting practices of so-called American sportsmen. In his *Sand County Almanac* (1949), Leopold demonstrated how deer hunters in their relentless pursuit of a legal buck often kill and abandon

several antlerless deer for every legal buck taken. "The illegal carcasses are left where they fall. Such deer-hunting is not only without social value but constitutes actual training for ethical depravity elsewhere."

The illegal deer kill may well equal the legal kill. Reports from farmers still verify the existence of this kind of behavior. The Germans have managed to do away with this degeneracy by requiring the passing of educational course work on high-quality hunting prior to licensing. Slob hunters who give the sport a bad name in this regard are all but eliminated.

The German educational course and examination prior to licensing has also made hunting more acceptable to the non-hunting population in Germany. Perhaps we too could short-circuit the antihunting sentiment that is currently so prevalent in this country by implementing a mandatory educational program prior to the hunt, a program which would go far beyond the voluntary hunter-safety program. We do not drive automobiles without driver training courses. Why do we take to the field without any required training in weaponry, marksmanship, the laws governing trespass, or in the habits and life history of the quarry itself?

The more one delves into this question, the more ridiculous our current situation becomes. Dan Trainer, the Dean of the College of Natural Resources at the University of Wisconsin—Stevens Point, vividly demonstrated the laxity of our hunting license requirement when a friend of his, who "is classified as legally blind, purchased a big game hunting license. It would seem logical that someone going into the woods with a high-powered rifle should be able to see, yet we do not require this in Wisconsin."

In Germany hunting is considered a privilege; in America it is considered a right. Which would you prefer? For my part, I view this eternal pursuit as a privilege with all the responsibilities, duties and self-education that it entails. In his *Meditations,* Ortega defined hunting in the following way: "In his mystical link with the game, a deeper connection develops, and the hunter starts to be like the animal he hunts; he becomes one with nature."

If we accept this definition of the hunt, we are all obliged to view hunting from the perspective of a privilege. Obviously, we need to maintain the right to hunt, but along with this right we must assume greater responsibility in educating ourselves for a proper deer-hunting ethic, an ethic which will preserve and foster the precepts of ecology, fair chase and conservation. The deer hunting ethic as it exists today, *without* an adequate hunter education program, *without* a basic examination prior to hunting, is governed wholly by self-interest, just as social ethics were more than a century ago.

Deer hunting in Germany remains a cherished tradition and a privilege; we can all profit, I submit, from their experience and tradition. Unfortunately, the American hunter will probably oppose the German attitude of mind toward hunting because of its self-imposed restrictions. But the genuine American sportsman will accept restrictions and establish cherished traditions. If he does not, if he does not police his own ranks, the public will do it for him and probably in a less desirable way for all concerned.

Leopold realized this problematic situation as early as 1933, when he pleaded with American hunters to "adhere to self-imposed restrictions which go further than

the law and further than group rules." Too frequently American deer hunters still merely obey the laws, rules and regulations of hunting while violating their spirit and ethics. Let us adhere to Leopold's basic moral precept and become the "advanced individuals" he envisaged over 40 years ago. Only then will we have a hunting and shooting fraternity worthy of the name.

To summarize: Managing the white-tailed deer in the absence of predator control demands an ethical restraint of the highest order. It is difficult to exaggerate the importance of this idea. In his *Sand County Almanac* Leopold developed the essential foundation for a deer-hunting ethic in an essay entitled *Wildlife in American Culture.* This marvelous essay of timeless quality needs to be read and re-read by all serious deer hunters. In it we find one of the most eloquent pleas for ethical restraint while hunting ever formulated. Its basic moral precept reads as follows: "A peculiar virtue in wildlife ethics is that the hunter ordinarily has no gallery to applaud or disapprove of his conduct. Whatever his acts, they are dictated by his own conscience, rather than by a mob of onlookers. It is difficult to exaggerate the importance of this fact."

Today's sportsman must realize that ethical practices are not only a question of personal responsibility and conscience, but are at the heart of the very idea of high-quality deer hunting and indeed at the heart of the future of the sport itself. As hunters we all need to fully recognize the rights and privileges of hunting, and treat the quarry, the magnificent whitetail, with profound respect.

While written creeds and moral codes will not necessarily make anyone ethical in his hunting practices, *The Creed of the Wisconsin Sportsman* as formulated by a 30-member citizens committee and chaired by a representative of the Department of Natural Resources in 1976, can surely provide guidelines against which the modern deer hunter can measure his conduct. It needs to be quoted in its entirety:

THE CREED
OF THE WISCONSIN SPORTSMAN

I will:

Set a personal example to broaden public understanding of sport hunting as a valuable form of outdoor recreation and an essential tool of wildlife management and recognize that my conduct is a reflection on the collective hunter image;

Go afield mentally equipped with a knowledge of the species I seek, the game laws and regulations I am pledged to obey, and the character of the habitat in which I hunt;

Go afield physically fit and equipped to demonstrate gun safety and marksmanship that will assure a safe, clean, conservative harvest;

Consider myself an invited guest of the landowner, seeking his permission, protecting property from damage and litter, and so conducting myself that I will be welcome in the future;

Recognize fully the rights and privileges of my fellow hunters, and of the nonhunting public, engaging in fair, honest sport, courteous relations, and sportsmanlike acceptance of results;

Shun hunting practices that degrade the safety and caliber of the sport: careless gun handling, road hunting, gang hunting, and other practices which are dangerous or unethical;

Treat my quarry, alive or dead with profound respect, engaging only in fair chase, retrieving all game, and utilizing it fully, seeking primarily a priceless outdoor experience, enjoying companionship and scenery as well as a beneficial hunting experience;

Support wildlife management projects, hunter control policies, and law enforcement programs that protect and increase the quantity of wildlife and the quality of the quest;

Support organizations offering public leadership in campaigns for broad environmental quality, energy conservation, and ecological education;

Respect the privilege of hunting and the ethic of its pursuit, and initiate hunters of all ages in that spirit.

It might be well to go back and re-read this Creed and reflect on its meaning. This is not bureaucratic jargon. Reflect on last year's hunting season. Were you a sportsman according to this Creed? Were you considerate of others, their property and privileges? Did you participate in any public hearings on proposed law changes? Did you work in any conservation projects? Did you read any current literature on ecology and wildlife management? Do you understand the Criminal Trespass Law? Developing and maintaining professional standards of ethical conduct in the field of sport hunting is a tremendous challenge.

This Creed in general represents an adequate beginning toward developing a deer hunting ethic. Unfortunately, the recommendations of the committee to require some type of basic examination prior to purchasing the first hunting license and to eliminate road hunting, which all too frequently leads to trespassing on private property, were defeated in the Legislature. Perhaps the greatest irony of the work of this committee, it seems to me, manifests itself in the following paradox: On the one hand, the last sentence of this Creed assumes that hunting is indeed a privilege rather than a right; and yet on the other, in the numerical ranking of study area items, "the failure to accept hunting as a privilege and not a right" gets a low final rank of importance of 63 out of 80

If you cannot get the shot you want, let the animal pass rather than shoot helter-skelter. Whitetails deserve your best behavior. *Photo credit Leonard Lee Rue III*

in the Final Report. How should one explain or interpret this paradox? Perhaps, it was assumed as a basic postulate not needing discussion? Maybe it was overlooked due to its low solvability? In any event, until this area of study gets the highest ranking of importance, we will never really develop, much less implement, an adequate deer-hunting ethic.

In this chapter I have argued that we should consider deer hunting as a privilege rather than a right, and that we should look toward Germany in this regard, not for a model of game management, but for the proper attitude of mind toward hunting. For like it or not, the major stockholder in American wildlife, by the weight of sheer numbers, is not the hunter but the non-hunting public. One of the advantages of defining deer hunting as a privilege rather than a right is that it will more likely encourage us to formulate and implement an adequate program of hunter education and to require from us a basic examination prior to the hunt. Both procedures would enhance our image in the eye of the non-hunting public. The German attitude toward hunting, beyond any doubt, heightens our awareness of the basic protocol, tradition, philosophy and responsibilities inherent in high-quality deer hunting, or in *der Hochwildjagd,* as the Germans would have it. Their complete program of hunter education goes far beyond our mere hunter-safety courses, and can serve as a basic prototype for us, with perhaps a lesser degree of control and severity.

What American environmental education must build today is an ethical underpinning for hunting, in general, and for deer hunting, in particular; what we need, as Leopold foresaw many years ago, is a new woodcraft of the highest cultural order.

An Afterword

by Fred Bear

For perhaps 3½ million years, man has been eating meat. First near Olduvai Gorge and Lake Rudolph in Africa and later in the Ice Age caves of Spain and southern France, where he recorded his hunts with what are believed to be religious-based drawings on the hidden recesses of caves.

In early days, man hunted these forest and plains animals with sharpened leg bones, then fire-hardened, pointed tree limbs, stone-headed spears and finally throwing sticks, or atlatls, to increase his hunting range beyond the length of his arm.

About 50,000 years ago, some enterprising hunter discovered that his fire-making bow could also be used for hunting if it were made larger and stronger. For most of that time, the bow and arrow has been man's only tools used with his growing intellect and group-hunting techniques to sustain his family unit.

With the development of gunpowder and then firearms, man's capability as a hunter greatly increased in range. Yet he still retained his group-hunting methods and built upon his hunting traditions.

Today, we are fortunate to have men such as Dr. Rob Wegner and Leonard Lee Rue III, among others, who have devoted much of their lives to recording this rich and deep tradition of hunting the white-tailed deer.

This book may well become a classic in American hunting literature, and I compliment everyone involved in the making of this excellent work.

—*Fred Bear, 1984.*

PART V
WHERE TO FIND
MORE INFORMATION

Chapter 23

Deer & Deer Hunting: An Annotated Bibliography, 1838–1984

"The Deer Hunter's Four Hundred"

A NOTE ABOUT THE BIBLIOGRAPHY

This bibliography is a comprehensive list of most books published in the English language on the subject of deer and deer hunting. I annotate the list with the hope that the reader will seek out memorable titles that appeal to his or her tastes.

An asterisk (*) indicates that the book is out of print. It will either have to be located in a used-book store or you will need to have an out-of-print book specialist search for it. A list of reputable book specialists in the field of outdoor literature follows this bibliography.

Most of the books without an asterisk should be available through your local bookstore. Privately printed titles may be difficult to locate, however, and could be another job for the out-of-print book specialist. For an ongoing comprehensive review of books and information pertaining to deer and deer hunting, read *Deer &*

Deer Hunting magazine, P.O. Box 1117, Dept. 5B, Appleton, WI 54912, telephone (414)-734-0009.

Adams, Chuck. *The Complete Book of Bowhunting.* New York: Winchester Press, 1978. 298 pp.

A comprehensive guide written by a well-known authority on the subject. Informative reading.

Alsheimer, Charles J. *New York State Big Buck Club Record Book: 1980.* New York: YFC Printers, 1980. 32 pp.

Patterned along the lines of the Pope and Young and the Boone and Crockett record books, this booklet indicates that more record heads were taken in the 1970s than during any comparable period in the history of New York. Contains not only a history of the New York State Big Buck Club but also fine chapters by Charles Alsheimer entitled "Empire State Whitetails," and "The Rut: A Scientific Approach." Second edition limited to 5000 copies.

The author has spent a great deal of his life finding, buying and reading books on the subject of deer and deer hunting. His collection of deer books includes more than 400 titles on the natural history of deer and the hunting of them, dating back to 1838. *Photo credit Robert Wegner*

Anderson, Luther A. *How to Hunt Whitetail Deer.* New York: Funk and Wagnalls, 1968. 116 pp.

A clearly written, simple, common-sense manual for the beginner.*

Angen, Snow. *Shooting with Snow: Adventures of a New Zealand Deerstalker.* New Zealand: Reed, 1982. 182 pp.

Great moments in the life of a New Zealand deer hunter who captures the essence of the sport in one stanza when he writes:

"I remember the stag with his great lofty
    head,
That wonderful beast, our magnificent red.
I remember the stalk and thrill of the chase,
Of that extra shot fired just in case . . .

The counting of points and admiring the
    head,
And wishing somehow this beast was not
    dead.
That head was shot during one fall
And it now hangs on the trophy room wall,
For it was too big for the passage or hall."

Angier, Bradford. *Home Book of Cooking Venison and Other Natural Meats.* Pennsylvania: Stackpole Books, 1975. 191 pp.

A fine reference volume on preparing and cooking venison. As Brad reminds us, "This republic came of age eating venison and wearing buckskin. We were weaned as a nation on deer meat, took our first venturesome steps in deerhide moccasins, and saw our initial daylight through buckskin-scraped thin as parchment, greased for transparency, and stretched over log cabin windows in place of glass. Today the multiplying descendants of these earlier whitetails add much to the pleasure of the dining room."*

Arsenault, Dick. ed. *The Maine Antler and Skull Trophy Club 4th Annual Big Game Records Publication: 1982.* Maine: Privately printed, 1982. 64 pp.

Another state records booklet. Describes and illustrates Maine's trophy whitetails.

Atkinson, G. G. *Red Stags Calling.* London: Reed, 1974. 164 pp.

An entertaining and historical record of pursuing trophy red deer in their rugged mountain haunts of New Zealand. Although deer hunting may change over the years, the mountains and the men who love them stay the same. This volume will be a joy for deer hunters who love great stags and their mountainous terrain. Delineates the hard work, the anxious moments as well as the comical ones of the chase.*

Balfour-Browne, V. R. *The Stalking Letters and Sketches.* Great Britain: Antony Atha Publishers, 1978. 131 pp.

Deer sketches, deer paintings and letters of a keen student of English deer and deer hunting. Contains charming descriptions of his memorable days afield pursuing deer between 1909 and 1957.

·What's happening? Subordinate and immature white-tailed bucks will sometimes sniff the rear and lick the genitals of dominant bucks. This picture captures a very rare occurrence in the life of white-tailed bucks. The photographer who took the picture tells us that during the rut "this buck was licking the genitals of the other deer and he did it on and off over a period of several hours. The other buck was the dominant buck. I have often seen deer sniff and occasionally lick each others' tarsal glands, but this one was licking the genitals. The two bucks were quite compatible: they showed no overt signs of aggression while I filmed them." Indeed, the sniffing of the tarsal gland of a dominant buck by a subordinate buck is a more frequent occurrence than genital licking. Subordinate and immature males will occasionally mount each other in an attempt to dominate the lesser individual, apparently believing that by subjecting the mounted individual to this relationship the mounter achieves a higher social standing. *Photo credit Leonard Lee Rue III*

Bare, Collen Stanley. *Mule Deer*. New York: Dodd, Mead, 1981. 56 pp.

Juvenile literature. Presents a year in the life of a young mule deer.

Bartlett, Ilo Henry. *Whitetails: Presenting Michigan's Deer Problem*. Michigan: Department of Conservation, 1938. 64 pp.

———. *Michigan Deer*. Michigan: Department of Conservation, 1950. 50 pp.

Two classic pamphlets in the history of deer management. Written by a man who probably walked more deer trails through Michigan's deer forests than any other man, dead or alive. Of great historical value in understanding modern-day deer problems.*

Basala, Allen C., ed. *Official North Carolina Records of the Dixie Deer Classic*. North Carolina: Wake County Wildlife Club, Inc., 1982. Volume I. 52 pp.

Entertaining and informative reading on the various aspects of the 1981 and 1982 Dixie Deer Classics.

Batten, H. Mortimer. *The Singing Forest*. London: Blackwood, 1955. 197 pp.

A true story of a Highland red deer who undergoes many changes and survives the dangers common to all deer. A book for young and old alike. The result of 40 years of deer stalking.*

Bauer, Erwin A. *The Digest Book of Deer Hunting*. Chicago: Follett, 1979. 96 pp.

Where and how to hunt deer by a noted writer and wildlife photographer.

————. *Erwin Bauer's Deer in Their World*. New York: Outdoor Life Books and Stackpole Books, 1983. 242 pp.

A beautiful book filled with spectacular photos of deer plus sound information on capturing them on film. Written by a master deer photographer. Contains an interesting discussion of using deer decoys.

Baynes, Ernest Harold. "Actaeon." *My Wild Animal Guests*. New York: The Macmillan Company, 1930. pp. 1–57.

A charming, biographical story of a white-tailed deer in the open New Hampshire countryside. Copiously illustrated with reproductions of exceptionally beautiful and interesting photographs.*

————. *Wildlife in the Blue Mountain Forest*. New York: Macmillan Company, 1931. 140 pp.

Light, entertaining stories about deer and deer hunting in the Corbin game preserve in the Sunapee Lake region of New Hampshire.*

Bear, Fred. *The Adventures of Fred Bear*. New York: Doubleday, 1976. 288 pp.

The exciting field notes of one of the world's most respected hunters and conservationists. Vividly portrays the rigors of the outdoor world, the thrills of the chase and the total excitement of the hunt. Provides us with a brilliant definition of the hunt: "I like to think that an expedition be looked upon, whether it be an evening hunt nearby or a prolonged trip to some far-off place, as a venture into an unspoiled area. With time to commune with your inner soul as you share the outdoors with the birds, animals, and fish that live there."

Beattie, Kirk H., and Moss, Bruce A. ed. *Proceedings of the Midwest Bowhunting Conference*. Wisconsin, 1983. 238 pp.

An excellent analysis of the problems facing the sport of modern bow hunting. The contributors come from a wide variety of backgrounds, including industry, state wildlife agencies, outdoor writing, university education, and bow-hunting organizations. Although the articles orient themselves toward bow hunting in the Midwest,

they apply to situations in virtually all states. Contains an excellent editorial entitled "On Crippling Sematics: An Opinion." Highly recommended.

Beck, B. B., and Wemmer, C. M. ed. *The Biology and Management of an Extinct Species: Pere David's Deer*. New Jersey: Noyes Publications, 1983. 193 pp.

This volume deals with the first large mammal to become extinct in the wild, but rescued by captive breeding. Emphasizes the diverse expertise required for the propagation of an endangered species. Contains charming notes on the animal's natural history.

Bender, Doc. "Nine Days to December." *Maker's Spring*. Wisconsin: Bristow Press, 1979. pp. 46–65.

A brooding, philosophical and introspective essay examining a nine-day Wisconsin deer hunting ordeal in the driftless hills of Vernon County. First appeared in *Gray's Sporting Journal*. High-level prose. Highly recommended for the serious, thoughtful deer hunter.

Benoit, Larry. *How to Bag the Biggest Buck of your Life*. Vermont: Whitetail Press, 1974. 158 pp.

A no-nonsense, hard-fact book written by a deer hunter from Vermont with a successful track record unequaled in modern times. Describes in detail how he tracked one trophy buck for 13 days—traveling well over 300 miles on foot before tagging the old monarch of the woods. An engaging book with impressive photos of trophy deer hunting activities in Vermont. As the author fondly notes, "Oh, a good buck track just sets me to quivering!"*

Bentley, Arthur. *An Introduction to the Deer of Australia:* Printing Associates, 1978. 350 pp.

The standard reference on Australian deer combining a detailed personal knowledge of deer and deer hunting with a deep respect for the potential of deer herd management. Based on scientific study and practical experimentation. Contains many snippets of deer lore from the early days of Australian settlement. A very unusual book.*

Bersing, Otis. *Bow and Arrow Big Game*

Hunting in Wisconsin. Wisconsin: Department of Conservation, 1973. 24 pp.

———. *Fifteen Years of Bow & Arrow Deer Hunting in Wisconsin.* Wisconsin: Department of Conservation, n.d. 52 pp.

———. *A Century of Wisconsin Deer.* Wisconsin: Department of Conservation, 1966. 272 pp.

Major references and records in the field of deer hunting statistics. Written by a 32-year veteran of the Wisconsin Department of Natural Resources. Provides a treasury of chronological facts on types and lengths of seasons, deer harvests, regulations, number of hunters, sex and age ratios of deer taken, number of deer taken per square mile, number of illegal seizures, number of hunting accidents, and innumerable statistical comparisons. A valuable statistical reference for other states as well.*

Block, George H., III. *Block's Buck Book.* Pennsylvania: Rainbow Graphics, 1983. 100 pp.

A short pamphlet on Pennsylvania deer and deer hunting. Emphasizes that ''states are going to have to make a decision between a herd managed for numbers or a herd managed for quality. You can't have both, and in most cases it's the numbers outlook that wins.''

Bone, Phyllis M. *Deer Talk.* Scotland: Michael Slains, 1962. 70 pp.

Juvenile literature. A story of two roe deer written by a famous English animal sculptor.*

Bowhunting Big Game Records of North America. Colorado: Johnson Publishing Company, 1975. 307 pp.

The records of the Pope and Young Club plus useful and interesting information for hunters, conservationists, outdoorsmen, researchers and wildlife managers.

Brady, Lillian. *Saga of a Whitetail Deer.* California: Amber Crest, 1981. 119 pp.

A story of a white-tailed deer set against the natural background of Wilderness Acres, a private Minnesota refuge created by the author and her husband.

Brandreth, Paul. *Trails of Enchantment.* New York: Watt, 1930. 318 pp.

A superb book written with great eloquence by a gentleman of high culture, a keen deer hunter and a devoted student of nature about hunting whitetails in the Adirondacks. Contains excellent photos and nostalgic memories. A classic in outdoor literature. Highly recommended.*

Bronson, Wilfrid. *Horns and Antlers.* New York: Harcourt, Brace & World, Inc., 1942. 143 pp.

Juvenile literature—ages 3 to 7. An enchanting view of North American deer and antelope for the young reader. Written in a lively and engaging style.

Brothers, Al, and Ray, Murphy E. *Producing Quality Whitetails.* Texas: Fiesta Publishing, 1975. 245 pp.

First-rate book for the layman on deer herd management. Written by two Texas wildlife biologists. Includes an excellent chapter on breeding and a common-sense explanation on the buck/doe ratio. Contains more than 100 superb pictures and illustrations, some dating back to the early 1900s. The bible of Texas deer hunters and landowners. Now available in paperback for $5.95. Can be ordered by writing to the author: Al Brothers, H. B. Zachry Ranches, Box 850, Laredo, TX., 78040.

Brown, Robert D., ed. *Antler Development in Cervidae.* Texas, 1983. 480 pp.

A comprehensive reference text for wildlife managers, wildlife researchers and anyone interested in the natural history of deer. Deals with social behavior, breeding and genetics, wildlife management, endocrinology, light cycles, as well as nutrition and diseases. An excellent companion piece to Richard Goss's *Deer Antlers,* although more technical in nature.

Browning, Meshach. *Forty-Four Years of the Life of a Hunter.* Philadelphia: Lippincott, 1928. 400 pp.

Classic reminiscences of a very successful Maryland deerslayer who hunted the Allegheny Mountain section of western Maryland during the years 1884–1928, and who managed to kill between 1800 and 2000 deer. If you are interested in the heroic, picturesque adventures of fighting with wounded bucks and catching deer barehanded in the snow, you will want to read this exciting, rustic volume. A most captivating narrative of old-time deer hunting scenes!*

Brunner, Joseph. *Tracks and Tracking*. New York: Macmillan, 1909. 217 pp.

A classic text on the subject. Identifies deer tracks in a most remarkable way with the nature of the animal's wound. Constructs nine fascinating illustrations in the process. The idea of determining the nature of the wound by analysis of the track never reappeared in the literature on deer and deer hunting.*

Bryant, Ken. *From the Kill to the Package*. Texas: Bryant Publishing, 1980. 52 pp.

A practical guide complete with illustrations, instructions and photos for processing your deer in the field. An excellent booklet for the beginner's knapsack.

Cadman, Arthur. *Dawn, Dusk, and Deer*. London: Country Life, 1966. 138 pp.

A fascinating mixture of facts about deer and reminiscences covering many years of experience in pursuing them. Who would disagree with his assessment that "to the sportsman naturalist there are few more rewarding activities than the study of deer. The very fact that such a study takes one into quiet places means that some thing of interest, be it animal, bird, insect or plant, is seen on almost every outing." Written by a forester, naturalist and authority on English deer. Beautifully illustrated.*

Calef, George. *Caribou and the Barren-Lands*. Toronto: Firefly Books, 1981. 176 pp.

A beautiful portrait of the animal and the vast landscape over which it roams. A fine example of combining scientific expertise with photographic genius.

Callender, Hollis, and Conway, Bryant W. *Successful Hints on Hunting Whitetail Deer*. Louisiana: Claitor's Publishing, 1967. 70 pp.

A transcription of tape-recorded "off-the-cuff" comments on Louisiana deer hunting.

Cameron, Allan Gordon. *The Wild Red Deer of Scotland*. London: Black & Sons, 1923. 248 pp.

An important contribution to the literature of the red deer. A charmingly written book for the serious student of deer. A fine com-panion piece to Colin Gibson's biography of Cameron.*

Candy, Robert. *Getting the Most from Your Game and Fish*. Vermont: Garden Way Publishing, 1978. 278 pp.

So you've shot that trophy buck? Now what do you do to get the most out of your deer? Read this book, for it addresses this question candidly and authoritatively. Fantastic illustrations on the whole process—from the field to the kitchen. Written by the chief of information and education for the Vermont Fish and Game Department.

Carhart, Arthur H. *Hunting North American Deer*. New York: Macmillan, 1946. 232 pp.

A fine handbook written by a Colorado game official and a well-known outdoor writer who first patented a white man's gadget for calling mule deer. Strong on our deer hunting heritage and on the history of deer populations. Rightly believes that while "a hunting trip may have the taking of the grand trophy as its climax, deer hunting, fundamentally, is one excuse for going into the outdoors, and a mighty good one." Basic reading for the thoughtful deer hunter.*

Carrick, Donald. *The Deer in the Pasture*. New York: Greenwillow Books, 1976. 30 pp.

Children's fiction—grades three to five. A deer who has become too friendly with man must be frightened and driven away for its own protection when the hunting season opens.

Carrighar, Sally. "The Mule Deer." *One Day on Beetle Rock*. New York: Ballantine Books, 1943. pp. 154–177.

A unique journey into the Sierra Nevadas. Offers an insightful excursion into the fascinating world of mule deer that inhabit Beetle Rock, a large cliff high in the Sierra Nevada Mountains. Written with great perception and sensitive insight. Fiction, yes, but fiction closely parallel with fact. Breaches the gap between science and art. As Aldo Leopold once remarked, "Beetle Rock is good ecology and good literature."

Cartier, John O. *The Modern Deer Hunter*. New York: Funk & Wagnalls, 1979. 310 pp.

A serious, well-rounded manual written by a long-term Midwest field editor for *Outdoor Life* magazine. Includes numerous personal experiences and anecdotes of his many years of Michigan deer hunting, as well as many fine points on maintaining a positive attitude while afield. A highly recommended how-to book.

Caton, John Dean. *The Antelope and Deer of America*. New York: Forest and Stream, 1877. 426 pp.

The first scientific treatise on deer to appear in America. Written by an ardent deer hunter and prominent judge from Illinois. Emphasis placed on the anatomy, physiology and natural history of deer. Includes an impressive chapter on the chase, in which the author discusses the true virtues of hunting and reminds us that "to the cultivated mind capable of understanding and appreciating the works of the Divine hand, the pleasures of the pursuit are immeasurably enhanced by a capacity to understand the object taken." Read that once again! Thorough and extraordinarily fine, this is a blue-chip deer book. Reprinted in 1974.

Chalmers, Patrick R., ed. *Mine Eyes to the Hills: An Anthology of the Highland Forest*. London: A. & C. Black, 1931. 368 pp.

A classy anthology of the best prose and poetry on the subject of English deer and deer hunting. Comprehensive and well chosen.*

———. *Deerstalking*. London: Philip Allan, 1935. 253 pp.

A classic treatise on deer hunting from the English "academy of spy, stalk and approach." Rightfully acknowledges that the deer hunter "seeks a becoming beast in a becoming setting and in a becoming manner. Which is to say that even modern luxury and modern rifles cannot rob deer stalking of what is ancient, primitive, in fact, and honorable." Indeed, the deer hunter finds himself in lands that belong to the Muse. Scarce.*

Chaplin, Raymond E. *Deer*. Dorset: Blandford Press, 1977. 218 pp.

An in-depth portrait of what it means to be a deer. Focuses on the survival problem of deer throughout the world. Rightly insists that "the world of deer, even of those on our doorsteps, is still largely unexplored and provides us with a major challenge." A wide-ranging primer which can be confidently recommended to the newcomer to the study of deer. A useful addition to the literature on the subject.

———. *Capreolous: The Story of a Roe Deer*. London: Collins, 1978. 80 pp.

The story of the early life of a roe deer. Highly recommended for young readers between the ages of 7 and 11.

Chapman, Donald, and Chapman, Norma. *Fallow Deer: Their History, Distribution, and Biology*. Suffolk: Terence Dalton Limited, 1975. 271 pp.

The definitive book on fallow deer. Interesting, readable and informative. Provides an overall picture on what is known of their natural history. Includes a chapter on the Persian fallow, a very rare and endangered species. A classy book on deer. Beautifully illustrated. One wonders why American publishers do not produce deer books of this quality and substance?

Clarkson, Ewan. *The Running of the Deer*. New York: Dutton, 1972. 217 pp.

Not only a first-rate story, but a very perceptive examination of the forces, both natural and man-made, that find themselves in opposition over deer and their destiny in today's world. An exciting and impressive portrait of the life of the red deer Rhus—following him from birth to maturity. Reaches the familiar conclusion that when man finally destroys himself on this planet, when civilization crumbles, deer will ultimately remain; for they live in harmony with their surroundings and in sympathy with the rest of the living world.

Clutton-Brock, T. H.; Guinness, F. E.; and Albon, S. D. *Red Deer: Behavior and Ecology of Two Sexes*. Chicago: University of Chicago Press, 1982. 378 pp.

This volume, primarily for the scientific researcher, synthesizes a 10-year study of the red deer population of Ruhm, an island off the Scottish coast, and represents a major contribution to work in sexual selection.

Cole, Harold. *I Think I'll Get One Hundred: Thirty Years of White Tail Deer Hunting with Shotgun, Rifle, and Bow*. Connecticut: Privately printed, 1982. 240 pp.

This book contains more than 80 stories about the deer Cole has taken while hunting in New Hampshire, Vermont, New York, and Pennsylvania. Communicates the excitement of the deer-hunting experience.

Collyns, Charles Palk. *The Chase of the Red Deer*. London: Lawrence and Bullen, 1902. 307 pp.

A descriptive account of the chase of red deer in the counties of Devon and Somerset between 1780 and 1860. A classic in this particular branch of the sport. A classy book with interesting anecdotes and incidents, containing beautiful illustrations.*

Colquhoun, John. *The Moor and the Loch*. London: W. Blackwood & Sons, 1897. 496 pp.

An attractive book of personal reminiscences written by a "gentleman for gentlemen, healthy in tone, earnest in purpose, and as fresh, breezy, and life-giving as the mountain air of the hills amongst which the sport it chronicles is carried on."*

Conatser, Dean. *Bowhunting the Whitetail Deer*. New York: Winchester, 1977. 171 pp.

A basic book for the novice bow hunter of the whitetail. Written by a Texas deer hunter. Includes fine illustrations of deer anatomy and imaginary angles of where to shoot.

Conway, James. *Forays Among Salmon and Deer*. London: Chapman and Hall, 1861. 248 pp.

A delightful narrative of red deer stalking on the Highlands of Scotland. Based on the author's journals, letters and notes written among the scenes they attempt to portray. Fascinating historical reading.*

Cooper, James Fenimore. *The Deerslayer*. Chicago: A. L. Burt Company, 1841. 564 pp.

A rich and intensely exciting story. Portrays hunting as a proper form of ecological consciousness. Standard reading for the woodsman.

Corder, E. M. *Deer Hunter*. New York: Jove Publications, 1979. 189 pp.

A fine example of the type of literature which is helping to destroy the sport of American deer hunting.

Cornish, John E. *Venison Cuisine*. New Zealand: C. H. B. Print, 1982. 43 pp.

This speciality booklet on the art of preparing, cooking and presenting venison in the New Zealand tradition is a must for the deer hunter who likes his saddle of venison marinated for days, braised in Chateau wine, garnished with glazed onions, chestnuts and sauteed mushrooms, and served with a heavy red wine. Underscores the idea that venison has a much lower fat content than other red meats. A fine cookbook for the deer shack!

Cox, Alex. *Deer Hunting in Texas*. Texas: Naylor, 1947. 105 pp.

A practical handbook for the Texas deer hunter. Written by a Texas hunter who harvested one of the largest whitetails ever recorded, in 1941. Dated.*

————. *Deer Hunting in Texas*. Texas: Privately printed, 1977. 106 pp.

A revised version of the 1947 edition.

Coziah, Calvin. *Bucks, Bows, and Campfires*. Idaho: Coziah Enterprises, 1981. 159 pp.

Me and "Doc" experiences of an Idaho mule deer hunter.

Crealock, Henry Hope. *Deer-Stalking in the Highlands of Scotland*. London: Antony Atha Publishers, 1981. 194 pp.

A magnificent edition of deer hunting reminiscences and lore, with many lavish reproductions of the author's pen-and-ink sketches. Full of life and vigor. A reprint of the original 1892 edition. Limited to 255 copies. A blue-chip deer book. Very expensive.

Crump, Barry. *A Good Keen Man*. Australia: Reed, 1960. 192 pp.

High comedy and slapstick farce about the deer hunting fraternity of New Zealand. A strange book about a deer hunter's inability to find a good keen man as a hunting partner.*

Daggett, David. *Sawyer Swampers*. Privately printed, no date. 58 pp.

A modern-day deer camp diary dealing with the years of 1966–1979. Represents a good portrait of the typical deer shack and its social activities. Although the activities take place in the hills and dales of Sawyer County, Wisconsin, the action could really be taking place anywhere in deer country.

Dahlberg, Burton L, and Guettinger, Ralph C. *The White-Tailed Deer in Wisconsin*. Wisconsin: Conservation Department, 1956. 282 pp.

The classic result of a deer research project that functioned continuously for more than 14 years. Designed for technician and layman alike. Provides a tremendous mass of facts and information on nearly all aspects of white-tailed deer and the hunting of them. Highly recommended for the hunter trying to gain a better understanding of the history and future of this remarkable animal. A gold mine of information.*

Dalrymple, Byron W. *The Complete Book of Deer Hunting*. New York: Winchester, 1973. 247 pp.

––––––. *Deer Hunting with Dalrymple: A Lifetime of Lore on the Whitetail and Mule Deer*. New York: McKay, 1978. 248 pp.

Two immensely helpful books for the deer hunter. Written by the "Old Master" with more than a half century of experience behind him. Solidly based on practical experience. Eminently readable. If you don't learn the ABCs of deer hunting after reading these two books, take up potato farming.

Dalrymple, Tom., ed. *Bowhunting in Arizona*. Arizona, 1980. 150 pp.

Records the finest trophies taken with bow and arrow in the state of Arizona. Patterned after the Pope and Young record book. Encourages bow hunters to pursue excellence, and to make their behavior while hunting an ethical example for future generations.

Darling, F. Fraser. *A Herd of Red Deer: A Study in Animal Behavior*. London: Oxford University Press, 1937. 215 pp.

An intimate, ecological study of a herd of red deer (a species closely related to the American wapiti). Presents a vivid picture of the delicate relationship between deer and their environment. The author's data on the reactions of deer to sudden changes in temperature, barometric pressure, wind, precipitation, light, darkness, humidity and other environmental conditions are of particular value and may profitably be used as yardsticks in the study of deer in other areas of the world. Despite the date of publication, the book remains fresh and stimulating. As Aldo Leopold once wrote: "A community biography of exceptional literary merit."*

Darner, Kirt. *How to Find Giant Bucks*. Missouri: Walsworth Publishing Company, 1983. 283 pp.

The hunting adventures and practical advice of one of this nation's top mule-deer hunters. If you are interested in trophy mule-deer hunting, you will want to read this remarkable account of the man who "rewrote the record book."

Dasmann, William. *Deer Range: Management and Improvement*. North Carolina: McFarland & Company, 1981. 168 pp.

For the deer hunter who would like to acquire a basic ecological understanding of deer and their habitat. Explains how deer range must be managed to maintain healthy herds in relatively stable numbers and in balance with their habitats. Highly recommended.

––––––. *If Deer are to Survive*. Pennsylvania: Stackpole Books, 1971. 128 pp.

An earlier version of the book mentioned above.*

Davidson, William R., ed. *Diseases and Parasites of White-Tailed Deer*. North Carolina: Tall Timbers Research Station, 1981. 458 pp.

A scientific reference text on the health status of white-tailed deer. Covers all known diseases and parasites of white-tailed deer. Intended primarily for game managers and deer biologists.

Davis, S. T. *Caribou Shooting in Newfoundland*. Pennsylvania: The New Ear Printing House, 1895. 212 pp.

A detailed account of personal experiences in hunting caribou among the White Hills of Newfoundland. Reaches the inevitable conclusion that we all reach: "Is it any wonder that when the leaves begin to change color in autumn, the hunter becomes restless under the yoke of arduous professional duties, and anxious to seek the habitat of fin, fur, and feather—to break the fatal strain on the nervous system from the daily routine of work and worry which has hurried so many good men to premature graves.''*

Dawson, Jim. *Whitetail Hunting*. Pennsylvania: Stackpole Books, 1982. 224 pp.

An elementary text for the beginner.

DeFalco, Joe. *The Complete Deer Hunt*. New York: Madison Publishing Company, 1981. 117 pp.

An introductory manual written by a Long Island deer hunter. Emphasizes field-dressing, butchering and preparing tasty venison.

de Nahlik, A. J. *Wild Deer*. London: Faber and Faber, 1959. 240 pp.

————. *Deer Management: Improved Herds for Greater Profit*. London: David and Charles, 1974. 250 pp.

The first of these two texts, *Wild Deer*, contains a fascinating chapter on the behavior of deer after being shot. The second, *Deer Management*, provides a practical guide to the economic management of deer herds. Bitterly opposes deer farming and insists that the wild nature of the herd must be preserved. Written by one of Britain's well-known deer managers. An important and valuable aid for those interested in the area of economic deer management.*

Dickey, Charles. *Deer Hunting*. Alabama: Oxmoor House, 1977. 110 pp.

When you hunt deer you are dealing "with a crafty, cagey, cautious combination of electric sight, radio ears, and radar nose, a misty spook that magically vanishes with the blink of your eye, a master of melting camouflage." So writes that delightful outdoorsman, Charley Dickey, in this essential manual on the ritual of the deer hunt. Well written, modestly priced and one of the best manuals of its kind.

Dixon, Joseph S. *A Study of the Life History and Food Habits of Mule Deer in California*. Reprinted from *California Fish and Game* by the Wildlife Division of the United States National Park Service. Volume 20. Numbers 3 and 4. July/October, 1934. 146 pp.

A magnificent study of mule deer written by a man who hunted and studied them in most of the mountain and foothill counties of California. Based on 30 years of personal observations. A standard reference volume to which one continually returns.*

Donne, R. E. *Red Deer Stalking in New Zealand*. London: Constable and Company, 1924. 270 pp.

A classic on the subject—like a good bottle of wine. Finds the true essence of the deer hunt to be contained in one word—*unselfishness*. The ideal deer hunting trip, the author writes, "consists of a good comrade, fine country, and very few trophies. . . . The best deer hunter is the man who finds the most game, kills the least, and leaves behind him no wounded animals. . . .''*

Donovan, Robert E. *Hunting Whitetail Deer*. New York: Winchester, 1978. 228 pp.

Another general how-to book. Strong on weapons and marksmanship. Correctly believes "that most deer hunters are interested in their quarry not simply as quarry and table fare, but as creatures with which we share this limited planet and as creatures without whom this world would be a much poorer place to live."

Drain, James A. *Stories of Some Shoots, or the Chronicles of a Gratified Gunner*. Washington, D.C.: Arms and the Man Publishing Co., 1912. 114 pp.

Memories of an American deer hunter who goes to Scotland to stalk the Scottish stag and soon learns "that the sportsman who puts the bag first is very poorly served by fortune in sports afield. To me the creatures I pursue and their capture are incidental to my pleasure. I gather my joy from the contact with nature.''*

Dugmore, A. A. Radclyffe. *The Romance of the Newfoundland Caribou*. Philadelphia: Lippincott, 1913. 191 pp.

A classy intimate account of the life of the caribou. Captures the very essence of the land of the caribou with romantic and nostalgic early vintage photos. A must for those interested in the wild creatures of Newfoundland.*

Ederer, Bernard F. *Hunting the White-Tailed Deer*. Minnesota: University of Minnesota Press, 1940. 78 pp.

An early handbook on all the essentials for the deer hunter. Contains a mixture of wisdom and adventure. Written by a Minnesota dentist who always found the lure of faraway places, deer tracks in snowy spruce swamps and the smell of gunpowder irresistible.*

Edminster, Frank C. *Hunting Whitetails*. New York: Morrow & Company, 1954. 192 pp.

A solidly based research manual on whitetail hunting. Written by a well-known wildlife researcher and one-time superintendent of game management for the New York Department of Conservation. Recommended for the seasoned deer hunter who wants to add the final touches to technique. Edminster's precise attention to details gives the book its special value.*

Edward, Second Duke of York. *The Master of the Game*. Edited by Wm. A. and F. Baillie-Grohman. New York: Duffield & Company, 1974. 302 pp.

The oldest and most important work on hunting in the English language. Written between 1406 and 1413. A real jewel for all lovers of sport hunting, nature and good books in general. No one can get the highest enjoyment out of deer hunting unless he can live over again and again in his library the keen pleasure he experiences in the field while pursuing his quarry. This book will help you do just that!

Edwards, Lionel. *Beasts of the Chase*. London: Putnam, 1950. 49 pp.

A vivid and colorful portrait of the roe deer, fallow deer and red deer by one of England's famous huntsmen.*

———., and Wallace, H. F. *Hunting and Stalking the Deer: The Pursuit of Red, Fallow, and Roe Deer in England and Scotland*. London: Longmans, 1927. 274 pp.

Pleasurable deer hunting experiences. Emphasizes the universal idea that the forest and the deer possess a charm which will never fade. An admirable work. Contains two excellent bibliographies on deer and deer hunting. Hard to find. Well illustrated.*

Einarson, Arthur S. *The Pronghorn Antelope and its Management*. Washington, D. C.: The Wildlife Management Institute, 1948. 238 pp.

A colorful and delightful treatise on those "phantoms of the grassland and sagebrush." Based on extensive field work in Oregon, Idaho, Nevada and California. Although a book of facts, the reader with an esthetic bent will not be slighted. Filled with lyrical vignettes. Authoritative, interesting and handsomely illustrated.*

Ellis, Mel. "Life in Wisconsin's Old-Time Deer Camps." In *Yarns of Wisconsin*, edited by Sue McCoy. Wisconsin: Tamarack Press, 1978. pp. 168–172.

Turn back the clock from the comfort of your easy chair and relive life in an old Sawyer County deer camp that symbolizes deer camps all across this land. Read this classic essay and discover why deer camp is "a place that shuts out the world and all the worry that goes with it." A brilliant and nostalgic characterization of the American deer camp and the feelings it evokes.

Elman, Robert., ed. *All About Deer Hunting in America*. New York: Winchester, 1976. 255 pp.

A compilation of tested techniques and secrets of this continent's expert deer hunters. Emphasizes regional differences. A standard anthology of deer hunting know-how. Contains a wealth of practical information for novice and veteran alike.

Epler, E. H. *Eighty Years in God's Country*. Illinois: Ink Spot, 1973. 116 pp.

Contains a brief but interesting historical description of the "BackTrackers Deer Camp" located near Eagle River, Wisconsin. Small printing. Hard to find.*

Evered, Philip. *Staghunting with the Devon and Somerset (1887–1901): An Account of the Chase of the Wild Red Deer on Exmoor*. London: Chatto & Windus, 1902. 378 pp.

Delightful scenes of the noble sport of stag hunting the red deer. Will appeal to all lovers of deer and deer hunting. Records a long chase in which a deer ran more than 20 miles in two hours and 10 minutes. Beautifully illustrated.*

Fadala, Sam. *Successful Deer Hunting.* Illinois: DBI Books, Inc., 1983. 288 pp.

A general guide primarily concerned with equipment.

Faulkner, William, *Big Woods.* New York: Random House, 1955. 198 pp.

Contains the famous hunting stories of William Faulkner, which present a profoundly moving and memorable tribute to the hunter and the hunted. Provides us with a brilliant and penetrating examination of the hunter's paradox: How can man kill the object he loves? Ultimately defines deer hunting as "the best game of all, the best of all breathing and forever the best of all listening." Unforgettable deer hunting tales in the dense thickets of the Mississippi River Delta!

Ffolliott, Peter F., and Gallina, Sonia., ed. *Deer Biology, Habitat Requirements, and Management in Western North America.* Mexico: The Institute of Ecology, 1981. 278 pp.

The papers included in this book present information relating to biology, habitat requirements and management of deer populations in Mexico and Arizona. Particular emphasis has been placed on reporting investigations conducted on La Michilia and the Beaver Creed biosphere reserves. An excellent reference work on the wise use and conservation of deer populations.

Fish, Chet., ed. *Outdoor Life Deer Hunter's Yearbook, 1983.* New York: Outdoor Life Books, 1982. 184 pp.

Reprints from *Outdoor Life.*

————., ed. *Outdoor Life Deer Hunter's Yearbook, 1984.* New York: Outdoor Life Books, 1983. 184 pp.

Like its predecessor, this yearbook entertains you while helping you to become a better deer hunter. Most of the chapters originally appeared in *Outdoor Life.* Contains John Madson's classic essay on why we hunt deer.

Fishchl, Josef, and Rue, Leonard Lee III. *After Your Deer is Down: Care and Handling of Big Game.* Oklahoma: Winchester, 1981. 137 pp.

Provides the hunter with a step-by-step photo essay illustrating everything you need to know to dress out, cape, skin, quarter, bone and cut up a deer. Contains three dozen venison recipes. Written by a professional meat cutter from Germany and one of America's most published wildlife photographers. Will help the amateur to process his deer properly, and at a big savings in money.

Flader, Susan L. *Thinking Like a Mountain: Aldo Leopold and the Evolution of an Ecological Attitude Toward Deer, Wolves, and Forests.* Missouri: University of Missouri Press, 1974. 284 pp.

An outstanding, detailed analysis of Aldo Leopold's ecological attitude toward deer. Strong on deer overpopulation. Provides a fascinating glimpse into the history of whitetailed deer management. Rewarding reading for the ecologically minded sportsman.

Flemming, Tom. *The Complete Book on Rattling Whitetails.* Indiana: Blue-J Inc., 1982. 96 pp.

An expensive 96-page pamphlet of pictures on how to rattle whitetails.

Flerov, K. K. *Fauna of USSR: Musk Deer and Deer.* Moscow: The Academy of Sciences, 1952. 257 pp.

Scrutinizes deer from many points of view in order to focus attention on their numerous features: their evolution, geographical dissemination and distribution, as well as specialization and adaptation. Provides an early system of classification.*

Fleuron, Svend. *Monarch of the Glen: The Adventures of a Roebuck.* Translated by E. M. Nielsen. New York: Henry Holt and Company, 1935. 210 pp.

The romantic adventures of Piet, a mighty monarch of the deer forest, and a blackbearded deerslayer named "the Quiet Rustler" with the deathpipe on his shoulder.*

Foote, Leonard E. *The Vermont Deer Herd: A Study in Productivity.* Vermont: Fish and Game Service, 1945. 125 pp.

An early analysis of the whitetail in Vermont. Written by a student of Aldo Leopold's. Contains an excellent discussion of crop damage to orchards.*

Forester, Frank. *The Deer Stalkers: A Sporting Tale of the South-Western Counties.* Philadelphia: T. B. Peterson & Brothers, 1843. 198 pp.

A short fancy sketch of early American deer hunting, not intended to convey any how-to instruction. Written by that prince of the sporting writers who became the model for the rising generation of ethical sportsmen of the late 19th century. Constructs a brilliant portrait of the chase. Based on the proposition "that there is not only much practical, but much moral utility, in the Gentle Science of Woodcraft."*

Fortescue, J. W. *The Story of a Red Deer.* London: Macmillan and Company, 1935. 144 pp.

The classical story of an Exmoor stag. Written from first-hand knowledge of the animal, the country and the hunt. Correctly believes that deer provide us with "the most worthy study" which the mind can undertake because of their nobility, subtlety and wisdom.*

Fortier, Roger. *The Whitetail Deer . . . From Field to Table.* Canada: National Meat Institute, Inc., 1980. 64 pp.

Through the use of illustrations and pictures, this practical booklet shows the successful deer hunter how to clean his deer, skin it, and how to get the best cuts of steaks, roasts or chops. The manual is packed from cover to cover with useful information on dealing with all aspects of venison. Reaches the inevitable conclusion that "it is not by accident that royalty of past decades jealously regarded deer hunting as their divine privilege and venison decreed for the king's table alone."

Fraser, Sir Hugh. *Amid the High Hills.* London: A. & C. Black, 1923. 224 pp.

Pleasant and delightful essay on deer and their ways. Written by an ardent deer hunter and hillsman. Successfully conveys his own intense enthusiasm for deer and deer hunting: "The fascination of deer hunting is largely due to the romance of the hill—the hill as it is known only to those who love it and understand something of its hidden mysteries. The lone day, all too quickly ended, with the silent but sympathetic stalker—alone with Nature in its most inspiring and elevating form—the ever-changing beauty of sky and hill—the joy of watching deer when they have no suspicion that they are being watched—the opportunities of seeing rare birds and finding rare plants—all these things apart from the difficulty and interest—and the greater the difficulty the greater the interest—of trying to outwit—in other words trying to get within shot of the particular stag one is after—go to make up the attractions of what some of us think is the very best of true sport."*

Fratzke, Bob. *Taking Trophy Whitetails.* Wisconsin: Target Communications Corporation, 1983. 124 pp.

An inexpensive booklet that emphasizes detailed scouting and the use of camouflage clothing.

Freeman, Edward H. *How to Hunt Deer.* Pennsylvania: Stackpole Books, 1956. 243 pp.

A work that expresses a great love for deer hunting. Written by a reformed poacher and a professional guide from Maine. Contains a summary of his deer hunting adventures in the farming section of Maine, as well as an excellent chapter on hunting accidents—the author himself being a statistic in the list of hunting casualties. Rightly concludes that "one of the most serious threats to deer hunting, as we know it, is the growing breach in the relations between hunters and landowners. While this situation may not be entirely the fault of the hunters, it can only be healed by the hunter's action. Each of us should lean over backwards in an effort to establish and maintain friendly relations with landowners." Informative and thoughtful reading.*

Gasset, Jose Ortega y. *Meditations on Hunting.* New York: Scribners, 1972. 152 pp.

One of the greatest books ever written on the philosophy of hunting. A classic! Based on the correct assumption that human nature is inseparable from the hunting instinct. Places hunting in the context of a limited privilege rather than an undeniable right. Believes that hunting "involves a complete code of ethics of the most distinguished design." Ultimately, defines hunting as the purest form of human happiness.*

Gates, Clayton. *Whitetail Deer Hunting: An Instructive Treatise on Deer Hunting Especially Applicable to the Whitetail Deer.* Chicago: W. F. Herr, 1941. 43 pp.

Short pamphlet dealing with deer hunting in the eastern and southern United States.*

Gathorne-Hardy, A. E. *Autumns in Argyleshire with Rod and Gun.* London: Longmans, 1900. 228 pp.

Pleasant recollections containing several chapters devoted to deer. Written by a practical roe stalker who had many fine trophies to his credit. Filled with entertaining thoughts. Here's one, for example: "Many deer are doubtlessly missed upon the hillside, but few in the smoking room."*

Geist, Valerius. *Mountain Sheep: A Study in Behavior and Evolution.* Chicago: University of Chicago, 1971. 383 pp.

A superb book for anyone interested in mammalian behavior, ecology and evolution. The definitive text on mountain sheep. Beautifully written and based on detailed field observations which Geist conducted in British Columbia, Alberta and the Yukon between 1961 and 1966. A classic study in animal behavior.

Genevoix, Maurice. *The Last Hunt.* New York: Random House, 1943. 281 pp.

A beautifully written account of the pursuit of a great red stag by two French hunters, one a killer, the other a sportsman. Pits the brutal, merciless poacher who kills for the sheer lust of it against the Gamekeeper who hunts for the love of the chase. An unforgettable novel of deer and deer hunting in a French forest. Brings terror to your heart as it takes you across the swamp through the bracken and over the hill with the hunted stag. A book of distinction and imagination. Succeeds as one critic wrote "partly because of a certain amount of literary artistry rare and welcome in animal fiction; partly

because of a skillful and nostalgic evocation of the wild, vast beechwoods of France and the deer that roam them." Needs to be read in the deer forest. A story of breathtaking, dramatic quality. A spellbinder.*

Gentry, Christine. *When Dogs Run Wild.* North Carolina: McFarland & Company, Inc., 1983. 195 pp.

This first book-length study of the effects of loose and stray dogs on our deer should be read by all deer hunters and dog owners. It discusses at length how free-roaming pets run down and chew up deer for sport. Due to the dog population in this country, we have reached a point where man's best friend is nature's worst enemy! The amazing losses of deer as a result of free-running dogs simply does not make an impression upon the general public. Read this book for an interesting discussion of this controversial problem.

Gibson, Colin. *Highland Deer Stalker.* London: Seeley, Service & Company, 1958. 243 pp.

The story of Allan Cameron, a famous Highland deer stalker.*

Glover, Ronnie. *More Than Luck: A Guide for Hunting the Trophy Buck.* Louisiana: A Big Buck Publication, 1980. 52 pp.

Practical advice for those who hunt deer in the hills and hollows of southwestern Mississippi.

Glover, Rosamond. *A Deer in my Kitchen.* Great Britain: Arthur H. Stockwell, 1978. 121 pp.

A true story of a roe deer.

Gorton, Audrey Alley. *The Venison Book.* Vermont: The Stephen Green Press, 1957. 78 pp.

A popular guide to handling venison. Gives the how and why for every step from the deer forest to the table. Written by a former food expert for the BBC and the *Manchester Guardian.* Essential reading for the venison connoisseur.

Goss, Fred. *Memories of a Stag Harbourer.* London: H.F. & G. Witherby, 1931. 224 pp.

Memories of one of England's most famous deer hunters. Contains an excellent chapter on the many-sided art of slots and slotting, in which the author admits that he knows few "things more fascinating than to find where a big stag has been feeding, to slot him into the wood, and afterwards to cast all round the wood along fences, lanes and roads, to see if he has walked out again. Slotting a stag this way from feeding-ground to resting place, and making sure by casting round that he has not moved, gives the hunter a confidence that not even a view of the stag at close quarters can strengthen."*

Goss, Richard J. *Deer Antlers: Regeneration, Function, and Evolution.* New York: Academic Press, 1983. 316 pp.

This is a great book about one of nature's most remarkable accomplishments. While this comprehensive account of antlerology might not answer all your questions about these unique appendages, it will surely arouse your curiosity about the many unsolved problems of how antlers grow, die and are shed in the course of a year. Indeed, this book addresses the following provocative questions: From what kinds of tissues do antlers develop? What morphogenetic mechanisms regenerate them every year? How are they influenced by hormones? How do seasonal day-length fluctuations regulate their annual replacement? Not since William Macewen's *The Growth and Shedding of the Antler of the Deer* (1920) and A. B. Bubenik's *Das Geweih (Antlers,* 1966), has a better book been published on the subject. Scientifically accurate and very readable. Highly recommended. A blue-chip deer book.

Grant, Norman B., Jr. *Records of Alaska Big Game: 1971.* Alaska Big Game Trophy Club, Inc., 1971. 111 pp.

A very valuable record book for the trophy hunter. The chapter by Professor Atamian entitlted "The Psychology of Fair Chase," in particular, is worth the high price of the book itself. In that chapter Professor Atamian emphasizes one basic proposition: "Hunting is a basic mechanism by which man's consciousness is expanded so that his innermost nature is more clearly perceived. He reconciles himself to what his humanity really is instead of weaving webs

of self deception with fantasies designed to falsify the realities of life and death. If hunters are less alienated than others (and I believe they are) it is because they sense something about the mystique of life and death instead of avoiding it. Everyone accepts the Socratic dictum 'know thyself'—the hunter does something about it." A blue-chip book on big-game hunting that contains a superb and remarkable statement on hunting ethics.*

Gregory, Tappan. *Deer at Night in the North Woods.* Maryland: Charles C. Thomas, 1930. 211 pp.

The exciting adventures of an early outdoor photographer. A classic in photographing deer. Provides enchanting reading for deer hunter and nature enthusiast alike. Includes a fantastic collection of photos.*

Grey, Zane. *The Deer Stalker.* New York: Harper, 1925. 243 pp.

The grim, gory story of Ranger Thad Eburne, who tries to protect a herd of 50,000 deer that are doomed to die. Revolves around the deer population of Bucksin Mountain in northern Arizona which had increased because of unrestrained slaughter of cougars. Underscores the paradox that deer protected in national forests against their natural enemies starve to death during the winter because of a limited food supply. Describes the government's miserable failure at trapping and transplanting deer, including an abortive attempt to drive thousands of deer down the Grand Canyon and across the Colorado River, which was led by author Zane Grey himself. Uses the deer irruption situation to illustrate the baneful effects of man's meddling with nature. Paramount Pictures, interestingly enough, tried to produce a film based on the story, but failed because of the studio's difficulty in obtaining footage of deer activity.*

Grimble, Augustus. *Deer-Stalking.* London: Chapman and Hall, 1888. 308 pp.

A famous manual of practical advice and reminiscences. Offers sound advice on every aspect of the sport, not the least of which is the problem of buck fever. On this subject the author writes: "The disease must run its course. Advice will not cure it, *neither will whiskey;* but after a course of downright bad misses the foresight of your rifle will by degrees cease to wobble round and round. The eye will see clearly that there *is* a stag within a hundred yards, and the brain begin to tell that it will be better to keep the sight steady if you wish to taste one of his haunches instead of sending him off to give a treat to a neighbour.''*

Grusendorf, W. F. *Fifty Years of White-Tailed Deer Hunting in Texas.* New York: Vantage Press, 1962. 79 pp.

Collected reminiscences of 50 years of Texas deer hunting.*

Hackmann, Georg. *Hunting in the Old World.* Hannover, 1953. 80 pp.

An essay written in the interest of American sportsmen hunting in Europe. Familiarizes us with European customs, gamekeeping and methods of hunting. Provides a basic introduction to red deer, fallow deer and roe deer. Views deer hunting as the "supreme of hunting delights." Portrays the values and attitudes of the *hirschgerechter Jäger,* the ethical deer hunter.*

Hamilton, Archibald. *The Red Deer of Exmoor: With Notes on Those Who Hunt Them.* London: Horace Cox, 1907. 363 pp.

A fascinating addition to the literature on the red deer. Strong on deer hunting history and tradition.*

Hammond, S. H. *Hunting Adventures in the Northern Wilds.* New York: Derby & Jackson, 1859. 340 pp.

————. *Wild Northern Scenes or Sporting Adventures with the Rifle and the Rod.* New York: Derby & Jackson, 1857, 341 pp.

Early American deer hunting adventures in the Adirondacks.*

Harper, Francis. *The Barren Ground Caribou of Keewatin.* Kansas: University of Kansas, 1955. 163 pp.

An excellent scientific treatise on this cherished and spectacular creature. Based on a 1947 expedition of southwestern Keewatin.*

Harris, Roy A., and Duff, K. R. *Wild Deer in Britain.* Great Britain: David & Charles, 1970. 112 pp.

Popular and illustrated guide to the six species of deer in Great Britain: red deer, roe deer, fallow deer, sika, muntjac and Chinese water deer. Written by two freelance wildlife photographers. Includes as many photos as pages of text. The photographs are in themselves beautiful wildlife studies.

Hart-Davis, Captain H. *Stalking Sketches.* London: Horace Cox, 1904. 67 pp.

Pleasant stalking reminiscences. Reaches the conclusion that "there is a poetry and a charm in hunting or stalking the stag in his own boundless and magnificent home, be it in the Rocky Mountains or be it in Norway. The camping out, the freedom from control and from the thraldom of civilization, the immensity of the area over which you may sport at your will—all these appeal most strongly to all and every sportsman.''*

Hart-Davis, Duff. *Monarchs of the Glen: A History of Deer Stalking in the Scottish Highlands.* London: Jonathan Cape, 1978. 249 pp.

A colorful and fascinating historical survey of hunting the red deer in the Scottish Highlands. Will be the standard work on the subject for years to come. Working from unpublished sources, the author weaves a wealth of superb anecdotes into a splendid piece of deer hunting history. A jewel of deer hunting nostalgia!

Hartmann, John. *A Deer in the Family.* London: Michael Joseph, 1954. 36 pp.

Juvenile literature. The true story of an unusual friendship between a human family and a family of deer.*

Harvey, Lieut.-Col. J. R. *Deer Hunting in Norfolk: From the Earliest Times.* Norwich: Norwich Mercury Company, 1910. 96 pp.

A fascinating history of the sport we love best—a spin with the deer. The sport of deer hunting, the author observes, "has stood the test of public criticism through a period of a thousand years, and may surely assert its claims to the title of a national pastime.''*

Hayes, Tom. *How to Hunt the Whitetail.* New York: A. S. Barnes and Company, 1960. 256 pp.

Another how-to book of an earlier vintage. Based on one important premise: "Lack of knowledge of the habits of white-tailed deer, or failure to take advantage of this knowledge, is the primary reason for lack of success among reasonably experienced hunters." Written by a Texas deer hunter and a widely recognized hunting authority. Important reading.*

Helgeland, Glenn., ed. *Archery World's Complete Guide to Bowhunting.* New Jersey: Prentice-Hall, 1972. 262 pp.

Reprinted articles from *Archery World* magazine.

Hendee, John C., and Schoenfeld, Clay. *Human Dimensions in Wildlife Programs: Reports of Recent Investigations.* Washington, D.C.: The Wildlife Management Institute, 1973. 193 pp.

An interesting collection of papers dealing with the human dimensions aspect of wildlife use. Contains five excellent essays on deer hunting behavior in the states of Washington, Montana, Colorado, Maryland and Massachusetts.*

Herbert, Harry John. *The Population Dynamics of the Waterbuck.* Hamburg: Verlag Paul Parey, 1972. 68 pp.

By elucidating ecological and biological questions, this critical monograph investigates the reasons for the alarming decrease of the waterbuck. Based on investigations made in a private nature reserve bordering the Kruger National Park. A basic reference work.

Herrigel, Eugen. *Zen in the Art of Archery.* New York: Pantheon Books, 1953. 109 pp.

An illuminating account of the art of archery. Highly recommended for the philosophically-minded deer hunter who likes to meditate on his bow hunting experiences and who likes to tune himself into the unconsciousness as he floats through the air in his oak tree.

Heuser, Ken. *The Whitetail Deer Guide.* New York: Holt, Rinehart and Winston, 1972. 208 pp.

A standard reference guide. Interspersed with those tiny gems of whitetail knowledge for which experienced deer hunters are constantly searching. Attempts to destroy the myth of the waiting game. "There is a great difference of opinion on whether to sit down and wait fifteen minutes to a half hour before pursuing wounded game or whether to pursue immediately. My advice is to pursue and push immediately! Don't wait around for a deer to lie down and stiffen up. Pure bunk!"

Hewett, H. P. *The Fairest Hunting: Hunting and Watching Exmoor Deer.* London: J. A. Allen and Company, 1963. 116 pp.

A historical account of the art of hunting red deer in England with Devon and Somerset stag hounds. A valuable work of reference which places deer hunting in its modern historical perspective.

Hine, Ruth L., ed. *White-Tailed Deer Population Management in the North Central States.* Wisconsin: The Graphic Printing Company, 1980. 116 pp.

This collection of papers examines such basic tools and techniques as aging deer, determining populations and measuring harvests. It also deals with the causes of mortality, the factors influencing productivity, as well as with the human dimensions of deer hunters, state administrators and John Q. Public. Sorts out the confusing pieces of the deer management puzzle in a logical and useful manner for game managers and deer hunters alike.

Hoff, Roy. *Roy Hoff tells it as it was . . . Forty years of archery and bow hunting.* California: Privately Printed, 1980. 186 pp.

A history of bow hunting containing stimulating episodes of some of the all-time greats. Written by the founder of *Archery Magazine.* Deals with humorous incidents, goofs and disappointments. Entertaining. Printed on a hand-operated Vandercook reproduction proof press.

Holden, Philip. *The Deer Hunters.* New Zealand: Hodder and Stoughton, 1976. 104 pp.

Captures the magic of New Zealand's outdoors while covering the deer hunting scene from Stewart Island to north of Auckland.*

Holmes, Frank. *Following the Roe: A Natural History of the Roe Deer.* Edinburgh: John Bartholomew and Son, 1974. 112 pp.

A fascinating scientific study of the roe deer written for the naturalist and all others with a genuine interest in deer. It's a shame American publishers do not provide the public with excellent material like this! Contains a superb chapter on "roe language."*

Hoover, Helen. *The Gift of the Deer.* New York: Knopf, 1968. 210 pp.

A wilderness tale of a deer, his mate, their offspring and two human beings. Vivid prose which describes the annual life cycle of deer living around a two-room cabin home in the bush country of the United States-Canadian border.

Hornaday, William T. "The Deer Family." *The Mentor* 8: 1–11. April 15, 1920.

An early survey of the deer family by a famous naturalist. According to Hornaday, "The pursuit of the deer of the world did more to create high-class rifles and promote good rifle shooting than had been accomplished by any other cause prior to 1914." The deer of the world have made keen woodsmen and trackers out of many men. Scarce.*

Houston, Douglas B. *The Northern Yellowstone Elk: Ecology and Management.* New York: Macmillan, 1982. 474 pp.

A superb ecological study of the feeding, breeding and social patterns of the northern Yellowstone elk herd and their impact on the northern range ecosystem. Employs a system of comparative historical photography. Also includes their seasonal distribution, population dynamics and their effects on other wildlife. A major contribution to wildlife management—based on 10 years of first-hand field research and painstaking scholarship.

Howard, John E., ed. *North American Big Game Hunting in the 1800's.* New Jersey: Amwell, 1982. 498 pp.

Another blue-chip deer book from The National Sporting Fraternity Limited. If you buy this jewel, you will never regret it, for this splendid memorial to an age which we will never see again provides the modern-day deer hunter with basic and essential reading. One of the finest books in my library. In reading through this anthology, one soon realizes that nothing changes. "Only the actors in the drama. The plot remains the same. The deer roams the hills. The man follows it. Only the name of the man changes. The deer changes too. But only the individual, not the species."

Hoyt, Vance Joseph. *Sequoia.* New York: Grosset & Dunlap, 1931. 272 pp.

Formerly published as *Malibu: A Nature Story.* Legend and story. Animal lovers and nature enthusiasts who like their natural history interwoven with fiction will enjoy Dr. Hoyt's yarn. Tells the story of his experiment with a puma cub and a fawn. Hoyt writes to tell the animal's side of life's struggles. The author is at his best when recounting the methods employed by the deer to evade pursuers and with the deer's capacity to reckon with scent both as a warning when it emanates from others and as a danger signal when it emanates from its own species.*

Hurd, Edith Thacher. *The Mother Deer.* Boston: Little Brown and Company, 1972. 32 pp.

Juvenile literature. Describes a year in the life of a doe from birth of her fawns to her mating again and the birth of another set of fawns.

International Union for Conservation of Nature and Natural Resources. *Threatened Deer.* Great Britain: Alden Press, 1978. 434 pp.

Proceedings of a meeting of the Deer Specialist Group of the Survival Service Commission. Includes case histories of various threatened species and guidelines on threatened species restoration. Contains an interesting chapter on the Columbian white-tailed deer *(Odocoileus virginianus leucurus),* the only deer still on the world threatened list in North America. Highly technical.

James, David, and Stephens, Wilson., ed. *In Praise of Hunting: A Symposium.* London: Hollis & Carter, 1960. 231 pp.

Deer hunting frequently becomes the subject of sensational publicity and ill-informed and malicious talk. This volume puts forth the question that seldom gets asked: Why do people of diverse outlooks, talents and interests enjoy hunting and consider it a worthwhile sport? Contains different lines of reasoning and differing points of view. Includes a strong argument in favor of deer hunting on Exmoor by noted deer authority G. Kenneth Whitehead. Basic reading for understanding the hunting-antihunting debate.*

James, M. R. *Bowhunting for Whitetail and Mule Deer.* New Jersey: Jolex, Inc., 1976. 224 pp.

A manual for improving your bow hunting skills. Contains a first-rate chapter on blood trails and a balanced discussion of the drug-tipped arrow.

Jefferies, Richard. *Red Deer.* London: Longmans, Green, and Company, 1892. 248 pp.

A delightful book on red deer and the hunting of them. Contains the following classic description of deer: "There is no more beautiful creature than a stag in his pride of antler, his coat of ruddy gold, his grace of form and motion. He seems the natural owner of the ferny coombes, the oak woods, the broad slopes of heather. They belong to him, and he steps upon the sward in lordly mastership. The land is his, and the hills, the sweet streams, and rocky glens. He is as natural as an oak." A famous book of delightful reading.*

Jenkins, Marie M. *Deer, Moose, Elk, and their Family.* New York: Holiday House, 1979. 128 pp.

A general description of all types of deer found throughout the world. A nice book to put in the hands of the beginning hunter and early deer enthusiast.

Jones, Burt. *Habits, Haunts, and Anecdotes of the Moose.* Boston: Alfred Mudge and Son, 1901. 143 pp.

A classy book on his Lordship—The Moose. Written by the founder of *The National Sportsman,* who tells us "that a trophy over one's fireplace is an object to be admired by one and all. It brings you back to a last hunting trip, and well do you remember, as

you gaze thereon, what a chase it had led you on in life, through bog and alder swamp, until at last an opportunity presented itself whereby the deadly missile from your rifle sends him to his death. As the blue rings of smoke from your brier pipe float up and away, you are carried in thought to the North Woods wherein he roamed."*

Jungius, Hartmut. *The Biology and Behaviour of the Reedbuck.* Hamburg; Verlag Paul Parey, 1971. 106 pp.

A critical monograph on this African antelope, whose secluded way of life is threatened due to the increasing destruction of its habitat. This comprehensive study was undertaken in Kruger National Park. Strong on social behavior and the ecological requirements of this species.

Kennedy, James Joseph III. "A Consumer Analysis Approach to Recreational Decisions: Deer Hunters as a Case Study." Ph.D. dissertation, Virginia Polytechnic Institute and State University, 1971. 181 pp.

Puts forth a conceptual model for analyzing deer hunting behavior. Emphasizes the idea that the real benefits of deer hunting are esthetic and that management judgments need to be based primarily on concern for quality. In other words, the wildlife manager's fetish with size and condition of deer herds is often of less consequence in providing hunter enjoyment than efforts in other aspects of management such as improving roads and trail access, improving sight distances and so on. Who would disagree with the author's contention that "Many expectations the day before deer season frequently exhibit an optimism transcending reality."

Kirschner, Bob. *Everything I Know About Bucks with a Bow.* Pennsylvania, 1974. 104 pp.

———. *The Art and Appreciation of Trophy Bowhunting.* Pennsylvania, 1981. 262 pp.

Two how-to manuals on hunting trophy bucks. Written by a deer hunter from Pennsylvania. Privately printed.

Kline, Lee., ed. *Colorado Bowhunting Records.* Colorado Bowhunter's Association, Inc., 1982, 215 pp.

While whitetails certainly do not serve as a threat to unseat mule deer as the top attraction to bow hunters in Colorado, whitetails are there and always have been. This well-researched record book documents the story from the alleged disappearance of whitetails in Colorado to their status today. Contains a scrapbook potpourri section of "hero" pictures.

Koller, Lawrence R. *Shots at Whitetails*. New York: Knopf, 1975. 359 pp.

An instructive, practical and invaluable book written by one of the old masters from the Catskill Mountains. Deals with all aspects of deer hunting—including everything from the woodcraft of hunting to equipping the deer camp itself. Strong on the nature and habit of the whitetail. A classic of wilderness lore.

Krausman, Paul R., and Ables, Ernest D. *Ecology of the Carmen Mountains White-Tailed Deer*. Washington, D.C.: Department of the Interior, 1981. 114 pp.

This technical report, a revised version of a doctoral dissertation, examines the ecology of the Carmen Mountains white-tailed deer in the Big Bend National Park of Texas. Discusses distribution, habitat, food habits, competition with mule deer and predator-prey relationships.

Krenz, Bill., ed. *Bowhunting Big Game Records of California: 1983*. California Big Game Club, 1983. 290 pp.

Records for California's mule deer and blacktails.

LaBarbera, Mark., ed. *Minnesota Deer Classic Record Book*. Minnesota Wildlife Heritage Foundation, 1983. 130 pp.

A fine reference work on Minnesota whitetails of extraordinary proportions. Includes some interesting rumors about new world records and an excellent chapter entitled "Minnesota's Rich Deer and Deer Hunting History" by John Ludwig and Tom Isley.

Laffin, W. Mackay. "Deer Hunting on the Au Sable." In *Sport with Gun and Rod in American Woods and Waters*, edited by Alfred M. Mayer. New York, 1883. pp. 233–255.

A brilliant historical description of Deer Camp Erwin on the banks of the famous Au Sable in northern Michigan. Nostalgic and unforgettable reading.*

Latymer, Lord. *Stalking in Scotland and New Zealand*. London: Blackwood and Sons, 1935. 256 pp.

A delightful characterization of the deer stalker of 1935, who in a spiritual sense, at least, remains quite similar to the American deer hunter of the 1980s. Indeed, "In matters touching the spirit—in the peace which descends on those who lift up their eyes to the hills, and in the deep thrill which stirs many men when they match their wit against the keen senses of wild deer—it is likely that our reactions are not, after all, so very different from those experienced by our forefathers." Written by an English nobleman with several record red deer heads to his credit.*

Laycock, George. *Whitetail: The Story of a White-Tailed Deer*. New York: Norton, 1966. 110 pp.

A sensitive, well-illustrated story of a deer's struggle to survive against great odds. Written by one of America's leading outdoorsmen. Excellent reading during the off season.*

———. *The Deer Hunter's Bible*. New York: Doubleday, 1963. 154 pp.

A standard guide for the beginner.

LeBastille, Anne. *White-Tailed Deer*. Washington, D.C.: The National Wildlife Federation, 1973. 32 pp.

A beautifully illustrated text for children between the ages of 1 and 6. Written by a well-known naturalist. A Ranger Rick book produced by the National Wildlife Federation.

Lees, J. A. *Peaks and Pines*. Oslo: Nortrabooks, 1967. 230 pp.

Reindeer hunting in Norway during the 1930s.*

Leopold, Aldo. *A Sand County Almanac*. New York: Oxford University Press, 1966. 269 pp.

A classic in the ethics of hunting and woodsmanship. A must for all members of the deer hunting fraternity, if this sport is to continue in the future. The essay entitled "Wildlife in American Culture" should be required reading before the issuance of any deer hunting license. A beautiful, heart-warming book!

Linsdale, Jean M., and Tomich, P. Quentin. *A Herd of Mule Deer*. Berkeley: University of California, 1953. 567 pp.

Field notes of a 13-year study. Contains a wealth of observations and data on black-tailed deer. It seems rather strange that the name "mule deer" was used rather than "black-tailed deer." Much of the material is repetitious and presented in an undigested form. Strong in reporting details, but lacks any coherent synthesis. Includes an excellent chapter on communication. Well indexed.*

Lippincott, Joseph Wharton. *The Phantom Deer*. New York: Lippincott, 1954. 192 pp.

———. *Long Horn: Leader of the Deer*. New York: Lippincott, 1928. 128 pp.

The first of these books about outdoor life tells the story of a friendship between a boy, a man and a Key deer—those miniature deer from the Florida Keys. Provides a stirring picture of animal courage in a tropical setting. The second title is intended for younger readers. Its story of a brave and handsome deer holds the reader's sympathy and interest to the end. Gives to readers young and old a moving and beautiful picture of deer. Written by a well-known author, publisher and sportsman.

Long, William J. *Following the Deer*. Boston: Athenaeum Press, 1901. 193 pp.

A classic story of following a cunning old buck throughout the seasons in the woods of Maine. Written for all deer hunters who rejoice in the autumn woods and who view killing as a minor part of the hunter's story. Underscores one important lesson: "An animal's life is vastly more interesting than his death, and that of all the joys of the chase the least is the mere act of killing." Tempers our deer hunting with humanity. As Long puts it, "The best things that a hunter brings home are in his heart, not in

his game bag." Should be read by all members of the deer hunting fraternity. Brilliant brier patch philosophizing about deer! A great companion to E. T. Seton's *Trail of the Sandhill Stag*. Highly recommended for boys of 20 and for boys of 60 and over.*

Lonsdale Library. *Deer, Hare and Otter Hunting*. London: Seeley, Service and Company, 1936. 255 pp.

A historical account of late 19th century and early 20th century deer hunting in England. Who would disagree with one of the editors when he writes that "to watch and enjoy them . . . to witness the wiles and craftiness of hunted deer, and to pit your wits against theirs, sometimes successfully, sometimes not, makes one realize some of the reasons why I have, for a quarter of a century, enjoyed hunting deer."*

Lumpkin, Courtney "Foots." *100 Deer*. Alabama: Privately printed, 1980. 158 pp.

A book of deer hunting stories and tales.

Lund, Fred. *I Mind: Memories of the Old Hunting Camp Days*. Minnesota: Privately printed, 1969. 78 pp.

Stories, incidents and facts of a Minnesota deer hunting camp called "The Homestead," a two-story log cabin located in beautiful deer country which lured the author back each fall. "I'm going back next fall and God willing, I'll go back again and again, because somewhere in that enticingly beautiful country that brings back countless memories there's a big buck. He has hoof prints as large as a small steer and a rack of horns the size of a rockin' chair. He's pokin' around those hills and potholes and he knows he's got my name on him. If I keep my eye peeled, I'll nail 'em."

Luxmoore, Edmund. *Deer Stalking: The Whys and Wherefores*. London: David & Charles, 1980. 143 pp.

A splendid account of modern-day deer hunting in England. Frequently referred to as the authoritative book on English deer stalking. Describes in detail modern methods, equipment and practices. Written by a successful lawyer who became "hooked" on deer in his childhood, and for whom deer have become a lifetime's addiction. Reaches the following conclusion: "One is very fond of the deer and, if they win sometimes, it adds a lot to the enjoyment. Deer stalking, like salmon fishing, would never be worth it in terms of pleasures if the quarry did not have his successes too—long may it remain so." A rare and timely book containing a skillful blend of entertaining, educational and scientific information.

Lydekker, Richard. *The Deer of all Lands.* London: Rowland Ward, 1898. 329 pp.

A comprehensive source book and popular history of the family *cervidae* which describes 11 genera consisting of 57 species and 48 subspecies. Extremely scarce and expensive. Frequently quoted at $300 or more.*

Macewen, William. *The Growth and Shedding of the Antler of the Deer.* Glasgow: Maclehose, Jackson & Company, 1920. 109 pp.

A scientific work and a real blue-chip deer book. Though dated in its biological information, it still furnishes us with one of the best descriptions of the processes involved in the growth and development of the antler—one of the most magnificent and intricate devices of nature. Exceedingly well illustrated. A standard work on the subject.*

Mackenzie, Evan G. *Grouse Shooting and Deer Stalking.* London: Love and Malcomson, Limited, 1907. 240 pp.

Light reading for the deer shack for those who enjoy the art of deer stalking, an art which grows on one as the author maintains. "For the second season in a deer forest is invariably more enjoyable than the first, and not until one has had a third or a fourth on the same ground are the full delights of deer stalking thoroughly appreciated." Rightly believes that as deer hunters we simply live through nine months of the year so that we may enjoy the other three in the deer forests we love so well.*

Macleay, W. A. *Rua: The Story of a Highland Red Deer.* London: Hutchinson's Books, 1945. 120 pp.

An unusual and absorbing story of a Highland red deer, written while in a German prison camp. Presents a vivid picture of the Highlands aided by Frank Wallace's illustrations.*

MacNally, Lea. *Highland Deer Forest.* London: J. M. Dent & Sons, 1970. 107 pp.

Personal encounters with the varied wildlife of the Highlands, especially with red deer and roe deer. Views deer hunting as the direct antithesis of the way of modern life, "in which the trend is increasingly to closet humanity from physical exertion and to insulate it from the realities of cold and wet, in overheated cars and habitations."*

————. *The Year of the Red Deer.* London: J. M. Dent & Sons, 1975. 112 pp.

A prominent British wildlife photographer and Scottish editor to *Deer: The Journal of the British Deer Society,* beautifully records the year's life cycle of the Highland red deer. Based on a lifetime's pursuit of watching and photographing red deer. Passionately maintains that there is no one with a higher regard for—indeed, at times an utter dedication to—his deer than the hunter. Superb photos. A pleasurable book to read.*

MacQuarrie, Gordon. *Stories of the Old Duck Hunters and Other Drivel.* Pennsylvania: Stackpole Books, 1967. 223 pp.

A sporting classic containing three excellent deer hunting stories which underscore one universal theme of the deer hunting experience: The means are greater than the end, and every deer hunter knows it. Warm and hilarious tales told by a master. Highly recommended! Currently available in paperback from Willow Creek Press, Box 2266, Oshkosh, WI 54903.

Macrae, Alexander. *A Handbook of Deer Stalking.* London: William Blackwood and Sons, 1880. 85 pp.

One of the earliest handbooks on the subject. Short and full of sensible advice, especially with regard to the element of wind. Written by an old English forester who, like many Englishmen, doesn't think too highly about deer drives: "This is a coarse sort of way of going to work, and depends for its success not so much upon knowledge as upon force."*

McConnochie, Alexander Inkson. *Deer*

Stalking in Scotland. London: H. F. & G. Witherby, 1924. 208 pp.

A delightful chronicle of deer hunting adventures in Scotland. Strong on after-dinner stalking yarns.*

———. *The Deer and Deer Forests of Scotland: Historical, Descriptive, Sporting.* London: H. F. & G. Witherby, 1923. 336 pp.

An excellent historical survey of British deer stalking.*

McCullough, Dale R. *The George Reserve Deer Herd: Population Ecology of a K-Selected Species.* Michigan: University of Michigan, 1979. 271 pp.

A scientific examination of the relationship of population density to birth and survival of whitetail offspring. Difficult reading for the layman, but interpersed with "golden nuggets" for the deer hunter and white-tailed deer enthusiast. Consider, for example, the George Reserve's regulations governing deer shooting: "Deer were to be shot either in the neck or the heart. No shot was to be taken at distances greater than seventy-five yards, and only standing or slowly moving deer were to be shot." Emphasizes sport hunting as the primary management tool and contains an excellent analysis of the integration of social and biological factors influencing sport hunting.

———. *The Tule Elk.* California: University of California, 1969. 209 pp.

A fascinating study of the history, behavior and ecology of the Tule Elk. Based on direct observation of elk in their undisturbed state.*

McGee, Richard C. *The Original Tree Stand Handbook.* Florida: Sportsman's Studios, 1982. 152 pp.

An excellent book dealing exclusively with tree stands and tree stand hunting. Summarizes most commercial stands and puts forth 25 tree stand ideas you can build. Well illustrated. Also contains a directory of tree stand manufacturers.

McGuane, Thomas. "The Heart of the Game." *An Outside Chance: Essays on Sport.* England: Penguin Books, 1982. pp 227–243.

Reflects with eloquence and simplicity on the morality of deer hunting. A vivid and personal account of the acclaimed novelist's deer hunting adventures in Montana. Gives deep meaning to the deer hunting experience. Lavish, high-level and hypnotic prose. Highly recommended.

McGuire, Bob. *Advanced Whitetail Hunting Techniques.* Tennessee: Bowhunting Productions, 1983. 124 pp.

A short booklet dealing with the techniques of mock scraping.

McNair, Jack. *Shooting for the Skipper: Memories of a Veteran Deershooter.* New Zealand: Reed, 1971. 153 pp.

Humorous and not-so humorous memoirs of a seasoned mountain man and deer stalker who was asked by the New Zealand Government to take up deer culling. Deals with a little-known and less understood period of New Zealand's deer shooting history. Appealing to those who enjoy true tales of deer, deer stalking and mountainous living. Contains excellent photos of New Zealand's deer hunting country.

Madson, John. "The Secret Life of the Cottontail Deer." *Out Home.* New York: Winchester, 1979. pp. 33–39.

A classic essay on the whitetail that compares his movement patterns to the flashy starts and circular movements of the cottontail rabbit. Speaks brilliantly to those aspects of the deer hunting experience that transcend geographical restrictions of time and place. Written by one of America's foremost nature writers. Highly recommended!

———. *The White-Tailed Deer.* Illinois: Olin Mathieson Chemical Corporation, 1961. 108 pp.

A marvelous book that every deer hunter should read before entering the deer forest. Deals with the animal's life history, its management, methods of hunting and the whitetail's future. Great outdoor literature.*

———. *The Elk.* Illinois: Olin Mathieson, 1961. 125 pp.

Vintage Madson—entertaining, educational and inspirational. Well illustrated.*

Marchioness of Breadalbane. *The High Tops of Black Mount.* London: William Blackwood & Sons, 1935. 252 pp.

A classic account of deer stalking in Argyllshire, written by a lady. A gem of fine writing. Glorifies the target: "All the years I have been deer stalking, throughout the whole season I have gone regularly to the target, holding that no amount of trouble is too great which may help to fewer wounded stags, fewer misses, and fewer disappointments to the hunter himself."*

Massey, Jay. *Bowhunting Alaska's Wild Rivers.* Alaska: Bear Paw Publications, 1983. 176 pp.

Whets the appetite of any deer hunter interested in bow hunting and wilderness river running. Rightly argues that "an increasing number of bow hunters are getting fed up with gadgetry and the New Archery and the archery manufacturers that produce it. More and more archers are coming to realize that success in bow hunting cannot be measured solely by numbers. More and more bow hunters are beginning to see that *how* an animal is taken is more important than how many were taken or the size of their racks." Highly recommended!

Matunas, Edward A. *Deer Hunter's Guide to Guns, Ammo and Equipment.* New York: Outdoor Life Books, 1983. 338 pp.

An authoritative guide on guns and equipment written by a highly qualified specialist on the subject.

Mattis, George. *Whitetail: Fundamentals and Fine Points for the Hunter.* New York: Van Nostrand Reinhold Company, 1980. 248 pp.

A newly revised edition of a classic work written by an active conservationist who hunted and observed whitetails for more than 50 years. Provides us with a fine collection of personal experiences together with much practical knowledge. A unique book—quite different from the regular how-to book in that it does not attempt to be all-inclusive, but rather puts forth with great conviction the author's own likes and preferences. Favors, for example, the solitude and challenge of still hunting. Illustrated with realistic drawings of hunting situa-

tions by renowned wildlife artist William Reusswig. Great educational reading.

Mednick, Murray. *The Deer Kill.* New York: Bobbs-Merrill, 1972. 96 pp.

Mystified drama centering around rural hippies, the local game warden and the issue of responsibility when the group's dog kills a young doe.*

Merrill, Lawrence. *Deer Trails and Camp Tales.* Michigan: Privately printed, 1983. 94 pp.

Deer-camp stories and incidents based on more than 30 years of deer-hunting experiences in the Deer Lake area of the Upper Peninsula of Michigan. Written in "lumberjack language" and "jargon slang," as the author himself admits.

Merrill, Samuel. *The Moose Book.* New York: E. P. Dutton, 1916. 366 pp.

A magnificent volume devoted exclusively to the history of the moose, "the grand prize in the lottery of American sportsmanship." Covers his habits, habitat and methods of hunting him. Beautifully illustrated with drawings and photographs by Carl Rungius and others. A great fireside companion.*

Mershon, William B. *Recollections of My Fifty Years of Hunting and Fishing.* Boston: The Stratford Company, 1923. 259 pp.

A classic in outdoor literature. Chats in an extremely interesting fashion of his experiences of many years with rod and gun. Contains a fine description of the famous Nichols Deer Hunting Camps on the Au Sable River in various parts of the Lower Peninsula of Michigan. Highly recommended.*

Millais, John Guille. *British Deer and their Horns.* London: Henry Sotheran and Company, 1897. 224 pp.

An exhaustive and accurate account of all English native deer. A monumental work that deserves a place on the bookshelf of any lover of deer. Written in a most engaging manner by an author of high standing, a skillful fisherman and a good shot with both gun and rifle. Beautifully illustrated. Rare and very expensive. Frequently listed in book catalogs at $400 plus.*

Milliken, Henry. *Hunting in Maine*. Maine: L. L. Bean, Inc., 1947. 186 pp.

Pleasant reflections of deer hunting adventures in the wilds of eastern Maine. Relates in real deer hunting lingo the Maine tradition of deer hunting. Entertaining.*

Milling, Chapman J. *Buckshot and Hounds*. New York: A. S. Barnes and Company, 1967. 132 pp.

A book on the deer drive as practiced in the Deep South. For the deer hunter who delights in "the music of hounds, the sound of a distant shot, the heart-thumping thrill of anticipation, and the clear plaintive note of the driver's horn on a golden autumn morning." A well-written book by a widely-recognized authority on South Carolina. Delightful reading for those who realize the advantages of the shotgun and certainly required reading for anyone planning to organize a deer hunting club.*

Mitchell, George J. *The Pronghorn Antelope in Alberta*. Canada, 1980. 165 pp.

A scientific treatise on the status, biology, ecology, behavior, population dynamics and management of this unique plains mammal.

Mitchell, John G. *The Hunt*. New York: Alfred A. Knopf, 1980. 242 pp.

A personal exploration of hunting in America today and an examination of the emotional attitudes it inspires among devoted deer hunters, nature lovers and those who abhor hunting. Alive with controversy, anecdotes and first-rate reportage on modern-day deer hunting activities. Challenges one's attitudes toward hunting to the very foundations. An extraordinary book written by the past editor-in-chief of Sierra Club Books. Required reading!

Mockler-Ferryman, A. F. *In the Northman's Land*. London: Sampson Low, 1896. 316 pp.

A charming description of reindeer hunting in Norway. In deer hunting, the author maintains, "The real enjoyment depends on the amount of difficulty and labour required for success. Deer stalking necessitates endurance, patience, perseverance, and when the time comes for drawing the proverbial bead, coolness. How many times, I wonder, has the want of coolness at the critical moment lost the finest head that ever bore antlers."*

Mowat, Farley. *People of the Deer*. New York: Jove, 1951. 303 pp.

An absorbing book on the primitive Eskimos and the caribou of the Canadian Barrens. Illuminates the material and spiritual bonds that exist between a people and their deer—the animals Mowat calls "the lifeblood of the land." Awes the reader with beautiful descriptions of caribou migrations. Teaches the modern deer hunter how the Eskimos totally utilize the carcass: skin for clothing and tents, lard for light, the deer forehead for boot soles, the neck for boots, and meat for existence. Summarizes for today's deer hunters the historical reasons for the hunt. Passionate and inspired writing.

Muir, John. "Shasta Game." In *John Muir Summering in the Sierra*. Edited by Robert Engberg. Wisconsin: University of Wisconsin Press, 1984. pp. 39–50.

A classic example of wilderness journalism at its all-time best. A spontaneous, direct and lyrical essay about hunting mule deer and sheep in the mountains of California in November of 1874. This is Muir's account of the only hunting expedition he ever joined. Filled with pointed barbs irreverently directed against the sport of hunting, though Muir found himself caught up in the intense, emotional excitement of the chase nonetheless. Characterizes his four hunting companions as "sterling fellows, who, instead of traveling tamely, guide-book in hand, mingle with hunters and trappers, and drink in the grandeur of our matchless wilds in magnificent enfranchisement from all conventions and creeds."

Murie, Olaus J. *The Elk of North America*. Wyoming: Teton Bookshop, 1979. 376 pp.

A reprint of the original classic by a foremost field biologist of his time. The definitive work on the American elk. Reflects a lifetime spent in an ecological study of the subject. Extremely significant and useful.

———. *A Field Guide to Animal Tracks*. Boston: Houghton Mifflin, 1974. 375 pp.

A classic field guide. Contains an excellent discussion on deer tracks and droppings. Suggests in an illustration that you can determine the sex of the deer by analyzing the shape of the pellet.

Murray, W. H. H. *Adventures in the Wilderness; or, Camp-Life in the Adirondacks.* Boston: S. E. Cassino, 1882. 236 pp.

A collection of advice and sketches about camping in the Adirondacks. Contains an interesting chapter on jack-shooting deer on a foggy night.*

Myers, Charles E. *Memoirs of a Hunter.* Washington: Shaw and Borden, 1948. 309 pp.

A delightful book of deer-hunting memoirs based on more than half a century of deer-hunting experiences in the mountains and fields of the Pacific Northwest. The entire narrative supports the idea "that good sportsmanship is one of the prime and basic qualities going to make up good citizenship." Filled with nostalgic and humorous incidents as well as practical comments on the sport of deer hunting. Highly recommended.*

National Rifle Association., ed. *Deer Hunter's Guide.* Washington, D.C.: The National Rifle Association, 1978. 160 pp.

A handbook of articles edited from the best of *The American Hunter.* Can be ordered from the NRA Book Service.

Nelson, Norm. *Hunting the Whitetail Deer.* New York: McKay, 1980. 212 pp.

Four decades of deer hunting experiences in the Great Lakes and the Pacific Northwest form the foundation and setting for this how-to book for the beginning deer hunter. Well illustrated.

Nesbitt, William H., and Wright, Philip L., ed. *Records of North American Big Game.* Virginia: The Boone and Crockett Club, 1981. 409 pp.

The eighth record book of the Boone and Crockett Club. Contains informative chapters by recognized experts on the record-keeping system as well as an interesting remembrance of Carl Rungius, the famous wildlife artist. Also includes the complete story behind the world-record typical whitetail, an excellent chapter annotating the books published by the Club, and a fascinating article on Lynn Rogers' deer research in northeastern Minnesota.

Newhouse, Joan. *Reindeer are Wild Too.* Great Britain: John Murray, 1952, 174 pp.

A study of the Lapps and how their society revolves around the welfare and necessities of reindeer herds.*

Newsom, William Monypeny. *Whitetailed Deer.* New York: Scribners, 1926. 288 pp.

A classic in deer and deer hunting literature that should be re-read every year before that magical day—the opening of the season. Strong on ethics, still hunting and tracking wounded deer. Contains excellent wildlife photographs of an early vintage and numerous illustrations of white-tailed deer nostalgia. As Joe Wilcox once remarked, "A deer book which is not a dull compendium of pomposity written by an ass! Mr. Newsom was an Englishman and his writing is excellent." A blue-chip deer book.*

Norris, Ralph S. *Science of Hunting the Whitetail Deer.* Maine: Privately printed, 1972. 116 pp.

A straightforward how-to manual written by a former game warden and guide from the state of Maine. Well illustrated. Contains a well-balanced chapter on the problem of wounded deer.*

North American Big Game. Washington D.C.: The Boone and Crockett Club, 1977. 367 pp.

The seventh records book of the Boone and Crockett Club. A valuable reference volume for the deer hunter with a serious interest in our native big game. Provides sufficient information to score your own trophies. Includes photographs of the top trophies in each category.

O'Connor, Jack. *The Art of Hunting Big Game in North America.* New York: Outdoor Life, 1967. 404 pp.

A standard reference on almost every aspect of big game hunting as it is practiced on this continent. Written by one of the most distinguished shooting editors this nation has ever produced. A complete and enlightening guide.*

Oklahoma Department of Wildlife Conservation. *Deer Hunter's Handbook.* Oklahoma: Department of Conservation, 1982. 24 pp.

A basic pamphlet for the Oklahoma deer hunter. Emphasizes the idea that deer hunting is a privilege rather than a right.

Old Stalker. *Days on the Hill.* London: Nisbet and Company, 1926. 262 pp.

Scottish deer hunting reminiscences. Reflects that rare combination of one who is skilled in a great field sport and who can write of what he has seen and known.*

Oleberg, Carl. *Guide to Deer Hunting in the Catskill Mountains.* New York: Outdoor Publications, 1968. 40 pp.

This booklet provides the sportsman with the kind of helpful material he should know about if he plans to deer hunt the Catskill Mountains. Read this booklet together with Koller's *Shots at Whitetails* before hunting deer in the Catskills.

Olson, Sigurd F. "The Swamp Buck." *Runes of the North.* New York: Alfred A. Knopf, 1974. pp. 73–83.

A stimulating, vibrant story of an old deer hunter who returns to the woods of the North to take up the trail of a white-tailed buck. Deeply expresses the haunting appeal of the wilderness and the tales and legends to be found there. Reaches the following conclusion with regard to trailing deer: "Old hunters have said that when they pursue a quarry for a long time, they begin to feel and think as the animal does, and Indians have told me that sometimes they become a part of the very creatures they seek to kill. The two days I trailed the buck gave me an intimation of what they knew." Written by one of this country's best-known woodsmen and naturalists. Highly recommended.

Ontario Bowhunters Association. *Bowhunting Notes.* Ontario: Privately printed, 1980. 209 pp.

An accurate and reliable source of information for the prospective bow hunter and the experienced bow hunter as well.

Ormond, Cylde. *Hunting our Medium Size Game.* Pennsylvania: Stackpole Books, 1958. 219 pp.

Despite the misnomer of the title, this basic how-to book of an early vintage by master outdoorsman Cylde Ormond deals essentially with deer and black bear huntig.*

Orr, Willie. *Deer Forests, Landlords and Crofters: The Western Highlands in Victorian and Edwardian Times.* Edinburgh: John Donald, 1982. 226 pp.

A historical and scholarly work on the development of deer forests and deer stalking in the western Highlands of Scotland.

Osgood, Wilfred H. *The White-Tailed Deer.* Chicago: Field Museum of Natural History, 1922. 12 pp.

An early pamphlet describing the natural history of the animal. Written by the curator of the Chicago Field Museum of Natural History. Rare.*

Outdoor Life's Deer Hunting Book. New York: Outdoor Life, 1974. 275 pp.

A basic anthology on the subject. Consists of reprinted articles from *Outdoor Life.*

Page, F. J. Taylor., ed. *Field Guide to British Deer.* England: Blackwell, 1971. 83 pp.

A basic field guide to the deer of Great Britain. Currently available from The British Deer Society.

Page, Warren. *Deer Hunting.* New York: Holt, Rinehart, and Winston, 1966. 127 pp.

General introduction for the beginner. Written by a veteran editor of *Field & Stream* who contributed nine heads to the records of the Boone and Crockett Club.*

Park, Francis E., Jr. *Deer Hunting.* New York: The Ronald Press Company, 1954. 96 pp.

An introductory guide for the "city guy." Written by a seasoned woodsman from Maine.*

Parrish, J. C. *Whitetails.* Michigan: Harlo Press, 1978. 152 pp.

Direct and boastful reminiscences and stories of a Michigan deerslayer. Provides light reading for the novice. Contains an interesting collection of photos of Deer Camp Parish—Chaney Lake, Wakefield, Michigan. Somewhat marred, however, with the perpetuation of technological gadgetry.

Perry, Richard. *The Watcher and the Red Deer*. London: William Hodge, 1952. 188 pp.

A vivid, graphic and sensuous tale of everyday life among the herds of red deer in the glens and on the mountain pastures of the Scottish Highlands. Emphasizes the eternal idea that the lure of deer will always call us. A genuine love for deer shines through its pages.*

Perry, Walter. *Bucks and Bows*. Pennsylvania: Stackpole Books, 1953. 223 pp.

An early nostalgic account of bow hunting and its Indian origins. Well illustrated. Of great historical interest.*

Peters, Roger. ''Wapiti and Deer.'' *Mammalian Communication: A Behavioral Analysis of Meaning*. California: Brooks/Cole Publishing Company, 1980. pp. 105–160.

A rare and excellent discussion of how deer communicate and available in paperback format. Deals with this little-known subject under four categories: Neonatal communication, integrative messages, agonistic messages, and sexual messages. Highly recommended.

Petersen, Eugene T. *Hunters' Heritage: A History of Hunting in Michigan*. Michigan: Michigan United Conservation Clubs, 1979. 55 pp.

An interesting book on the history of deer hunting in Michigan. Written by the superintendent of the Mackinac Island State Park Commission. Beautifully illustrated with deer hunting photographs of an early vintage. Fascinating reading. Can be ordered through the Michigan United Conservation Clubs, Box 30235, Lansing, MI 48909.

Peterson, Randolph L. *North American Moose*. Canada: University of Toronto Press, 1955. 280 pp.

An outstanding reference on this animal, which all students of deer will want to read. Painstakingly researched and based on detailed field work as well. An intense volume of facts. Well illustrated. Still available in paperback.

Phillips, Archie, and Phillips, Bubba. *How to Mount Deer*. Pennsylvania: Stackpole Books, 1981. 127 pp.

Covers every detail from skinning and preparing the hide to final grooming and painting the finished mount. Assists the hobbiest in creating his own mount easily and inexpensively. Hundreds of photographs clearly illustrate the process in detail. A first-rate how-to book on the art of taxidermy written for both the professional and amateur taxidermist.

Phillips, W. E. *The Conservation of the California Tule Elk*. Canada: The University of Alberta Press, 1976. 120 pp.

A socioeconomic study of a survival problem. Deals with two central questions in the fight to save a threatened species: (1) Who benefits from survival?; and (2) Who pays the costs? All those concerned with the survival of deer should read this book.*

Pope, Saxton. *Hunting with the Bow and Arrow*. New York: Popular Library, 1974. 232 pp.

A famous book of philosophical thoughts on hunting that greatly inspired Fred Bear, Art Young and Aldo Leopold. A classic statement revealing the true excitement of bow hunting. Emphasis placed on woodcraft and on outsmarting wild animals. Written by one of the founders of modern-day bow hunting. Delightful reading! Can be ordered through The Fred Bear Sports Club, Rural Route 4, Gainesville, FL 32601.

Popowski, Bert. *Hunting Pronghorn Antelope*. Pennsylvania: Stackpole Books, 1959. 225 pp.

A fine contribution toward pronghorn lore. Based on reams of Pittman-Robertson project reports. Describes the pronghorn's history, habits and habitat, and explains how it was threatened with extinction, and how, by a system of live-trapping, transplanting and proper conservation, the species has been saved. A basic and authoritative work.*

————. *The Hunter's Book of the Pronghorn Antelope*. Oklahoma: Winchester, 1982. 356 pp.

A revised and updated version of the 1959 classic. The definitive book on pronghorn and pronghorn hunting. The final project of a renowned outdoorsman whose outdoor writing career spanned half a century. Thorough and entertaining.

Poulos, D. W. *Venison: The Choice of Kings.* Michigan: Privately printed, 1980. 41 pp.

A fine 41-page pamphlet devoted exclusively to the preparation of venison. A handy reference work for the inexperienced wildlife cook. Can be ordered by writing to the author at 146 N. 5 Mile Rd., Midland, MI 48640.

Pratt, Jerome J. *White Flags of Apacheland.* New York: Vantage Press, 1966. 126 pp.

A revealing study of the Coues deer that relates its dramatic past to the Apache way of life. Written in factual and non-technical terms, yet written by a professional wildlife manager. Of great interest to the lay naturalist and deer hunter alike.*

Prichard, H. Hesketh. *Hunting Camps in Wood and Wilderness.* London: Sturgis and Walton, 1910. 274 pp.

Big game hunting in Patagonia, Newfoundland and Labrador. Correctly believes that "The hunter's ideal is a chase in which he can see his quarry in the open, can match his intelligence against its instinct, and win or lose the day on his merits." Unique photographs and illustrations of old-time deer camps.*

Prior, Richard. *Living with Deer.* London: Andre Deutsch, 1965. 150 pp.

This history of British deer offers practical advice toward solving the problems of living with deer on an overcrowded island. Written by one of those rare characters who occur from time to time in English letters: a naturalist who can write graphic and elegant prose and a sportsman who knows his wildlife ecology. An enjoyable book for the general reader. Combines history, anecdote, natural history and practical advice on deer management.*

———. *The Roe Deer of Cranborne Chase: An Ecological Survey.* London: Oxford University Press, 1968. 222 pp.

A very delightful study of the fascinating and delightful roe deer based on a lifetime's interest and five years of uninterrupted field research. Written by a professional game biologist. Covers all aspects of the natural history and ecology of the roe deer. Discusses an interesting phenomenon called "post-rut wandering," whereby bucks apparently leave their normal locality and move into outlying crops for a brief time in September. An excellent book for the deer hunter and the nature enthusiast.*

———. *Roe Stalking.* London: Percival Marshall, 1963. 90 pp.

An excellent introduction to the hunting and stalking of roe deer.*

———. *Trees and Deer: How to Cope with Deer in Forest, Field and Garden.* London: Batsford, 1983. 208 pp.

This book, produced in association with the British Deer Society, sets forth a detailed policy for the successful integration of forestry with the management and control of deer. Contains sound practical advice on the art of deer stalking. Draws from the writings of T. S. Van Dyke. A timely and valuable contribution to the problem of deer damage. Provides the researcher with an excellent chapter on deer fences.

Prishvin, Mikhail. *The Root of Life.* New York: Macmillan, 1980. 115 pp.

A fanciful novel dealing with the timeless rites and mysterious processes of nature and with a young Russian soldier who captures and raises a herd of wild spotted deer. Written by one of Russia's most popular nature writers.

Puckett, Riley. *Advanced Bowhunting for the Modern Archer.* Virginia: Privately printed, 1983. 75 pp.

A short essay on the sport of bow hunting written by a champion archer from Virginia. Rightly insists that "once in a tree stand during the rut, never come out until dark. . . . When you come out of that tree before dark, your chances of killing a deer, especially a large buck, become microscopic.

Rae, William E., ed. *A Treasury of Outdoor Life.* New York: Outdoor Life Books, 1982. 458 pp.

An excellent anthology of hunting and fishing stories that includes several fine articles on deer and deer hunting, especially John Randolph's article entitled "Deer Camp."

Rawlings, Marjorie Kinnan. *The Yearling*. New York: Scribners, 1938. 428 pp.

A Pulitzer Prize-winning novel of the relationship between a young boy and his tame fawn. A classic work of American literature. The author weaves the texture of this book out of such humble material as the zest of a hunting expedition, the stir of spring in the deer forest and a suddenly glimpsed dance of grave, stately cranes. Reaches a peak of poignance and tragic power. Still available in paperback.

Reiger, John F. *American Sportsmen and the Origins of Conservation*. New York: Winchester, 1975. 316 pp.

Thoroughly demonstrates how sport hunters were among the first to challenge the exploitative pioneer attitudes toward our natural resources and documents the fact that hunters and fishermen originated the environmental movement. A devastating rebuttal to Cleveland Amory and his anti-sportsmen followers. An eloquent and compelling portrayal of the role of the American hunter and the conservation movement. Contains a superb picture album of sport and conservation in early America. Enlightened reading.

Reneau, Jack, and Reneau, Susan. *Colorado's Biggest Bucks and Bulls*. Colorado: Colorado Big Game Trophy Records, Inc., 1983. 275 pp.

An excellent reference volume filled with a wealth of where and how-to information based on the experiences of some of Colorado's most successful deer hunters. Contains a superb chapter on rare photographs of special interest. If you are collecting and reading the various state record books on trophy deer, you will want to add this fine volume to your collection.

Rhodes, Cecil E. *Adventures in Deer Hunting*. New York: Carlton Press, 1979. 62 pp.

A distillation of 10 years of deer hunting experiences. Written by a Tennessee deer hunter. Focuses on the exciting moments in the career of one white-tailed deer hunter, rather than on how-to information. Episodic in nature.

Riley, Perry G. *Outwitting the Whitetail*. Illinois: Privately printed, 1981. 85 pp.

A brief pamphlet of deer hunting experiences written for the beginner.

Roberts, Major Ned H. *Big Game Hunting: White-Tailed Deer and Black Bear*. Chicago: Paul, Richmond & Company, 1947. 160 pp.

A how-to manual of an early vintage. Emphasis on deer rifles, cartridges, sights, scopes, mounts, equipment and accessories. Based on 65 years of deerslaying experience. Focuses on eastern and northeastern deer hunting.*

Robinson, Rollo S. *Shots at Mule Deer*. New York: Winchester, 1970. 209 pp.

Fine one-volume work on hunting mule deer. Written by a biologist/zoologist with more than 40 years of mule deer hunting experience. Entertaining, instructive, practical.*

Rogers, Robert. *Great Whitetails of North America*. Texas: Privately printed, 1981. 221 pp.

Contains pictures and stories of more than 100 of the largest whitetails taken in North America.

————. *Big Rack*. Texas: Privately printed, 1980. 168 pp.

A book of pictures and stories of various classifications of Texas trophy whitetails. Reaches five conclusions: (1) the average distance of kill is only 50 yards; (2) the average weight is 147 pounds; (3) the average time of day for the kill is 10:00 a.m.; (4) half of the hunters were in pursuit of a particular deer; and (5) in the remaining hunts the deer were taken purely by chance. Apparently, a little luck never hurt anyone.

Roosevelt, Theodore; Van Dyke, T. S.; Elliot, D. G.; and Stone, A. J. *The Deer Family*. New York: Macmillan, 1924. 334 pp.

An early work on the natural history of deer, as well as on the methods of the chase that according to Roosevelt consisted of two chief elements: (1) the chance to be in the wilderness; and (2) the demand made by the particular kind of chase upon the qualities of manliness and hardihood. Dated in its biological information, but entertaining reading nonetheless.*

Rosenberry, Marvin B. *A History of Deerfoot*

Lodge: Memories of Happy Hunting. Wisconsin: Privately printed, 1941. 70 pp.

A detailed description of a famous Wisconsin deer camp dealing with the years 1910–1935. Written by a chief judge of the Wisconsin State Supreme Court. Recreates in a vivid manner the atmosphere of the traditional deer camp. Contains exciting and humorous stories, maps and photos of deer camp activities, as well as lyrics for deer hunting songs. Strong on ethics, tradition and camaraderie. A must for the deer camp enthusiast. Extremely rare.*

Ross, John., ed. *The Book of the Red Deer.* London, 1925. 161 pp.

A classic collection of essays on stalking deer in Scotland and elsewhere. Edited by an authority on the subject. Correctly prophetized as early as 1925 that deer hunting would gradually come into its own again. In the words of one of the contributors, ''I am hopeful of the future, for I cannot believe that this grandest of all sports will ever cease to appeal to a man with an ounce of poetry or romance in his being.''*

Rothhaar, Roger. *In Pursuit of Trophy Whitetails.* Indiana: Blue-J Inc., 1982. 112 pp.

A trophy bow hunter from Ohio shares his deer hunting experiences. Most of the material originally appeared in *Bowhunter* magazine. Well worth reading in the event that you missed the magazine articles. Strong on scrape hunting and the study of breeding areas. A fine companion volume to the books on trophy whitetail hunting by Wensel, Wootters and Benoit.

Ruark, Robert. ''Mister Howard Was a Real Gent.'' *The Old Man and the Boy.* New York: Holt, Rinehart, and Winston, 1957. pp. 59–80.

This first-rate portrait of a deer hunt in the woods of North Carolina represents one of the finest essays ever written in American outdoor literature. Its insights and in-depth feelings warrant reading and rereading it every year when the deer season beings.

Rue, Leonard Lee III. *The Deer of North America.* New York: Crown, 1978. 463 pp.

———. *The World of the White-Tailed Deer.* New York: Lippincott, 1962. 137 pp.

Two classic texts illustrated with breathtaking photos. Written by one of America's leading wildlife photographers and naturalists. Absolutely first-rate. Authoritative, readable, convincing. The best two books on the subject I have read. Highly recommended!

Russell, Franklin. *The Hunting Animal.* New York: Harper and Row, 1983. 211 pp.

While reading this enlightening little masterpiece, I felt time and again my gun in my hands and repeatedly saw deer fall to the forest floor. Few books create such an impression! Indeed, few books on hunting are written with such grace and style. A powerful book. Written by a professional naturalist who writes beautiful prose and knows how to make his specialized knowledge fascinating to the layman. Documents the thesis that existence in the natural world is an endless hunt.

Rutledge, Archibald. *An American Hunter.* New York: Frederick A. Stokes Company, 1937. 461 pp.

A superb collection of hunting tales, many of which deal with deer and deer hunting in the South. Written by the poet laureate of South Carolina who not only shot 299 bucks in 78 years of deer hunting, but who wrote more than 80 books in between deer hunts. Will always be remembered as the most eloquent chronicler of deer hunting adventures in the South Carolina low country. Vastly entertaining throughout.*

Ryan, Pat. *Deer Hunting: Current Evidence and Advanced Techniques.* New York: Privately printed, 1982. 52 pp.

A basic pamphlet for the beginning deer hunter to read and digest.

Ryden, Hope. *The Little Deer of the Florida Keys.* New York: Putnam, 1978. 62 pp.

Juvenile literature, geared for grade levels four to seven. The story of the threatened survival of the Key deer. Anthropomorphic in tone, with a strong antihunting bias. Is there any wonder why deer hunting is in trouble in this country?*

Safari Magazine. *Deer of the World.* Arizona: 1983. 112 pp.

An excellent although brief analysis of deer and deer hunting world-wide. Filled with beautiful photographs of deer by Erwin and Peggy Bauer and includes an interesting chapter on deer artists.

Salten, Felix. *Bambi: A Life in the Woods.* New York: Simon and Schuster, 1928. 293 pp.

The life story of a red deer for children. Regrettably, its vision is deflected by a sentimental transference of human characteristics to the animal mind. Anthropomorphism at its all-time worst.*

Schaller, George B. *The Deer and the Tiger: A Study of Wildlife in India.* Chicago: University of Chicago Press, 1967. 370 pp.

An eloquent plea for wildlife management and for relating the basic problems of animals to the problems of human ecology. Written by a naturalist of first rank. Absorbing reading.

Schmidt, John, and Gilbert, Douglas L. *Big Game of North America: Ecology and Management.* Pennsylvania: Stackpole Books, 1978. 494 pp.

A comprehensive reference volume from the Wildlife Management Institute devoted to the ecology and management of North American big game. Written in a style accessible to amateur naturalists and deer hunters alike. In-depth information. Highly recommended for the eager-to-be-informed deer hunter.

Schuh, Dwight. *Bugling for Elk. A Complete Guide for Early-Season Elk Hunting.* Montana: Stoneydale Press, 1983. 162 pp.

A personal approach to elk hunting based on numerous actual experiences in Colorado, Oregon, Arizona, Montana and Idaho. The first book to deal with the subject of bugling for elk during the early season. Of interest for those dreaming about or planning an elk hunt on the public land of the West.

Schuyler, Keith C. *Bow Hunting for Big Game.* Pennsylvania: Stackpole Books, 1974. 256 pp.

A practical book on advanced bow hunting, written with the gun hunter in mind. Directed toward the deer hunter who wishes to vary his local hunting with trips far afield

for other big game. Tips and hunting anecdotes abound. Condemns the poisoned arrow and attempts to destroy the myth of animals' suffering. Written by a Pennsylvanian deer hunter who pens the column "Straight from the Bowstring," which appears in the *Pennsylvania Game News.*

Scrope, William. *The Art of Deer Stalking.* London: John Murray, 1838. 436 pp.

The first work devoted to the subject. A classic—often reprinted. If Scrope did not invent modern methods of deer stalking, he was the first individual to describe the process in great detail. His great enthusiasm for chasing deer shines forth from the book like polished antlers in the sun:
"My heart's in the Highlands, my heart is not here,
A chasing the wild deer, and following the roe,
My heart's in the Highlands wherever I go."
Full of anecdotes on the habits of deer.*

Seabury, Joseph Stowe. *Reflections of a Moose Hunter.* Boston: Privately printed, 1921. 68 pp.

A personal, poetic resumé of the serious and picturesque aspects of life in deer country. Beautiful descriptions of the "joy of striking off alone with an old backwoodsman to sleep in a distant logging camp and at evening to watch the fishhawks and deer." A delightful and powerful journey through the various stages that most serious deer hunters go through.*

Seaby, Allen W. *The White Buck: A New Forest Story.* London: Thomas Nelson, 1939. 214 pp.

A fictional account of a white fallow deer, for young and old.*

Sell, Francis E. *The American Deer Hunter.* Pennsylvania: Stackpole Books, 1950. 174 pp.*

————. *Advanced Hunting on Deer and Elk Trails.* Pennsylvania: Stackpole Books, 1954. 156 pp.*

————. *Art of Successful Deer Hunting.* Wisconsin: Willow Creek Press, 1980. 192 pp.

Standard works in the fine art of trail watching, by one of America's foremost deer hunters. Particularly strong in the implications of hunting directly on deer trails and in understanding thermal air movements and weather conditions. Essential reading.

Seton, Ernest Thompson. *The Arctic Prairies: A Canoe-Journey of 2,000 Miles in Search of the Caribou.* New York: Harper and Row, 1981. 415 pp.

In 1907 Ernest Thompson Seton set out on a six-month journey by canoe into the remote reaches of the Canadian northwest. His goal was to observe caribou and to prove their continued abundance. This outstanding nature classic documents his exploration.

————. *The Trail of the Sandhill Stag.* New York: Scribners, 1899. 93 pp.

One of the most thought-provoking, sensitive, moving tales ever written of the long, endless pursuit of a black-tailed stag. Should be read by every deer hunter at least once in his lifetime—preferably after the mellowing-out stage. Challenges and examines the basic philosophy of the chase.*

————. *Lives of Game Animals.* New York: Doubleday, 1929.

One of the first detailed accounts of the whitetail to be published in this century. Written by one of America's best-loved naturalists. Reaches the conclusion that "the whitetail is the American deer of the past, and the American deer of the future.''*

Shaffmaster, Allen Dyer. *Hunting in the Land of Hiawatha.* Chicago: M. A. Donohue and Company, 1904. 183 pp.

A delightful diary of incidents peculiar to deer camp life in the northern woods of Michigan. Written by an editor and eloquent outdoor writer. Captures the history and philosophy of the sport as few books do. Reading this diary allows you to relive the savory and pungent odors of a North Woods deer camp. Contains a superb collection of old Kodak exposures on many aspects of deer camp life. Rare.*

Sheldon, H. H. *The Deer of California.* California: Museum of Natural History, 1933. 67 pp.

An early scientific treatise on deer by a well-known naturalist. Makes an interesting comparison between football and deer hunting. "Just as a knowledge of the rules of football, and an acquaintance with the players, increases the interest and the pleasure of those who watch the game, so an intelligent understanding of game laws, and intimacy with characteristics and habits of the quarry adds zest to the deer hunt.'' Rightly admits that skill in deer hunting is born not of genius, but of practical experience.*

Shepard, Paul. "Fellow Creatures." *Man in the Landscape.* New York: Alfred A. Knopf, 1967. pp. 190–213.

The classic argument for killing animals for their own good and ours as well. Following Leopold, Shepard believes that "Hunting is a reenactment of a historically important activity when contact with the natural environment and the virtues of this contact were less obscured by modern urban life." Basic reading, if modern man is ever to understand the essence of hunting.*

Shields, G. O., ed. *The Big Game of North America.* London: Sampson Low, 1890. 581 pp.

A famous anthology that places deer hunting in the context of natural history. Argues that the sportsman studies and observes the deer's characteristics, not merely because they interest him and provide food for thought while on the hunt or around the campfire, but because he realizes that he must know all the resources of the animal in order to succeed in the hunt. The last chapter, entitled "The Ethics of the Field Sports," by Judge Caton, is worth the price of the book alone; in it he formulates a classic deer-hunting ethic and suggests that deer biologists have much to learn from deer hunters. A great book!*

Shiras, Geroge III. *Hunting Wildlife with Camera and Flashlight.* Washington, D.C.: The National Geographic Society, 1898. Two volumes.

A classic in wildlife photography. Written by one of America's most widely-known and appreciated field naturalists and the inventor of flashlight photography of wild animals. Includes some of the most extraordinary photos of deer ever taken. Provides a detailed description of his Whitefish Lake deer camp.*

Shoemaker, Henry W. *Pennsylvania Deer and Their Horns*. Pennsylvania: The Faust Printing Company, 1915. 120 pp.

A choice piece of whitetail nostalgia that contains one of the finest collections of photos of Pennsylvania's greatest deerslayers. Deals with the picturesque side of the chase, including tales of notorious stags that held the veritable army of Pennsylvanian "red coats" at bay for days on end. Describes, for example, the wild adventures of "Black Jack" Schwartz, who presided over deer drives that encompassed a radius of 30 miles or more. Brilliant Pennsylvania deer hunting history.*

Siegler, Hilbert R., ed. *The White-Tailed Deer of New Hampshire*. New Hampshire: Fish and Game Department, 1968. 256 pp.

Provides the non-professional with insights into the complexities and inter-relationships that must be considered to produce intelligent evaluations of proposals for changes in regulations governing deer harvests and other aspects of deer management. An excellent reference volume edited by a student of Aldo Leopold's.*

Sisley, Nick., ed. *Deer Hunting Across North America*. New York: Freshet Press, 1975. 281 pp.

An anthology written by some of the most experienced and knowledgeable deer hunters in the country. Includes first-rate chapters on everything from chasing Coues and Columbian blacktails to hunting whitetails in Potter's County, Pennsylvania; from Adirondack deer hunting to outwitting Michigan whitetails; from solo hunting in Wisconsin to Dixie hunting, southern style; from bow hunting mule deer to Texas trophy hunting. Thoroughly enjoyable. Basic reading.

Smith, Richard P. *Deer Hunting*. Pennsylvania: Stackpole Books, 1978. 256 pp.

A how-to book that combines hunting deer with bow, gun and camera. Draws on the wealth of information and experience that the author gained as a professional guide in Michigan.

Soper, Eileen A. *Muntjac: A Study of These Small Elusive Asiatic Deer which Colo-nized an English Garden*. London: Longmans, 1969. 142 pp.

A rare account of the life history and behavior of these secretive and largely nocturnal deer. Describes how the author succeeded over a period of eight years in establishing a colony of them in her own wildlife sanctuary. Conveys the charm of these elusive creatures and the excitement of observing them.*

Spaulding, Edward Selden. *Deer!* Privately printed, 1968. 133 pp.

A very unusual book of West Coast deer hunting episodes. Rare and quite expensive. Rightly acknowledges that "of all the larger mammals of the North American Continent, it is the deer that have had the greatest influence upon us."*

Spiess, Arthur E. *Reindeer and Caribou Hunters: An Archaeological Study*. New York: Academic Press, 1979. 312 pp.

A published Ph.D. dissertation, which attempts to explain the man-caribou relationship by studying detailed accounts of human caribou-hunting patterns. Contains an interesting discussion on the deer-drive fence used to funnel deer into ambush.

Spinage, C. A. *A Territorial Antelope: The Uganda Waterbuck*. London: Academic Press, 1982. 334 pp.

A scholarly treatise on the waterbuck with special emphasis on the role of territorial behavior.

St. John, Charles. *Wild Sports and Natural History of the Highlands*. London: John Murray, 1893. 319 pp.

A classic in the highest tradition of true sportsmanship. Encourages the idea that a fondness for observing the habits of animals confers a greater pleasure than the mere shooting of a great quantity of game. Teaches us to study and admire the deer we pursue. A most readable book—once started, it's hard to put down. Strong on natural history. Contains the famous account of the Muckle Hart of Benmore—the most famous stag ever shot in Scotland. Written by a fascinating specimen of that old breed, the shooting naturalist.*

Stadtfeld, Curtis K. *Whitetail Deer: A Year's Cycle*. New York: The Dial Press, 1975. 163 pp.

A fascinating and comprehensive biological study written in the form of a nonfiction novel by a Michigan professor of journalism and writing. Follows a Michigan doe throughout the four seasons. Documents the propensity of deer to overpopulate in the absence of their natural predators. Examines the ethics of deer hunting, and ultimately accepts hunting as necessary and humane. Well researched and beautifully written. Basic reading in the ecology of the whitetail.

Staines, Brian. *The Red Deer*. Great Britain: Blandfort, 1980. 43 pp.

Juvenile literature—an intelligible guide on the red deer for pupils between the ages of 9 and 13.

Stanton, Don C. *A History of the White-Tailed Deer in Maine*. Maine: Department of Inland Fisheries and Game, 1963. Game Division Bulletin #8. 75 pp.

An interesting and romantic account of the whitetail's story as it bounds across Maine's history from pre-colonial days to the present. "We have seen it match its wits against wolves," the author relates, "Indians, the pioneer whites, lumbermen and pulp cutters, farmers, market and hide hunters, dogs, sportsmen, legislators, poachers, game wardens, and biologists. We have seen it contend with too much forest and too little forest, with fires and Maine winters, with sporting camps and automobiles—with feast and famine. More often than not, it has come out on top"*

Stephen, David. *Six-Pointer Buck*. London: Lutterworth, 1956. 255 pp.

The biography of a roe buck in the Scottish Highlands. Makes you feel his pattern of life and death, his struggles for survival and his instincts for self-preservation. Contains a large number of unfamiliar Scottish words for the American reader. Nonetheless, will appeal to nature lovers and sportsmen. The result of patient watching and living among deer.*

Stokes, Bill. "A Haunted Night in a Deer Yard." In *Hi-Ho Silver, Anyway*. The Milwaukee Journal: no date. pp. 32–35.

The interesting tale of how a *Milwaukee Journal* outdoor writer and columnist spent a night in the deep snow and severe cold of a winter deer yard. A devastating experience with temperatures of 30 degrees below zero.

Straight, Lee. *How to Hunt Deer and Other Game*. Canada: Saltaire, 1974. 160 pp.

A basic book on big game shooting by the popular fish and wildlife columnist for the *Vancouver Sun*. Views deer hunting as a cradle-to-the grave pursuit.*

Strung, Norman. *Deer Hunting*. Philadelphia: Lippincott, 1973. 239 pp.

A comprehensive guide that includes an eloquent argument for the usefulness of hunters. Makes it clear why men deer hunt. "Elimination, removal, control, killing—call it what you will—reduction of the deer population by hunting is the best route to maximum-sized herds of heathly deer in balance with their environment." Written by an outdoor writer and a guide of extensive experience. Teaches us to move with the rhythm of nature. Highly recommended.

Stuart, John Sobieski, and Stuart, Charles Edward. *Lays of the Deer Forest with Sketches of Olden and Modern Deer Hunting*. London: William Blackwood, 1848. II Volumes. 560 pp.

A charming description of deer hunting that emphasizes the wholesome tradition of the past. Captures the romance and excitement of deer hunting in Scotland up to 1848. Indeed, the authors wallow unashamedly in romantic nostalgia of the golden era of Scottish deer hunting. Vividly describes hunting a roe buck with a single hound for three entire days—stopping only for periods of rest during the darkness. Entertaining and opinionated history. Finds the ultimate meaning of deer hunting in poetical meditation: "Abounding with long intervals of repose, in the watches of the pass or the evenings of the winter hut, the life of the deer hunter has many vacancies in which the mind is left to its own workings." Volume II contains many detailed personal observations on the habits of deer.*

Swift, Ernest. *A History of Wisconsin Deer.* Wisconsin: Department of Conservation, 1946. 96 pp.

A basic history of Wisconsin deer by one of Wisconsin's well-known conservationists. Needs to be revised, updated and brought back into print. Rare.*

Swigget, Hal., ed. *Hal Swiggett on North American Deer.* New Jersey: Jolex, 1980. 272 pp.

A Jolex outdoor manual that attempts to present the North American deer hunting picture in one volume. Written by the associate editor of *Gun World.*

Taylor, Walter P., ed. *The Deer of North America: Their History and Management.* Pennsylvania: Stackpole Books, 1956. 668 pp.

An exhaustive, scholarly study on the life history, habits and management of whitetails, blacktails and mule deer. Written by leading deer biologists, conservationists and wildlife managers. Copiously illustrated. A standard reference work on deer and deer hunting. Hard to locate and quite expensive. Authoritative throughout.*

Tegner, Henry. *The Roe Deer: Their History, Habits, and Pursuit.* London: Batchworth, 1951. 176 pp.

A very informative and entertaining book on one of England's loveliest mammals. A pleasure to read. Strong on natural history. Written by one of Britain's leading deermen and a deer stalker who studied the roe deer for more than 25 years. Few Americans probably realize, as Tegner points out, that Felix Salten's *Bambi* was not the tale of a Virginian white-tailed deer, but the tale of a roe buck. An enthusiastic and colorful account of the gazelle-like elegance and beauty of these little deer. A collector's piece.*

––––––. *Game for the Sporting Rifle.* London: Herbert Jenkins, 1963. 191 pp.

If you are interested in excellent and high-quality deer hunting, read this volume. "Although it is said," the author writes, "that there is something of the hunter in most men, the true sportsman is not a blood thirsty person in any sense. It is always the stalk, or the chase itself, rather than the kill which is the attraction in all forms of hunting, be it fox-hunting or the pursuit of a wily roebuck in the English woodland.'"*

––––––. *The Buck of Lordenshaw: The Story of a Roe Deer.* London: Batchworth, 1953. 174 pp.

A beautiful story of a roe deer set in the countryside of northern England.*

––––––. *The Tale of a Deer Forest.* London: Geoffrey Bles, 1957. 157 pp.

Autobiographical sketches of a lifetime's experience of hunting deer. Lucid, free-running and laced with an abundance of anecdotes. Author's life epitomized the finest traditions of a 19th century sporting naturalist and hunter, perhaps the last specimen of this breed. Effectively illustrated by Frank Wallace.*

Tenney, Horace Kent. *Vert and Venison.* Chicago: Privately Printed, 1924. 155 pp.

One of the greatest testaments ever written on the deer hunting call:

"Hear it humming, partridge drumming; Daylight's almost here: Greet the morning, hunter's warning, Rouse and hunt the deer."

A classic. Rare and very expensive.*

Thomas, Jack Ward, and Toweill, Dale E., ed. *Elk of North America: Ecology and Management.* Pennsylvania: Stackpole Books, 1982. 698 pp.

Traces the history of elk in North America and chronicles the events and circumstances of the animal's decline and remarkable recovery. A compendium of the latest and best scientific data. A remarkable book.

Thomson, Joff A. *Deer Hunter: The Experiences of a New Zealand Stalker.* New Zealand: Reed, 1952. 194 pp.

The adventurous experiences of a deer culler for the Government of New Zealand. Gives us a vivid description of what the deer shooter's country of New Zealand is really like. Believes that happiness and camaraderie constitute the essence of deer hunting. Includes many superb deer camp photos of high-country life.*

———. *Deer Shooting Days*. Australia: Reed, 1964. 166 pp.

Another memorable collection of New Zealand's backcountry deer hunting lore and legend. Written by a Canterbury New Zealander who took to the high hills in pursuit of deer at an early age.*

Thornberry, Russell. *Trophy Deer of Alberta*. Alberta: Green Horn Publishing, 1982. 299 pp.

A catalog listing of more than 600 of Alberta's greatest trophy mule deer and whitetails. Contains stories of some of the hunters who bagged these trophies and illustrates unusual and freak antler formations in a chapter entitled "Oddities of Nature." Describes Alberta's unusual hybrid deer. Adds a new category between typical and non-typical deer. A fine reference volume.

Tillett, Paul. *Doe Day. The Antlerless Deer Controversy in New Jersey*. New Jersey: Rutgers University Press, 1963. 126 pp.

Explores the problems New Jersey had with deer overpopulation and how attempts in the late 1950s to control the deer population lead to conflicts of interest between landowners, hunters, farmers, wildlife managers, state agencies and journalists and eventually involved the State Supreme Court. Written by a New Jersey deer hunter and a professor of political science. Basic reading for the "barbershop biologists" who think they know everything. A classic case study in the politics of deer management.

Tinsley, Russell. *Hunting the Whitetail Deer*. New York: Outdoor Life Books, 1965. 144 pp.

A practical, straightforward and comprehensive how-to book. Explores the subject of hunting storm fronts in some detail. Strong on field-dressing and butchering. An invaluable guide for beginning and experienced hunter alike.

Tome, Philip. *Pioneer Life: or, Thirty Years a Hunter*. New York: Arno, 1971. 238 pp.

The hair-splitting adventures of an early 19th century deer hunter from Pennsylvania.

Contains everything from fire hunting deer to capturing grown elk alive on the waters of the Susquehanna. All lovers of the hunt will surely enjoy these exciting deer hunting scenes. Originally published in 1854.

Townsend, M. T., and Smith, M. W. *The White-Tailed Deer of the Adirondacks*. New York: Bulletin of the Roosevelt Wild Life Experiment Station, 1933. 385 pp.

A standard scientific study on the life history of the white-tailed deer of the Adirondacks. Contains superb photos of Adirondack deer, hunting country and an interesting discussion of "stump chewing" by whitetails. Highly readable, but difficult to find.*

Underwood, Lamar., ed. *The Deer Book*. New Jersey: Amwell Press, 1980. 460 pp.

This custom-bound volume contains many of the best articles on deer hunting ever assembled. If you enjoy the rich treasure of prose on deer hunting, you will enjoy this book. These great stories and reflective essays by Jack O'Connor, Ted Trueblood, Theodore Roosevelt, John Madson, Larry Koller, Archibald Rutledge, Gene Hill and Sigurd Olson—to mention but a few names—will allow your mind to slip into the enchanting world of deer hunting as you read in front of the fireplace. As Gene Hill once remarked, the book "fulfills all our needs for understanding ourselves as hunters and the deer as an extraordinary lure for us." Highly recommended for the connoisseur of deer hunting stories and articles.

Van Dyke, Theodore S. *The Still-Hunter*. New York: Macmillan, 1923. 389 pp.

An unsurpassed classic on all aspects of deer and deer hunting. Exhaustive in deer knowledge and still hunting techniques without being exhausting itself. If the American deer hunters read this classic *en masse*, the future of the sport would be ensured. A blue-chip deer book with no equal.*

Vowles, Alfred. *Stag Hunting on Exmoor*. Taunton: Barnicott and Pearce, 1920. 50 pp.

Notes on the noble pastime of hunting red deer, a game that the author maintains, "is a stayer's game, not a matter of one hunt or one season but of many years, only understood to the full by a few and by them loved dearly.''*

————. *Wild Deer of Exmoor: History, Haunts, Habits.* England: Cox, Sons and Company, 1936. 47 pp.

A short treatise on the subject of deer which, as the author concludes, is inexhaustible. Deals with the natural history of the red deer of West Somerset and North Devon.*

Wallace, H. Frank. *Happier Years.* London: Eyre and Spottiswoode, 1946. 288 pp.

Frank and fascinating reminiscences of one of England's leading authorities on deer stalking. Entertaining accounts of stalking deer, elk and chamois. A charming book. Exudes a spirit of good port, good sport and good breeding.*

————. *British Deer Heads.* London: Country Life, 1913. 112 pp.

An illustrated record of the Exhibition of trophy British deer heads held in London in 1913. A most valuable account of record heads and the various collections then in existence. The accompanying historic and nostalgic remarks about each head underscore the author's idea that the chase ''is surrounded by an atmosphere of romance which no other sport can rival, and calls into play many of those qualities which we admire most. Long may it continue!''*

————. *Hunting Winds.* London: Eyre & Spottiswoode, 1949. 351 pp.

More beloved memories and reflections about deer stalking by one of England's greatest deer hunters. Standard reading for the deer shack.*

————. *A Highland Gathering: Being Some Leaves from a Stalker's Diary.* London: Eyre & Spottiswoode, 1935. 192 pp.

A romantic and nostalgic characterization of the charms of deer hunting. Written by a big game hunter of international repute and a very skillful writer and artist. Enjoyable reading after a day's hunt. Includes a valuable account of record roe heads.*

Wallack, L. R. *The Deer Rifle.* New York: Winchester, 1978. 243 pp.

Practical knowledge of how to select and

use the arms and ammunition appropriate to your needs. Provides a wealth of material on bores and ballistics. Tells you how to set up and sight in your rifle. Written by an expert deer hunter and a well-known firearms consultant.

Wallmo, Olof C., ed. *Mule and Black-Tailed Deer of North America.* Nebraska: University of Nebraska, 1981. 605 pp.

The definitive volume on the predominant deer of western North America. Topics range from the history of management to deer physiology, predation, hunting, behavior and interactions with various habitats. Of great interest and value to everyone with an appreciation for deer.

Walrod, Dennis. *More than a Trophy.* Pennsylvania: Stackpole Books, 1983. 267 pp.

An excellent manual on field dressing, skinning, quartering, butchering, preparing and cooking venison, tanning the hide, making soap, and doing your own taxidermy. Conveys the message of down-to-earth self-sufficiency. A highly recommended how-to book of the first order.

Wambold, H. R. *Bowhunting for Deer.* Pennsylvania: Stackpole Books, 1978. 223 pp.

A classic book of hunting wisdom for the seasoned deer hunter. Puts forth a pioneering theory relating blood volume and shock to the traditional myth of the ''waiting game.'' Offers fresh advice for trailing wounded animals. Written by a lifelong bow hunter from Pennsylvania and a member of the Pope and Young Club. Based on research. Strong on deer anatomy. Highly recommended.

Warner, Charles Dudley. *A-Hunting of the Deer and Other Essays.* New York: Houghton, Mifflin and Company, 1878. 85 pp.

A literary celebration of the early army of deerslayers of the Adirondacks and of the deer itself, who according to the author is ''simple in his tastes, regular in his habits, affectionate in his family. Unfortunately for his repose though, his haunch is as tender as his heart.''*

Waters, Frank. *The Man Who Killed the Deer.* New York: Pocket Books, 1971. 217 pp.

A novel about the Hopi Indians in the Southwest, whose deer-hunting ethic we need to follow: "Nothing is simple and alone. We are not separate and alone. Man, the breathing mountains, the living stones, each blade of grass, the clouds, the rain, each star, the beasts, the birds, and the invisible spirits of the air, we are all one indivisible— nothing that any of us does but affects us all. In the old days we all remember, we did not go out on a hunt lightly. We said to the deer we were going to kill, we know your life is as precious as ours; we know we are all one life and the same mother earth beneath the same plains of the sky. But we also know that one life must sometimes give way to another so the one great life of all may continue unbroken. So we ask your permission, we obtain your consent of this killing."

Watson, Alfred E. T. *Red Deer*. London: Longmans, 1896. 320 pp.

A nostalgic and romantic account of red deer stalking in England. Puts the whole sport in its cultural persepctive. Includes a superb chapter on the cookery of venison. Enchanting. Hard to find.*

Weiss, John. *The Whitetail Deer Hunter's Handbook*. New York: Winchester, 1979. 265 pp.

A well-balanced handbook that illustrates the finer points in understanding whitetail behavior. Written by an Ohio deer hunter and freelance writer. Contains an excellent chapter on deer movement. Enthusiastically believes that a "good tracking snow, the challenge of a whitetail's cunning, and thoughts of prime roast venison are things that just might help a man life forever."

Weitz, Chauncey. *A Game Warden's Diary: 1933–1965*. Wisconsin: The Willow Creek Press, 1983. 132 pp.

Great reminiscences from a crusty old Wisconsin game warden that include humorous anecdotes and serious encounters in the daily business of deer shooting and poaching. Light reading after a day spent afield.

Wensel, Gene. *Bowhunting Rutting Whitetails*. Montana: Privately printed, 1981. 152 pp.

An unusual deer hunting book with an original approach. Refreshing. Written by a chiropractor who obviously spends a great deal of time deer hunting. "He has *not*," as Joe Wilcox rightly observed, "broiled up and served a lot of old articles from *Outdoor Life* which were summarized from others in *Field and Stream*." Filled with insights as to how trophy whitetails live and react. Highly recommended for those interested in hunting trophy white-tailed bucks.

Weston, Dr. Frederick H. *Hunting the White-Tailed Deer in Texas*. Texas: Privately printed, 1954. 148 pp.

A rare book based on 40 years of deer hunting experiences. Written by a game biologist for the Texas Game and Fish Commission. Provides us with a brilliant explanation of what makes a deer hunter tick, of the individualistic characteristics of deer hoofs, as well as a brilliant analysis of deer beans. Superbly illustrated. Highly recommended, but difficult to find.*

Whelen, Major Townsend. *Big Game Hunting*. Colorado: Outdoor Life Publishing Company, 1923. 93 pp.

In this handbook on big-game hunting, Whelen argues that the sportsman should limit himself to one good head of each species, thereafter turning to wildlife photography and the study of the habits of deer. In this later stage of deer hunting the author writes, "he will find quite as much to excite, interest, spur him on, and call him back year after year as in hunting with the rifle."*

Whisker, James B. *The Right to Hunt*. New York: North River Press, 1981. 173 pp.

Examines the historical, religious, ethical, legal and practical aspects of hunting wild animals. Contains an excellent commentary on Ortega's *Meditations on Hunting*. Demonstrates that morally, historically, religiously and legally there is embedded in our civilization a right to hunt and a right to bear arms. Concludes his brilliant defense of hunting by arguing that hunting deer represents man's most direct and satisfying way of communing with the natural world. Read this volume and learn what deer hunting is all about in a philosophical sense.

Whitehead, G. Kenneth. *The Deerstalking Grounds of Great Britain and Ireland*. London: Hollis & Carter, 1960. 552 pp.

A gold mine of statistical information, with some historical commentary. Written by a leading authority on deer who has hunted and photographed deer world wide.*

————. *Hunting and Stalking Deer Throughout the World*. London: Batsford, 1982. 336 pp.

A book for the deer hunter who travels the world in pursuit of his quarry. Comprehensive coverage of deer hunting areas all over the world. "No single person," Whitehead writes, "no matter how widely he may have traveled the world, can claim to be an authority on the subject of deer hunting in any country other than perhaps his own." Yet, Whitehead is such a person, for he has hunted deer worldwide for more than 40 years. A definitive reference work that makes fascinating reading.

————. *Hunting and Stalking Deer in Britain Through the Ages*. London: Batsford, 1980. 304 pp.

A history of English deer hunting over the last 1000 years, from the days before the Norman Conquest up to the present. A unique book recording the old and noble sport of deer hunting and stalking. Colorful. Essential for those whose interest in deer extends beyond observation and day-to-day management. Will remain a basic reference for a long time to come.

————. *The Deer of Great Britain and Ireland: An Account of their History, Status, and Distribution*. London: Routledge and Kegan Paul, 1964. 597 pp.

A monumental history of England's deer. Will undoubtedly remain the standard reference on the subject.*

————. *Deer and Their Management*. London: Country Life, 1950. 370 pp.

Another indispensable reference work dealing with park deer and their management. Written by one of the founding members of The British Deer Society.*

————. *Deer of the World*. London: Constable, 1972. 194 pp.

A useful and authoritative book that re-places Richard Lydekker's *The Deer of All Lands*. Covers all 40 species of deer and many of the subspecies, which run to nearly 200. Provides us with a general summary of the deer family. Well illustrated, outstandingly attractive. Winner of the 1975 literary prize of the Conseil International de la Chasse.*

Whitlock, Ralph. *Deer*. Great Britain: Wayland, 1974. 80 pp.

This book describes and illustrates for children the various types of deer across the world. An excellent book for the young reader.

Wileden, Arthur F. *The Buckshot Story, 1928–1972*. Privately printed. Madison, Wisconsin. 20 pp.

A detailed record of a Wisconsin deer camp in the area west of Cable, covering the period 1928–1972. Written by a retired professor of rural sociology from the University of Wisconsin. Captures the essence of deer camp as a closely-knit social group. Contains detailed records of who hunted and specific information about their kills. Well illustrated with photos. A delightful booklet.*

————. *A Lifetime of Hunting and Fishing Experiences*. Wisconsin: Privately printed, 1982. 211 pp.

More stories by Professor Wileden of his deer-hunting adventures in northwestern Wisconsin. The last chapter deals with "why" man hunts deer. After a successful career as a rural sociologist and after a lifetime spent in the deer forest, he makes observations on why man hunts, reflecting the current findings of The Human Dimensions Study Group.

Williams, Glenn H. *The Bucks Camp Log, 1916–1928*. Wisconsin: Wisconsin Sportsman Publication, 1974. 111 pp.

A deer camp diary revealing the true and ageless spirit of the deer hunt. Includes exciting hunting adventures, tragedy, rare humor, woodsmanship, as well as philosophical reflections on the sport. A fascinating glimpse into our deer hunting past. Colorful and humorous.

Williams J. H. *The Spotted Deer*. London: Rupert Hart-Davis, 1957. 261 pp.

Focuses on the delicate trust that can be built up between man and deer, as exemplified in the beautiful incident of the spotted deer that the main protagonist meets in a jungle on the North Andaman.*

Williamson, Henry. *The Wild Red Deer of Exmoor*. London: Faber & Faber, 1931. 64 pp.

A digression on the logic and ethics of deer hunting. Sets forth all points of view—both for and against—in a particularly interesting way. By means of a commentary on the verbatim report of a protest meeting, a meeting with heated arguments, interruptions and noises of the divided and disorderly audience, and by glowing descriptions of his own experiences, Williamson submits to our judgment all aspects on the ethics of deer hunting.*

Winans, Walter. *Practical Rifle Shooting*. New York: G. P. Putnam's Sons, 1906. 98 pp.

A pugnacious combination of memoirs and practical advice on deer hunting. Contains an interesting chapter on deer drives in which he tells us that "deer will not be *driven;* if they think they are being forced, they will break back, however thick the beaters are . . . Instead of being called deer driving, it ought to be called (coining a word in the German manner) deceiving-the-deer-into-going-where-you-want-them-to."*

———. *Deer Breeding for Fine Heads*. London: Rowland Ward, 1913. 105 pp.

A one-of-a-kind book on an unusual subject by a country gentleman who rightly insists that "I think the deer, if asked, would rather have a scamper through the fields occasionally than spend all his life shut up in a small pen in a menagerie."*

———. *The Sporting Rifle*. New York: Putnam, 1980. 217 pp.

Memoirs and advice on shooting and driving deer. Written by one of the most bizarre figures in the history of deer hunting, who maintained a great passion for deer drives which he indulged in on a gigantic scale. His massive and grandiose operations required a small army of beaters. One photograph records the illustrious presence of 17 ponies, 35 deer hunters and nearly 20 dead stags.*

When not in the deer forest, the deer hunter dreams of super-racked bucks and tracking them in the snow. There is no better substitute for being in the deer forest than to collect and read blue-chip deer books.
Photo credit Leonard Lee Rue III

Wootters, John. *Hunting Trophy Deer*. New York: Winchester, 1977. 251 pp.

A basic manual for the deer hunter who wants to track down and collect a "harvey wallhanger." Includes a first-rate analysis of whitetail movement patterns as related to weather conditions. Develops the thesis that by the time a buck is in the trophy class, his habits and patterns of movement have become so different from those of ordinary deer that he evades the common hunting methods without any effort. Profusely illustrated with photos of giant-racked bucks by wildlife photographers Jerry Smith and W. A. Maltsberger. Serious reading for the serious deer hunter.

Wormer, Joe Van. *The World of the Pronghorn*. New York: Lippincott, 1969. 191 pp.

Another fine text in the Living World Series. Contains magnificent photos, fascinating facts, personal anecdotes and little-known Indian legends.

Yoakum, James D., and Spalinger, Donald E., ed. *American Pronghorn Antelope: Articles Published in The Journal of Wildlife Management, 1937–1977.* Washington, D.C.: The Wildlife Society, 1979. 244 pp.

An excellent reference volume complete with bibliography and index.

Zumbo, Jim. *Hunting America's Mule Deer.* Oklahoma: Winchester, 1981. 358 pp.

A how-to book that discusses the best ways to hunt mule deer. Filled with personal anecdotes. Contains an enormous store of deer hunting knowledge. Includes a state-by-state directory of mule deer with facts on natural history, present status, population estimates, recent harvest figures and hunter success rates.

Zumbo, Jim, and Elman, Robert., ed. *All American Deer Hunter's Guide.* New York: Winchester Press, 1983. 320 pp.

Another general anthology.

ADDENDA

The following books, theses and privately printed publications on deer and deer hunting crossed the author's desk as this book went to press:

Adams, Chuck. *The Complete Guide to Bowhunting Deer.* Illinois: DBI Books, Inc., 1984. 256 pp.

Cartier, John O., ed. *20 Great Trophy Hunts.* New York: McKay, 1980. 269 pp.

Eberle, Irmengarde. *Fawn in the Woods.* New York: Thomas Y. Crowell Company, 1962. 43 pp.*

Haight, Austin D. "I Kill My First Deer." In *The Biography of a Sportsman.* New York: Crowell, 1939. pp. 71–85.*

Halls, Lowell K., ed. *White-tailed Deer.* Pennsylvania: Stackpole Books, 1984. 864 pp.

Herron, John S. C. "Deer Harvest and Wounding Loss Associated with Bowhunting White-Tailed Deer." Unpublished master's thesis. University of Wisconsin-Madison, 1984. 36 pp.

Hull, Russell. *Trophy Bowhunting: The Supreme Challenge.* Kansas: Privately printed, 1984. 131 pp.

Kesel, James Alan. "Some of the Characteristics and Attitudes of Michigan Deer Hunting Violators." Master's thesis. Michigan State University, 1974. 36 pp.

McMath, Neil. *Continuing the Story of the Turtle Lake Deer Club.* Michigan: Privately printed, n.d. 49 pp.*

Manierre, Franny. *The Story of the Clow Deer Hunt.* Michigan: Privately printed, 1938. 22 pp.*

Marburger, Rodney G. *The King of Deer.* Texas: Privately printed, 1983. 272 pp.

Maynard, Roger. *Advanced Bowhunting Guide.* New Jersey: Stoeger Publishing Company, 1984. 22 pp.

Michmerhuizen, Lewey. *Grandpa Recalls . . . Deer Hunting Stories.* Michigan: Lew Publishers, 1964. 46 pp.*

Millen, George W. *Blizzard Bound—1914: An Account of Deer Hunting at Camp Newton.* Michigan: Privately printed, 1914. 17 pp.*

New, Harry S. *The Story of the Turtle Lake Deer Club.* Michigan: Privately printed, 1923. 36 pp.*

Parker, Willie J. "The Deer Hunters." In *Chesapeake Assignment.* Maryland: Tidewater Publishers, 1983. pp. 100–109.

Perry, Oliver Hazard. *Deer Hunting Expeditions of Oliver Hazard Perry.* Cleveland: Privately printed, 1899. 246 pp.*

Potter, Arthur G. *The 1907 Hunt of the Forest City Deer Hunting Club in the Wilds of Northern Maine.* Maine: Privately printed, 1908. 111 pp.*

Rogers, Robert., ed. *The Professional Guide to Whitetail.* Texas: Privately printed, 1984. 170 pp.

Wilcox, Sidney W. *Deer Production in the United States, 1969–1973: Data Relating to Deer and Deer Hunters.* Arizona State University, 1976. 77 pp.*

Wood, F. Dorothy. *The Deer Family.* New York: Harvey House Inc., 1969. 48 pp.*

Out-of-Print Booksellers Who Specialize in Outdoor Literature

Kenneth Andersen Books
38 Silver Street
Auburn, MA 01501
(617) 832-3524

Angler's and Shooter's Bookshelf
Goshen, CT 06756
(203) 491-2500

Judith Bowman Books
Pound Ridge Road
Bedford, NY 10506
(914) 234-7543

Seymour Brecher
The Woodland Gallery
Box 987
Monticello, NY 12701

Callahan & Company Booksellers
Box 704
Peterborough, NH 03458
(603) 924-3726

Chestnut Ridge Books
Box 353
Rutherford, NJ 07070
(201) 438-5850

Charles Daly Collection
66 Chilton St.
Cambridge, MA 02138
(617) 547-8228

Dutchman Books
Box 111
Mason, OH 45040
(513) 398-1294

Gamebag
Box 1020
Mundelein, IL 60060
(312) 362-6562

Gary L. Estabrook—Books
Box 61453
Vancouver, WA 98666
(206) 699-5454

Fine Sporting Books
Howard & Janet French
284 Redwood Dr.
Pasadena, CA 91105
(213) 254-2759

Colonel J. Furniss
Old Police House
Strathpeffer
Ross-shire
England

Grayling Books
Lyvennet, Crosby Ravensworth, Penrith
Cumbria CA10 3JP
England

Gunnerman Books
P.O. Box 4292
Auburn Hills, MI 48057
(313) 879-2779

E. Chalmers Hallam
Earlswood, Egmont Dr.
Avon Castle, Ringwood
Hampshire, BH24 2BN
England

Morris Heller
Box 46
Swan Lake, NY 12783
(914) 583-5879

Henderson & Park
Fifth and Main
Greenwood, MO 64034
(816) 537-6388

Patricia Ledlie—Bookseller
Box 46B
Buckfield, ME 04220
(207) 336-2969

Jerry Madden
Campfire Books
7218 Hogue Rd.
Evansville, IN 47712
(812) 425-8549

Melvin Marcher Bookseller
6204 N. Vermont
Oklahoma City, OK 73112
(405) 946-6270

Piece of Time
Jack Ragonese
North Stonington, CT 06359
(203) 535-1375

Pisces & Capricorn Books
302 S. Berrien St.
Albion, MI 49224
(517) 629-3267

Ray Riling Arms Books Co.
6844 Gorsten St.
P.O. Box 18925
Philadelphia, PA 19119
(215) 438-2456

Ray Russell—Books
111 East Fourth St.
Rochester, MI 48063
(313) 651-2525

Lou Razek
Highwood Farms Books
P.O. Box 1246
Traverse City, MI 49684
(616) 271-3898

Sporting Book Service
Box 177
Rancocas, NJ 03073

Thunderbird Books
Box 2129
Sidney, B.C.
Canada V8L 3S6
(604) 656-5170

Trophy Room Books
4858 Dempsey Ave.
Encino, CA 91436
(213) 784-3801

University Microfilms International
Dissertation Copies
P.O. Box 1764
Ann Arbor, MI 48106
(To order by phone and credit card, call
800-521-3042, toll-free).

John Valle
550 Mohawk Road
West Hempstead, NY 11552
(516) 887-3342

Watkins Natural History Books
Rebecca & Larry C. Watkins
R.D. #1
Belden Corners Rd.
Dolgeville, NY 13329-9526
(518) 568-2280

R.E. & G.B. Way, A.B.A
Brettons

Burrough Green
Newmarket
Suffolk
CB8 9NA
England

Index